PLANNING CURRICULUM
FOR SCHOOLS

J. Galen Saylor
University of Nebraska

William M. Alexander
University of Florida

HOLT, RINEHART AND WINSTON, INC.

New York   Chicago   San Francisco   Atlanta
Dallas   Montreal   Toronto   London   Sydney

ONU Rev. record

Library of Congress Cataloging in Publication Data

Saylor, John Galen, 1902–
Planning curriculum for schools.
Parts of this book have been published in 1954 under title:
Curriculum planning for better teaching and learning, and
in 1966 under title: Curriculum planning for modern schools.
Includes bibliographical references.
1. Curriculum planning—United States. I. Alexander,
William Marvin, 1912–   joint author. II. Title.
LB1570.S29   1974   375'.001   73–7843
ISBN: 0–03–085352–4

PREFACE

Planning Curriculum for Schools is a guide for planning the curriculum of the schools from early childhood levels of maturity to young adulthood. It is intended to be a basic text for students engaged in professional study of the scope and nature of curriculum and its planning, and a reference for all persons who participate professionally in planning the program of a school. This book is comprehensive in its treatment, presenting models of the process of planning and analyzing the factors and steps involved.

The 1970s and the decades ahead will be crucial but exciting times for the schools of this nation. Many citizens want them to continue to serve primarily as the guardians of the traditional social values and institutions. Some believe they should take a leading role in the solution of our national problems and in building the new America of the future. Others feel that the schools are unresponsive not only to the nature of the

iii

times but to the educational needs of children and youth—that the curriculum lacks relevancy, that the structure for schooling is outmoded. Yet everyone acknowledges the necessity of providing the best schools possible for the education of their students. The issue is: What should be the nature and character of the curriculum of the schools of the future? It is our hope that this book will assist educators in grappling effectively and insightfully with this basic issue.

The models, concepts, and principles draw on a variety of sources in addition to our own knowledge and understanding of curriculum planning. Research studies and theoretical works of philosophers and scholars in the field of professional education and cognate areas of study have been examined critically. Concepts and generalizations garnered from the experience of teachers, administrators, and other practitioners have been utilized extensively. Also, we have turned to the writings, editorials, speeches, and comments of students, parents, concerned citizens, official task forces, and coworkers in curriculum planning for insights, points of views, reactions to both old and new practices and programs in the schools, and recommendations.

Curriculum planning, by its very nature, constitutes choices—choices among values, social aims, social theories, and psychological systems. Many alternative approaches to schooling are possible. Hence, we have cited a large body of literature, often presenting differing points of view, on many of the topics treated within the models. Readers are urged to draw on many sources, including those cited, in formulating their own concepts about the nature of schooling, developing their personal models of the process of curriculum planning, and proceeding with the job at hand. We believe that the concepts and recommendations presented in this book will provide an adequate base, both as to the scope and nature of the curriculum and the processes to be used in its planning, for students and specialists to develop further their competencies in this most important of all professional responsibilities.

The basic models and supporting theory are presented in Chapter 1, and further explicated throughout the book. In Chapter 2, procedures for planning the curriculum are described, and the roles and responsibilities of all who should participate are explained.

As the basic model shows, the starting point in a complete program of planning is the gathering of data and the formulation of generalizations from the major factors that should and do shape the curriculum. The kinds of data and concepts needed by planners are treated in Chapter 3. The second aspect of educational planning is the definition of goals, and, derived from these, the subgoals and the objectives that guide planning for the various domains of the curriculum. Chapter 4 deals with this process of goal definition.

With purposes defined in broad scope, planners must determine the nature, scope, and organization of the educational program. This is encompassed within the designs selected for organizing curriculum and instruction. The various approaches to design are analyzed in Chapter 5. Implementation of the curriculum within the broad domains and designs is treated in Chapter 6. Various modes for planning instruction and guiding principles for selecting appropriate ones are presented. Chapter 7 deals with the final aspect of curriculum planning—the evaluation of the curriculum.

The concluding chapter, utilizing the theories and concepts elaborated throughout the book, offers principles and guidelines for planning the kinds of schools we believe this nation needs, not only now but in the decades ahead.

Among the many esteemed persons with whom we have worked in the professional field of education, the most revered is Hollis L. Caswell. His contributions to the theories and practices of curriculum planning over a period of more than thirty-five years constitute the basis for valid and forward-looking planning in the future. It was our great privilege to have the opportunity to study and work with him during his brilliant career.

Lincoln, Nebraska   J. Galen Saylor
Gainesville, Florida   William M. Alexander
September 1973

CONTENTS

List of Tables

List of Figures

1

CURRICULUM PLANNING IN THEORY AND PRACTICE

This book presents no single, simple formula for curriculum planning. Any such presentation would be a dangerous oversimplification of a highly complex field. We will instead review various theories of the curriculum and its planning, explain and illustrate some principles and practices we consider especially relevant, and leave to readers the development of their own formulas for use in particular curriculum planning situations.

This chapter is an overview of the field of curriculum planning and an introduction to the book. Although some theoretical considerations are both necessary and inevitable, we are mindful of such criticisms of curriculum theory as Schwab's assertions that the field of curriculum is "moribund" and that it "has reached this unhappy state by inveterate, unexamined, and mistaken reliance on theory."[1] In this book the curricu-

---

[1] Joseph J. Schwab, *The Practical: A Language for Curriculum* (Washington, D.C.: National Education Association, Center for Study of Instruction, 1970), p. 1. Also see John I. Goodlad, "Epilogue: Perspective on Curriculum Design," in Richard W. Burns and Gary D. Brooks, eds., *Curriculum Design in a Changing Society* (Englewood Cliffs, N.J.: Educational Technology Publications, Inc., 1970). Goodlad decried the absence of adequate theory in curriculum planning.

lum is viewed both as a conceptual scheme and as the changing, living happening it can be and is in the school and community of real people. Similarly, curriculum planning is viewed both as the system it can be and as the combination of operations, however inadequate and unrealistic, it is in actual school situations.

CONCEPTS OF THE CURRICULUM

The authors of the many books and other publications on curriculum that have appeared since the first in 1918, Bobbitt's *The Curriculum,* have usually presented a particular conception of the curriculum. Many of these conceptions have contained similar elements, if not phraseology, and some efforts at their classification have been made. Particularly helpful are the classifications by Lewis and Miel and by Posner, both published in 1972. Lewis and Miel's classification of curriculum concepts is presented in Table 1. They define the curriculum as "a set of intentions about opportunities for engagement of persons-to-be-educated with other persons and with things (all bearers of information, processes, techniques, and values) in certain arrangements of time and space."[2]

Posner compared various definitions as to their emphasis on processes or product, on the temporal relation of curriculum to instruction (prior to or concurrent with), and on description or prescription (programmatic). He preferred a definition that "(a) is product-oriented, (b) places curriculum prior to instruction, and (c) is descriptive," and noted that such definitions had been found in the literature for the past forty years.[3]

Our own analysis of past and present concepts of the curriculum benefits from and relates to those just cited but employs somewhat different categories.

The Curriculum as Subjects and Subject Matter

Historically and currently, the dominant concept of the curriculum is that of subjects and subject matter therein to be taught by teachers and learned by students. In high schools and colleges the term "curricu-

[2] Arthur J. Lewis and Alice Miel, *Supervision for Improved Instruction: New Challenges, New Responses* (Belmont, Calif.: Wadsworth Publishing Company, Inc., 1972), p. 27.

[3] George J. Posner, "Education: Its Components and Constructs," paper presented at the Annual Convention of the American Educational Research Association, Chicago, April 1972, pp. 2–5.

Table 1
A Classification of Concepts of the Curriculum*

CURRICULUM AS SOMETHING INTENDED			CURRICULUM AS SOMETHING ACTUALIZED		
Course of study (Subject matter)	Intended learning outcomes	Intended opportunities for engagement	Learning opportunities provided	Learner's actual engagements	Learner's actual experiences
Traditional, persisting meaning					
Phenix, 1958[1]	Johnson, 1967[2]	Miel, 1968[3]	Saylor and Alexander, 1966[4]	Mackenzie, 1964[5]	Caswell and Campbell, 1935[6]
					Many others, current

* From *Supervision for Improved Instruction: New Challenges, New Responses* by Arthur J. Lewis and Alice Miel. © 1972 by Wadsworth Publishing Company, Inc., Belmont, Calif. Reprinted by permission of the publisher.

[1] Philip H. Phenix, *Philosophy of Education* (New York: Holt, Rinehart and Winston, Inc., 1958), p. 57.

[2] Mauritz Johnson, Jr., "Definitions and Models in Curriculum Theory," *Educational Theory*, 17, No. 2 (1967).

[3] Alice Miel, "Curriculum Design and Materials—Pressure or Release?" *Childhood Education*, 44, No. 7 (1968).

[4] J. Galen Saylor and William M. Alexander, *Curriculum Planning for Modern Schools* (New York: Holt, Rinehart and Winston, Inc., 1966).

[5] Gordon N. Mackenzie, "Curricular Change: Participants, Power, and Processes," in Matthew B. Miles, ed., *Innovation in Education* (New York: Teachers College Press, 1964).

[6] Hollis L. Caswell and Doak S. Campbell, *Curriculum Development* (New York: American Book Company, 1935).

lum" has been and still is widely used to refer to the set of subjects or courses offered, and also to those required or recommended or grouped for other purposes; thus such terms as the "college preparatory curriculum," "science curriculum," and "premedical curriculum" are commonly used. In curriculum terminology, *program of studies* is more properly used in these connections.

Despite efforts for over a half century to achieve broader and different curriculum foci, the concept of curriculum as subject matter persists as the basis of the dominant curriculum design (see Chapter 5). It was central to and emphasized by the wave of curriculum development in the subject fields that began in the late 1950s under the stimulus of the Russian advance into outer space and subsequent pressure to improve American education. The steps in the processes of curriculum revision as developed by Zacharias and White for the Physical Science

Study Committee's work in physics, and as it influenced many national curriculum projects, embodied completely the concept of curriculum as subject matter:

> the process of determining the precise boundaries of the educational unit that will be treated;
> the process of identifying the subject matter which is to be dealt with within that educational unit;
> the embodiment of that subject matter in material form, as text, laboratory or classroom materials, and other learning aids; and
> the preparation of teachers in the new subject matter and in the use of the materials.[4]

In his 1968 edition of *Curriculum Theory*, Beauchamp insisted that a curriculum should be a written document and noted that "a most commonly included feature is an outline of the subject matters to be taught." He also explained that "subject matter embraces whatever is to be taught in the school: in school subjects, in selected disciplines, in problems of living, or in a pattern organized in any other way," but emphasized that "whatever the mode of expression, the subject matter is the substantive hard core of the curriculum."[5]

Although we agree with Beauchamp that the curriculum plan must encompass subject matter, the latter term is too closely associated with the organized subjects to be considered identical with what we prefer to call curriculum content. Content as learning opportunities utilizing both knowledge classified in subjects and knowledge and experiences that cut across or are independent of subjects is a concept more compatible with theories of curriculum planning that we can accept.

The Curriculum as Experiences

The concept of the curriculum as the experiences of the learner, including those utilizing organized subject matter, was introduced in early curriculum publications. Bobbitt defined curriculum as *"that series of things which children and youth must do and experience* by way of developing ability to do the things well that make up the affairs of adult life. . . ."[6] Caswell and Campbell embraced the experiences concept of

---

[4] Jerrold R. Zacharias and Stephen White, "The Requirements for Major Curriculum Revision," in Robert W. Heath, ed., *New Curricula* (New York: Harper & Row, Publishers, 1964), p. 69.

[5] George Beauchamp, *Curriculum Theory*, 2d ed. (Wilmette, Ill.: The Kagg Press, 1968), pp. 83–86.

[6] Franklin Bobbitt, *The Curriculum* (Boston: Houghton Mifflin Company, 1918), p. 42. [Bobbitt's italics]

the curriculum as they observed the sterility of instruction based on text-books and courses of study outlining subject matter. In their popular *Curriculum Development* (1935) they gave this concept wide exposure, holding the school curriculum "to be composed of all the experiences children have under the guidance of teachers."[7] Many subsequent pub-lications utilized similar definitions. As noted by Lewis and Miel (see Table 1), in an earlier edition of this book (1966) we also used a definition Lewis and Miel classified with Caswell's as "something actualized." Our intent, however, is to emphasize the curriculum *as a plan* rather than as a record or even an observation of learning opportunities; but along with Caswell and others we reject concepts of the curriculum that focus solely on subjects or objectives. For the curriculum to have the vitality Caswell and Campbell and subsequent authors sought, the curriculum plan must be based on consideration of "all elements in the experience of the learner."[8]

The Curriculum as Objectives

Early efforts at curriculum improvement made much use of aims and objectives as bases for curriculum planning, and Tyler contributed through the Eight-Year Study of school-college relations and his later publications a model (see pages 9–10) that systematized this approach. Instruction tended to be subsumed under curriculum, although the term "curriculum and instruction" was commonly employed to include both curriculum designs and instructional strategies. However, methods courses tended to remain apart from curriculum courses in teacher education and certification. A series of research studies in instruction paralleled the search for new curriculum content beginning in the late 1950s, and many writers began to separate more definitely the study of curriculum and the study of instruction. One result was a definition of curriculum as con-sisting solely of objectives or ends and instruction as the means of their attainment. This view of the curriculum, described by Posner as "antici-patory," was clearly stated by Johnson:

> Curriculum is concerned not with what students will *do* in the learning situation, but with what they will learn (or be able to do) as a con-sequence of what they do. Curriculum is concerned with what results, not with what happens. And it stands in an anticipatory relationship to the learn-ing process, not in a reportorial relationship, after the fact. It deals with expectations or intentions, and, more specifically, with the learning outcomes

[7] Hollis L. Caswell and Doak S. Campbell, *Curriculum Development* (New York: American Book Company, 1935), p. 69.
[8] Caswell and Campbell.

intended to be achieved through instruction, that is, through the experiences provided, through what happens and what learners do.[9]

The issue posed by this concept has to do with the relation of planning ends and means. Seeing the curriculum as a plan, we would place our concept of the curriculum in the classification by Lewis and Miel as "something intended," but we believe that the intention should include both ends and means. Certainly means and ends, that is, curriculum objectives and instructional strategies, need at some points to be considered separately. And in a particular curriculum planning situation it is to be expected that objectives, designs, instruction, and evaluation will at points be studied and planned separately. But the relation is so inextricable that we find it inadvisable—indeed virtually impossible—to plan curriculum and instruction separately as though they were really discrete.

The Curriculum as a Plan

For the reason just cited, in this book we treat curriculum as a plan. Specifically, we define curriculum as *a plan for providing sets of learning opportunities to achieve broad goals and related specific objectives for an identifiable population served by a single school center.* Thus we regard the curriculum as anticipatory or intended. It includes specific plans (really subplans) for whatever learning opportunities are anticipated. It is focused on but not confined to aims and objectives, and it includes those elements identified later in this chapter as curriculum design, implementation (that is, instruction), and evaluation, which are essential to consideration and use of the plan for a specific population. As we see it, a plan never exists in an abstract sense; it is made for a particularized situation. Further, as a total plan for a situation, the curriculum includes many smaller plans. Thus, a curriculum plan is always made for an identifiable population (that is, particular students) served by a single school center (that is, the school or the educational agency or institution responsible for providing educational opportunities for this population).

All important in curriculum theory and curriculum planning and improvement is the role of the individual school. It is here that the curriculum plan unfolds; thus the plan should be tailor-made for the school, insofar as is feasible and desirable by the persons associated with that school center. The theory and research of John Goodlad, reported in a discussion of the League of Cooperating Schools (see pages 89–90),

[9] Mauritz Johnson, "Appropriate Research Directions in Curriculum and Instruction," *Curriculum Theory Network*, Winter 1970–1971 (No. 6), p. 25.

strongly supports this conviction. In presenting some of the "influencing notions" of the League, Goodlad stated:

> 1. The key unit for educational change is the individual school with its principal, teachers, students, parents, and community setting. The basic ingredients for learning and teaching are here. Anything from elsewhere must find its way into the school or is impotent.[10]

THEORIES OF CURRICULUM PLANNING

These various concepts of the curriculum have been reflected in theories and processes of curriculum planning. We give brief attention here to several theories before turning to our own model.

In reviewing theories of the curriculum and its planning, one notes that writings in the field have used such terms as "curriculum planning," "curriculum development," "curriculum construction," "curriculum improvement," and "curriculum revision" synonymously and interchangeably. We do not perceive discrete meanings for each of these terms, but some particular emphases cause us to reject other terms and to accept *curriculum planning* as the appropriate term to describe the process of creating a curriculum. Our definition of the curriculum as a plan leads us naturally to this usage. "Curriculum development" is little different and has been widely used in the same sense. But currently the term is frequently used to describe the creation of curriculum materials, including materials for use by students, that are products of curriculum planning but not in themselves curriculum plans. The terms "curriculum construction" and "revision" have been so traditionally used to describe writing and revising courses of study as to cause us to reject them here, while "curriculum improvement" describes a goal rather than a process of curriculum planning.

Theories Concerning Subjects and Subject Matter to Be Taught

The concept of the curriculum as subjects and subject matter has been reflected in a plethora of theories relating to principles for selection, sequence, and grade placement of subject matter. Compre-

---

[10] John I. Goodlad, "Educational Change: A Strategy for Study and Action," *National Elementary Principal*, 48, 9 (January 1969). See also John I. Goodlad with Maurice N. Richter, Jr., *The Development of a Conceptual System for Dealing with Problems of Curriculum and Instruction*, HEW Contract No. SAE-8024, Project No. 454 (Los Angeles: University of California and Institute for Development of Educational Activities, 1966).

hensive statements of the theory underlying curriculum planning for a subject curriculum are of relatively recent origin, perhaps because the process was so long unchallenged and in a general sense is well known. Curriculum planning for a subject curriculum follows a fairly common formula:

1. Use expert judgment (based on various social and educational factors) to determine what subjects to teach.
2. Use some criterion (difficulty, interest, sequence, for example) to select the subject matter for particular populations (grouped, for example, by state, district, age, or grade) and subjects.
3. Plan and implement appropriate methods of instruction to ensure mastery of the subject matter selected.

Even with the more sophisticated theories and processes now available, we ourselves tend to reject as inadequate any theory of the curriculum which confines schooling to the fields of organized knowledge. Earlier, when subject planning and materials development were less well done than they are today, curriculum theorizing generally tended to be focused on moving away from the subject design.

The Theory of a More Functional Curriculum

From John Dewey's laboratory school model at the turn of the century to the "school without walls" model exemplified some seventy years later in Philadelphia's Parkway Program, the most frequent and common assumption of curriculum theories, however inadequately developed and implemented, has been that a more functional or relevant curriculum can be developed than that of the traditional subjects. Each of the other curriculum designs was originally a breakaway from the subject design. As one examines the activity analyses, aims and objectives, child-centered school, social functions, and other designs of the 1920s and beyond, one notes that they seem to have the common elements constituting a theoretical approach to curriculum planning which Rugg identified in the 1927 Yearbook of the National Society for the Study of Education as "The Tasks of Curriculum-Making":

There are three definite jobs involved in the task:
First: The determination of fundamental objectives, the great purposes of the curriculum as a whole and of its several departments.
Second: The selection of activities and other materials of instruction, choice of content, readings, exercises, excursions, topics for open-forum discussions, manual activities, health and recreational programs.
Third: The discovery of the most effective organization of materials and their experimental placement in the grades of the public schools. All three tasks are of vital importance to the proper construction of the

curriculum. Consciously or implicitly, the curriculum-maker is always guided by his objectives in the selection of activities or other materials of instruction, and in their organization and grade-placement.[11]

In reviewing forty-five years later the contributions of this Yearbook, Tyler said its unique ones were that it provided a "comprehensive outline for curriculum-making and the emphasis upon the use of objective studies rather than armchair reflection to furnish the data on which plans are built and decisions are made."[12] We can add that it predicted the nature of most curriculum planning efforts, apart from the subject approaches, for the next two decades. In some cases these approaches described curriculum plans that seem to us more forward looking than many that are in effect today; their general failure to influence practice significantly was due to many factors, a critical one being the lack of adequate direction for research and practice. As goals for curriculum improvement, the theoretical statements of the 1920s and 1930s are still excellent models for study and development, as we shall point out in Chapter 5.

Tyler's More Comprehensive Model

In commenting on Rugg's outline cited above, Tyler in 1971 related it to the model of curriculum planning with which he had become associated a decade after publication of Rugg's description:

> This outline is similar to the one developed in 1936 for the work of the Eight-Year Study, but the latter study developed specifications for formulating objectives that provided a clear transition from objectives to learning experiences. Furthermore, a fourth task was recognized, namely, the evaluation of the curriculum being developed, using the results of evaluations as a basis for continuing revisions to effect continuing curriculum improvement.[13]

As director of evaluation for the Eight-Year Study of school-college relations and later as a professor and curriculum leader at the University of Chicago, Tyler developed a model for curriculum planning that is generally regarded as having significantly influenced the field

[11] Harold Rugg, Chairman, *The Foundations and Techniques of Curriculum-Making*, Twenty-sixth Yearbook, National Society for the Study of Education (Chicago: University of Chicago Press, 1927), Part I, *Curriculum-Making: Past and Present*, p. 51.

[12] Ralph W. Tyler, "Curriculum Development in the Twenties and Thirties," in Robert M. McClure, ed., *The Curriculum: Retrospect and Prospect*, Seventieth Yearbook, National Society for the Study of Education (Chicago: University of Chicago Press, 1971), Part I, pp. 31–32.

[13] Tyler, "Curriculum Development in the Twenties and Thirties," p. 31.

since the 1930s. His description of the work of the Eight-Year Study emphasizes his beliefs concerning the interrelations of objectives, learning experiences, instructional organization, and evaluation; he noted that the products of subject-matter committees "were not effectively utilized in the schools until teachers and pupils were more deeply involved in developing, or modifying, or trying out ideas and materials." As to evaluation, he concluded:

> Finally, the Eight-Year Study demonstrated the importance of evaluation as an essential part of curriculum-making. As new courses were being formed and resource units developed, the evaluation staff of the Eight-Year Study was helping teachers and specialists to clarify their objectives, to define them in terms of behavior, and to identify situations in which students' behavior could be appraised. This inclusion of evaluation in the curriculum process helped to clarify curriculum objectives and thus to furnish a clearer guide for selection of content and learning experiences.[14]

Tyler stated his rationale for evaluating a curriculum in 1949 in terms of four questions "which must be answered in developing any curriculum and plan of instruction":

> 1. What educational purposes should the school seek to attain?
> 2. What educational experiences can be provided that are likely to attain these purposes?
> 3. How can these educational experiences be effectively organized?
> 4. How can we determine whether these purposes are being attained?[15]

Our own model requires planners to answer the same questions, but it also calls for the deliberate use of essential data as the basis for planning, a systematization of objectives and plans within *curriculum domains* (broad, goal-oriented areas), and more specific provision for instructional plans (implementation). Although Tyler's model has undoubtedly been widely utilized and there have been many adaptations and expansions of it by such associates of his as Herrick, Taba, and Goodlad, it has also been criticized[16] on various bases such as inade-

[14] Tyler, "Curriculum Development in the Twenties and Thirties," p. 43.

[15] Ralph W. Tyler, *Basic Principles of Curriculum and Instruction* (Chicago: University of Chicago Press, 1949), p. 1.

[16] See Elliott Eisner, "Educational Objectives: Help or Hindrance," *School Review*, 75, 250–266 (Autumn 1967); Herbert M. Kleibard, "Curricular Objectives and Evaluation: A Reassessment," *The High School Journal*, 51, 241–247 (March 1968); Robert M. W. Travers, "Towards Taking the Fun Out of Building a Theory of Instruction," *Teachers College Record*, 69, 49–60 (October 1966); and George Willis, "Curriculum Theory and the Context of Curriculum," *Curriculum Theory Network*, Winter 1970–1971 (No. 6), pp. 41–59.

quacies in conceptions of objectives, curriculum design, and instructional organization. In our judgment, the model was chiefly useful in that it further turned attention from separate treatments of objectives, content, and methods toward a more comprehensive view of curriculum, one that emphasized the importance of evaluation.

Theories Concerning Analysis of Curriculum and Instruction

Theory development during the 1960s tended, as we have noted, toward separation of curriculum and instruction. Among such efforts we consider especially useful an analysis by Macdonald, who dealt with curriculum, instruction, teaching, and learning as four related, overlapping systems (see Figure 1). He distinguished between curriculum and instruction by considering them as "essentially two separate action contexts, one (curriculum) producing plans for further action; and the other (instruction) putting plans into action."[17] Macdonald explained the interrelation of all four systems as follows:

[17] James B. Macdonald, "Educational Models for Instruction—Introduction," in James B. Macdonald, ed., *Theories of Instruction* (Washington, D.C.: Association for Supervision and Curriculum Development, 1965), p. 5.

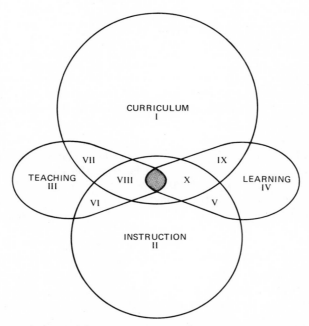

FIGURE 1   Action space of four systems: curriculum, instruction, teaching, and learning. (*From James B. Macdonald, "Educational Models for Instruction—Introduction,"* in Theories of Instruction, *1965, p. 4*)

Thus, teaching is defined as the behavior of the teacher, learning as the change in learner behavior, instruction as the pupil-teacher interaction situation and curriculum as those planning endeavors which take place prior to instruction.

Another way of putting this might be: learning is the desired response, teaching is the act of systematically presenting stimuli, and/or cues; instruction is the total stimulus setting within which systematic stimuli and desired responses occur, and curriculum represents the major source of stimuli found in instructional settings to be utilized systematically. When the appropriate sources are utilized in a productively structured setting, and presented in an effective manner, then the desired responses will hopefully occur and the shadowed space, the convergence of all four areas, has been entered.[18]

Our model of curriculum planning is essentially similar to Macdonald's. We see instruction as the implementation of the curriculum plan, and as usually but not necessarily involving teaching, which we see as the pupil-teacher interaction phase of instruction. We also see the desirability—and later writings of Macdonald cited later in this chapter suggest his agreement—of a systems approach to curriculum planning.

RELATING CURRICULUM THEORY AND CURRICULUM SYSTEMS: SOME VIEWPOINTS

The preceding discussion of theories of curriculum and its planning may indicate why some writers tend to deprecate the state of curriculum theory. For example, Johnson summed up his view of the state of the field as follows:

Most doctoral candidates in curriculum and instruction are convinced that they are dealing with the heart of the educational enterprise, but sooner or later they recognize that their field is characterized by a paucity of well-established knowledge, a meager, inconsistent theoretical base, an unclear structure, and a lack of any widely accepted standard mode of inquiry.[19]

Although some writers would simply improve on the quantity and quality of theoretical statements, others would turn to more systematic constructs. For example, Schwab would change the focus from the theoretic, "such as the pursuit of global principles and comprehensive

[18] Macdonald, "Educational Models for Instruction—Introduction," p. 6.
[19] Johnson, p. 24.

patterns, the search for stable sequences and invariant elements, the construction of taxonomies of supposedly fixed or recurrent kinds," to what he calls the "practical," "quasi-practical," and "eclectic." His definition of the "practical" seems to us similar to the use of a systems concept of the curriculum:

> The method of the practical . . . is, then, not at all a linear affair proceeding step-by-step, but rather a complex, fluid, transactional discipline aimed at identification of the desirable and at either attainment of the desired or an alteration of the desires.[20]

In a later article Schwab explained further his rejection of the simple and direct application of theories from the behavioral sciences to practical problems and proposed instead the use of "polyfocal conspectus" in studying curriculum problems.[21] This approach would involve the examination of educational situations and problems in the perspectives of more than one doctrine, preferably not less than three.

In his presidential address to the American Educational Research Association in 1968 John Goodlad cited Conant, Dewey, and Schwab in emphasizing the need for a continuing interplay of theory, research, and practice and added his own notion:

> Inventing or innovating in the practice of education involves a blending of theoretical-deductive and empirical-inductive inquiry, however primitive in their development the two modes of thought may be. Invention in practice provides articulation of persistent educational problems. And it poses alternative concepts, modes, and principles for conducting practice. In effect, invention provides for educational *practice* a kind of fluid inquiry in that old concepts and old ways of doing things are challenged. Is it not conceivable, then, that the study of invention would provide for educational *science*, also, a much needed stimulus to fluid inquiry?[22]

We cited earlier in this chapter Goodlad's critique of the status of curriculum theory and his emphasis on the role of the individual school in curriculum improvement.

Arguing for more rather than less development of curriculum theory, Beauchamp held that "progress in curriculum theory has been

---

[20] Schwab, *The Practical: A Language for Curriculum*, p. 5.

[21] Joseph J. Schwab, "The Practical: Arts of Eclectic," *School Review*, 79, 493–542 (August 1971).

[22] John I. Goodlad, "Thought, Invention, and Research in the Advancement of Education," *Educational Forum*, 33, 11 (November 1968).

slow and meager."[23] He defined curriculum theory as "a set of related statements that gives meaning to a school's curriculum by pointing up the relationships among its elements and by directing its development, its use, and its evaluation."[24] For theory development he identified three major uses of the term "curriculum" and a corresponding subtheory relating to each use: a curriculum plan, a curriculum development system, and curriculum as a field of study. As we see it, Beauchamp was dealing with a systems approach to curriculum development in his treatment of the "curriculum system" as "curriculum engineering." "Curriculum engineering," he wrote, "consists of all of the processes necessary to make a curriculum system functional in schools," and the term is used to represent both the system for decision-making and its internal dynamics. The primary functions of the system are "(1) to produce a curriculum, (2) to implement the curriculum, and (3) to appraise the effectiveness of the curriculum and the curriculum system."[25] Thus Beauchamp would, in effect, classify the notion of a curriculum system as one of several sets of statements considered curriculum theories.

Macdonald asserted that "the development of the curriculum in the American public schools has been primarily a historical accident."[26] He discounted oversimplified statements of curriculum theory:

> Too often, educators talk as if curriculum development were a completely rational-technical process based upon scientific and/or technical data abstracted from foundation areas (especially the behavioral sciences) and tested by educational research. This, of course, is only a statement of an ideal that some educators share. The danger in this rhetoric is that it fails to take into account that this ideal is essentially unfruitful in explaining how we got where we are or the developments taking place today.[27]

Emphasizing as he does that curriculum development is a "very complex and dynamic process" and not "a simple rational one," Macdonald sees the challenge ahead as "one of taking curriculum development out of the 'accidental' category and introducing some form of general rational input into planning, but maintaining the participation and integrity of the

[23] Beauchamp, p. 55.

[24] Beauchamp, p. 66.

[25] Beauchamp, p. 108.

[26] James B. Macdonald, "Curriculum Development in Relation to Social and Intellectual Systems," in McClure, Chap. V, p. 95.

[27] Macdonald, "Curriculum Development in Relation to Social and Intellectual Systems," pp. 111–112.

persons and groups involved."[28] His very brief description of the process of planning through "planned happenings" at different levels seems also to suggest a more systematic approach to curriculum planning than in the past.

One of the most comprehensive and constructive formulations concerning the state of the curriculum field is given by Joyce in the 1971 Yearbook of the National Society for the Study of Education. Joyce, too, finds the field in confusion and dilemma:

> The curriculum field is still relatively undefined. Curriculum planners have no agreed upon set of concepts or modes which are known and used by all hands. There is no lack of "prescriptive" curriculum theories —that is to say, ideas about what school programs ought to be. . . .
>
> The curriculum field has no overarching "metasystem," known to all or most of its practitioners, which enables comparisons of and choices between all the alternative approaches which are taken. This is not to say that there are no knowledgeable people who are acquainted with the alternatives. On the whole, however, curriculum planners "do their own thing."[29]

To correct the situation, Joyce proposes various "positive propositions," following his review of three "negative theses." His first proposition follows:

> The curriculum field should develop a set of working, engineering theories about the improvement of education. We need some generic engineering theories that can embrace many different types of education missions and many different kinds of strategies for teaching them. In addition, we need sets of subtheories, which deal with particular assumptive worlds, particular media, and are addressed to particular types of educational problems.[30]

These working theories Joyce would have "institutionless," since he holds that "most existing curriculum theory and subtheories are straight-jacketed by the existing structure of the school and the ubiquitous teacher role," and he would have developed sets of engineering propositions to bring about a variety of educational environments. To build the propositions, "systems planning procedures can be turned to this end if they are used to generate alternative goals and means rather than to identify the most economical path to given ends"; in fact, he rates sys-

---

[28] Macdonald, "Curriculum Development in Relation to Social and Intellectual Systems," pp. 111–112.

[29] Bruce R. Joyce, "The Curriculum Worker of the Future," in McClure, Chap. XIII, pp. 312–313.

[30] Joyce, "The Curriculum Worker of the Future," p. 330.

tems procedures as "the curriculum field's most powerful program-planning tool" because they can generate more options needed in the curriculum field, which "has long normed on a few curriculum alternatives rather than generating wide ranges of solidly rooted, testable possibilities."[31]

In *Supervision and Curriculum Renewal: A Systems Approach,* Feyereisen, Fiorino, and Nowak attempted to project a comprehensive systems approach to curriculum and instruction. Their description of the approach is relevant:

> The systems approach to supervision and curriculum renewal is grounded in modern organization theory. We lay no claim to its discovery or invention but rather to the adaptation of its concepts to school organization. Specifically, we have conceptualized and detailed a curriculum and instruction system with a supervisory subsystem in an organizational setting which is self-regulating, self-adapting, and self-renewing.[32]

Particularly useful analyses and proposals by these authors are discussed in Chapter 2.

Rather than cite still other authors who have taken positions on the usefulness of curriculum theory and/or systems models in curriculum planning, we will examine the points of agreement among those we have considered and then state our own position. Despite some points of clear disagreement among the various writers, we note some substantial agreement as follows:

1. Although curriculum theory is inadequate and the field itself confused, efforts should be continued, in fact increased, to develop theories as sets of statements which describe, explain, and predict particular curriculum arrangements. These theories should recognize fully the changing nature of schooling and the curriculum and should attempt to set forth realistic and useful formulations that can be tested and modified as needed. Thus the notion of the curriculum as a system is itself a theory, but the focus is on action rather than mere exposition.

2. Even among the several relatively like-minded authors quoted above there are differences as to concept of curriculum. But there does seem to be agreement on the importance of a definition that emphasizes

---

[31] Joyce, "The Curriculum Worker of the Future," pp. 330–331.

[32] Kathryn V. Feyereisen, A. John Fiorino, and Arlene T. Nowak, *Supervision and Curriculum Renewal: A Systems Approach* (New York: Appleton-Century-Crofts, 1970), p. vii.

the role of goals and objectives. We interpret this agreement as generally supportive of our statement that a curriculum is a system—a set of components so related and organized as to attain the goals for which the curriculum is planned.

3. Although only two (Feyereisen, Fiorino, and Nowak and Joyce) of the sources we have cited clearly advocate use of a systems model in curriculum planning, others offer planning procedures which have many elements of a systems approach. We ourselves have long advocated a systematic set of procedures for curriculum planning, and we have presented a systems model in an earlier publication.[33] Current usage of systems models in business and government and increasingly in education incline us to use of this approach wherever appropriate in curriculum planning. We turn now to a model of curriculum which indicates further our views concerning use of a systems approach in curriculum planning.

CURRICULUM AS A SYSTEM

Considering a system as a set of components so related and organized as to attain the ends for which the system is established, we can refer to curriculum as a system. We defined curriculum as "a plan for providing sets of learning opportunities to achieve broad educational goals and related specific objectives for an identifiable population served by a single school center." The "set of components" in the system is the "plan for providing sets of learning opportunities," and the "ends" of the system are the "broad educational goals" for the school population served.

Use of the systems concept offers advantages to curriculum planners. Past efforts to plan the curriculum have tended to lose sight of the integral relation of goals and learning opportunities; with a systems approach the objectives are central in decision-making activities, including those major ones relating to choice of learning opportunities. In the past, too, attempts to plan the curriculum have also tended to be piecemeal and fragmentary; with a systems approach the planners are concerned with all relevant factors as they work out the steps to be taken to achieve the goals.

[33] See William M. Alexander, J. Galen Saylor, and Emmett L. Williams, *The High School: Today and Tomorrow* (New York: Holt, Rinehart and Winston, Inc., 1971), p. 126.

Two Central Assumptions

Educators of the 1970s are faced with the sobering knowledge that past theories and practices of curriculum planning, however much some of them may be revived in current demands and movements, have not worked either to effect education that is good enough for the times or to bring about professional unanimity concerning what makes for good education. In our judgment most mistakes of past and present curriculum planning are generally attributable to the failure to make paramount in all plans two central assumptions that underlie the theory we present here.

1. *The central goal of schooling, and therefore of the curriculum and its planning, is the most complete development educationally feasible and socially acceptable of the self-directing, continuing learner.* Statements of this goal abound in the literature, but the hard facts of practice all but deny its existence. In fact, observers infer very opposite goals of schooling (see page 28). In the report of his study of U.S. schools, Silberman observed that they were suffering from "mindlessness," and no wonder, since he viewed the purpose of education as "to educate educators—to turn out men and women who are capable of educating their families, their friends, their communities, and, most importantly, themselves."[34]

Gardner has said that the ultimate goal of the educational system is "to shift to the individual the burden of pursuing his own education":

> This will not be a widely shared pursuit until we get over our odd conviction that education is what goes on in school buildings and nowhere else. Not only does education continue when schooling ends, but it is not confined to what may be studied in adult education courses. The world is an incomparable classroom, and life is a memorable teacher for those who aren't afraid of her.[35]

Weinberg and his associates gave heavy weight to the educational experiences which would give students joy and meaning, turning them on to continuing learning; thus Joyce emphasized the role of curriculum workers in creating options:

[34] Charles E. Silberman, *Crisis in the Classroom* (New York: Random House, Inc., 1970), p. 114.

[35] John W. Gardner, *Self-Renewal: The Individual and the Innovative Society* (New York: Harper & Row, Publishers, 1964), p. 12.

Our efforts should be to increase on a continual basis the options that are available to the population and the flexibility with which they can be made available. As more options are developed, making more and more kinds of education commonplace, and giving students the power to educate themselves in increasingly human ways, then the curriculum worker will be making his contribution to the search for an increasingly humanistic education.[36]

2. *The individual learner is actively involved in planning his own curriculum, in an open process that eliminates a "hidden curriculum."* A 1957 brochure of the Association for Supervision and Curriculum Development stated:

More recently the philosophy of democratic participation and the recognition of the dynamic nature of learning have led to emphasis upon teacher-pupil planning. For the past 20 years schools have been experimenting with ways to improve the process by which children and young people help set the goals, plan the activities and evaluate the results of their work with the leadership of the teacher.[37]

Perhaps it was the post-Sputnik clamor for academic excellence beginning late that same year which made this movement somewhat short-lived, at least until student dissatisfactions with schooling became outspoken, even violently so, in the late 1960s. A high school student whose article was included in a 1969 anthology, *How Old Will You Be in 1984?*, asked:

Why can't we make school worthwhile enough from the standpoint of the student? Why can't we institute more relevant courses, and after very basic requirements, which even less intelligent students realize as necessary, allow students to judge for themselves what will benefit them? You can tell them what's good for them, but you can't make them like the subject. And those that do like something can take advantage of it without worrying about room for it on a schedule including non-helpful studies. Maybe we'll interest more people in school if we give them a choice—if we give them responsibility.[38]

[36] Bruce Joyce, "Curriculum and Humanistic Education: 'Monolism' vs. Pluralism," in Carl Weinberg, ed., *Humanistic Foundations of Education* (Englewood Cliffs, N.J.: Prentice-Hall, Inc., 1972), p. 199.

[37] Prudence Bostwick, Chairman, "One Hundred Years of Curriculum Improvement, 1857–1957" (Washington, D.C.: Association for Supervision and Curriculum Development, 1957), p. 7.

[38] Bob Weinzimmer, "Compulsory Education—Good or Bad?" in Diane Divoky, ed., *How Old Will You Be in 1984?* (New York: Avon Books, 1969), pp. 88–89.

This demand for relevance has been a powerful factor in educational change in the late 1960s and 1970s. A paper prepared for the 1971 White House Conference on Youth pointed out that this demand did not come just from some small group of student radicals but "from the significantly larger minority of high school and college students who view the present educational systems as an institutional form sufficiently anachronistic to require, as the only adequate change, a reform culminating in transformation." The paper further described these youth and their motivations:

> The "revolution" to achieve relevance, then, will be led not by the minorities (unless their aspirations are crushed), nor by white working classes (there is now no populist movement), but by middle-class youth of the persuasion just cited. They are the alienated people of the technological society. As they see it, the new world is not the old world of work, nor is it the working man's; he still clings to the concept of identity through industrial or corporation roles. Meanwhile, the nation moves into cybernetics and a social context in which work as conventionally defined will not provide the basis for human fulfillment. These youth sense that the character of human satisfactions is changing, that old ones are no longer persuasive, albeit new ones are not yet fully perceived.[39]

Schools were strongly indicted for not trusting students by Macdonald in the 1971 Yearbook of the ASCD:

> The vast majority of schools, teachers, and other concerned persons do not trust students. The basic assumption of the schools' orientation to students is that students will do the wrong thing (what you do not want them to do) unless you make them do the right thing. If this were not so, most school policies and classroom disciplinary procedures would not be justified. Surely, faith in the worth, dignity, and integrity of individuals is not in evidence.[40]

We find the conclusion inescapable that past curriculum planning has failed to involve students adequately. A strong contrast has resulted between the curriculum planned for and the curriculum had by students. Evidence of this dichotomy is found in the existence of a

---

[39] Warren Bryan Martin, "The Relevance of Present Educational Systems," in *Education Task Force Papers*, prepared for the White House Conference on Youth (Berkeley, Calif.: University of California, 1971), pp. 6–7.

[40] James B. Macdonald, "The School as a Double Agent," in Vernon F. Haubrich, ed., *Freedom, Bureaucracy and Schooling* (Washington, D.C.: Association for Supervision and Curriculum Development, NEA, 1971), p. 237.

"hidden curriculum" of student strategies to pass successfully the hurdles of the formal or planned curriculum, as well as of other student-invented or student-structured systems of various "hidden" curriculums we allude to in appropriate sections of this book. Testimony as to the importance of the hidden curriculum was given by the M.I.T. psychiatrist Benson Snyder:

> I have found that a hidden curriculum determines to a significant degree what becomes the basis for all participants' sense of worth and self-esteem. It is this hidden curriculum, more than the formal curriculum, that influences the adaptation of students and faculty. I know of no kindergarten, high school, or college that is without a hidden curriculum which bears on its students and faculty. Though each curriculum has characteristics that are special to the particular setting, the presence of these hidden curricula importantly affect the process of all education. The similarities in these hidden curricula are at least as important as the differences.[41]

Recognizing fully that schools differ in their methods of evaluating student progress, we can state that students by and large learn fairly early in their school careers to attach much importance to the system of marks, promotion, credits, and reports. In high school and college these paraphernalia may become such dominant student concerns as to indeed create a hidden curriculum of student communication, devices, and tactics—strategies—for succeeding in the planned curriculum. Thus the means of meeting requirements, passing examinations, and earning teacher favor may become the ends of the student's curriculum rather than the objectives envisioned by the teachers. A fundamental change in goal setting and curriculum planning which enhances the student's role is essential in such situations.

Curriculum planning as it should be cannot result in the existence of two curriculums, the school's and the student's. The development of the lifelong learner envisioned in our first assumption necessitates the end of this dualism by bringing students into the planning process early, openly, and fully.

Model of the Curriculum as a System

The accompanying figures present a model of the curriculum as a system. Note that in Figure 2 the process of the system—the curriculum—is viewed as a plan consisting of a series of educational continuums (one or more for each curriculum domain) developed, implemented, and

[41] Benson Snyder, *The Hidden Curriculum* (New York: Alfred A. Knopf, 1970), pp. iii–xii.

INPUT

(Students
to Be
Educated)

OUTPUT

THE CURRICULUM—A PLAN
(For a Series of Educational Continuums, Set by
Curriculum Domains) Planned, implemented, and
evaluated for a particular population served by an
individual school center

(School Leavers
and Graduates Who
May Continue in
These Continuums in
Other Educational
Situations)

FIGURE 2   The curriculum system concept.

evaluated for a particular school center. Shane described a curriculum continuum as "an unbroken flow of experiences planned with and for the individual learner throughout his contacts with the school" and used the analogy of the Procrustean bed to compare individualized instruction and a personalized curriculum continuum:

> The individualized, and sometimes nongraded, approach to instruction was a distinct improvement, since it endeavored to shorten or lengthen the Procrustean bed to fit the child. The personalized curriculum continuum, on the other hand, is one in which the child, with teacher guidance, is encouraged—indeed expected—to build his own bed.[42]

In our view the curriculum is better thought of as planned in terms of a few broad areas of human development, or life activities, designated as continuums for planning purposes, with each learner having his own personalized set of learning opportunities within each domain chosen or fashioned by the learner.

Our model (see Figure 3) does not tie curriculum to a ladder of schooling as has been done for the past century with the graded school; nor does it confine curriculum to formal schooling in the sense of a specific building called a "school." Rather, we use the term "school center" to connote the facility in which the arrangements are made for a student's schooling, which may then take place in a "school," community facilities, at home, or in some combination of these places. Other critical terms and concepts implicit in the model are defined in the following paragraphs.

[42] Harold Shane, "A Curriculum Continuum: Possible Trends in the 70's," *Phi Delta Kappan*, 51, 390 (March 1970).

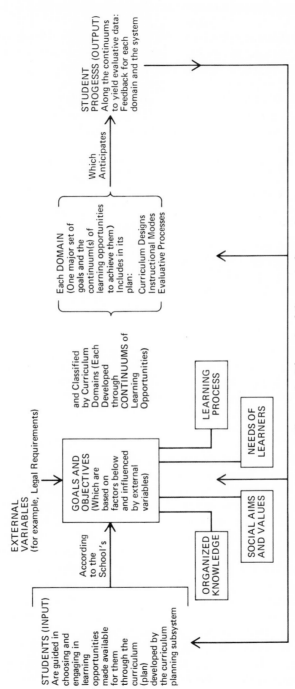

FIGURE 3 Elements of the curriculum system.

23

Curriculum   As we explained earlier, the curriculum is conceived of as *a plan for providing sets of learning opportunities to achieve broad educational goals and related specific objectives for an identifiable population served by a single school center*. We have also noted that the curriculum is organized on the basis of sets of educational continuums, each set belonging to a *curriculum domain* (see below). Our view is that in the actual learning situation each learner has his own set of educational continuums, that is, his own curriculum or, in Shane's language, his "personalized curriculum continuum." The curriculum as a plan anticipates sets of continuums and student progress thereon.

Our definition of the curriculum as a plan dictates that the curriculum anticipates the provision of learning opportunities for a particular set of objectives and a particular population. That is, the curriculum is not just any plan; it is a total plan for the program of a particular school. We shall frequently refer to this plan—the curriculum —as the "curriculum plan," since this phrase is synonymous with our definition and may convey our meaning more fully to readers who have different concepts of curriculum. The curriculum plan usually incorporates many smaller plans for particular portions of the curriculum. A (partial) plan can be appropriately developed for a single set of related goals, a domain, although most curriculum plans tend to be more global, for example, general curriculum guidelines for a state or district, or more specific, for example, a course of study for one subject and level. Generally, particular plans for individual aspects of the total curriculum plan are written in such diverse forms as programs of studies, lists of activities, schedules, policy statements and handbooks, courses of study, syllabi, units of work, and learning activity packages. The total curriculum plan is rarely written as one document. In the school the most vital and influential plans may be sets of agreements reached by the faculty and by relatively small groups of teachers for achieving series of objectives formulated for particular groups of students; these agreements are rarely written down in their entirety and certainly not in a single document. A teacher's own plan for achieving particular objectives in working with a class, small group, or individual is also an aspect of the total curriculum plan.

The total curriculum, then, is a plan which represents a series of choices (particular, partial plans) by the planners among the *internal variables* available as curriculum designs, instructional modes, and evaluative procedures. These variables are identified in later sections of this chapter and are treated fully in Chapters 5–7.

Curriculum Domain   Traditionally, curriculum components have been identified as subjects, with only passing attention given to the nonsubject curriculum areas of activities, services, and special programs and groupings. But many of the most important educational goals, especially those of an affective nature, are not really sought through the subjects or even the conventional nonsubject areas. To facilitate more functional groupings of learning opportunities, we use in this book the concept of a *curriculum domain* to describe *a grouping of learning opportunities planned to achieve a single major set of closely related educational goals with corollary subgoals and specific objectives.* Since planning has rarely so tied goals and curriculum, we hope that use of this approach to curriculum will help to make planning more systematic. Later in this chapter we indicate a taxonomy of domains we consider appropriate for emphasis, and in Chapter 4 further attention is given to the relation of domains and goals.

To illustrate our concept of a curriculum domain, we see the domain of continued learning skills as embracing the various educational goals having to do with skills and processes essential for present and future learning and including such varied learning opportunities as the following, each of which might be developed as a *continuum*:

> Specific instruction in reading and other initial learning skills
> Programmed instruction in use of library tools and sources
> Individual, student-choice reading in school and community libraries
> Use of group-process skills in laboratory sessions for their development and in teacher- or student-directed groups and community groups
> Use of television at school and at home
> Interviewing of peers in instructional situations and in school and community for information acquisition
> Teacher-guided mastery of skills unique to particular subjects and activities.

A domain can thus include a plethora of learning opportunities to be planned by continuums as appropriate and without needless restriction as to school subjects, learning locales, group organization, and other factors that have frequently limited goal setting and curriculum planning in general. The domain defines a broad area of the curriculum; it can be used as a set of guidelines to facilitate moving across former boundaries of subjects, activities, and services to make certain that the goals which set the domain are reflected in a plan which can be implemented and the goals achieved, regardless of whether the goals fit conventional subjects and activities.

Curriculum planning is a subsystem of the curriculum and it involves developing, monitoring, and evaluating the total curriculum plan. It is in this subsystem that the systems model becomes highly relevant, for here there is great need for the careful relating of all elements that this model is intended to provide. Planning must properly assess the various bases from which goals and objectives are chosen; weigh the impact of external variables against the possibilities of the internal ones and choose the combinations of curriculum designs, instructional modes, and evaluative procedures that are calculated best to attain the goals; review feedback from the plan in effect through instruction and make changes as indicated; and study evaluative data about the progress of learners on the continuums of the curriculum and about the total plan itself and replan the elements of the plan as the data indicate necessary.

A *systems approach* to curriculum planning is viewed as desirable in many situations. The less technical term "systematic approach" can be useful in any curriculum planning situation, and therefore it is used more frequently in this book. Whatever term is used, we describe and analyze plans and planning organizations in terms of the relations of ends and means, the attention to pertinent factors and data, and the flow of activities or procedures from beginning to end.

Other concepts and terms involved in the theories of curriculum and curriculum planning presented in this book are usually explained at the point of initial use.

THE CURRICULUM PLANNING PROCESS

Figure 4 shows a conceptual model of the curriculum planning process. Some of the major gaps between the conceptual model and actual processes can now be identified, and these may serve as guidelines for developing the curriculum planning system.

Past and current practice in curriculum planning is fully described in Chapter 2, but we should note that presently it ranges from being sporadic and inadequate in far too many schools to being systematic in approach, incorporating many of the processes described in· this book as forward looking, in others. Most models of curriculum planning followed by U.S. schools seeking continuing curriculum improvement have relied on processes of cooperative efforts at state, district, and local school levels, with input from various external agencies and from members of the school community. Unfortunately, the use of these processes elsewhere has been spasmodic and ineffectual rather than continuing and influential. In *Behind the Classroom Door* Goodlad and his associates summarized their investigations of the first four years of instruction in

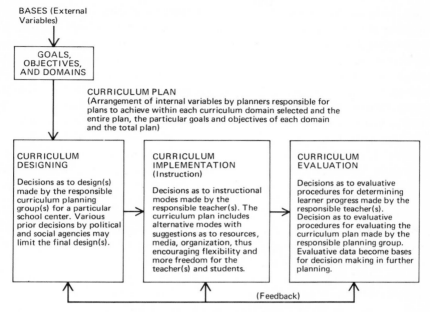

FIGURE 4   The curriculum planning process.

school, years for which cooperative and effective planning is frequently assumed to exist, as follows:

> We endeavored to secure evidence of curriculum plans being developed by the school faculty as a whole or by committees of that faculty. We encountered only one example but, admittedly, evidence here was very difficult to obtain. Nonetheless, neither observations nor interviews with teachers and principals revealed faculties at work on curriculum problems and plans. In general, each class operated as an individual unit, taking curricular direction from textbooks, courses of study, and teachers' experience.[43]

Our observations and investigations[44] indicate a similar state of affairs in most schools above the primary level. These studies yield two other observations that are pertinent here. On the negative side, one sees

[43] John I. Goodlad, M. Frances Klein, and associates, *Behind the Classroom Door* (Worthington, O.: Charles A. Jones Publishing Company, 1970), p. 64.

[44] See William M. Alexander, Vynce A. Hines, and associates, *Independent Study in Secondary Schools* (New York: Holt, Rinehart and Winston, Inc., 1967); and William M. Alexander and others, *The Emergent Middle School*, 2d enlarged ed. (New York: Holt, Rinehart and Winston, Inc., 1969), Chaps. 9 and 10.

many schools in which the obsession with scheduling time to plan obscures the fundamental goals and processes of planning, frequently reducing the planning process to a series of rapid-fire decisions on immediate problems with little effort made to relate present crises and tasks to long-range goals. On the positive side, those cases, admittedly rare, in which comprehensive planning has been done by the individual school faculty, with adequate representation from the community and student body, give much hope that systematic planning at the school level can and does make a difference. For this difference to occur, the planning process must be based on an adequate conception of the roles of goals and objectives, and of feedback and evaluation, in relation to the curriculum plan and its implementation and to continuing efforts in planning year after year.

Goals and Objectives

Examination of past and present practices of curriculum planning indicates a frequent lack of a continuing focus on goals and objectives which is essential to systematic curriculum planning. Indeed, one can infer that the actual as well as the "hidden" objectives are frequently quite contrary to what is written in the curriculum guides. Feyereisen, Fiorino, and Nowak comment as follows on objectives that could be so inferred from the difference between the system's input and output:

> One objective must be to dull the curiosity of our students, because most children leave school less curious than when they entered. Another objective would be to diminish or extinguish the desire to learn, because most students enter school with a much stronger desire to learn than when they leave. . . . We would have to agree that these may not be the "real" objectives of the curriculum—but if these are not, what are they? The implication here seems clear. While we in education have given lip service to the need for a statement of clearly defined objectives, little has been accomplished.[45]

The problem seems to be the failure to relate the various components of the curriculum to long-term goals as well as to short-term specific objectives. For example, a widely cited goal of curriculum planning is to develop educational programs which help learners become increasingly self-directing. Curriculum plans that reflect this goal would need to include curriculum designs and instructional modes which extend over the entire period of schooling, and the evaluative procedures would need to appraise the growth of self-direction over an extended period as well as for short-term instructional units. But most curriculum plans are

[45] Feyereisen, Fiorino, and Nowak, pp. 131–132.

for relatively short periods, and evaluation arrangements rarely include such goals as this one, and even more rarely do they cover multiyear periods.

In fact, the concept of the curriculum plan as relating to a particular set of goals and objectives within a specific curriculum domain differs rather sharply from most curriculum planning practice. A curriculum plan, in practice, tends to be a course of study or an instructional system within a subject field for achieving varied objectives, typically cognitive ones, relating to a particular body of subject matter. In his treatment of curriculum design, Beauchamp describes a curriculum as "a written document" and notes that "a most commonly included feature is an outline of the subject matter to be taught."[46] One can infer from some courses of study that the objectives were determined by the subject matter rather than the reverse.

The concept of curriculum content as consisting of "learning opportunities" is also at variance with much practice. The typical curriculum guide is a schedule of subject matter and activities presented as a sequence for a class of students rather than a set of suggested alternative programs and activities that may be chosen for and/or by individual students as their own learning experiences.

Dynamic and Realistic Goals and Objectives

Educational goals and curriculum objectives should be as changeable as are their sources: social conditions and needs and the nature of learners and learning. Undoubtedly a major explanation for student dissatisfaction with schools and colleges in recent years stems from the continued adherence by these institutions to specific goals and objectives and hence programs that are no longer relevant in a rapidly changing society. Young people today are not only conscious of the shortcomings of society and the schools but outspoken about what they feel. Especially they want diversity, Toffler says in *Future Shock*:

> One basic complaint of the student is that he is not treated as an individual, that he is served up an undifferentiated gruel, rather than a personalized product. Like the Mustang buyer, the student wants to design his own. The difference is that while industry is highly responsive to consumer demand, education typically has been indifferent to student wants.[47]

Put another way, statements of objectives and thus curriculum plans frequently do not reflect the most influential learning experiences

[46] Beauchamp, p. 83.
[47] Alvin Toffler, *Future Shock* (New York: Bantam Books, 1970), p. 272.

created by the school. Note the emphasis given to the indirect but effective curriculum by Silberman in the popular report of his observations of American education:

> What educators must realize, moreover, is that how they teach and how they act may be more important than what they teach. The way we do things, that is to say, shapes values more directly and more effectively than the way we talk about them. Certain administrative procedures like automatic promotion, homogeneous grouping, racial segregation, or selective admission to higher education affect "citizenship education" more profoundly than does the social studies curriculum. And children are taught a host of lessons about values, ethics, morality, character, and conduct every day of the week, less by the content of the curriculum than by the way schools are organized, the way teachers and parents behave, the way they talk to children and to each other, the kinds of behavior they approve or reward and the kinds they disapprove or punish. These lessons are far more powerful than the verbalizations that accompany them and that they frequently controvert.[48]

In addition to encouraging practices that lack present relevance, some schools still fail to relate goals and programs. Although many major goals are permanent, specific applications and programs must be appropriate to a time and place. Continuing failure to base the curriculum on dynamic and realistic goals and objectives underlies the serious concern of many citizens and educators for the survival of public education. Undoubtedly, much of the gap between educational goals and the actual curriculum of the schools is attributable to the impact of various external factors that are not properly weighted in a systematic process of curriculum planning. We turn now to these factors.

External Forces Affecting Curriculum Planning

In addition to the recognized forces of legal structures, educational research, and professional relations that constitute established sources of data for curriculum planning, many external forces operate on the curriculum planning process as variables that must also be considered in local situations. Several of these major forces are briefly identified below.

National Curriculum Projects The role of national curriculum projects is described in detail in Chapter 2. The projects have constituted one of the chief realities of curriculum planning since the late

---

[48] Silberman, p. 9. On this same point see Michael Scriven, "Values and the Valuing Process," Diablo Valley Education Project, Curriculum Planning Workshop. ERIC Document No. ED 059932, 1971.

1950s when most of them got started as part of the post-Sputnik effort to upgrade U.S. education, especially in the sciences. Special funding through the National Science Foundation, the National Defense Education Act, and other federal sources gave early priority to curriculum development in science, mathematics, and foreign languages, but the model of these projects as means of updating, reorganizing, and disseminating curriculum content spread to other fields. There developed a continuing relation among the projects, government and philanthropic foundations, and publishers that has led to wide adoption of the "new" subject sequences and materials. Through the output of these projects local curriculum planners have a wider variety of curriculum materials in the standard subject fields as well as in some emergent ones than was true earlier. The planning groups, however, must continue to face the problems of teacher readiness to use the materials and the possibility of the "new" subject matter becoming frozen and out of date.

Tradition With opinion polls and other community interaction devices, curriculum planners today are not as powerless to evaluate the force of tradition as in the past when the argument "they won't let us change" was an ever-powerful deterrent to curriculum change. Nevertheless, the beliefs of parents, students, and community power groups reflect their experience and its traditionalizing effects, and these beliefs must be considered in curriculum decision-making. Reliance on tradition perpetuates the status quo, but disregard of it may hasten regression.

Accreditation The intent of accreditation is to maintain some acceptable, at least minimum, level of education. Originally accreditation was largely a school-college relation that was regionally initiated at the turn of this century to facilitate college admission. The impact of regional accrediting associations on high school programs lessened with the advent of more rigorous state standards and accrediting procedures. State accreditation is a means of enforcing state regulations regarding schools, but it is also used in some states as a means of improving local educational planning processes. In any event the local curriculum planning group must deal with the realities of accreditation requirements of whatever bodies accredit their schools; frequently whether a major change can be made in a school's program depends on whether an exception can be made in these requirements, and fortunately most accrediting plans have procedures to encourage experimentation. In some states local initiative is being encouraged through new patterns of accreditation and planning. In Colorado, for example, school districts may set their own standards in contracts with the state department of education. The 1972 Florida legislature required each school district (the county unit in Florida) to develop a comprehensive annual and long-term plan for meeting its educational program needs. The implementing regulation of the state board of education included a provision for waiving state regulations that conflicted with a district's comprehensive plan:

> Upon the written request of a district school board the Commissioner is authorized to waive specifically identified State Board Regulations for a specified period of time when, in the opinion of the Commissioner, the evidence presented by the district board is sufficient to show that the regulation is preventing the attainment of a valid objective identified in the district comprehensive plan.[49]

The Preparatory Syndrome   The ladder system of education has brought with it what we consider almost a syndrome of illnesses related to the notion that the student must prepare at each rung of the ladder for the next, with the college and especially now the graduate school at the top being the great determiner of educational purposes and programs below. Despite all of their services to the schools, colleges and universities have had an impact on curriculum planning that has often augured against the interests of students and that is inconsistent with our first assumption, that the central purpose of education is the development of an independent learner. Current changes in educational patterns toward more varied community college programs, intermittent study-work programs, adult education, and changing patterns of college admission may make possible lessened emphasis on presumed requirements for college preparation. In any event, more systematic processes of curriculum planning will utilize continuum concepts rather than grade norms. Hopefully, they will also involve systematic input and feedback from many sources, not just the level above, and will include in planning groups representatives of various levels.

Public Opinion   Since 1969 annual Gallup polls have given educational planners data as to national trends in public opinion, and many local polls on specific issues provide more relevant data for local curriculum planners. Certainly this elusive force of public opinion is one to be appraised seriously in formulating educational goals and means of achieving them. Suggestions regarding citizens' participation in curriculum planning are included in Chapter 2 and at other appropriate points in this book.

Special Interest Groups   Many special interest groups in the United States are constantly seeking to affect curriculum decisions.

---

[49] Cited in Florida Department of Education, *Guidelines for District Comprehensive Educational Planning, 1973–1974* (Tallahassee, Fla.: The Department, 1972), p. 4.

Whenever some group—patriotic, political, religious, economic, or whatever—wishes to impress the group's views and purposes on others, it almost inevitably decides that the school should be requested, aided, or pressured into getting its point of view into the school program. Accordingly these groups, usually with the highest and generally worthy motives, work to affect the curriculum through such steps as the passage of laws, the adoption by local boards of policies or prescriptions, public statements and news releases, provision of free and inexpensive materials, and contacts with teacher groups and individual teachers to urge the use or elimination of particular materials. The operation of such groups is clearly valid within the processes of American democracy, but their uncontrolled or unregulated impact on the school curriculum can be calamitous. Systematic processes of curriculum planning regularize the input of these groups and provide for the screening of their requests while at the same time utilizing the unique contributions many have to make. Effective community councils and other plans of total community representation tend to minimize the pressure of individual groups.

The "Knowledge Industry" Textbook publishers have been joined by a variety of commercial organizations aiming to produce materials and equipment—software and hardware—for the very large school market. "Learning kits," "curriculum packages," and other terms have been used to describe the considerable output of this relatively new "knowledge industry." These organizations are active in their type of research and development of materials and aggressive in their pursuit of sales. Many have marketed the products of the curriculum projects described above, and many have long utilized professional educational assistance in the development of their products. Resulting from these efforts is a very large body of instructional materials from which curriculum planning groups may select. A major challenge to the curriculum planning system is a means of keeping abreast of the supply of materials and equipment and a sound pattern for their selection and evaluation.

Testing Programs Tests produced by many publishers, and others sponsored by professional organizations, accrediting agencies, and colleges and universities, also have a significant impact on curriculum planning. This relation is described and analyzed in Chapter 7.

Philanthropic Foundations Private philanthropy, especially through foundations, has supported many fundamental educational improvements on a national, regional, and local basis. Through their support of particular research projects and specific programs within school districts these foundations may have a rather direct influence on curriculum planning. The curriculum planning system must provide for obtaining data about possible sources of support and for utilizing and evaluating support received in light of the goals of the system.

Phases of the Curriculum Plan

As indicated in Figure 4, the principal phases of the curriculum plan—as a whole and within each curriculum domain—are curriculum designing, curriculum implementation (instruction), and curriculum evaluation. Chapters 5–7 deal with these components in detail. If this conception were clearly translated into practice, the plan for achieving any set of major educational goals would include the grouping of learning opportunities in some type of design or pattern, a selection of instructional modes, and a plan for evaluation. Actually, even the more complete plans rarely include more than the beginning of an evaluation plan, and many have very incomplete descriptions or only designations of possible instructional modes.

Another set of factors to be considered in the curriculum planning process relates to school organization. At what points in the educational continuum are particular opportunities to be made available, and at what points on their own continuums would different learners be helped to accept certain opportunities? Such questions relate, of course, to the vertical organization of schooling and also to the matter of individual sequences in learning. Traditionally, curriculum plans have assumed a graded school ladder and have been differentiated as to the level of school and even the grade; thus, a characteristic curriculum plan would be for elementary school mathematics, grade 5. It might be further differentiated for slow, average, and fast learners. But the continuum notion (see Figure 2) in curriculum planning is incompatible with a graded school system; plans influenced by the continuum concept focus on objectives or competencies to be achieved instead of time and ground to be covered. Shane noted the following implications of the curriculum continuum notion for traditional practices relating to student progress:

> There would be no failure or "double promotion."
> "Special education" and "remedial work" would cease to exist.
> Annual promotion would become a thing of the past.
> There would be no dropouts.
> Compensatory education would terminate.
> Report cards and marks would vanish.[50]

Feedback and Evaluation

As noted above, the entire component of curriculum evaluation is missing in many curriculum plans and inadequately provided for in most. In addition, the systematic provision for feedback from each step

[50] Shane, p. 391.

in the curriculum system—and from learners in each instructional situation—is frequently lacking. Feedback and evaluation constitute a major contribution of the systems model to curriculum planning, and they also constitute the major basis of continuing curriculum improvement. More ingenious, frequent, and significant uses of feedback are possible in most curriculum systems.

Current arguments for and approaches to "accountability" in education stem in part from the inadequate provision for evaluation in curriculum plans of the past. Lessinger, a leading proponent of accountability plans, explained the concept in part as follows:

> With the advent of major federal aid to education, taxpayers increasingly ask, "What are we getting for our money?" Traditional answers in terms of resources employed, teachers available, and buildings provided are no longer sufficient. The public wants to know, for a start, whether young people can read, can get and hold a job, can go as far in higher education as their abilities warrant. This is a call for accountability in results, a growing demand for changes in the way that schools are managed.[51]

The Locale of the Curriculum

Our curriculum planning system would be designed to allocate learning opportunities to the places where they can most appropriately take place. The selection of instructional modes involves decisions as to places and personnel. Undoubtedly, many learning opportunities can be better provided in community facilities rather than in schools on both independent study and group-inquiry bases. Joyce blamed much of the "impotence" of the curriculum field on its past focus on schools and teachers: *"By focusing on a certain kind of educational institution (the school) and by focusing on functionaries (teachers) whose roles have developed within the constraints of that institution, the curriculum field has forced itself to operate within parameters so restrictive that it has been unable to develop strong, validated theory and it has been impotent to improve education."*[52]

Typical curriculum plans rarely assume a locale other than the school, because the curriculum has traditionally been what happens in school. Future designing, we believe, will take into much fuller account the possibilities of curriculum happenings outside the school. Toffler's predictions include change in the locale of schooling made possible by advanced technology:

---

[51] Leon M. Lessinger, *Every Kid a Winner: Accountability in Education* (New York: Simon and Schuster, Inc., 1970), pp. 8–9.

[52] Joyce, "The Curriculum Worker of the Future," p. 314. [Joyce's italics]

A good deal of education will take place in the student's own room at home or in a dorm, at hours of his own choosing. With vast libraries of data available to him via computerized information retrieval systems, with his own tapes and video units, his own language laboratory, and his own electronically equipped study carrel, he will be freed, for much of the time, of the restrictions and unpleasantness that dogged him in the lockstep classroom.[53]

Chapter 6 on instructional modes assumes a wide range of locales for the implementation of the curriculum.

Flexibility in Curriculum Plans

Some curriculum plans anticipate considerable flexibility in teachers' choices of subject matter and activities, whereas others assume one basic route to achievement of the objectives or coverage of the topic. Few plans anticipate adequately the wide range of individual differences within learning groups and a correspondingly wide choice of alternative learning opportunities. A flexible curriculum plan is flexible in all aspects: alternative curriculum designs, instructional modes, and evaluative procedures.

Such flexibility is possible only as curriculum planners build into their plans many alternatives and as the users of the plans—teachers and students—choose freely from the alternatives. Such an "open access curriculum," as advocated by Wilson, would have among other characteristics "guidelines for study (but not prescribed and controlled routes) that permit students to commit themselves to fully personalized projects, to pursue them as long as their interests dictate and their success warrants."[54]

Adoption of Externally Developed Plans

In our judgment the most serious gap between the theory and practice of curriculum planning occurs as local planning groups and individual teachers adopt without study and adaptation specific plans made external to the school center and population concerned. This practice is perhaps most obviously represented by blind adherence to a textbook as *the* curriculum plan for a particular subject. The uncritical use of commercially prepared curriculum packages is little different. The curriculum plan as we have presented it, designed for a particular population and for particular goals and objectives, would rarely be identical

[53] Toffler, p. 275.
[54] L. Craig Wilson, *The Open Access Curriculum* (Boston: Allyn and Bacon, Inc., 1971), p. 16.

from one school situation to another. Uniform curriculum plans for different school centers are not consistent with the concept of systematic curriculum planning processes.

COMPONENTS OF THE CURRICULUM

The curriculum system is a set of components, we noted earlier, for achieving broad educational goals. These components comprise plans for a program of learning opportunities arranged within curriculum domains and include suggestions for curriculum designs, instructional modes, and evaluative procedures. These concepts are briefly defined in the following paragraphs.

Curriculum Domains

Earlier we defined a curriculum domain as "a grouping of learning opportunities planned to achieve a single set of major educational goals." Thus the identity of the domains for which plans are made for a particular school center is dependent upon the major educational goals selected by the planners. We recognize, of course, that many factors determine the goals of a particular school center, and it is to be expected that goals will differ among centers. Nevertheless, we suggest as a broad classification of goals by domains for our reference in this and other chapters of this book four sets of goals that seem to us to be of great present and future significance: personal development, human relations, continued learning skills, and specialization. That these domains may be perennial is indicated by two somewhat similar classifications made in past decades. The analyses and deliberations regarding U.S. life and education by the Educational Policies Commission resulted in this 1938 classification of educational purposes:

1. The Objectives of Self-realization
2. The Objectives of Human Relationship
3. The Objectives of Economic Efficiency
4. The Objectives of Civic Responsibility[55]

This report describes these purposes in detail, listing many subpurposes and objectives.

Studies conducted during the 1950s at the Midwest Administra-

---

[55] Educational Policies Commission, *The Purposes of Education in American Democracy* (Washington, D.C.: National Education Association, 1938).

tion Center of the University of Chicago concerning the task of public education resulted in the following conceptual framework:

A. Intellectual Dimensions

1. *Possession of Knowledge*: A fund of information, concepts.
2. *Communication of Knowledge*: Skill to acquire and transmit.
3. *Creation of Knowledge*: Discrimination and imagination, a habit.
4. *Desire for Knowledge:* A love for learning.

B. Social Dimensions

5. *Man to Man*: Cooperation in day-to-day relations.
6. *Man to State*: Civic rights and duties.
7. *Man to Country*: Loyalty to one's own country.
8. *Man to World*: Inter-relationships of peoples.

C. Personal Dimensions

9. *Physical*: Bodily health and development.
10. *Emotional*: Mental health and stability.
11. *Ethical*: Moral integrity.
12. *Aesthetic*: Cultural and leisure pursuits.

D. Productive Dimensions

13. *Vocation-Selective*: Information and guidance.
14. *Vocation-Preparative*: Training and placement.
15. *Home and Family*: Housekeeping, do-it-yourself, family.
16. *Consumer*: Personal buying, selling, and investment.[56]

Although each of these taxonomies includes domains similar to our own, we consider that of the Educational Policies Commission inadequate for current use because it subsumes under other purposes the skills of continued learning. Too, both of them ignore phases of specialization other than the economic, productive ones, important as these are. For the 1970s and beyond, educational goals that relate to lifelong learning (our domain of continued learning skills) and to multifaceted interests, career and otherwise (our specialization domain), are significant and seem to us deserving of central emphasis in curriculum planning.

     Personal Development   In a very general sense the entire purpose of education is to aid the development of the person. Somewhat less generally, we see much schooling that seeks in many ways at all levels to aid the individual in attaining his personal objectives, solving his personal problems, and above all establishing his concept of self. This major category of goals has been stated in many ways: "to enable

[56] Lawrence Wm. Downey, *The Task of Public Education: The Perceptions of People* (Chicago: Midwest Administration Center, University of Chicago, 1960), p. 24.

the individual to achieve his potential"; "to help the individual develop a favorable self-concept"; "to guide the individual's search for self-actualization"—or "self-direction"—or "independence." Despite the controversy concerning whether the school should be interested in the "whole child," the well-recognized fact is that progress in school, academic and otherwise, is inextricably related to the total growth and development and well-being of the learner.

The personal development domain includes a vast array of learning opportunities: basic communication skills; most opportunities relating to the so-called general education objectives; value assessment and development; guidance and counseling services; health and physical education; exploratory subjects; activities and opportunities that give each individual chances to discover areas of interest for later specialization; and others.

Human Relations   American educational goals have generally given emphasis to citizenship education, social welfare, human rights, and similar phrases which we encompass under the term "human relations." Certainly a continuous and essential goal of education in a society of human beings, and especially in one which prizes democratic values and processes, is ever-improving human relations.

This domain, too, includes a plethora of curriculum possibilities: the various knowledge areas included in the social sciences and humanities; languages; social interaction and organization within the schools themselves; the participation of students in the various social groups and institutions of their communities; and specific studies and skill-development activities related to particular human relations problems within the school and community, such as those involved in cultural differences and conflicts, and, again, valuing processes.

Continued Learning Skills   In practice much schooling has been preparatory for further study; the assumption seems to have been that the more knowledge a person acquires in school the better prepared he will be for acquiring still more knowledge at higher levels. Beyond reading and some other knowledge-acquiring skills, traditionally little attention has been paid to the skills learners need to learn effectively outside of and after school. With the ever-increasing changes in today's society, it is futile to expect individuals to store up during twelve to sixteen years enough information to solve future problems of adjustment. Instead, there is now wide agreement that the central mission of schooling is to develop lifelong learners—individuals who are motivated to continue learning and who have the basic skills to do so.

This curriculum domain includes such standard plans as instruction in reading, listening, viewing, and speaking. It encompasses as well plans generally yet to be made for teaching more advanced learning skills: interviewing, discussing, interacting; using various information-retrieval systems, including those made possible by computers; analyzing issues, selecting alternatives, trying out ideas, and other problem-solving skills; locating sources for continued study; evaluating sources and ideas; generalizing; and others. Especially needing emphasis in future curriculum plans are the learning skills related to use of the media, group interaction, and the computer.

Specialization   The specialization domain is even more difficult to categorize than the others, for what is specialized education for one individual may be exploratory or general education for another. American education clearly seeks to provide a wide and varied range of opportunities for individual students to work in depth in the areas they choose for themselves on the bases of interests and qualifications. Specialization for career purposes is generally delayed until after high school, yet many adolescents terminate, at least for some years, their education before or upon finishing high school. Even elementary school children develop strong interests in music, art, sports, and other areas that can be the basis of extended instruction and independent study. Thus this domain includes such traditional school areas as those generally classified as prevocational or vocational and, in addition, almost any area that can be pursued in depth by an individual selecting it for specialization. In this case specialization includes such cut-across learning opportunities chosen on the basis of individual interest as work experience, community service, or extended study in another school center, community, state, or nation.

In the 1970s the emphasis on education for earning a living was revived as "career development" or "career education" through the leadership of the then U.S. Commissioner of Education, Sidney P. Marland, Jr. Marland noted his preference for the term "career education," since it implies a structured preparation program as an integral part of a student's academic course work throughout his school and college years. He stated: "Inherent in the concept is the principle that our schools and colleges are accountable to students not only for developing their problem-solving skills, self-awareness, and social consciousness, but for equipping them as well to earn a living in a personally satisfying career field."[57] Certainly we would agree that the goal of career development and many programs for career education should be prominent in the specialization domain.

These four domains—personal development, human relations,

---

[57] Sidney P. Marland, Jr., "The School's Role in Career Development," *Educational Leadership*, 50, 203 (December 1972). "Education for Career Development" is the theme of this issue, which includes various articles on the theory and practice of career education.

continued learning skills, and specialization—represent a classification of major educational goals and related learning opportunities that seems fairly universal and therefore useful for the purposes of this book. It is not assumed that each school center in the United States would necessarily have curriculum plans within each of these domains, nor that additional domains cannot be developed. In Chapter 4 we deal fully with the process of defining goals and domains and indicate various classifications of goals that have been made in American education. There we also give attention to other levels of goals and objectives, especially the development and use of objectives for particular learning opportunities.

Curriculum Designs

We see designing as the somewhat creative aspect of curriculum planning, analogous to the role of the architect in building or the fashion designer in clothing or the menu planner (not the recipe maker) in cooking. The planning group responsible, for example, for developing plans in the human relations domain for a population of middle school children, having collected and analyzed essential data and identified goals, would need to create or select a general pattern—a design—for the learning opportunities to be provided. Among their alternatives would be (1) a subject design utilizing specific studies in the social sciences and humanities; (2) a scope and sequence plan built around a selection of persistent human relations (scope); (3) an analysis of the essential skills of human relations to be taught as the basis of activity and skills groups; (4) a selection with the students of individual interests and problems related to human relations in the classroom, school, and community; (5) and others, including combinations of the foregoing. The design plan ultimately anticipates the entire range of learning opportunities within the domain for this population, or at least the points of further planning.

Instructional Modes

The curriculum system, as we have viewed and presented it, includes the implementation of the curriculum design, or instruction. Each learning opportunity involves some mode, that is, way of happening. We present in Chapter 6 our classification of instructional modes.

Evaluative Procedures

The curriculum system also includes a plan for evaluation of the curriculum in relation to its goals. Our treatment of evaluation (Chapter 7) recognizes both formative and summative evaluation. Formative procedures are the feedback arrangements which enable the planners and implementers of the curriculum to make adjustments and improvements throughout the planning, or implementing, process. The summative evaluation comes at the end and deals directly with the evaluation of the total curriculum plan; this evaluation becomes in effect feedback for the planners to use in deciding whether to repeat, modify, or eliminate the plan with another population.

WHO PLANS THE CURRICULUM?

Chapter 2 deals with specific roles of various persons in the curriculum planning process. At this point we emphasize certain major postulates of our theory of curriculum planning.

The Student in the Leading Role

As indicated in the two central assumptions stated at the beginning of this chapter, we see the student as being actively involved in planning his own curriculum. Indeed, we see him as having the lead in the drama of his engagement with the learning opportunities he selects from the planned program of them provided by his school center for the population of which he is a member. Whether he spends his school day in an elementary or middle school or in and out of his high school or college or as a continuing learner having only infrequent contact with a school center, it is the learner himself who must finally embrace or reject the opportunities his school curriculum presents. As a member of the student population he also has opportunities related to his level of maturity to help in planning the total program; in this process of curriculum planning he participates but does not necessarily have the lead.

Other Roles in the School Center

Supporting the leading actor in the individualized curriculum drama are all the teachers, resource specialists, community educators, and others who share in teaching and guiding individual learners. For more dependent learners, hopefully limited to the earlier spans of the curriculum continuum, this support is quite active, providing incentives and careful guidance. For more independent learners, support is more on call of the learner. We consider especially important for more personalized curriculum planning the role of directors or counselors for personal development, an idea we develop in some detail in Chapter 8.

Our major concern in developing curriculum plans is to project a total program of learning opportunities keyed to the total population of the school center and reflecting the major goals it serves. Here the leaders are those with expertise in a systematic approach to curriculum planning: persons who can move from goals to curriculum domains to curriculum designs, instructional strategies, and evaluation schemes. These leaders are variously classified as teachers, resource specialists, curriculum directors and coordinators, counselors and directors of personal development, and administrators. Whatever their titles, their roles are those needed in the systematic process of curriculum planning.

External Participants

Various persons outside the school center also have significant roles to play in planning a program of learning opportunities for its students. Curriculum, instruction, and evaluation specialists from the district offices, community educators and resource specialists, parents, and others in the school community are needed in the system. A systematic process may involve the services of a curriculum designing unit outside the individual school centers, this unit staffed to provide the expertise needed by several school centers or possibly all centers within the district.

We prefer to think of all the organizations and individuals associated with various external forces affecting curriculum planning as resources for the curriculum planners rather than as a part of the planning group. That is, the project directors, authors, publishers, testers, accreditors, pollsters, lobbyists, and philanthropists we identified earlier as related to curriculum planning have much potential to affect this process, but systematic planning should elicit this potential as it is needed by the system.

The Teacher as Curriculum Planner

Past and present educational practice has enthroned the teacher as the final curriculum planner for his "class." Now that school organization is rapidly abandoning the notion of a standard-size class as the instructional unit and substituting varied size groups with much individualized instruction, the role of the teacher in planning is also changed. We see the teacher as a very active participant in the planning of the total program of the school center and of the learning opportunities within his particular domain(s) of the curriculum. In many school centers the teacher will have no "class" of his own but will instead be responsible for various groups and individuals within his domain(s). His planning responsibility then increasingly becomes one of continuing development of the particular learning programs through which he guides his students and of planning with individual students for their continuing progress through these programs. Whether he has a set group of students for guidance over an extended period of time or a rapidly changing group as programs are completed, or both patterns, depends on the plan of instructional organization developed by the planning groups involved.

THE MARKS OF A "GOOD" CURRICULUM (PLAN)

In closing this chapter we present a checklist whereby a visitor to a school center or a person employed there could investigate the quality of the school's curriculum (plan). No rating device is suggested although the person using the checklist could develop some scale if this seemed appropriate. In general, we would assume that affirmative answers to these questions, hopefully all of them, would indicate a good curriculum:

1. Are such essential data as are suggested in Chapter 3 available to the planning groups responsible for the curriculum of the school?
2. Are the goals of the school clearly stated and understood by all concerned? Are the goals sufficiently comprehensive, balanced, and realistic? Is there provision for modifying, dropping, and adding goals as needed?
3. Do the learning opportunities anticipate a progression from dependent, other-directed learning to independent, self-directed learning in accordance with the level of students served by the school center?
4. Do students and teachers mutually understand the specific plans in the total curriculum plan which affect them? Do students participate, as their maturities permit, in making the plans? Do they generally understand and agree as to what is expected of them, and why?
5. Are sets of related major goals grouped accordingly, with the learning opportunities in each set or domain selected for achieving these goals? Have sets of learning opportunities been checked as to their relation to the goals, with gaps and overlappings identified and remedied? Do the learning opportunities seem to be the best possible choices for this group of students at this time to achieve the goals set for them?
6. Within each domain or set of goals and related learning opportunities is there a pattern or patterns reflecting conscious attention to curriculum designing? Are all appropriate and feasible types of learning experiences utilized?
7. Is the plan tailor-made for the particular school center? Are any plans developed externally, adapted to the population and

facilities of the school center? Are the learning opportunities planned truly relevant to the educational needs of this population and community?

8. Are demands of external forces screened through a process that keeps them in acceptable balance?

9. Is the total curriculum plan comprehensive? Does it anticipate instruction and evaluation as well as include goals and designs of learning opportunities?

10. Are the responsible planning groups representative of all persons concerned, including students, parents, general public, and professional staff?

11. Does the plan have adequate provision of feedback from students and other concerned groups as well as means for making modification as indicated?

12. Can the plan and each of its parts be explained sufficiently clearly to the students, parents, and other lay persons to be understood by them?

13. Is there some representative council or curriculum evaluation unit or other group or individual responsible for identifying problems and collecting problems identified by others that develop in the planning process? Is there a clear channel of communication of such problems to those who can resolve them and a plan for reporting back to the problem identifiers the resolutions made? Similarly, is there a systematic way of securing, monitoring, and reporting action regarding suggestions for change and innovation?

14. Does the plan anticipate full use of the educational resources of the school center, the community, and the media?

15. Is flexibility built into the curriculum plan by adequate provisions for alternative learning opportunities, instructional modes, and student and teacher options in general?

ADDITIONAL SUGGESTIONS FOR FURTHER STUDY

Alexander, William M., "Curriculum Planning as It Should Be," in J. Galen Saylor, ed., *The School of the Future Now*. Washington, D.C.: Association for Supervision and Curriculum Development, 1972, Chap. 7. Somewhat more abbreviated treatment of some concepts presented in Chapters 1 and 2; see especially pages 118–125 on "Facilitating Curriculum Planning."

Briggs, Leslie, *Handbook of Procedures for the Design of Instruction*. Pittsburgh, Pa.: American Institutes for Research, 1970. A systems-based model for designing instruction and instructional materials, complete with practice exercises and self-tests.

Broudy, Harry S., *The Real World of the Public Schools*. New York: Harcourt

Brace Jovanovich, Inc., 1972. Advances the level of criticism of the public schools and offers provocative suggestions as to their future.

Curriculum Theory Network. Ontario, Canada: Ontario Institute for Studies in Education. An occasional journal, published beginning Summer 1968, devoted to curriculum theory and aiming to bring together "people interested in formulating a theoretical and methodological base for curriculum development and a coherent curriculum theory."

Frymier, Jack, *A School for Tomorrow*. Project sponsored by the Association for Supervision and Curriculum Development. Berkeley, Calif.: McCutchan Publishing Corporation, 1973. See especially Chapters 2–5 in relation to our Chapter 1 curriculum model.

Hillson, Maurie, and Joseph Bongo, *Continuous-Progress Education: A Practical Approach*. Chicago: Science Research Associates, 1971. Contains specific suggestions, formulas, and materials to aid in implementing the continuum concept of the curriculum through a nongraded, continuous progress system.

Hughes, John F. and Anne O., *Equal Education: A New National Strategy*. Bloomington, Ind.: Indiana University Press, 1972. Critically reviews the programs funded under Title I of the Elementary and Secondary Education Act and other federal efforts toward equal education and proposes a new national strategy for achieving equal educational opportunity.

Leeper, Robert R., *Curricular Concerns in a Revolutionary Era*. Washington, D.C.: Association for Supervision and Curriculum Development, 1971. Readings from *Educational Leadership* that emphasize, especially, forces for curriculum change such as value conflicts, individualization, social involvement, integration, ethnic studies, and student rights and responsibilities.

Lengrand, Paul, *An Introduction to Lifelong Education*. Paris: UNESCO, 1970. Describes forces calling for lifelong education and stresses the necessity to link together the objectives and processes of education for children, adolescents, and adults.

Martin, John H., and Charles H. Henderson, *Free To Learn: Unlocking and Ungrading American Education*. Englewood Cliffs, N.J.: Prentice-Hall, Inc., 1972. Criticizes past education and outlines a plan for community-based programs aiming to "rearrange the assembly-line classroom into a sophisticated and highly efficient version of the one room school house."

2

PROCESSES
AND ROLES
IN CURRICULUM
PLANNING

Many processes—from the most casual to the most highly organized—are utilized in curriculum planning for American schools, and many groups and individuals play diverse roles—from very minor to primary ones—in these operations. In this chapter we describe and to some extent classify these processes and roles, so that our readers, present and prospective curriculum planners, may choose their own processes and roles or fashion new ones. Attention is first turned to the products of curriculum planning.

THE PRODUCTS OF CURRICULUM PLANNING—
THE PLANS

As explained in Chapter 1 (see Figure 3), the curriculum plan is regarded as an arrangement of internal variables (curriculum designs, instructional modes, and evaluation procedures) intended to achieve the particular goals and objectives of the curriculum domain(s) involved. The plan may be global, encompassing all goals and domains, or specific for an individual goal and domain or some phase thereof. Typically it is written; otherwise it is unlikely to serve as a reference for implementation and evaluation.

Broadly speaking, the products of curriculum planning include much more than written curriculum plans, or curriculum guides. Ideally, the products include changes in the behavior of learners, and, to achieve these, changes in the practices of teachers and the teaching environments which affect learners. The direct products of planning which we can analyze here are the plans to affect the people and things that constitute teaching-learning situations. We cannot lose sight of the fact, however, that changes in learner behavior are the ultimate products sought and that the goal of the curriculum planning process is to enable teachers to effect these changes. We heartily concur in Alice Miel's classic thesis that curriculum change is "a type of social change, change in people, not mere change on paper."[1] Certainly the increased understanding of the curriculum and of the teaching and learning which generally accrues from systematic curriculum planning is an important product which almost in itself justifies the process. Teachers who are themselves becoming more knowledgeable, more skillful, and more dynamic can serve increasingly effectively as guides to learners. Hence ultimate changes in learners and their teachers are inextricably related to the plans that are direct products of the curriculum planning process.

Curriculum Plans and Levels of Planning

The nature of curriculum plans is influenced by the levels at and/or for which they are developed: national, state, school district, individual school, group of teachers, individual teacher. Various kinds of plans developed at these levels are identified in a subsequent section on levels of planning.

Curriculum Guides

Most curriculum plans developed by state and local school agencies are ultimately put in written form, thus becoming curriculum guides. One can obtain an idea of their number and variety from the hundreds of guides exhibited at each annual conference of the Association for Supervision and Curriculum Development and the annual published list of the guides exhibited. A sample of titles is shown in Figure 5. The

[1]Alice Miel, *Changing the Curriculum* (New York: Appleton-Century-Crofts, 1946), p. 10.

FIGURE 5   Sample of curriculum guide titles.

many thousands of such guides in published form can be roughly classified as follows.

General Statements   Many school districts and even individual schools find it desirable to prepare statements of their philosophy and program of education. Such general guides usually contain one or more of the following types of materials: philosophy and objectives; scope and sequence of learning opportunities, usually organized by subject fields; suggestions for organizing instruction; policies relating to the curriculum. Guides for self-study, assessment programs, preparation of curriculum materials, and other purposes are also prepared.

Courses of Study   Most curriculum guides deal with the content of the curriculum areas. For the elementary and middle schools and much less frequently for high schools and in combined vertical presentations, these guides may indicate suggestions for organizing instruction in all curriculum areas. Many guides deal with a particular field for all levels of instruction, although separate courses of study for each high school subject are also quite common. Frequently the guides are prepared for levels: primary, intermediate, middle, junior high, and senior high school years. Their nature varies from very prescriptive outlines and minimum essentials of content to be taught to very general suggestions to teachers as to possible guidelines for selecting content and organizing instruction.

Specific Teaching Aids   Although the more useful courses of study are usually replete with specific suggestions as to materials and techniques, many publications focus on aiding teachers in particular ways. Thus resource units may be made available for helping teachers plan their own units of work with reference to some broad curriculum topic or theme. Various types of curriculum packages (see pages 74–75), such as learning activity packages (LAP's), may be prepared externally and by teachers for student use. Detailed listings of materials, especially audiovisual ones, and guides to community resources are frequently provided. General guides to teaching, with specific suggestions on many teaching responsibilities, are also issued by some state and larger local systems.

Descriptions of Practice   Any of the above types of curriculum guides may contain descriptions of practice within the school district, but some districts also publish bulletins wholly devoted to describing curriculum opportunities and teaching practices within these districts. Although frequently directed primarily to parents and the general public, such bulletins also serve useful purposes in helping the teachers who prepare them and others who read them develop common concepts about the school program.

Undoubtedly some curriculum guides are not put to good use, but we would not abandon the important process of preparing guides just because of faulty procedures or poor products in some situations. The growth that can come from cooperative work by school personnel in developing guides is perhaps one of the major reasons for maintaining the production of these materials. Furthermore, good guides, well planned and well written, can be of much direct assistance to school personnel. We suggest the following considerations for their development:

1. Each guide should clearly indicate its intended use. Generally, there are two uses by professional school personnel: (a) orientation and reference with respect to the total curriculum and the curriculum policies of the school district; and (b) specific guidance of teachers in planning instruction.

2. Guides written to give specific help to teachers should suggest a wealth of possibilities from which the teacher may derive ideas for exploration in his own situation. The presentation of suggestions should be in such form as to aid the teacher in understanding and evaluating them, and also to emphasize the teacher's responsibility and opportunity to make the best plan possible for his situation.

3. The guides should be attractive in format, clear in presentation, and arranged to facilitate teachers' use for reference purposes. For the more specific types of guides, a looseleaf notebook arrangement is probably preferable so that the teacher can insert additional materials. Tabs, paper of different colors, write-in sections, and other mechanical aids are helpful.

4. Most general guides are probably best used as bases of discussion. Accordingly, they should be brief, cogent, and specific as to issues and positions. References to other sources for further study and even questions for discussion may be useful in materials which are likely to be discussed in parent or teacher study groups and in faculty meetings.

DECISION-MAKING IN CURRICULUM PLANNING

The curriculum planning process involves many decisions of various types made at one or more levels. These levels, the major types of decisions, and some factors affecting the decisions are shown graphically in Figure 6, to which specific reference is made at appropriate points in this chapter. The extralegal forces were described in Chapter 1 and various social controls over the schools are treated in Chapter 3.

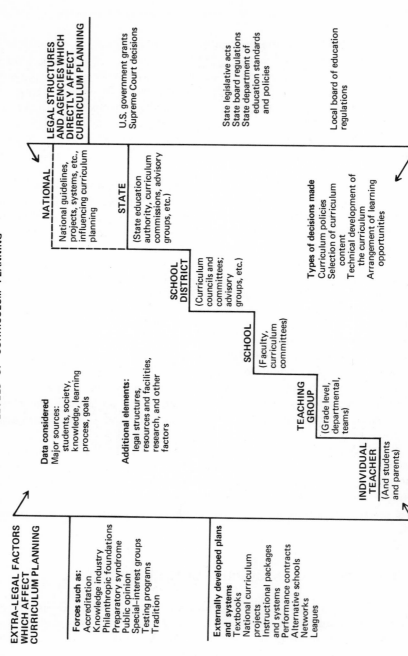

FIGURE 6 Decision-making in curriculum planning.

Levels of Curriculum Planning

Although the types of curriculum decisions made at various points vary from one school situation to another, the organization of U.S. public education is sufficiently uniform to permit a classification of the levels at which curriculum planning occurs. Although the United States has fifty state systems of public education, there are many instances of national curriculum planning in addition to the legal force of Supreme Court decisions and the guidelines of federal grants affecting states and districts which accept such grants. Within the state systems there is the direct relation of state education authority, local district, school, teaching group, and individual teacher, with plans usually existing at each of these levels.

Although Figure 6 is arranged in ladder style, it should not be assumed that curriculum plans are uniformly passed either up or down this ladder. Certainly some set of state requirements influences local planning, and certainly the plans of the individual teacher are nearest the learning situation. But between the state authority and the individual teacher great variation exists as to the activities at other levels and their relations.

Planning at the National Level

Although education was left to the states by the U.S. Constitution—hence the broken lines in Figure 6—there is much curriculum planning of an interstate and national type. The many curriculum studies supported by the federal government and various national organizations, the National Assessment of Educational Progress and other projects emanating from or supported by the Education Commission of the States, the conferences convened by the U.S. Office of Education, the projects of the National Education Association and other national professional organizations, and even some of the special subsidies to certain curriculum areas appropriated by Congress constitute significant efforts toward national curriculum planning. The national curriculum projects (see pages 72–74) have developed and are still developing curriculum plans for particular subject fields, plans that generally are implemented through textbooks and teaching aids that can be adapted to local curriculum plans. Instead of creating their own curriculum plans, many districts simply adopt complete programs developed and sold by regional education laboratories and other organizations. Other externally developed plans described in this chapter include textbooks and teaching aids developed without the guidance of national curriculum projects that also may be adapted or adopted in local situations.

An extension of some curriculum projects and the development of others through agencies originally funded by the federal government is the growing group of instructional systems and curriculum packages, as they are variously called, produced and disseminated on varying bases by the research and development centers and the regional educational laboratories and their successor organizations. For example, a special issue of the *D & R Report,* a periodical of the Council for Educational Development and Research, Inc., on "Elementary Education" in October 1972 included descriptions or announcements of such varied sets of curriculum materials as the following that were in process of development or already available:

> Aesthetic Education Program (5 instructional packages)—CEMREL, Inc., St. Louis, Mo.
> *Teaching of Science: A Self-Directed Learning Guide* (7 manuals) —Research and Development Center for Teacher Education, University of Texas, Austin.
> Achievement Competency Training Package (ACT)—Research for Better Schools, Inc., Philadelphia.
> *Individually Guided Motivation: Guidelines for Implementation*— Wisconsin Research and Development Center for Cognitive Learning, University of Wisconsin, Madison.
> "Innovative Social Studies—Urban Elementary Schools"—Mid-Continent Regional Educational Laboratory, Kansas City, Mo.
> Minicourses for Teacher Training (various materials available through The Macmillan Company)—Far West Laboratory for Educational Research and Development, Berkeley, Calif.
> Instructional Profiles Cards (9 areas)—Center for Urban Education, New York, N.Y.
> Comprehensive School Mathematics Program—CEMREL, Inc., St. Louis, Mo.
> Oral Language Program (OLP) (150 lessons)—Southwestern Cooperative Educational Laboratory, Inc., Austin, Tex.

This list is merely a sample of the great variety of curriculum and instructional materials in various stages of preparation, publication, or use that have come out of the research and development centers and regional educational laboratories originally created by federal funds in the mid-1960s.

Planning at the State Level

The fifty states have varied in the ways their educational agencies influence the curriculum of their local schools and in the extent of their influence. Perhaps the most easily identifiable influences are state constitutional provisions, legislative acts, and state board or department of education regulations which prescribe subjects to be taught, graduation requirements, time allotments, and special programs and emphases. These prescriptions generally stipulate a basic program of studies for the elementary school, including the customary subjects of language arts, arithmetic, U.S. history, geography, science, health, physical education, art, and music; but they may make more specific requirements of some but not all individual subjects for the high schools. The most common requirements for the high schools have been in English and in U.S. history, with many states also prescribing mathematics, science, health, and physical education. Other more specific requirements of individual states have included state history, driver education, conservation, and drug education.

Planning at the state level may control or restrict local curriculum planning through regulatory measures other than these curriculum prescriptions. State textbook adoption still prevails in several states. The state may set special requirements to be met in order for schools to receive state support for special programs. State accreditation standards define many curriculum policies relating to such matters as the program of studies, extraclass activities, library and other learning resources, organization of classes, and many others. State supervision and inspection may have almost the effect of regulation. State examination systems, such as the Regents' examinations in New York, may influence very greatly local curriculum plans. State legislative investigations and reports have at times inhibited local experimentation.

As we see it, to ensure an adequate and indeed excellent program throughout the state, the state should set a broad framework of the school program and provide sufficient general support, with standards to be met in order to receive that support. Regulatory measures are undoubtedly needed, but if the state educational agencies stop with regulations and standards, local decision-making is not aided in moving beyond requirements and minimums to ever-improving educational programs. Thus, we consider the most important function of planning at the state level to be that of working with local leadership in making plans which will aid local school districts in moving forward with their own curriculum planning. Some significant steps in this direction follow:

1. Use of state curriculum commissions, committees, and advisory groups, representing educational groups throughout the state, in determining state curriculum policies, such as those we have identified, and also in recommending ways and means whereby local systems may

organize their own curriculum improvement programs. Curriculum guides may be produced through these endeavors to help local districts move into new areas of curriculum development.

2. Establishment of state curriculum evaluation commissions to carry on deliberate and informed evaluation of curriculum proposals from many sources and to serve liaison functions with such commissions in other states and with national and regional curriculum studies and projects.

3. Stimulation of professional development and school innovation through conferences, consultations, surveys, studies, and other means[2] of focusing the attention of local educational leaders on systematic processes of change.

4. Sponsorship of curriculum research and development studies in the state, with financial and other aid to the schools serving as research centers, with adequate arrangement for field testing and dissemination.

5. Working with state-wide organizations interested in but outside the field of education in order to develop understanding and support of the educational program of the state, and also to secure suggestions for its improvement.

Curriculum Planning at Local Levels

Because of the great importance and prevalence of curriculum planning at the local levels (school district, school, teaching group, individual teacher; see Figure 6), subsequent sections of this chapter deal primarily with locally employed processes.

In addition to overall plans or organization for the entire program, school district plans may encompass such diverse areas as priority goals, or official programs of studies (courses for which graduation credit is given) of all secondary schools; subjects taught in elementary and middle schools, perhaps with some agreement as to time allocations among them; programs of studies for any special groups of students; systems for determining and evaluating student progress in the curriculum; provisions for experimental curriculum projects; agreements as to priorities in the content of any curriculum domain or area; curriculum opportunities to be provided cooperatively or otherwise shared between schools; content of educational television programs for in-school use; arrangements

---

[2] See Henry M. Brickell, *Organizing New York State for Educational Change* (Albany: New York State Department of Education, 1961), for an example of a state-wide effort toward educational change that was influential in stimulating other state programs in the 1960s. Also see Brickell's chapter (20) in Matthew B. Miles, ed., *Innovation in Education* (New York: Teachers College Press, 1964).

for computer-assisted instruction; selection and plans for use of textbooks and other learning resources; and so on.

Any of the plans just identified may be within the decision-making province of the individual school. In addition, school plans include deviations, experimental or otherwise, from district-wide programs of studies and other curriculum plans; agreements as to all-school programs, projects, and emphases; policies concerning the use of school and community facilities and resources in the curriculum; nature and schedule of special activities involving relatively small groups of students; intramural athletics and other activities; agreements as to placement of curriculum content by area and/or level; organization of instructional groups and schedules; and so on.

Any of the plans may be within the province of the teaching group which is especially responsible for specific agreements as to scope and sequence of its curriculum areas; priorities in these areas; preparation of instructional objectives, curriculum prescriptions, teaching and resource units; agreements as to individual responsibilities within the group; details of requirements or expectations of students, syllabi, bibliographies, worksheets, examinations; and so on.

Local policy may leave many of these plans to the individual teacher. In addition, each teacher usually has decisions to make as to year-long, periodic, and daily plans of scope and sequence in his areas of responsibility; units or blocks of work; materials for student use; and plans for individual learners.

Types of Decisions

Instead of presenting hard and fast rules concerning the distribution of decision-making responsibility among boards of education, professional educators, academic scholars, laymen, parents, or students, it may be more useful to recognize the major types of curriculum decisions and to suggest general guidelines as to individuals and groups who contribute to each type. In particular situations, as each aspect of the curriculum planning job is completed, persons are used as their contributions are available. Four major types of decisions are involved in the process of curriculum planning.

Policy-making is perhaps the most difficult kind of curriculum decision-making. In part it is made difficult by the clamor of everyone to participate in it, since almost all citizens as well as professional educators feel they have a stake in the educational process. In the United States curriculum policy-making involves professional organizations and more particularly legally constituted groups, namely, state and local boards of education. Nevertheless, we recognize fully that decisions concerning what to teach and what not to teach in local school districts must be shared not only by the local board of education and the professional staff but by the taxpayers and parents and the students themselves. The challenge of curriculum planning is to determine orderly processes whereby the wishes of all concerned may be considered in the final determination of curriculum policy by legally constituted authority.

Curriculum designing, once a task only of textbook writers, is also an area in which many individuals and groups seek to participate. Certainly the academic scholars have great contributions to make in the organization and presentation of knowledge. Authors and editors, too, have much to contribute in providing materials to fit various designs. The aims of special interest groups, the interests of taxpayers and parents, and the readiness and interests of students themselves also enter into this major task. We believe, however, that the final selection of curriculum organization and opportunities for particular students, classes, and schools should be—indeed, must be—the responsibility of the professional educators who know the population to be educated as well as the potentials of their school organizations and facilities.

Technical development of the curriculum involves decisions having to do with the conduct of curriculum research and evaluation and the preparation of curriculum guides, syllabi, resource units, packages, instructional systems, and many other types of materials which give guidance to teachers and students. The technician is also involved in the selection of teaching-learning aids, the use of computerized instruction, educational television, programmed instruction, and other aspects of instructional technology. In these more technical tasks there is real need for specialists in curriculum development, whether they are classified as curriculum directors, media specialists, educational technologists, consultants in instruction, research and development specialists, or other terms. The specialists serve as powerful resources and, indeed, as catalytic agents in the process of curriculum planning. However, the job is not one for the expert alone: administrators, classroom teachers, resource persons in the community, and professional people in publishing and other industries may contribute to these significant aspects of curriculum development decisions.

Curriculum implementation, or instruction, is the central job of the teacher. Decisions as to the nature and content of learning experiences involve much more than the telling by lecture, television, recitation, or other means, which has characterized so much classroom practice. The aspect of curriculum planning which we might designate as presentation is the link between the planning done external to and also prior to the interaction of teacher and pupil. It is at this point of interaction that the teacher decides almost from minute to minute, and from student to student, how to aid and abet the learning experiences of individual boys and girls.

Data for Decision-Making

Although there is little information that does not in some way relate to curriculum planning, the types of data listed in Figure 6 and discussed in detail in Chapter 3 are of particular importance to any individual or group responsible for planning some aspect of the program of the schools of a state, of a school district, or even of an individual school, classroom, or student.

ROLES OF VARIOUS GROUPS IN LOCAL CURRICULUM PLANNING

In addition to the leading roles of students and teachers in the curriculum planning drama, important supporting actors include the members of lay advisory groups, curriculum councils and committees, teacher teams, and curriculum development units. As shown in Figure 6, all of these roles are affected by their interaction with various groups and agencies outside the curriculum theater: authors and publishers, testing agencies, accreditation associations and units, legally constituted control bodies, pressure groups of many types, and the other influences we identified in Chapter 1. In this section we consider the leading and supporting roles directly involved in the curriculum planning process.

Role of Students

Students or their parents as representatives can and do participate effectively in almost all decisions regarding the curriculum. The one notable exception is that of setting the broad goals and domains of the curriculum, this being essentially a political decision determined by legislatures, boards of education and other bodies controlling the schools, and all the pressure groups and societal forces which affect official decisions. Hopefully, parents and students have influence on and through some of these political bodies. But whether or not the school actually provides a curriculum plan in the human relations domain, for example, is not a decision in which students usually have a direct voice. Once goals and domains are defined, students should and in some schools do have many ways of affecting decisions regarding the curriculum opportunities actually provided.

Two types of student participation in curriculum planning are envisioned. One is the involvement of students of appropriate maturity in decisions concerning the basic curriculum plan. High school students can sit in on planning groups, and their contributions are prized in a growing number of high schools that are seeking to increase student involvement. Although curriculum is only one of many areas of complaint students have singled out in their underground newspapers,[3] open demonstrations, and strikes, it has been and remains an area of contention. More general participation of students in curriculum decision-making, through membership on planning groups, consultation and even referendum on critical issues, and involvement in *ad hoc* studies of various types would be positive methods of reducing the need for underground and confrontation techniques of participation. Increased involvement of younger children may be best secured through the use of parent advisers and members of planning groups, although teacher interviews of children and polling on many questions may also be useful; obviously the physical presence of young children on adult planning groups would rarely bring out student interests and needs as clearly as with more mature students.

The more universally possible type of student participation is direct consultation of the learner about his own personal curriculum continuum. Here there is no adequate substitute for a close relation between teacher and individual student. At the elementary school level this possibility was always present in the self-contained classroom arrangement, and now even with the use of team teaching and specialized instruction in elementary schools there generally remains some arrangement whereby each child has one teacher who is his first adviser. Although some middle schools follow the departmentalized pattern of the secondary school organization, many utilize some sort of home-base arrangement in which each student has his own teacher-counselor. At the high school level such arrangements are more infrequent but equally desirable. (See Chapter 8 for our proposal to use "directors of personal development" for this counseling purpose.)

Role of Teachers

Along with students, teachers are the most important actors in the curriculum planning theater. We use "teachers" in the generic sense to include all educational personnel who work with learners: teachers,

---

[3] See Diane Divoky, ed., *How Old Will You Be in 1984?* (New York: Avon Books, 1969); and John Birmingham, ed., *Our Time Is Now* (New York: Frederick A. Praeger, Inc., 1970), for many illustrative complaints and criticisms in the underground press.

administrators, and such varied specialists as counselors, librarians, audio-visual coordinators, curriculum and instruction consultants, activity directors, and others. These persons make up the curriculum committees and councils to be discussed shortly. Each of them has direct opportunity to influence and help students in their choices of learning opportunities and activities.

Teacher participation in curriculum planning has too frequently been minimal or nonexistent. When teachers had little education themselves beyond the high school and minimal if any preparation for teaching, curriculum planning was the province of textbook authors in colleges and universities and of state and district supervisory personnel. But beginning in the 1920s, as teacher preparation became more common, teachers have had increasing participation in the development of educational objectives and curriculum guides. The widespread practice of textbook adoption, and beginning in the late 1950s of adoption of materials from the national curriculum projects, frequently overlooked teacher participation and perhaps made it all too easy for teachers simply to follow plans made externally to the learning situation. By the 1970s, however, teacher organizations were frequently demanding the voice in curriculum planning most curriculum leaders would have had for them many years ago.

Some division of opinion among educators regarding the role teachers should play in curriculum planning reflects conflicting views concerning where curriculum decisions should be made. The person who perceives curriculum planning as a function of the state or the school district fails to recognize the integral relation of curriculum designing and implementation as presented in this book. Even curriculum designs prepared externally to the individual school can be effectively implemented only as the teachers of each school concerned have the opportunity to criticize, modify, and adapt these plans. Thus the learning kit as well as the textbook can be misused by teachers who have not related these materials to their own plans for their own particular students.

Thus, we see the teacher as having a dual role in curriculum planning. First, each teacher takes part in planning the total program of the school, possibly at district and state levels as a member of committees, councils, and other planning groups, and always as a member of the faculty of a particular school. Second, and more important, the teacher is the final decision-maker concerning the actual learning opportunities to be provided his students, although the student has the final choice concerning the opportunities provided. It is at this point that the curriculum is implemented, and it is the teacher who decides how each learning opportunity is presented, guided, and evaluated for the particular learners involved. The best-designed opportunities as well as the poorest owe their ultimate success or failure to the quality of the teacher's own planning and implementation.

Curriculum Councils

A popular organization for coordinating planning in school districts is the council on curriculum and/or instruction. Early examples of such councils in Battle Creek, Michigan, Glencoe, Illinois, Kingsport, Tennessee, Milwaukee, Wisconsin, and Minneapolis, Minnesota, were described in 1950 by Caswell and his associates.[4] Twenty years later a book on a systems approach to curriculum development and supervision contained a chapter entitled "The Systems Design Component and the Curriculum Council." It defined the curriculum council as "a representative or composite group that is responsible for the planning of general policies for the curriculum of all the schools in the system," recommending such a council as "eminently qualified to serve as the control unit of the systems-design subsystem."[5]

Although individual schools may also have curriculum councils, the chief utility of the organization we are describing is in its coordination of curriculum planning activities of the various schools. Alexander described the operation of the Battle Creek, Michigan, organization as follows:

> *The Council on Instruction* consists of teacher repersentatives from each building, who, together with representatives of the administrative and supervisory staffs, are responsible for: (1) reporting problems from each building regarding which city-wide policies and plans are needed; (2) reporting to the buildings policies and plans recommended by the Council, for building faculty consideration; (3) delegating specific jobs such as bulletins, guides, and conferences to instructional committees and/or the Division of Instruction. Thus, the Council is responsible to the building faculties.[6]

A somewhat similar role is indicated in the 1969–1970 annual report of the Great Neck, New York, Curriculum Development Council:

> The council maintains a role in decision making on curriculum change, and serves as a clearing house for receiving and disseminating

[4] See Hollis L. Caswell and associates, *Curriculum Improvement in Public School Systems* (New York: Bureau of Publications, Teachers College, Columbia University, 1950).

[5] Kathryn V. Feyereisen, A. John Fiorino, and Arlene T. Nowak, *Supervision and Curriculum Renewal* (New York: Appleton-Century-Crofts, 1970), Chap. 13.

[6] Quoted by William M. Alexander in Chapter 6, Caswell, p. 123, from a Battle Creek Public Schools mimeographed bulletin dated August 1947.

information relative to the staff and community through its relationship with Curriculum Area Committees and Building Faculty Curriculum Groups.

The minutes of the Council are sent to the Board of Education, all members of the staff, all P.T.A. presidents, the editors of the four student newspapers, and members of the community requesting them.

The focus of the Council's work this year has been in refining itself as a prime source for communication, encouraging research and development, and establishing a broader role as an initiator for constructive curriculum change.[7]

These statements concerning two district curriculum councils, one as of the late 1940s and the other as of 1969–1970, are representative of the councils we have known for more than twenty-five years. They are also consistent with Feyereisen, Fiorino, and Nowak's relatively recent statement regarding the functions of such a group in a systems approach to curriculum renewal:

A curriculum council's primary function is the coordination of the curriculum-renewal and policy-making activities for the total school system. To accomplish this the council normally meets monthly to do the following:
1. Screen the problem input.
2. Assign problems to planning teams or study groups.
3. Hear progress reports and provide guidance and assistance.
4. Consider and approve recommendations of planning teams and study groups.
5. Forward recommendations to superintendent for authorization.[8]

Different districts have organized these councils in various ways. Our own observation affirms the wisdom of representation from each school unit and from the central office. Whether community and student representation should be through this council or through separate advisory bodies is a question that needs to be thought through in each district, we believe. Districts having more schools than can be individually represented in a group small enough for effective group discussion (probably not over twenty-five persons) may find feasible some plan of subdistricts and subdistrict councils which would, in turn, be represented on a district-wide council. However organized, the essential role of the council is to serve as a clearinghouse for exchange of information and ideas about problems in the schools (and subdistricts) and to prepare recommendations to the district administration and the individual units. This role is a very important aid to communication and toward problem resolution and curriculum change in the school district.

[7] Great Neck Public Schools, "Curriculum Development Council, Annual Report, 1969–70," mimeographed.
[8] Feyereisen, Fiorino, and Nowak, p. 288.

Curriculum Committees

The committee approach to problems and tasks is widely used in curriculum planning. At the school level, committees of students, parents, and faculty, sometimes separately and sometimes jointly, are used for many purposes: investigating specific curriculum problems; developing plans for particular curriculum purposes; steering faculty planning and coordination; articulating instructional programs between teams, grades, subjects, and schools; organizing staff-development activities; conducting curriculum research and experimentation. At the district level curriculum councils get much of their work done, as we noted, by organizing committees or task forces, including persons from the council and from outside it, to perform particular tasks such as developing innovative proposals; working on problems submitted through the communications channels of the council; preparing curriculum plans in new areas; evaluating existing programs; and searching literature, practice, and research for information relative to any aspect of curriculum and instruction agreed upon as needing such review. Committees of parents and of students are organized to parallel or join in with staff committees for similar purposes, and especially for securing feedback regarding established or proposed curriculum practices. Our experience with curriculum committees for all of these purposes suggests the following guidelines:

1. *Ad hoc* committees, organized for particular tasks and composed of the persons best qualified to perform the tasks, are generally more effective than standing committees without specific tasks to perform.

2. Committees created by a curriculum council or a school faculty or the curriculum administrator should be given as clear definition as possible of their task, even if it is to propose their own role, with some timetable as to dates for committee reports.

3. Each committee should be given as much help as the situation permits in terms of time for meetings, resources of personnel and materials, and other specific needs the task involves.

4. Recognition for committee work is desirable and in such forms as are appealing to committee members and feasible in the situation: publication of reports, presentation to boards of education and other status groups, in-service requirement credits, reduced teaching loads, additional employment (summer), points for salary increase, direct compensation, leaves of absence, and others.

Teacher Teams

We think of "teacher team" in a generic sense as describing any group of teachers who are teamed together for curriculum planning for a particular population of students taught by members of the team. This concept differs from that of the "teaching team," whose members plan, teach, and evaluate together. Thus a teacher team may be a group of teachers at a grade level, or within a subject department, or representing several subject areas for a section or block or little school of students or a teaching team. The teacher team thus focuses its planning on a portion of the entire population of the school. Observation indicates that most so-called teaching teams tend to plan together and not teach together, so that "teacher team" or "team planning" is probably a more accurate term than "teaching team."

Regardless of these differences in terminology, many roles in curriculum planning can be and are filled by groups or teams of teachers: selecting goals and subgoals for the grade, subject, section, little school, or other basis of organization; designing appropriate learning opportunities to achieve these goals; assigning of responsibility for particular programs and students; procuring needed materials; scheduling instructional groups and facilities; defining student evaluation procedures; and planning for and conducting evaluation of particular instructional programs and, indeed, the entire curriculum plan for which the team is responsible. Whether interdisciplinary, intradisciplinary, or simply a planning group for grade or departmentalized teaching, the teaching team has fundamental decisions to make within the particular curriculum domain(s) concerned. Teams have especially significant decisions to make regarding curriculum implementation: what instructional modes they will use, and when and how; individualized self-teaching; guided independent study; laboratory-type experience; group discussion, inquiry and analysis; or combinations of these.

Increasing use of team teaching in elementary and middle schools makes even more important the provision of adequate time, leadership, and facilities for team planning. As several teachers who are working together in planning, teaching, and evaluating instruction for the same groups of learners are able to share their experience and expertise, better plans should emerge. This is the goal of such planning systems as Individually Guided Education (IGE), described later in this chapter.

Curriculum Designing Units

Groups of personnel especially organized for curriculum development have long been used in school districts and even in individual schools. For example, many curriculum guides have been prepared by groups of personnel employed during the summer for this purpose. Large school districts have also arranged for the release of personnel during the school year to work with a central curriculum bureau or department to prepare curriculum guides, conduct curriculum studies, serve as executive secretaries of curriculum councils and committees, and perform similar tasks relating to the central purpose of curriculum designing (see Chapter 5).

During the 1960s a somewhat different approach to curriculum designing was employed by such organizations as national curriculum projects, intermediate or regional units usually supported at least initially by Title III, Elementary-Secondary Education Act funds, and commercial organizations making performance contracts (see page 77) with school districts. The general approach used in these various types of units is exemplified in our later description of the national curriculum project method of curriculum development; that is, the curriculum design is prepared by a group of specialists in the curriculum area and from outside the school district and is tried out in the schools, with extensive materials and staff-development programs accompanying the designing, tryout, and finalizing stages.

In their work on a systems approach to curriculum development, Feyereisen, Fiorino, and Nowak referred to a "curriculum-design component" in the school district, although detailed description was not given of the organization and operation of such a unit. Their concept of a systems approach involves the development of *instructional packages that can be conceived of as units of study*":

> A package is designed to include broad topics, problems, or skills, such as poetry, how to combat poverty, nuclear energy, or how to use reference materials in a library. Each instructional package is composed of a set of procedures designed to achieve the objectives of the package. An instructional package designed to develop skill in using library reference materials might include procedures to teach the types and use of available materials, how to use an encyclopedia, how to use the *Reader's Guide to Periodical Literature*, and any other procedure appropriate to the maturity level of the student.[9]

The designing procedures suggested by these authors include the employment of a systems analyst, an in-service education program to prepare the staff for their involvement in the process, and the preparation of packages for individual "subsystems" (horizontally, subjects; vertically, grades):

> Since much of the content of the existing curriculum will remain relevant to the redesigned curriculum, it will be utilized in the subsystem selected for implementation, and new content will be added as dictated by the new objectives. This process should result in a clear definition of the subsystem

---

[9] Feyereisen, Fiorino, and Nowak, p. 145.

to the package level. The design of procedures would be accomplished through the cooperation of the instructional staff and the personnel of the curriculum-design component. The newly designed subsystem is then ready to be tried experimentally. On the basis of the results of the trial, any dysfunctions can be adjusted, and the subsystem can be adopted for general use.[10]

These authors also point out that "in situations where the curriculum-design component has a large staff, the process could be accelerated by designing and implementing multiple subsystems" and also that "the purchase of appropriate and increasingly available, commercially produced multimedia packages would decrease the time needed to design and implement the subsystems."

In the early 1970s many school districts were using curriculum development procedures quite like those of the systems approach just cited. As we shall later consider more fully, various forms of instructional systems and packages are in widespread use. Unfortunately, in many situations these packages are not the result of a real systems approach within the district and are fitted, or sometimes misfitted, into the curriculum plan rather than being an integral part of it as envisioned by Feyereisen, Fiorino, and Nowak and by us, who advocate a systematic approach to curriculum planning. We see the advisability of creating curriculum designing units within school districts, units that would be staffed by professional personnel trained for this purpose and released from other responsibilities to design particular packages and other types of materials needed within the complete design of the curriculum plan hammered out in individual schools. Regional centers or intermediate units may also play very useful roles in developing curriculum materials for several contiguous school districts. And certainly well-prepared commercial packages can be useful in achieving many curriculum objectives.

We emphasize, however, that many curriculum goals cannot be achieved by the usual types of curriculum packages. These are the subtle, frequently the affective, but also many times the higher cognitive objectives. For these, determined planning of learning opportunities by teachers for their particular students and groups is essential.

Community Participants

We envision important roles in curriculum planning for many persons in the school community other than those actually employed by the school. Help is needed at each stage: goal setting, designing, implementing, and evaluating.

At the goal-setting stage of curriculum planning various types of

[10] Feyereisen, Fiorino, and Nowak, p. 150.

community advisory groups may be used. The board of education may set up a general advisory group of community representatives to advise it on many educational problems, including the goals of its system. Or it may appoint advisory groups on specific problems such as curriculum, finance, facilities, and others. Advisory groups for particular curriculum areas such as vocational education, human relations, health education, and others are also used. Even without formally organized groups of this type, the district may use some existing organization such as the PTA Council for advisory functions. And individual schools may choose to use PTA committees, homeroom parents' organizations, Dads' clubs, and other existing organizations to seek suggestions and feedback regarding school goals.

At the curriculum designing stage various interests in the community can be consulted for specific help in planning learning opportunities. Work-experience programs require arrangements with local businesses and industries for the work assignments to be conducted. Indeed, learning opportunities outside the school of all types need to be planned with representatives of the various agencies, organizations, businesses, and industries in which the opportunities may be made available. As the school without walls idea[11] gains wider acceptance, new boards or councils for community education may be needed to provide closer cooperation and coordination of educational opportunities available through schools, community libraries and museums, television and radio, scout troops, youth clubs, travel tours, churches and social welfare agencies, and other community institutions.

The human relations domain of the curriculum in particular requires extensive community participation. Perhaps each school should have a community advisory council with competent specialists advising the participants on the many problems incident to opening up the community to student participation in the enterprises appropriate for student learning experiences. Such councils could sponsor community-student forums on social problems and issues in the community, as well as suggest resource persons representing all facets of community life to work with students.

Community participation in the instructional program is anticipated in the planning just described. Community resource persons assist individual students and various types of student groups with the par-

---

[11] John Bremer and Michael von Moschzisker, *The School Without Walls: Philadelphia's Parkway Program* (New York: Holt, Rinehart and Winston, Inc., 1971); Richard W. Saxe (ed.), *Opening the Schools: Alternative Ways of Learning* (San Francisco: McCutchan Publishing Corporation, 1971); and Donald William Cox, *The City as a Schoolhouse* (Valley Forge, Pa.: Judson Press, 1972). Also see "Community Education: A Special Issue," *Phi Delta Kappan*, 54, 145–224 (November 1972).

ticular expertise gained through their professions, hobbies, travels, and unique experiences. Community agencies and institutions make their resources available for the learning opportunities planned. Businesses, industries, and various community institutions provide work-experience opportunities. Especially helpful services are provided by the various types of school volunteers.[12] Parents of children in school, college and university students, and other community residents help man offices, classrooms, lunchrooms, health clinics, libraries, and other school facilities.

Curriculum evaluation cannot be adequately done without extensive community involvement. Parents' reports on their children's progress in reaching objectives, as revealed in their behavior at home, work supervisors' reports on the performance of students engaged in work experience, and other types of data from home and community are essential for evaluating many educational goals. Furthermore, a major source of data in evaluating the curriculum plan is the opinions of school patrons and community participants and observers. Comprehensive evaluation plans generally use opinion polls on both specific and broad questions relating to the school curriculum.[13]

No single formula for community participation will work for all of the thousands of U.S. communities. We would recommend as a general principle in any school community, large or small, the organization and consistent use of one or more curriculum advisory councils. Existing organizations may suffice or new ones may be needed. Answers should be sought to such questions as the following: How can the school get participation by the parents and other citizens it serves in providing the best curriculum possible for the student population? Is one general council needed or one for each curriculum domain within the plan? How can the council members be fully enough informed of school policies, goals, and programs to give school personnel reactions and suggestions useful in curriculum improvement? How can the school utilize most effectively the educational resources of the entire community?

USE OF EXTERNALLY DEVELOPED
CURRICULUM PLANS AND SYSTEMS

So far in this chapter primary consideration has been given to processes and roles in local curriculum planning, although we have noted the relation of local to state and national planning and the influence of

---

[12] See Barbara Carter and Gloria Dapper, *School Volunteers: What They Do—How They Do It* (New York: Citation Press, 1972).

[13] See, for example, the citizens' opinion survey in Tulsa, Oklahoma, reported in *A Single Step*, Report of the Superintendent, Tulsa Public Schools, 1972, pp. 8–9.

various external forces and agencies, including the possibility of curriculum designing units outside the school and district. In the 1970s, however, many school districts and schools are modeling their curriculum planning on prototypes outside the districts and schools and are even adopting, in somewhat wholesale fashion, models, plans, and systems developed elsewhere. We ourselves believe that curriculum planning should remain a local function, albeit one that is discharged more satisfactorily than has been true in many situations in the past, but we must here identify the possibilities and practices of using externally developed plans and systems. Historically and perhaps still today the textbook is the most commonly used externally developed plan, and we consider this practice first.

Textbooks as Curriculum Plans

As late as 1961, elementary and secondary school principals surveyed by the NEA Project on Instruction ranked highest the textbook as a useful resource in developing a teaching program.[14] Although many other types of instructional materials have been developed and widely used in the ensuing years, the practice of textbook adoption on both state and local levels continues. It must be pointed out that the system of providing free textbooks to students involves great expenditures of funds and also, with all its intent of equalizing educational opportunity, tends to limit the use of varied materials and flexible curriculum plans.

Unfortunately, the adopted textbook has too frequently been the only curriculum plan used in many classrooms. The weakness in these situations is not inherent in the textbook but rather in the absence or disregard of a curriculum plan which facilitates the proper use of the textbook in relation to the objectives of the instructional program. Curriculum planning of recent decades has tended to correct this abuse of textbooks, and greatly improved textbooks and many other instructional aids have facilitated the new plans, but no person knowledgeable about curriculum practices in U.S. schools would deny that the textbook is still the curriculum plan in many classrooms.

In such situations the curriculum plan, if one could really call it that, follows a pattern: (1) adopt the objectives of the textbook author; (2) adopt the scope and sequence of the textbook as the design of the curriculum; (3) use whatever instructional strategies the textbook (or the accompanying manual or guide) suggests; (4) make evaluation a series of tests (sometimes also provided by the publisher) of learners'

---

[14] Project on the Instructional Program of the Public Schools, *The Principals Look at the Schools* (Washington, D.C.: National Education Association, 1962), p. 24.

mastery of the textbook. Ignored in general are the aspects of curriculum planning described in this book such as the studying of data about the learners involved, the relating of the curriculum goals and design to the needs of learners and the social factors operating in the community, the mapping of instructional strategies in relation to goals and learners, and the provision for continuing feedback concerning the effectiveness of the learning opportunities provided.

When other teaching-learning materials were generally lacking, when teachers had little preparation for their jobs, and when students had little competition from other media for their interests, the basic textbook was certainly a great advance as a curriculum plan over memorization of dictated and copied material. Today greatly improved in format, content, and accompanying aids, it can still be a great resource for the instructional program, but it ought not to be used to prescribe that program for widely varying learners, classrooms, and schools. That is, we question the use of any national curriculum plan as the exact plan for any situation, and the textbook used as just described is such a national plan.

Probably most efforts toward curriculum improvement in this century have sought to diminish the use of the textbook as the curriculum plan. The curriculum movement itself, beginning in the 1920s with the aims and activity-analysis approaches of Bobbitt and Charters (see pages 199–201), was begun and continues as a system of planning which relates instruction to educational goals and objectives rather than to textbooks alone. Each of the designs described in Chapter 5 would utilize a curriculum plan other than that of any single textbook. But the designs were reflected in textbooks, and the local plans frequently either began with the adopted textbooks or utilized them to the exclusion of all other sources of curriculum content. As we see it, the most influential and widespread departure in local curriculum planning using councils, committees, and other means we have described came in the late 1950s with the national curriculum projects. Many districts and schools sought to incorporate or adopt the "new curricula" in their plans. Many of these projects, too, resulted in textbooks. Although developed differently and including new curriculum content sometimes presented in whole kits of materials, like textbooks the new materials can also be misused by being incorporated wholesale into local curriculum plans. Hence we doubt if curriculum planning should assume that any plan, however creatively designed, cannot at some point be reflected in a textbook or learning kit that will in some classrooms become the curriculum plan. The inferences we draw from this observation are that (1) the curriculum plan should include alternatives as to instructional materials and strategies; (2) teachers should be helped through preservice and inservice training to make wise choices of the alternatives; and (3) whatever materials are developed and/or purchased should be the best available, so that if alternatives are still ignored and externally developed materials are still used without adaptation, learners have as good a chance as possible under such circumstances—and the chances are poor—to have good learning experiences. In other words, if all else fails and textbooks (and kits) constitute the plans, find the best ones possible!

National Curriculum Projects

The facts of the national curriculum project movement of the late 1950s and thereafter have been related in numerous sources[15] and will be only reviewed here. More than 100 of these projects were identified in the various publications cited of the Association for Supervision and Curriculum Development. Many of these projects were still actively developing curriculum plans and materials in 1973, and an uncounted number of additional projects were in various stages of development. In 1971 Eisner noted that over $100 million had been used in curriculum development in science and mathematics alone and that over fifty projects in social studies were then listed, with one of them (Man: A Course of Study) having an annual budget of about $3 million.[16]

The projects came into being as an answer to the criticisms of the school curriculum, originally especially in science and mathematics, that followed the Russian launching of Sputnik in 1957. Federal appropriations through the National Defense Education Act (1958) and the National Science Foundation and other educational support provisions made possible a great acceleration of curriculum development, improved facilities, and teacher education in science, mathematics, and foreign

[15] For full identification of the projects and descriptions of the movement see William M. Alexander, *Changing Curriculum Content* (Washington, D.C.: Association for Supervision and Curriculum Development, NEA, 1964); Elliot W. Eisner, ed., *Confronting Curriculum Reform* (Boston: Little, Brown and Company, 1971); Robert S. Gilchrist, *Using Current Curriculum Developments* (Washington, D.C.: Association for Supervision and Curriculum Development, NEA, 1963); John Goodlad with others, *The Changing School Curriculum* (New York: Fund for the Advancement of Education, 1966); Robert W. Heath, ed., *New Curricula* (New York: Harper & Row, Publishers, 1964); Glenys G. Unruh, ed., *New Curriculum Developments* (Washington, D.C.: Association for Supervision and Curriculum Development, NEA, 1965); Glenys G. Unruh and Robert R. Leeper, *Influences on Curriculum Change* (Washington, D.C.: Association for Supervision and Curriculum Development, NEA, 1968); and "At the Edge and Still Cutting," *NASSP Curriculum Report*, 2, 1–12 (February 1973). Most of these sources also include detailed lists of publications of or about the various projects, and many articles and reports in the literature of the major subject fields also report particular projects.

[16] Eisner, p. 2.

languages initially. The impetus given these subjects and widespread concern for updating curriculum content in general stimulated project development in all fields in time. Along with the interest in new content and additional trained manpower in the fields first of national defense and then of specialization in general, an accelerated effort was made to utilize more fully new technology in education.

The national curriculum project method of curriculum development is illustrated in Figure 7. The original approach was described by the leaders of one of the early and highly influential projects, the Physical Sciences Study Committee, as consisting of the steps in a "logical process of curriculum revision" we cited in Chapter 1.[17]

Each project initially aimed at the content of one subject field, for example, physics, biology, or chemistry, and frequently a year-long course, although broader projects and even interdisciplinary projects developed later. Each has generally been funded by the federal government and/or an educational foundation and sometimes has involved contributions from a university or school district. Most result in curricu-

[17] See pages 3–4.

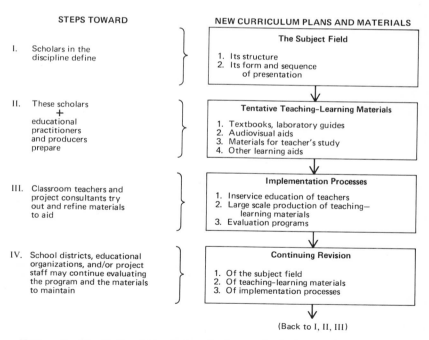

STEPS TOWARD

NEW CURRICULUM PLANS AND MATERIALS

The Subject Field

I. Scholars in the discipline define
1. Its structure
2. Its form and sequence of presentation

Tentative Teaching-Learning Materials

II. These scholars + educational practitioners and producers prepare
1. Textbooks, laboratory guides
2. Audiovisual aids
3. Materials for teacher's study
4. Other learning aids

Implementation Processes

III. Classroom teachers and project consultants try out and refine materials to aid
1. Inservice education of teachers
2. Large scale production of teaching—learning materials
3. Evaluation programs

Continuing Revision

IV. School districts, educational organizations, and/or project staff may continue evaluating the program and the materials to maintain
1. Of the subject field
2. Of teaching-learning materials
3. Of implementation processes

(Back to I, II, III)

FIGURE 7   The National Curriculum Project method of curriculum planning.

lum materials that are in the public domain and published by commercial publishers or through the project or some quasi-public educational laboratory.

Local curriculum planning groups have used the projects in any of these ways:

1. The general approach of the project in defining its field, usually through the selection of basic concepts, principles, and processes —the so-called structure of the subject (see Chapter 5)—may be followed or at least consulted in the development of the local curriculum plan for this field.

2. Textbooks and perhaps related learning aids which have been influenced by a project's definition of the content of a field may be selected for some use in the local curriculum plan.

3. The entire program, kit, or "package" developed by the project or its publishers may be adopted and used locally as the curriculum plan; such adoption may involve education of the staff responsible for the use of the materials.

This third approach is not much different from the practice of adopting a basic textbook as the curriculum plan. To the extent that teachers are trained in the use of the materials, and to the extent that the materials facilitate adaptation to the individual differences of learners, classrooms, and teachers, the use of the project materials can be a useful aid to local groups in developing their own instructional program. Used without adaptation to local objectives, designs, and learners, the projects can be almost as sterile and irrelevant as the worst of the textbook-alone "plans."

Instructional Packages and Systems

Current publications and publishers' advertisements hopelessly confuse such terms as "packages," "packets," "kits," "instructional systems," and related ones. The terms are used almost interchangeably to cover two very different concepts: (1) a total system of learning activities and related materials for a broad area of content or a series of objectives; and (2) a particular assembly of materials for one segment of such a system, or even of a subject or other curriculum component that is not fully systematized. To eliminate the confusion here we use "instructional system" for the first, broader concept and "package" for the latter, narrower one. We consider "system" as appropriate to the former, since the more advanced instructional systems use a systems approach; we prefer "package" for the latter because of the widespread use of the term in local curriculum planning to refer to locally produced materials for specific curriculum objectives, such as the LAP (learning activity package). In this section our reference is to the use in local curriculum planning and implementation of systems and packages developed externally, primarily the first type above.

In a 1970 article Unruh gave an excellent description of instructional systems, as we use the term, although she referred to "well-designed teaching learning packages . . . built as instructional systems":

1. *The emphasis is on individualization in the emerging concept of teaching-learning packages.* Pretests or means of assessment may be used to determine what the student already knows and placement can be arranged for him into personally tailored instructional processes and content. Options are offered to accommodate for differences in learning rates, past achievement, interests, motivation, and other diversities. All students are not expected to complete all of the procedures as in older programs.

2. *Instructional systems packages are based on broad concepts organized into manageable coordinated modules.* The total package is comprehensive and frequently encompasses basic substance and a wide range of materials of a defined area of study as opposed to the type of package intended as supplementary materials to accompany a textbook or previously entrenched course of study.

3. *Clearly stated instructional objectives convey to the student the quality of performance expected of him.*

4. *Multimedia learning materials of varying types are included to provide a choice of vehicles for learning for various steps in the process.* The package recognizes that people learn in different ways and that a variety of media may provide more effective learning.

5. *The package not only provides diversified materials, but also provides for diversified learning activities, particularly student-student interaction and teacher-student interaction.* The range of activities may include large group and small group instruction, field trips, model building, role playing, simulation, laboratory experimentation, independent study, and others. The package has built-in self-evaluation processes designed to provide continuing feedback to assist the student in determining his progress toward achievement of the instructional objectives.

6. *The role of the teacher-instructor is significantly changed.* His function as a dispenser of information is considerably reduced as the student moves into a more active role in the learning process. Teachers become diagnosticians of learning and find themselves developing professional competence in helping each individual learner find success. Teachers have more time for effective instructional planning to solve learning problems and to provide enrichment for individual students.[18]

[18] Glenys G. Unruh, "Can I Be Replaced by a Package?" *Educational Leadership,* 27, 765 (May 1970).

Many instructional systems have been developed in recent years by commercial publishers and the large producers of educational software and hardware, frequently called learning industries, and by regional educational laboratories (see pages 53–54) and other organizations. Obviously these systems vary in the extent to which they exemplify Unruh's characteristics. Even more variation is probably exhibited in the skills with which teachers use the systems, especially in relation to the alternatives emphasized by Unruh: variety of media; diversified learning activities; and teacher behavior.

Commercially or other externally developed instructional systems offer new resources to local curriculum planners. For those goals which the school or district shares with the developers of the systems, the latter may represent better plans of curriculum implementation than local groups can readily and efficiently develop. But the processes involved in the original selection of a system and its use are critical: if the right system is selected and it is used in the way any "right" system should be —that is, with careful choice for particular learners of appropriate media, activities, and teacher behavior—the system may indeed be the right plan. As to the choice of instructional systems, an extended study by a committee of the ASCD of guidelines to assist local school officials in making decisions about "instructional units" (a term similar to our "instructional system") seems relevant. This committee described the following as factors that should be considered in selection:

> Objectives of the unit: those of the producer as well as yours
> Relevance and validity of unit's content
> Compliance of units with principles of human growth and development
> Time and space (organizational) considerations
> Personnel factors
> Community factors
> Cost analysis of the unit
> Instructional and curricular factors
> Evaluative procedures
> Dissemination
> Implementation.[19]

Full consideration of these factors, including not only the many subquestions suggested by the Committee but also others important in a local school or district, would in itself be a rather comprehensive type of

[19] Richard I. Miller, *Selecting New Aids to Teaching* (Washington, D.C.: Association for Supervision and Curriculum Development, NEA, 1971), p. 7.

curriculum planning, and one that seems to us of critical importance whether the instructional system is to be purchased on these bases or ultimately to be developed locally.

CURRICULUM MODELS FROM OTHER GROUPS

Performance Contracts

In the late 1960s and early 1970s as public concern for results in education and accountability therefor mounted, the performance contract came into use in education. Under this plan the school district contracts with some outside agency, usually a commercial firm, or even a group of its own employees, to achieve specified results, with provisions for payment and penalties according to the results. Lessinger, a leading advocate of this approach, has described the process as follows:

> A performance contract is a legal agreement between a local school board and a supplier of instructional programs providing that the amount and schedule of payment will depend not on what services are said to have been provided, but on the degree of increase in student accomplishment, as independently audited, in the field of the program. In requesting bids for such a contract, the board specifies the results it wants, leaving the various firms to propose what methods they would use. In selecting a firm, the board could, of course, reject any proposal resting on a method that it did not approve of and that in its opinion failed to deal with local conditions adequately. But the method of instruction, after approval by the board and within supervision by the MSG (management support group), is the business of the winning firm; and at the conclusion of the program, what the board reviews is not the process of instruction, but the accomplishment of the students, their performance on specified tests. Especially if the students do well, the board will take a keen interest in *how* the results were produced, but in any case the payment will depend on an evaluation of the product, not of the process which led to it.[20]

Lessinger cited these benefits of performance contracting:

1. Use of a more sophisticated technology of instruction.
2. Introduction of greater resources and versatility into the schools.
3. Opportunity for experimentation in "an orderly, responsible manner with low costs and low political risks."
4. Help in desegregation by accelerating skills development of previously segregated children.

[20] Leon M. Lessinger, *Every Kid a Winner: Accountability in Education* (New York: Simon and Schuster, Inc., 1970), pp. 67–68.

5. "Performance contracting, as part of a competitive program, can call forth a high quality both of proposals and of work."[21]

The purported benefits of performance contracting came into question in the early 1970s as evaluative studies failed to show improved performance by the students involved. A review of the evidence appearing in *Education U.S.A.* included these reports and observations:

Performance contracting in education failed its $5.7 million test with the Office of Economic Opportunity (OEO). After months of delay and the use of three different analysis systems to evaluate the test results of 18 experimental programs, OEO finally concluded that performance contracting is no more successful than traditional classroom methods in improving the reading and math skills of disadvantaged children. "Neither approach did well" during the year-long experiment, the OEO officials said at a Washington, D.C., press conference. . . .

OEO's reading of the results was uniformly grim. "Not only did both groups (experimental and control) do equally poorly in terms of overall averages but also these averages are very nearly the same in each grade, in each subject, for the best and worst students in the sample, and, with few exceptions, in each site," OEO's report said. Thomas Glennan, OEO's acting assistant director for planning, research and evaluation, said the wide variety of learning systems used in the experiments gave no clue as to which technique works better than another. "They all did badly," he said. He admitted, however, that a five-year span for the experiment may have come up with different results. Continuing his pessimistic view of performance contracting, Glennan disclosed that four of the six companies involved in the experiment have given up performance contracting and that five of the companies are now involved in a complicated dispute with OEO over how much money is due them. . . .

The OEO projects at the 18 districts involved 13,000 pupils in the experimental program. They were selected from the most "academically deficient" student bodies. They were compared with 10,000 "control" pupils, who were selected because they had the "next lowest" scores in reading and math. Participating school districts were New York City; Philadelphia; Seattle; Dallas; Anchorage; Fresno, Calif.; Grand Rapids, Mich.; Hammond, Ind.; Hartford; Jacksonville; Las Vegas; Portland, Maine; Wichita, Kan.; Athens, Ga.; McComb, Miss.; Rockland, Maine; Selmer, Tenn.; and Taft, Texas. The six firms: Alpha Learning Systems, Singer/Graflex, Westinghouse Learning Corp., Quality Educational Development, Learning Foundations and Plan Education Centers. Despite the bad news in the OEO report, about 100 performance contracts are now in effect in various forms—69 in Michigan alone. Meanwhile, OEO officials say they have given up performance

---

[21] Lessinger, pp. 68–70.

contracting and "will go back to the drawing boards" to experiment with other alternatives to traditional systems—including the voucher plan.[22]

Our interest here is in the possibilities of performance contracts in the curriculum planning activities of the school and district. As we see it, the contract is primarily a matter of implementing, through instruction directed by the contractor, a plan for which objectives and to some extent design have been set by the school and/or district. The fallacy of such planning, we believe, lies in the separation of planning for instruction from the planning of objectives and design. First, instructional strategy and resources are closely related to design, so that turning over the total plan for instruction to an outside contractor means that the district is relinquishing some of its control over the scope and quality of learning activities provided learners. Second, one wonders whether the school can possibly give emphasis commensurate with their importance to the objectives it assigns to contractors and to the objectives it retains for its own program. Third, learning opportunities typically may relate to more than one objective, even cutting across domains, and division of responsibility for different objectives, such as those in reading and social studies, might well mean that students lack the opportunity to work on reading skills, for which the contractor is responsible, in the social studies program, for which the school retains responsibility.

Nevertheless, it is entirely possible that continued experimentation with performance contracting will result in finding useful applications for particular objectives and programs that can be planned for by the curriculum planners of the district and school. Especially interesting is the use of contracts with the district's own personnel as a means of incentive to teacher and school performance with hard-to-attain objectives. Contracts with two teacher groups in Dade County, Florida, were reported in the fall of 1972 as having resulted in greater student achievement in reading and math and at less cost than comparable contracts in that district with a commercial contractor.[23]

Alternative Schools

In the late 1960s and early 1970s widespread dissatisfaction with the established public schools and other factors, undoubtedly including

[22] *Education U.S.A.*, Washington Monitor, "OEO Flunks Performance Contracting," (Washington, D.C.: National School Public Relations Association, February 7, 1972), pp. 125–126. Copyright © 1972 National School Public Relations Association. Also see Ellis B. Page, "How We All Failed at Performance Contracting," *Phi Delta Kappan*, 54, 115–117 (October 1972), for a commentary on the OEO experiment.

[23] "Teacher Contractors Outdo Business Firm in Landmark Dade County Schools Experiment," *Phi Delta Kappan*, 54, 218 (November 1972).

for some parents resistance to desegregation and school busing, resulted in a plethora of so-called alternative schools. An article describing this movement in 1970 stated that "over 700 independent schools have been founded during the past three years, as teachers, parents, and students seek alternatives to the stultifying climate of so many public schools" and that "two or three new alternative schools are born every day, and every day one dies or gives up its freedom."[24] A year later the same author, Donald W. Robinson, asserted that the alternative schools were having marked influence on the established schools:

> Alternative schools may not survive in large numbers, though that will depend in large part on how widely the voucher plan is adopted and how it is administered. Already they have had tremendous influence comparable to the manner in which minor parties have through the years influenced American social legislation. They have forced the establishment into a greater awareness of the urgency of the need for reform.[25]

Robinson's assertion, and one he cited to the same effect from *The Handbook of Private Schools*, that the first result of the increased formation of alternative schools "will be to force both public and private education to be more competitive on their terms," seems to us supported by the subsequent movement of public school systems to set up their own alternative schools. Before examining this movement, we should note some of the characteristics of the nontax-supported alternative schools.

Generalizations about these alternative, nonpublicly supported schools are difficult because of their highly diverse nature. Some such schools were the storefront academies established first in New York City, described in part by one writer in this statement:

> The orientation of the academy program from its inception has been socio-psychological, demanding a twenty-four-hour-a-day commitment to its students. Much of the academy's success is undoubtedly attributable to its image as an *alternative* to public school education. It functions personally, tutorially, remedially. It has the leisure and the dedication to explore education in the broadest of contexts—the total life of its students. Ideally, this should be the function of a public school education as well, but the danger of the academy's doubling back into the school system is that this uniqueness and intense personal involvement may be lost.[26]

[24] Donald W. Robinson, " 'Alternative Schools': Challenge to Traditional Education," *Phi Delta Kappan*, 51, 374 (March 1970).

[25] Donald W. Robinson, "Alternative Schools: Is the Old Order Really Changing?" *Educational Leadership*, 28, 605 (March 1971).

[26] Jonathan Black, "Street Academies: One Step Off the Sidewalk," *Saturday Review* (November 15, 1969), p. 100.

The alternative schools also include, perhaps as their most numerous variety, many types of schools set up by parent and other community groups for various age levels, sometimes any age under 20. Many of these have been established in California; a Los Angeles reporter in 1972 described these schools as follows: "Free schools, alternative schools, radical schools or new schools. Whatever you call them, they have at least one thing in common: wild flight from the precepts and practices of the cumbersome public institution they scorn as the 'big gray schoolhouse.' "[27]

This writer also cited these "windows on what alternative schools believe in":

> No grades, no competition, no "invidious comparisons among students through exams, honors, prizes."
> No "institutionalized coercion" regarding behavior or curriculum, no demerits or detention, and the schools' rules usually are made by the students or drawn up with their participation.
> No grade-level separation of students, no promotion or flunking. "Classes and projects often include wide age ranges."
> Teachers are chosen for individual abilities and character rather than for formal training or certification.[28]

But not all alternative schools are so free of the practices of the public school establishment. For example, many alternative schools established in the South and elsewhere for parents and students—at least in part seeking to escape desegregation, school busing, discipline problems, and other aspects of public school education—have followed more traditional patterns of education. Wiles' study of new independent schools in Florida noted a close relation between the curriculums of these schools and those of public schools:

> When the schools were asked to "describe the curriculums," 27 of the 58 schools answering the question described their curriculum as "general," while another 25 schools reported a "college prep" program. That 52 of the 58 schools described a program which is parallel to that of the public schools is generally characteristic of the new independent schools. This duplication of programs is even carried to the use of identical textbooks when possible.[29]

[27] Lynn Lilliston, "A Wild Flight from Public Education," *Los Angeles Times,* March 19, 1972, p. E1.

[28] Lilliston, pp. E1 and E12. These "windows" are based on criteria the author cited as used by the New Schools Exchange of Santa Barbara, California, in listing the more than 400 schools in its national directory.

[29] Jon Whitney Wiles, "Southern Alternative Schools: A Portrait," *Educational Leadership,* 29, 535 (March 1972).

By contrast, the so-called free schools of inner cities, as described by Kozol, serve children of the ghetto and avoid the stereotype of the public school as far as possible, although basic skills are taught. Kozol defines free schools as follows:

> I am, then, speaking for the most part about Free Schools (1) outside the public education apparatus, (2) outside the white man's counter-culture, (3) inside the cities, (4) in direct contact with the needs and urgencies of those among the poor, the black, the dispossessed, who have been the most clearly victimized by public education, (5) as small, "decentralized," and "localized" as we can manage, (6) as little publicized as possible.[30]

Thus, curriculum planning groups in established public and private schools can find no common curriculum plans in alternative schools, but they can draw one central implication for their own planning models: consult our clients! This implication arises from the single common denominator one finds in the alternative school movement, namely, the aim of escaping the public school. This motive, combined with the threat of the voucher plan still being tested for feasibility as this book goes to press, has put great pressure on public school systems to look to their clientele for dissatisfactions that might be the basis for reforming practices from which students, parents, and teachers were escaping. The voucher plan itself, as originally proposed,[31] would give the parent a voucher for his child's tuition at any school of his choice within whatever criteria and requirements the state laid down. Thus the result might be to make formerly public and nonpublic schools fully competitive for tax dollars.

By 1973 many school districts had created their own alternative schools within the system, and others were planning them. Outstanding examples are the Parkway Program in Philadelphia; Metro High School in Chicago; Murray Road School in Newton, Massachusetts; Adams-Morgan School in Washington, D.C.; and the twenty-four alternative programs developed by the Berkeley, California, Unified School District in its federally subsidized Experimental School Program.[32] In March 1972 the Educational Alternatives Project at Indiana University reported that at least 60 public school districts were developing or operating about

---

[30] Jonathan Kozol, *Free Schools* (Boston: Houghton Mifflin Company, 1972), p. 16.

[31] See George R. LaNove, *Educational Vouchers: Concepts and Controversies* (New York: Teachers College Press, 1972), for various readings on the background of the voucher plan, the proposals, and their pros and cons.

[32] See Berkeley Unified School District, *Alternative Education: Experimental Schools Program* (Berkeley, Calif.: The District, October 1972), for a brief description of the twenty-one Experimental Schools operating as of the fall 1972.

200 alternative schools.[33] A National Consortium of Alternative Schools was organized which publishes *Changing Schools,* "An Occasional News-letter on Alternative Schools." The project director described the pros-pects of the movement in these terms:

> The educational alternative provides the most promising vehicle for school reform in this decade. The conceptualization and development of alternative schools is a possible avenue for the self renewal of public educa-tion. New alternative schools will provide new opportunities for the coopera-tive teacher training programs for alternative schools as they develop. The community and the profession can develop new relationships as the alter-native schools develop. New means of evaluation and accountability can be built in as the alternatives develop rather than being added on later as is currently being attempted with existing schools.[34]

The Educational Research Service published in June 1972 descriptions of forty-seven alternative high school programs serving students in thirty-eight school systems, noting that these programs did not represent a comprehensive national survey and that "programs are springing up every day." These excerpts cite some common aspects of planning in the schools:

> Parents and other community members are vitally involved—in the planning, in the teaching, and in an all-around display of interest in the program. The students have had a very key role in planning, developing, and evaluating the school and its program; this degree of student participation manifests itself in continuing development and governance of the school. . . .
> Student self-evaluation is an important part of the evaluation of student progress in the academic and social aspects of his school program. . . . There is a low student-counselor ratio and regular meetings with the counselors are part of each student's program. Most schools and classes are nongraded. Most offer (or even require) students to take a part in work-study programs or community service volunteer work as part of their school program and for credit. In all cases individualization of instruction is the primary concern.[35]

We see two major influences on local curriculum planning of the alternative school movement: (1) the planning system must have

---

[33] "Alternative School Seen as Key to Reform," *Education U.S.A.*, March 20, 1972, p. 159.

[34] Vernon H. Smith, "Alternative Schools: A Rationale for Action," *Changing Schools*, No. 002 (n.d.), p. 13.

[35] *Alternative High Schools: Some Pioneer Programs*, ERS Circular No. 4, 1972 (Washington, D.C.: Educational Research Service, American Association of School Administrators and NEA Research Division, June 1972), pp. 1–2.

adequate participation and feedback mechanisms to insure the identification of student and parent interests, problems, and dissatisfactions with the school program; and (2) the alternative school within the system can be an excellent means of developing and trying out curriculum alternatives. We question the establishment of alternatives only as palliatives for the dissatisfied, although temporary conditions may necessitate such an approach. But the long-term use of alternatives is built into the planning system we propose a little later in this chapter.[36]

Networks

Although their proposals of various "networks" were intended as substitutes for schools, which they would eliminate as now known, Illich and Reimer have really suggested still another type of curriculum plan which might be developed externally to the school or possibly by a group of schools. The networks proposed are these:

1) Reference Services to Educational Objects—which facilitate access to things or processes used for formal learning. Some of these things can be reserved for this purpose, stored in libraries, rental agencies, laboratories, and showrooms like museums and theaters; others can be in daily use in factories, in airports, or on farms but made available to students as apprentices or on off-hours.

2) Skills Exchanges—which permit students to list their skills, the conditions under which they are willing to serve as models for others who want to learn these skills, and the addresses at which they can be reached.

3) Peer Matching—a communications network which permits persons to describe the learning activity in which they wish to engage in the hope of finding a partner for the inquiry.

4) Reference Services to Educators-at-Large—who can be listed in a directory giving the addresses and self-descriptions of professionals, paraprofessionals, and free-lancers, along with conditions of access to their services. Such educators, as we will see, could be chosen by polling or consulting their former clients.[37]

---

[36] In addition to references cited in this section on the alternative school movement, readers may wish to consult Allen Graubard, *Free the Children: The New Schools Movement in America* (New York: Pantheon Books, Inc., 1973); Steve Bhaerman and Joel Denker, *No Particular Place To Go: The Making of a Free High School* (New York: Simon and Schuster, Inc., 1972); George Dennison, *The Lives of Children: The Story of the First Street School* (New York: Random House, Inc., 1969); and "Alternative Forms of Schooling," *Educational Leadership*, February 1972 issue.

[37] Ivan Illich, "Education Without School: How It Can Be Done," in Daniel U. Levine and Robert J. Havighurst, eds., *Farewell to Schools???* Contemporary Educational Issues, National Society for the Study of Education (Worthington, O.: Charles A. Jones Publishing Company, 1971), pp. 39–40. See also Ivan Illich, *Deschooling Society* (New York: Harper & Row, Publishers, 1971); and Everett Reimer, *School Is Dead: Alternatives to Education* (New York: Doubleday & Company, Inc., 1971).

The central weakness in the Illich-Reimer proposals of substituting the networks for schools is exposed in this critique by Havighurst:

> But it is impossible for this writer to understand how the children and adults and communities who need education most could get a fair deal in this kind of subsystem. On the contrary, those who are best able to take care of their own education would make the best use of the four networks, while those disadvantaged by illiteracy and poverty would be neglected. Eventually, people with a social conscience would work through political and economic measures to set up educational institutions to serve the disadvantaged people better, and a school system would emerge again, as it did in the nineteenth century in the present developed countries.[38]

We agree with another reviewer of the Illich-Reimer proposals who states: "Skills centers, networks for the provision of 'equal opportunity for learning and teaching,' storefronts stocked with cassettes, poor matching, and the rest are certainly innovative."[39] We would note, however, that these so-called innovations, like most other practices so designated, are already in existence, though not as networks. Every learning resource center in a school has its "reference service to educational objects" and many communities and/or school districts their museums and libraries and other repositories of "things" that are frequently, but probably not frequently enough, catalogued for accessibility to students. Effective teachers have long arranged for skills instruction by peers and other types of pairing or "peer matching," although these arrangements could be much more systematically planned by the school than at present or as we would expect to happen if developed as loosely as Illich and Reimer propose. Placement bureaus, consulting firms, directories of professional organizations, in effect, advertise individual educators and their services, and various types of alternative schools advertise their programs and depend on their students and parent clients to do much of their promotion. But again more systematic directories of human resources available in a community, such as those compiled by an increasing number of schools and school districts as community resources and volunteer aides are sought, can be effectively used in curriculum planning and implementation. *Yellow Pages for Learning Resources* (see Table 2), published in 1972 through the cooperation of the MIT Press, Educational Facilities Laboratories, Inc., and the GEE! Group for Environmental Education, Inc., sought "to turn people on to learning in the city and to assist them in taking advantage of the wealth of available learning oppor-

---

[38] Robert J. Havighurst, "Prophets and Scientists in Education," in Levine and Havighurst, pp. 89–90.

[39] Maxine Greene, "To the Deschoolers," in Levine and Havighurst, p. 101.

Table 2
Table of contents from Yellow Pages for Learning Resources*

* SOURCE: *Yellow Pages for Learning Resources,* Richard Saul Wurman, ed. Developed under a grant from Educational Facilities Laboratories, Inc., and published by The MIT Press, Cambridge, Mass., and London.

tunities."[40] For each of the items listed in the Table of Contents, its entry answers the general question, "What can you learn about _____?" and frequently gives specific questions students might investigate about the item.

A proposal we consider relevant to this notion of networks and intended as a positive thrust for greater utilization of university resources comes from Bentley Glass:

> I can see three new types of organized effort. One of these, as at my own branch of the State University of New York at Stony Brook, we may call an Instructional Resources Center. Here instructional design, use

[40] Richard Saul Wurman, ed., *Yellow Pages for Learning Resources* (Philadelphia: GEE! Group for Environmental Education, Inc., 1972), p. 1.

of visual methods and audio tapes, computer-assisted instruction, and other novel experimental educational methods may be combined with facilities for scientific testing of the reliability and validity of such methods. A second organized unit we may call a Center for Curriculum Development. This is an institute in which task forces of scholars and scientists together with experienced teachers give continuing thought to the design of new educational programs, especially those particularly needed for the renewal of education. In this center the advanced methods of the new educational technology are to be brought together with the significant new developments of subject matter, and continuously new syntheses are evolved for actual teaching. No such program would be worth much without the final practical tests in the classroom and laboratory. The third organized unit, a Center for Continuing Education, is therefore necessary not only to satisfy the needs for the renewal of education of professional groups and of adults in general, but also to serve as the site where the new methods and ideas are to be put to the test. A steady flow of suggestions and criticisms from the staff and the students in the Center for Continuing Education will provide invaluable feedback for the Center for Curriculum Development and the Instructional Resources Center. This should be a true educational cybernetic system. Here may well be born the fresh, vital influence that will ultimately sweep away the timeworn methods of instruction and the moldy subject matter that so sadly characterizes much of our university teaching.[41]

Curriculum planning groups in schools and school districts could be greatly aided by such university centers. Here national curriculum projects could be continuously renewed, and here staff development could take place. The network could well be of affiliated schools and such centers that would build up their "reference services to professional objects" and "reference services to educators-at-large" for use by the schools and their learners and teachers.

We see the networks concept and the related university center idea as being of great relevance to our own discussion later in this chapter of the school center as a management system for curriculum and instruction.

Leagues of Schools

The final type of external planning model to be considered in this section is the concept of a league, that is, a relatively informal association of schools formed to help one another. Less formally organized than the school district with its legal status, the league cuts across district

[41] From Chapter 2 of *The Timely and the Timeless: The Interrelationships of Science, Education, and Society*, by Bentley Glass. © 1970 by Basic Books, Inc., Publishers, New York.

and even state lines. Planning models of this type have long been used in education, and we believe that they have more utility than ever before. For example, the Eight-Year Study involved an association of thirty schools and had ties with colleges and universities which entered into the agreement about the admission of the graduates of the schools. More recently the federally subsidized research and development centers and the regional educational laboratories have utilized various types of networks of participating schools. As we noted earlier, some of these organizations have emerged from a regional laboratory pattern to widely affect the school curriculum through their various projects; for example, the Education Development Center's popular *MAN: A Course of Study* is used in many schools. The supplementary educational centers financed by Title III of the Elementary and Secondary Education Act of 1965 and its supplements have generally served a specific group of schools and in some states have melded into intermediate units. The Union Boards of New York State and similar sharing arrangements among local districts in other states have provided special tax support for cooperative educational services shared by cooperating school districts. Local organizations too can have national impact, as evidenced by the extensive curriculum publications of the Educational Research Council of Greater Cleveland.

A useful example of the use of the league notion for planning curriculum and instruction is given by the "Individually Guided Education" (IGE) plan developed by the Wisconsin Research and Development Center for Cognitive Learning in conjunction with the model of the multi-unit elementary school. This plan has been concurrently implemented by IDEA (Institute for Development of Educational Activities, Inc.), an affiliate of the Kettering Foundation, through leagues of elementary schools, and later in leagues of middle schools, with plans projected for high schools as well. The components of the system were described as follows by the director of the Wisconsin Center, Herbert J. Klausmeier:

> 1. An organizational pattern for instruction, building-level administration, and central-office administration. Together, these elements constitute what we call the multi-unit school—elementary (MUS-E).
> 2. A model of instructional programming for the individual, with related guidance procedures. This model is designed to provide for differences among students in their rates and styles of learning, levels of motivation, and other characteristics. Based on educational objectives of the school, it is used to develop curriculum materials and implement IGE. . . .
> 3. A model for developing measurement tools and evaluation procedures. The model includes pre-assessment of children's readiness, assessment of programs and final achievement with criterion-referenced tests, feedback to the teacher and the child, and evaluation of the IGE design and its components.

4. Curriculum materials, related statements of instructional objectives, and criterion-referenced tests and observation schedules. The R & D Center in 1971–72 is developing materials and instructional procedures in reading, pre-reading, mathematics, environmental education, and motivation.

5. A program for home-school communications that reinforces the school efforts by generating the interest and encouragement of parents and other adults whose attitudes influence pupil motivation and learning.

6. Facilitative environments in school buildings, school system central offices, state education agencies, and teacher education institutions that encourage IGE practices.

7. Continuing research and development by center and school personnel to generate knowledge and to produce curriculum materials and instructional procedures.[42]

Expanding participation in this program was reported by Klausmeier:

In 1967–68 there were nine MUS-Es in Wisconsin; in 1970–71 there were 99. In 1968–69 the first three MUS-Es were started in Ohio and Pennsylvania; in 1970–71 there were 164 MUS-Es in seven states. This year there will be about 400 new schools.[43]

Another illustration of the league approach is that of the League of Cooperating Schools organized in 1966 by John Goodlad as Director, Research Division of IDEA. This league initially involved eighteen California schools and the University of California at Los Angeles in an effort to test and refine a strategy for continuous school improvement. In late 1972 Goodlad reported that "IDEA is no longer involved, the League has grown to 22 schools, and the education of teachers has become a major function."[44] The assumptions Goodlad stated as underlying the formation of this league constitute an excellent statement of the rationale of the league approach to influencing curriculum and instruction:

1. The initial assumption was that the individual school, with its principal, teachers, pupils, and, less intimately, parents and citizens is the largest organic unit for educational change.

2. The second assumption was that the individual school is not sufficiently strong, within existing constraints, to overcome the prevailing and, in large measure, necessary conservative (in the classic sense of preserving or conserving) characteristics of the surrounding school district. [Hence each League school was from a different school district.]

[42] Herbert J. Klausmeier, "The Multi-Unit Elementary School and Individually Guided Education," *Phi Delta Kappan*, 53, 181 (November 1971).

[43] Klausmeier, pp. 182–183.

[44] John Goodlad, "Staff Development: The League Model," *Theory Into Practice*, 11, 211 (October 1972).

3. A third assumption was that persons about to take risks are more willing to do so when some elements of success already are built into the structure. [Hence the association with IDEA and UCLA initially.]

4. A fourth assumption was that some screening, legitimizing, and communicating of ideas, beyond what individual schools might do informally, must be built into the new social system. [Hence a "hub" at the offices of the Research Division of IDEA in West Los Angeles.][45]

We ourselves believe that collaboration of schools in such ventures is a great incentive and aid to curriculum planning. Actually, the plans are not developed wholly externally to the school, since through the league there is typically much opportunity for participation in planning for any common curriculum designs and much opportunity for mutual support, feedback, and modification during implementation. The league may be organized with little aim of developing common curriculum plans, as was true in the Eight-Year Study with the great freedom each school had in developing its own plan, but with the expectation of sharing, criticizing, and observing the plans of individual schools. Thus the Florida League of Middle Schools was established in 1973 as an association for mutual aid with this original statement of purposes:

1. To facilitate continuing curriculum improvement, inservice education, and other phases of middle school education.

2. To serve as a clearinghouse for exchange of ideas, materials, and personnel needed for middle school development.

3. To assist in developing plans for evaluation of middle schools in Florida.

4. To help secure and maintain support of agencies and groups in the state interested in educational improvement.

5. To represent the middle schools in professional and public discussions of educational programs and problems.[46]

The systematic process of curriculum planning with which we now close this chapter would make full provision of such sharing and collaborating among schools with common needs and interests.

TOWARD A SYSTEMATIC PROCESS OF CURRICULUM PLANNING

So far in this chapter we have described usual products, processes, and roles in local curriculum planning, and we have also noted

[45] Goodlad, pp. 210–211.

[46] "Florida Middle Schools Get Together: Proposed Plan for a Florida League of Middle Schools," mimeographed, September 29, 1972.

some of the planning processes and systems developed externally to the local school and district. Later chapters deal in detail with the substance of curriculum planning—goals, essential data, designs, instruction, and evaluation. We need at this point to highlight some processes and roles, both those long in use and those only recently developed or awaiting development, which seem essential to a systematic process of curriculum planning in individual school centers and in the districts or other formal organizations to which they belong.

This section includes a description of the characteristics of cooperative curriculum planning followed by three subsections, the school district or other formal organization of schools, the school center, and the teacher. It must be emphasized that these three levels of planning are closely related and that the division of responsibilities among them may and should vary in accordance with the complexity of the organization and the flexibility of its personnel. We assume that each organization of schools should draw up its own planning chart to build in optimum flexibility.

Characteristics of Cooperative Curriculum Planning

Effective curriculum planning, we believe, is always cooperative, involving group decision-making. Although its various stages frequently include intensive activity by individuals, at times working alone, the individual is responsible to the group of planners who review his proposals and tentative plans and with whom he shares responsibility. Thus even the individual teacher who ultimately plans a particular instructional program for a particular group of learners is responsible to his colleagues in the planning group. He must be able to relate his own program to other instructional programs the learners have experienced in the past, are currently experiencing, or will experience in the future, and he shares responsibility with his colleagues for the total instructional program. The teacher is responsible, too, for involving in the planning process the learners themselves in ways and for purposes appropriate to their maturity. Whatever the level of planning and the group of learners, certain characteristics of cooperative planning are to be sought.

Common Goals Whatever the planning group and the problems for immediate focus, the common goal in curriculum planning is to provide maximally appropriate learning opportunities for the students concerned. This general goal may be broken down into many subgoals for the particular population of students for the specific phases of planning involved. but always the central focus of any planning group has to be the creation of appropriate learning opportunities. The group's effectiveness in planning learning opportunities directly relates to the clarity of its definition of subgoals, its earnestness in adhering to its goals, its consistent evaluation of the goals, and its own operation in terms of the central goal and the group's own subgoals. Thus a teaching team planning learning opportunities for the development of skills for continued learning sets up particular skills as subgoals and devises plans whereby these skills can be acquired by the students taught by the team; other items for planning and discussion are ruled out, and intermittently the group reviews its plan in terms of relevance and feasibility for skills development by the learners concerned. That is, the group keeps asking: "Will this plan or plans accomplish our goal of appropriate learning opportunities for our students to become better equipped for self-directed learning?"

Adequate Representation and Organization   Two basic principles are involved here: (1) all persons directly involved in the consequences of decisions made by a group should be represented in the decision-making; and (2) the group should have whatever organization is most promising for achievement of its goals. As to the first, all curriculum decisions have direct consequences for the students, school personnel, and community involved. Whether the educators can adequately represent student and community concerns depends on such factors as the significance of the decision to students and community, the ability of the students and community to understand and deal with the issues involved, and the integrity of the educators. As we see it, many decisions are of such critical consequences to students and community that they should be directly represented, and many others are so technical and relatively insignificant that student and community representatives would not wish to be involved. For example, a decision on whether sex education is to be provided in a school program ought to be made with adequate representation of students (at early levels through their parents) and community. On the other hand, a choice of commercial instructional materials ought to be made on such technical bases as to preclude the use of student and community judgment, except as usability might be tested out with representative students or as possibly controversial content might be checked out with community representatives.

We deal elsewhere in this chapter with the organization for curriculum planning, but here it should be said that each planning group should work out for itself an effective organization for achieving its goals. Items most groups need to plan for include the choice of a chairman, the system of recording, the schedule of meetings, the channeling of feedback, the use of subcommittees, the plan for reporting plans to other groups, and the process of modifying plans and making them final.

Competent Group Leadership   Curriculum planning groups, like groups in general, need leaders competent in directing the group process. The leader recognizes that every individual in the group is a potential leader who may at any time direct group thinking by questions, observations, and suggestions. The leadership person provides every opportunity for all potential leadership within the group to exert itself. At the same time this person gives personal leadership to the group enterprise when this seems critical. Among the specific tasks of leadership, not necessarily of a single person designated as chairman but of all who share the leadership role, are the following:

1. Maintain a comfortable environment.
2. Secure frank, full expression of ideas.
3. Summarize faithfully agreements or decisions reached and group progress from time to time.
4. Help record keepers in the maintenance of adequate notes as to the flow and results of discussion.
5. See that alternative courses of action and positions on issues are identified.
6. Determine the consensus when appropriate.
7. Recognize fully the contributions of group members.

Open and Clear Communication   Open and clear communication may be expected within a group when the leader operates as just described. But in curriculum planning there are continual needs for communication with other groups and individuals—the committee to the faculty, the teacher to the class, the committee or the school or district administrator to community groups and boards of education, for example. The communications network needs careful attention so that all concerned understand recommendations and actions and especially so that there is clear consideration of feedback from these persons.

Analysis of curriculum planning activities indicates that in both the planning and implementation phases a major block to action is the failure of persons concerned to understand each other. Implementation of plans made by persons other than the implementers is obviously impossible unless the plans are clearly communicated and fully understood and accepted. Even face-to-face communication breaks down because of semantic and perceptual difficulties. The use of written communications alone eliminates opportunity for discussion and constitutes an inadequate basis for curriculum planning at all levels. Systematic channels for communication clearly understood by all concerned, with information fed back to those who make suggestions, and maximum opportunity for proposals to be made and feedback about them to be gathered and considered, are essential in the planning process.

Use of Relevant Data   Curriculum planning does not have to be a matter only of sharing opinions. Although there are points when judgment may have to be speculative, there are many others when judgments can and should be based on interpretations of facts. Facts are available and should be considered regarding the student population, community expectations, goals of the school, and all of the other items described in Chapter 3 and elsewhere in this book as basic to curriculum planning. Furthermore, research reports are available on many problems, and these are becoming increasingly easier to locate through ERIC (Educational Research Information Clearinghouse Service) and other sources. If the school uses a systematic process of curriculum, much input is to be considered as it is channeled from the various feedback channels that give students, faculty, and the community opportunity to make their needs, wishes, and suggestions known.

The critical characteristic of effective planning is its reliance on such data. Instead of the curriculum planning group simply polling its members on what they think ought to be done, readiness for this question is developed through consultation of the data from the available sources. The question, "What do you think?" is more properly, "What do these data tell us needs to be done?" In the absence of data, the question may even become, "How can we find what ought to be done?"

Group Decisions   Groups which possess the characteristics we have described are almost certain to make decisions that reflect the best judgment of the group as a whole, or certainly of a majority of the group. The one pitfall frequently observed is a lack of awareness on the part of the group concerning the limitations of its decision-making powers. Committees that have worked out a careful plan for trying out a particular curriculum innovation in their school or district need to keep in mind that their recommendation is only a recommendation, that it must be considered by the larger faculty or community group that is responsible for the total school program. Groups are sometimes frustrated by not understanding what decisions they can make or what the force of their recommendations may be. Consequently, it is as important for the group leader to clearly identify the scope and force of the group's decision-making power as it is for him to guide the group to a decision that genuinely reflects the best judgment of group members.

Adequate Time and Facilities for Planning   Entirely too much curriculum planning, especially at the school level, has in the past had to be done within crowded time schedules and in crowded rooms. Although pleasant surroundings and adequate time do not guarantee good planning, they can certainly help. Increasingly schools are scheduling time for planning, with the groups meeting in conference rooms in the building. Spaces where planners can operate without interruption, in which boards or charts can be used to record items for all members to see, and in which audiovisual equipment can be readily used help greatly. Rapid duplication services, and perhaps dictating equipment, may expedite record keeping and the review of written materials.

Large blocks of time in which to meet are essential at many points in the group planning process, so that whole days—hopefully weeks, perhaps summer periods—should be set aside for this purpose. Summer workshops aided by adequate resources and needed data can be especially productive.

Curriculum Planning for the School District

As already indicated, the curriculum council provides a potentially effective clearinghouse for planning for a school district or other official organization of schools under a single administrative board or head. For larger districts, some plan of subdistricts, each with its curriculum council represented on an interlocking district-wide council, is desirable and frequently used. The council should represent each individual school, with some plan to insure representation also of the central administration, community, parents, and students served. This latter representation may be secured through parallel community and student councils, with an arrangement for liaison between the school's curriculum council and the community and students' advisory councils.

The effectiveness of the role of the curriculum council in planning for the district depends to a large extent on the quality of the arrangements made for it to receive problems and proposals from the constituent units and the opportunity given these units to review recommendations made to them by the council. It is particularly important for specific aspects of planning to be assigned to task forces, each created for a particular purpose and each reporting back to the council. Such tasks of planning include review of data regarding curriculum needs, selection of instructional systems or national curriculum project packages for district-wide use, creation of alternative schools for particular purposes, the setting of curriculum domains for district-wide curriculum designing, consideration of the possibilities of performance contracts, the planning of staff-development programs relating to curriculum needs, identification of problems for research, and, especially, review of feedback from various sources on the curriculum and instructional program of the district. Task forces should include personnel who are not members of the council and should have the facilities of consultant help, special services such as research and evaluation units, and others as needed for expeditious discharge of their assignments. Task forces may be created to design experimental units or even total instructional systems, but again their products should be subject to review and modification by the curriculum council and its constituent school units and advisory groups.

The school district also needs input from outside the district, and this may be made available through membership in leagues, through the services of supplementary educational centers and other sharing arrangements, through the organization of search parties to visit other schools and districts where needed resources have been identified, and through the services of consultants employed for particular services. The school district also needs specialized research and evaluation services to carry on its evaluation programs. It may very wisely identify and staff pilot curriculum centers and experimental units for the development and testing of innovative curriculum models with provision for dissemination through the council and other means. In all of these endeavors there is need for some feedback mechanism which provides critiques of the various operations by those concerned.

Curriculum Planning for the Individual School

A critical requirement for effective curriculum planning at the individual school center is strong leadership. In the past many persons who advocated centralizing curriculum planning justified their position by decrying the quality of curriculum leadership at the school and even the district level. Debates over whether the curriculum and instructional leader should be the principal or the curriculum coordinator or the assistant principal for curriculum and instruction have not resulted in providing the leadership needed. The important point is that the educational program of a school requires some one qualified person to be responsible for enlisting the resources, facilitating the processes, and advising the entire staff and other participants in planning, implementing, and evaluating the program. To this end the training of qualified persons and their assignment to individual school centers must be accelerated. Whether the school district gives this responsibility to the principal or to the curriculum coordinator, the assistant principal, or one or more unit or team leaders, the person selected must meet several qualifications. As a minimum, these qualifications should include training in group process, goal-setting, team planning and teaching, use of instructional resources, individual instruction and counseling, curriculum theory and research, and community relations. Undoubtedly, each district would modify and expand these qualifications to conform to local needs. Our thesis is that a systematic process of curriculum planning necessitates the presence of a qualified curriculum leader, whatever his actual title, in every school center.

As a management center for curriculum and instruction, the individual school needs a variety of information about the students for whom it is responsible. It should also have a complete inventory of all the learning opportunities available within the community and not just those planned for implementation within the school. In addition, the management system needs some trustworthy device for accurate matching of student needs and learning opportunities. Perhaps in time computer matching of learners and opportunities will be available. Until then the best possible arrangement appears to be a good counseling system. A teacher-counselor who is knowledgeable about his advisees and about the learning opportunities available, serving as we suggested earlier as home base adviser or director of personal development, would seem to be the best possibility. These advisers would need help from trained counselors and also the assistance of the curriculum leader to coordinate their activities.

Curriculum and instructional designing within the center would be largely accomplished by the teams of teachers responsible for particular curriculum domains. These planning teams would require the special help of the curriculum leader in setting up their programs, and they might well benefit from the input of the curriculum council and of any league of schools or other sharing organization with which they are affiliated. Increasingly schools are setting up special centers for instruction in the skills and specialization domains, and here are needed the specialists who can work closely and effectively with individual students. Their planning may need to be in concert, too, and they should have all the help possible in the form of instructional systems, special equipment and laboratory-type situations, and work and other experience in the community.

Feedback mechanisms at the school center must rely heavily on the data from students as they accept, modify, and reject the learning opportunities planned for them. Close interaction of teachers and students is imperative, but students also need the opportunity to appraise objectively their experiences and to suggest other types of learning opportunities they would like to see incorporated into their personal curriculums. Student representatives on school planning councils and special curriculum task forces are successfully used in many high schools. Middle school students are also involved in planning groups with their teachers and parents, and parents of younger elementary school children are widely used as representatives of their children. Opinion polls may be advantageously taken on many curriculum issues in the school.

The Individual Teacher

The professionally committed teacher is accustomed to carefully planning his instructional program, whether long-term, short-term, daily, or event by event. He needs much assistance from the planning groups of the district and school to mesh his plans with the goals and objectives of the district, the school, the team, and the individual students taught. Resource units which the teacher has helped develop can be very useful; further development of the system of computerized storage of resource units may eventually be very helpful in rapidly matching learning experiences and student needs.[47] Curriculum guides such as we described early in this chapter may also give the teacher considerable assistance. Instructional systems, even textbooks, that the teacher has had opportunity to study and work with and that he has freedom to adapt to his own situation may be indispensable in some teaching situations.

Teachers need consultant help, too, and frequently the best help may come from other teachers in the building, the district, or even other schools in the league. We consider the concept of "peer-intervention strategy" applicable to the planning and improvement processes of teachers. In the League of Cooperating Schools operated by the Research Division of the Kettering Foundation (see pages 89–90), individual teachers advertised through a newsletter their needs for help and also their expertise:

> The classified ads in the *Changing Schools* newsletter alert teachers to their new source of expertise. The types of assistance they offer or request run the gamut of educational concerns from the physical aspects of classroom management to the psychological factors that give a youngster a sense of confidence in his own ability to achieve.
>
> Perhaps even more interesting, however, is the tone that emerges if one reads between the lines of those ads. Here are professionals freely admitting that they're having trouble or announcing with pleasure that they think they have a good idea and suspect someone else would like to know about it. A quiet pride is evident beneath those words. It is the pride of professionals who are convinced they know enough about education to tackle the continuing job of improving instruction by themselves without waiting for a consultant to tell them what to do. /I/D/E/A/ is banking on that pride and sense of self-determination to make innovation a way of life for the schools.[48]

Similarly, effective teacher planning requires continuing assessment of the teacher's own needs for help and his abilities to give help to others. Peer intervention seems a highly promising way of advancing teacher cooperation and sharing for better plans and their execution. The curriculum leader will perhaps be of most assistance to individual teachers

---

[47] Robert S. Harnack, *Evaluation of an Innovation in Education—Computer Based Curriculum Planning*, Special Report of the Center for Curriculum Planning, State University of New York at Buffalo; Joseph M. O'Connell, ed., February 1970.

[48] */I/D/E/A/ Annual Report, 1970* (Dayton, O.: Institute for Development of Educational Activities, Inc., 1970), p. 12.

through bringing them together across the building and across schools for this purpose. We turn attention now to the role of the curriculum leader for a group of schools.

ROLE OF THE CURRICULUM LEADER

Our reference in this final section is to the individual who has assigned responsibility for leadership in guiding and coordinating the curriculum planning process in a school district or other group of schools. We noted earlier the importance of group dynamics in curriculum planning, and we also fully acknowledged the contributions of all persons who from time to time assume leadership for particular jobs. But we firmly believe that the curriculum planning process will not be systematic or effective unless there is, for whatever group of schools comprise the system, a responsible and competent individual officially designated as the curriculum leader. It matters little whether his title is assistant superintendent for instruction, director of curriculum, director of instruction, curriculum coordinator, or any other title used to designate his official function.

The management of a curriculum planning system involves many tasks, but the central one is the coordination of all of the processes described in this chapter. More than almost any other educator, the curriculum leader must be able to keep straight the relation of the trees and the forest. As he works with individual teachers and principals, school faculties, district councils, curriculum designing units, and lay groups, he not only helps each individual and group to make a contribution to curriculum planning but sees to it that these contributions mesh well with each other. In an early article Caswell emphasized this function of the curriculum leader:

> He must be in a position administratively to work with all groups affecting instruction. He must work cooperatively, depending upon the modification of viewpoints as a means of progress and thus must be in position to lead in the development of an in-service educational program for workers in the school system. He must be in position to coordinate supervision and to relate it to the evolving program. He must have opportunity to bring the findings of guidance workers to bear on the revision of the curriculum.[49]

This statement remains an excellent definition of the role of the curriculum leader. In the 1970s new demands arising from public discontent

[49] Hollis L. Caswell, "The Function of the Curriculum Director," *Curriculum Journal*, 9, 249 (October 1938).

with the schools and new resources through systems analysis and computer management make the role more complex but also potentially more challenging and rewarding.

In closing this chapter on roles and processes, we cannot emphasize too strongly the all-important roles of the curriculum leader of the school district and the principal of the individual school. These persons in particular must be inventive and visionary and able to articulate their visions to lead their colleagues and communities to evaluate and try out new ideas and innovations. We do not discount the roles of teachers, students, and others, but our observations are conclusive as to the beneficial impact of able leadership. Without it progress is rarely possible.

ADDITIONAL SUGGESTIONS FOR FURTHER STUDY

Alexander, William M., *The Changing High School Curriculum: Readings*, 2d ed. New York: Holt, Rinehart and Winston, Inc., 1972. See various selections in Chapters 8–12 on the processes of curriculum improvement.

Alternative Schools: Pioneering Districts Create Options for Students. Education U.S.A., Special Report. Washington, D.C.: National School Public Relations Association, 1972. Describes alternative schools within public school districts, with examples selected from some 200 schools reported as being operated or planned by 60 districts.

"Alternative Schools: Special Issue," *Phi Delta Kappan*, 54, 433–485 (March 1973). An editorial and seven articles offer analyses, criticisms, and observations regarding the alternative school movement, and seven other articles describe particular practices and schools.

Bushnell, Davis S., and Donald Rappaport, eds., *Planned Change in Education: A Systems Approach*. New York: Harcourt Brace Jovanovich, Inc., 1971. Chapters by various authors deal with organizing for change, accountability, performance contracts, instructional organization, and systems approaches to use of educational resources. See Chapter 1 for a useful model of the change process.

Doll, Ronald C., *Leadership to Improve Schools*. Worthington, O.: Charles A. Jones Publishing Company, 1972. Focuses on five major task areas of educational leadership; see especially Chapters 5–7 on curriculum leadership.

Eisele, James E., and others, *Computer Assisted Planning of Curriculum and Instruction: (How to Use Computer-Based Resource Units to Individualize Instruction)*. Englewood Cliffs, N.J.: Educational Technology Publications, 1973. Describes how computers are used to retrieve resource unit materials appropriate to various subjects to meet specific needs of individual students.

EPIEGRAM. New York: Educational Products Information Exchange Institute. Reviews current educational products. Published twice monthly, October through June (18 issues per year).

"The Future of Nonpublic Schools," *School Review,* 81, 155–232 (February 1973). Four articles on this theme are entitled, respectively, "The Trailblazer in an Age of R & D"; "Alternative Schools: Better Guardians Than Family or State"; "Public and Nonpublic Schools—Losers Both"; and "The Outcome of Catholic Education."

Goodlad, John I., and Harold G. Shane, eds., *The Elementary School in the United States.* Seventy-second yearbook of the National Society for the Study of Education, Part II. Chicago: University of Chicago Press, 1973. See especially, in regard to curriculum planning processes, Chapter X, "The School's Curriculum"; Chapter XIV, "Effecting Change in Elementary Schools"; and Chapter XV, "Prospects and Prerequisites for the Improvement of Elementary Education: 1973–1985."

Graubard, Allen, *Free the Children.* New York: Pantheon Books, 1973. Describes and evaluates the free school movement and its implications for public school improvement.

Kapfer, Philip G., and Glen F. Ovard, *Preparing and Using Individualized Learning Packages: For Ungraded, Continuous Progress Education.* Englewood Cliffs, N.J.: Educational Technology Publications, 1971. An instructional guide for teachers to learn to prepare and use individualized learning packages. Includes suggested learning activities, progress checks, post-tests, and suggestions for further study.

Kopp, O. W., and D. L. Zufelt, *Personalized Curriculum: Method and Design.* Columbus, O.: Charles E. Merrill Publishing Company, 1971. Emphasizes personalizing the program of the elementary school, with a useful chapter (4) on the curriculum development processes involved.

Sarason, Seymour B., *The Culture of the School and the Problem of Change.* Boston: Allyn and Bacon, Inc., 1971. Examines the problem of change in terms of the culture of the school, yielding especially helpful analyses of the roles of principals and teachers.

3

SOURCES OF
DATA FOR
CURRICULUM
PLANNING

Schools are social institutions established by a society to facilitate the education of young people; hence curriculum planning always takes place within a social structure and is designed to contribute in major ways to the education of an identifiable group of children, youth, and young adults. It follows logically that those who plan the curriculum must take into account certain basic factors within this broad structure of social function if the schooling provided students comprising the group is to be appropriate, proper, and valid. In this chapter we will identify and consider briefly the most essential types of data that educators, students, and citizens need as a basis for planning.

DATA ESSENTIAL FOR PLANNING

The models and the discussion of them in Chapter 1 have already shown the kinds of information essential for valid curriculum planning. The data will be obtained from four major sources: (1) the students to be educated; (2) the society which provides and operates the schools; (3) the nature and character of the learning process; and (4) the accumulated knowledge available and feasible for educating students.

Subsidiary to these primary sources, but nevertheless of great importance in planning an educational program, are these additional elements: (1) the legal structures within which schools must be established and operated; (2) resources and facilities for carrying on a school program; and (3) research reports and professional advice.

We will consider briefly the nature of the data desired from each source and some of the more important methods and means of obtaining them. The treatment will be limited, first, because of space limitations in a book on the entire process of curriculum planning, and, second, data obviously must be obtained for a particular group of students and for individual students who are to be educated for membership in a particular social group at a particular time in its history.

It should be recognized that much curriculum planning for today's schools does not follow the models and the processes we present in this volume. Often planners plunge right into the preparation of guides, instructional materials, or instructional plans without overtly and deliberately moving through all of the steps listed in Chapter 1 as necessary in a systematic approach to educational planning. Further, goals and objectives for the program, for example, frequently are written without thorough consideration of the fundamental factors listed above. The result of such sketchy, and often unrealistic, planning, as Mark Shedd stated,

> is that a great deal of what we have now *is not* working, and the breakdown is particularly acute in the urban sector . . . [Further, he charged] that most schools and school systems have become anachronistic. They are out of phase with everyday realities of their students' lives. They do not illuminate the concerns of youngsters. They appear disconnected from the "real" world. They are irrelevant.[1]

We recognize that highly educated professionals, such as teachers and other school staff personnel, have a broad and often deep knowledge of many of these factors basic to planning; they have studied psychology, sociology, philosophy, history, science, literature, and the like. They start with a professional's set of insights, understandings, and competencies. Nevertheless, we think the nature and character of the problems we face in the schools today, and the necessity of providing a

---

[1] Mark R. Shedd, "The Kinds of Educational Programs We Need—for Later Adolescent Years," in J. Galen Saylor, ed., *The School of the Future—Now* (Washington, D.C.: Association for Supervision and Curriculum Development, 1972), pp. 53–64.

program of education that is truly appropriate and valid for each student, require that on occasion, at least, all pertinent data for specific groups of students be systematically identified and brought up to date. Such information must then be considered fully and insightfully in all planning efforts.

DATA ABOUT STUDENTS

As Dewey pointed out three quarters of a century ago, "the fundamental factors in the educative process are an immature, undeveloped being; and certain social aims, meanings, values incarnate in the matured experience of the adult. The educative process is the due interaction of these forces."[2]

This is the basic position from which to start the collection of data and information for curriculum planning. Obviously, it is the young for whom we plan, although we recognize the role of the school in life-long education, and such planning cannot be complete or valid, except on a hit-and-miss basis, unless essential information about the educational needs of the learners is known and utilized in the development of the design. Let us consider, then, the kinds of data needed about the students to be schooled. Broad categories of data will be identified.

Pupil Population Data

Table 3 lists some of the more important kinds of enumerative and statistical information that should be available. Some sources from which the data may be obtained are suggested, although it is recognized that these may vary among school systems or that other sources may be available. The importance of the information for curriculum planning is indicated in the column headed "suggested uses." Such a list is not exhaustive nor are the recommendations spelled out in detail.

Much of the statistical data about the student body of the school, the population characteristics of the children of the district, and follow-up studies can be compiled or be made by staff members of appropriate research or personnel bureaus; other data may be compiled by administrators or counseling personnel of the individual school. Curriculum planning committees and individual teachers should readily have available this information without spending a great deal of their time in collecting it. Interpretations of the data, however, should be made by all of those involved in the planning process, including parents.

[2] John Dewey, *The Child and the Curriculum* (Chicago: University of Chicago Press, 1902), pp. 7–8.

Table 3
Kinds of Information Needed about Pupil Population

ITEM	POSSIBLE SOURCES	SUGGESTED USES
1. Population and enrollment data: numbers, trends, births, age distribution; race or ethnic background; projected birth rates and rates of population growth; projected enrollments.	Census data by tracts; pupil data records; individual school records; national and state reports on vital statistics; decennial census reports; forecast of population.	Facilities, staff, equipment, and materials needed; class size; teacher load; budget-making; planning desirable integration by racial and ethnic characteristics; locating buildings.
2. School progress: normal, retarded, or accelerated progress by grade, multiunit, or level.	Pupil records in individual schools; achievement as measured by tests.	Analyze and evaluate promotion and class assignment practices; diagnose individual needs; plan programs to meet special needs; plans for multilevel or ungraded groupings.
3. Dropouts: rate, causes, characteristics of the dropouts; school status; postschool status.	Pupil records, by schools and system-wide; follow-up studies; conferences; guidance records; student input before entering and after leaving school.	Critical assessment of curriculum and instruction in terms of genuine relevancy for all students; identification of potential dropouts and use of positive counseling measures; desirability of alternate types of educational programs for some students; planning part-time and informal programs for those who drop out; parent involvement; stimulating community action for better school programs.

Planning groups may benefit greatly from the use of research studies, reports, and interpretative studies published by many governmental agencies, study commissions, school survey committees, and similar groups. Listed below are some of the more important types of publications available. Obviously, these studies do not provide direct interpretations of data gathered for the local school system, but they are useful in showing the situation nationally, projecting trends and data for the nation, usually including figures by states, or stating findings that may assist school staffs in interpreting their own data. Also, some of the reports illustrate methods of collecting data and the nature of generalizations made.

U.S. Office of Education

(All government publications are available from the Government Printing Office, Public Documents Distribution Center, 5801 Tabor Ave., Philadelphia, Pa., 19120.)

Statistics of State School Systems. A biennial survey of school enrollment, number of staff members, finances, and the like, by states.

Statistics of Public Elementary and Secondary Day Schools. Published annually, but is preliminary data that may be revised and extended in the biennial report.

Statistics of Local Public School Systems. Published annually; based on questionnaire data from a representative sample; some data for individual schools in the sample are included.

Digest of Educational Statistics. Published annually. Comprehensive summary of data on schools collected from other reports of the Office.

Projections of Educational Statistics. Published annually. Projects pupil population data, staff requirements, and expenditures for ten ensuing years.

Statistics of Nonpublic Elementary and Secondary Schools. Published on occasion. Greater efforts are being made to collect and publish such data regularly.

National Assessment of Educational Progress. Test results from the national program of assessment of student achievement. Reports published on various subject areas as results become available (see also Chapter 7).

Research in Education. Published monthly with an annual compilation. Lists by subject, author, and institution many research reports and papers and gives instructions for obtaining copies. An invaluable aid in locating studies on any topic in the educational literature. By subscription.

U.S. Bureau of the Census

Various volumes reporting the decennial census, and special reports. Published each decade following the census. The main report is titled *Population.* It contains an extensive array of data on "general characteristics," "general social and economic characteristics," data on metropolitan areas, and other subjects. A special report on *Education* has been published in recent decades. Others on economic status, migration, and minorities are usually available. A school system could obtain computer tapes that provide data for as small a local area as a census "block" or for larger census areas of a city such as the area comprising a zip code section.

Current Population Reports, Series P-20 and P-25. Brief circulars published frequently during the year. Very useful in supplying data during the interim between censuses.

Characteristics of American Youth, 1971. P-23 Series of Technical Studies. A very useful special study of numbers, educational attainments, school enrollment, migration, marital status, income, occupations, and the like.

White House Conference on Children

Held each decade; reports prepared for the conference and of the proceedings are rich sources of information and data of many kinds. *The Profiles of Children,* prepared for the 1970 conference, contains a great deal of data related to children. Although prepared prior to the 1970 census, the book illustrates in depth the kinds of studies that may and should be made not only at the national level but for the local school district as well.

Youth in Transition

An extensive longitudinal study of over 25,000 adolescent boys in about 100 high schools made by the Institute for Social Research, University of Michigan, Ann Arbor 48106. The "blueprint" for the study was published in 1967, with a revision in 1971 (Volume IV). Reports of data and findings were published in the early 1970s. Volumes include *The Impact of Family Background and Intelligence on Tenth-Grade Boys* (Volume II); *Dropping Out—Problem or Symptom?* (Volume III); *Drugs and American Youth* (Special Report).

School Dropout Studies

The Mink Scale. A scale developed for a project on dropouts in Appalachia directed by West Virginia University, Morgantown. It differentiates significantly between potential dropouts and nondropouts at the junior high school level. See ERIC Documents ED 044 431 and ED 044 444.

Barbara J. Chance and Joseph A. Starthory, "Dropout Prevention: A Model for Educational Change," *High School Journal,* 55, 208–218 (February 1972).

Jerald G. Bachman, Swayzer Wirtanen, and Ilona Wirtanen, *Dropping Out—Problem or Symptom?* See "Youth in Transition" project above.

Growth and Developmental Characteristics and Status

Another major category of data needed about the students to be educated is the nature and status of their growth and development. Much of the insight and understanding curriculum planners need in this aspect of student data will utilize known generalizations about infants, children, and youth. It will, of course, be necessary to check this knowledge against the population for whom a particular curriculum plan is being prepared and instruction is being provided. In fact, personalization of instruction based on the developmental status of students is essential.

Table 4 lists some of the important types of information desired in this category.

Table 4
Kinds of Information Needed about Student Growth and Development

ITEM	POSSIBLE SOURCES	SUGGESTED USES
1. Physical development: health status; body development; physical abnormalities; family genetic history; motor skills; diseases; special physical needs.	School health examinations and records; tests of physical condition; conferences with parents; immunization record; nonconfidential reports of doctors and staff members; observation; books, research reports; health surveys.	Development of programs for students with exceptional needs, corrective programs, and programs of physical and health education; counseling on individual problems; recommendations for referral to appropriate person or agencies; special facilities and equipment needed; programs in family life education; teaching units on genetic counseling; remediation programs.
2. Emotional and social development: mental health status; self-directiveness; relations with fellow students, teachers, and parents; psychoneurological problems; nature and causes of aggressive behavior; stages in life cycle of development.	Widely accepted studies and literature on the subject; studies of individual children and youth (the child study movement); clinical studies; questionnaires; interviews; conferences with student and parents; personality interests; keen observation; nonconfidential medical records.	Development of programs for students with special needs; planning of curriculum and instruction that provide involvement and participation; humane relations throughout the school; inclusion of units on emotions and mental health in curriculum; teacher compassion; guidance plans and activities; parent conferences; family life programs for students and parents.
3. Psychological needs: developmental tasks; drives; basic needs of human beings; unmet needs; status of self-identity; status of ego development and needs; identification of realities of life for individual life-styles.	Same as above.	Program planning (schools without failure concept); instructional methods that involve participation; individualization of instruction; planning guidance and counseling services; therapy; student participation in school planning; provisions for psychological services.

ITEM	POSSIBLE SOURCES	SUGGESTED USES
4. Intellectual and creative development: current status of development; levels of readiness; capabilities and potentialities; levels of achievement; deficiencies; status of cognitive development; experiential background; special talents; absorbing interests.	Variety of tests; research studies; observation; achievement in school subjects; conferences; use of concepts and generalizations; level of rational thinking; ability to be self-directive; comparative data on basis of national tests.	Scope of opportunities for development of all individuals; comprehensive curriculum; work with parents in selecting school activities and programs; planning and guiding out-of-school experiences; having adequate types of learning resources available; antecedent factors in evaluation; nature and character of testing program and use of test results.
5. Personal traits: character; personality; values; moral traits; attitudes; motivational levels; concepts of self; aspirations; self-esteem; behavior; anxieties; relations with others, especially parents; extent and nature of use of drugs, narcotics, and alcohol; antisocial tendencies; student alienation and activism; factors in alienation, disillusionment, and rebelliousness and extent of these.	Same sources as for (2) and (4) above; observation is especially important; autobiographical sketches; appropriate tests of proven validity; guidance records on behavior; police, court, and probation records and reports.	Same as (3) and (4) above; programs for development of values, attitudes, and morals; programs in drug education; school practices and policies on behavior and dress; cooperation with appropriate community agencies; establishing "listening posts," nonschool counseling centers or services, halfway, wayward, or refuge houses; establishing and/or supporting "free form" and other types of alternative schools for some students.

Literature on the nature and status of the growth and development of children and youth is voluminous. Only a few sources which we consider to be of great significance are listed here; again, these publications not only provide important knowledge about the development of children and youth but they illustrate the kinds of information needed for valid curriculum planning.

White House Conference on Children

> *Report to the President.* This compilation of the reports of the 26 forums, the vote on a list of "overriding concerns," and the recommendations of the 1970 Conference is a significant document.

An Annotated Bibliography on Children. A 75-page list of selected references on children and their education.

Jean Piaget

The writings of this famous psychologist should be known to all curriculum planners. Concise summaries of his writings are:

Jean Piaget and Barbel Inhelder, *The Psychology of the Child,* translated by Helen Weaver (New York: Basic Books, Inc., 1969).

Herbert Ginsburg and Sylvia Opper, *Piaget's Theory of Intellectual Development* (Englewood Cliffs, N.J.: Prentice-Hall, Inc., 1969). Extensive citations to Piaget's writings are also included.

Richard M. Gorman, *Discovering Piaget: A Guide for Teachers* (Columbus, O.: Charles E. Merrill Publishing Company, 1972).

Educational Resources Information Center (ERIC)

Research in Education (see previous citation)

"Newsletter, Early Childhood Education," 805 West Pennsylvania Ave., Urbana, Ill. 61801. This ERIC clearinghouse publishes a newsletter that contains brief items about children and cites important research studies.

Intelligence

A great deal of controversy has developed in recent years about the nature of intelligence and the factors that shape its development. The following will provide at least a starting point in considering this whole aspect of development.

Joy P. Guilford, "Intelligence: 1965 Model," *American Psychologist,* 21, 20–26 (1966).

Arthur R. Jensen, Genetics and Education (New York: Harper & Row, Publishers, 1972).

"Heredity, Environment, Race, and I.Q.," Special Supplement, *Phi Delta Kappan,* 53, 297–312 (January 1972). A "debate" on heredity versus environment between William Shockley and N. L. Gage.

Herbert Ginsburg, *The Myth of the Deprived Child: Poor Children's Intellect and Education* (Englewood Cliffs, N.J.: Prentice-Hall, Inc., 1972).

J. McVicker Hunt, *The Challenge of Incompetence and Poverty* (Urbana: University of Illinois Press, 1969), Chap. 5.

General

"Twelve to Sixteen—Early Adolescence," *Daedalus,* Vol. 100, No. 4 (Fall 1971). An entire issue of 315 pages is devoted to adolescent development. Excellent.

John P. Hill and Jev Shelton, eds., *Readings in Adolescent Development and Behavior* (Englewood Cliffs, N.J.: Prentice-Hall, Inc., 1971).

Robert J. Havighurst, *Developmental Tasks and Education,* 3d ed. (New York: David McKay Company, Inc., 1972).

Lee Cronback and Richard E. Snow, *Final Report: Individual Differences in Learning Ability as a Function of Instructional Variables*, ERIC Reproduction Services, Bethesda, Md., ED 029 001, 1969. A very significant study of individual learning styles and an extensive review of research on the whole area of individual differences in relation to learning achievement.

Central Advisory Council for Education (England), *Children and Their Primary Schools*, 2 volumes (London: Her Majesty's Stationery Office, 1967). The world-renowned Plowden Report on children and education in England. Chapter 2, Volume 1, contains the findings about "Children: Their Growth and Development," and Appendix 10, Volume 2, contains a lengthy report on a national survey of children born in 1958. The findings in both chapters are highly significant summaries. The Council's use of such data in curriculum planning is a remarkable example of our point of view on basic data sources.

National Institute of Child Health and Human Development

This federal agency carries on research and funds research by other persons or agencies on human development. Its publications are excellent. See particularly *Child Health and Human Development: Research Progress*, Government Printing Office, issued periodically.

National Program on Early Childhood Education

A federally established and funded program that includes the National Coordination Center, 10646 St., Charles Rock Road, St. Ann, Mo. 63074, the ERIC Clearinghouse on Early Childhood Education (see above), and seven research and development centers at universities. The program encompasses three aspects: (1) knowledge base development, (2) prototype development and applied experimentation, and (3) model development. The program changes in activities and publications over a period of time; contact individual agencies.

Journals

A number of journals are devoted to human development. They publish research reports and scholarly articles on the development of children and youth:

Adolescence. Quarterly, Libra Publishers, Inc., Box 165, 391 Willets Rd., Roslyn Heights, N.Y. 11577.

Child Development. Quarterly, Society for Research in Child Development, Inc., University of Chicago Press.

Children. Six times annually, Office of Child Development, Children's Bureau, U.S. Department of Health, Education and Welfare.

Youth and Society. Quarterly, Sage Publications, 275 S. Beverly Drive, Beverly Hills, Calif. 90212

Home, Family, and Community Conditions

The family of a child is the single most significant factor in the whole process of education. It is also highly important in the schooling of youth, although at this age the peer group and the influence of the neighborhood as a social force also loom large. The relation between socioeconomic aspects of family life and school achievement, further education, and career choices has been well established by research. The emotional climate of the home and the nature and character of filial relation are also important considerations. Concept development, curiosity, use of language, interest in reading, experiential background, and many such aspects of development are closely related to the home life of the child.

Educators need to be aware of such relations and then give consideration to these factors in planning both the curriculum and instruction. Table 5 lists the kinds of information needed in this area.

Table 5
Kinds of Information Needed about the Family and Home and Community Conditions of Students

ITEM	POSSIBLE SOURCES	SUGGESTED USES
1. Family and home conditions: socioeconomic status of family; social class; occupations; composition and status of family; aspirations; educational level of parents; cultural and intellectual climate; community activities; personal relations; emotional climate; nature and extent of any disadvantagedness.	Pupil personnel records; home visitations; conferences with parents; conferences with social welfare staff members if involved with family; talks with pupils; observation.	Determining nature and scope of program and instruction; use as antecedent factors in evaluation; need for outside assistance, especially on health matters (glasses, and so on); teacher's relations with individual children; alerting welfare agencies and possibly police, especially in cases of child abuse, malnutrition, and so on; broadening child's experience out of school—trips, neighborhood activities; active and aggressive parents' association; adult classes and special activities for parents; topics for parent conferences; need for child-care centers and other child services; special programs for counteracting any disadvantagedness.
2. The constituency of the school: social, cultural, and economic	Census data for tracts included in attendance	Determination of curriculum units and special problems and topics for study;

ITEM	POSSIBLE SOURCES	SUGGESTED USES
characteristics of neighborhoods or groups served; the nature of the peer culture, especially at adolescent level; recreational facilities and opportunities for cultural and intellectual activities; incidence of deliquency and crime.	area; home visitations; welfare, court, and police records; survey of recreation facilities, libraries, community centers, and so on; conferences with staffs of neighborhood agencies of all kinds; discerning observation.	implementation of community school concept; establishment of community center with broad program of activities; establishment of community coordinating council; need for recreational and cultural services and programs; close liaison with other agencies, especially welfare and youth-serving ones.
3. The community: same as above, expanded to entire community.	Same as above, expanded to entire community.	Scope and nature of school's program; possible need for alternative kinds of educational opportunities or schools; need for a citizens' school advisory council; effective parents' organization community-wide; need for child-care centers and other services for children and youth.

A variety of professional literature is available on matters listed in Table 5. We cite only a few important items here, but they suggest the types of references that may be helpful in collecting and interpreting data in this category:

A. Harry Passow, ed., *Urban Education in the 1970's* (New York: Teachers College Press, 1971).

Mario D. Fantini and Gerald Weinstein, *The Disadvantaged: Challenge to Education* (New York: Harper & Row, Publishers, 1968).

James S. Coleman and others, *Equality of Educational Opportunity* (Washington, D.C.: Government Printing Office, 1966).

Frederick Mosteller and Daniel P. Moynihan, eds., *On Equality of Educational Opportunity: Papers Deriving from the Harvard University Faculty Seminar on the Coleman Report* (New York: Random House, Inc., 1972).

Martin Deutsch, Irwin Katz, and Arthur R. Jensen, eds., *Social Class, Race, and Psychological Development* (New York: Holt, Rinehart and Winston, Inc., 1968).

"The Imperatives of Ethnic Education," special issue, *Phi Delta Kappan*, 53, 265–328 (January 1972).

Christopher Jencks and others, *Inequality: A Reassessment of the Effect of Family and Schooling in America* (New York: Basic

Books, Inc., 1972). The highly significant but controversial report on factors affecting success in life.

James A. Banks and Jean D. Grambs, eds., *Black Self-Concept: Implications for Education and Social Science* (New York: McGraw-Hill Book Company, Inc., 1972).

Burton L. White and others, *Experience and Environment: Major Influences on the Development of the Young Child,* Vol. 1, Early Childhood Series (Englewood Cliffs, N.J.: Prentice-Hall, Inc., 1973). A major research report on how child-rearing practices affect social and intellectual competence of children.

Helaine Dawson, *On the Outskirts of Hope: Educating Youth from Poverty Areas* (New York: McGraw-Hill Book Company, Inc., 1968).

White House Conference on Children, *Report to the President,* 1971. See especially for this category of information Report of Forum 14, "Changing Families in a Changing Society," Forum 15, "Children and Parents: Together in the World," and Forum 17, "Developmental Child Care Service." See previous citation.

Juan B. Cortes and Florence M. Gatti, *Delinquency and Crime: A Biopsychosocial Approach* (New York: Seminar Press, Inc., 1972). Although summarizing research and stating theories relative to delinquency, the section on the role of the family in the moral and social development of the child is superb.

Children and Their Primary Schools. The Plowden Report, cited in the previous list.

Rodger L. Hurley, *Poverty and Mental Retardation: A Casual Relationship* (New York: Random House, Inc., 1969).

Urie Bronfenbrenner, "Reunification with Our Children," *Inequality in Education,* No. 12 (Cambridge: Harvard Center for Law and Education, July 1972), pp. 10–20.

Robert M. Hauser, *Socioeconomic Background and Educational Performance,* Arnold M. and Caroline Rose Monograph Series (Washington, D.C.: American Sociological Association, 1972).

Ray C. Rist, "Student Social Class and Teacher Expectations: The Self-Fulfilling Prophecy in Ghetto Education," *Harvard Educational Review,* 40, 411–450 (August 1970). An extensive analysis of research and other evidence on this subject.

Career Planning

Planning and preparing for a career is an important aspect of schooling. Curriculum planning, not only at the elementary and middle school levels, but at the high school level, must take into account vocational preparation in one way or another. Hence, a major category of data needed is the nature and character of career opportunities, potentialities for particular types of occupations, and interests and needs of individual students. Table 6 lists the kinds of information needed in this category.

Table 6
Kinds of Information Needed about Career Potentialities

ITEM	POSSIBLE SOURCES	SUGGESTED USES
Career plans: extent of continuation in college and other postsecondary institutions; current career choices and plans; career patterns of graduates; mobility among young persons; occupational patterns in the community; occupational trends, locally and nationally; opportunties for career education in the community or area; situation among minority groups in postsecondary schooling and occupational opportunities.	Follow-up studies of graduates; guidance records; conferences; census data by tracts; Department of Labor studies for U.S. and local and/ or state on occupations, manpower needs, employment trends, occupational outlook.	Courses to be offered; cooperative work-study programs; guidance programs; providing post-secondary opportunities for occupational preparation; establishing close working relations with collegiate institutions; programs to provide scholarships and special opportunities for members of minority groups.

Useful books and reports for obtaining and interpreting occupational data include:

U.S. Department of Labor

The United States Department of Labor Manpower Report of the President, including a Report on Manpower Requirements, Resources, Utilization, and Training. Published annually. Extensive sets of data and interpretation of employment and unemployment, occupational needs and trends, and special reports on dropouts and similar subjects. Invaluable for guidance purposes.

Occupational Outlook Handbook. Published biennally. The "bible" for career counseling.

Bureau of Labor Statistics Reports. Published irregularly during the year. Special reports on a variety of subjects related to employment; particularly helpful studies on status of minority groups and other subjects.

Monthly Labor Review. By subscription. Data on current employment and manpower conditions and outlook, but also excellent articles on these subjects.

State Employment Office

Often a state employment agency publishes studies on the status of employment, manpower needs, and outlook in the state.

The Center for Vocational and Technical Education

The ERIC Clearinghouse for Vocational Education at Ohio State University publishes considerable material on this subject as well as collects research reports and documents from many sources.

Research Coordinating Unit for Vocational Education

Most state education agencies have established a research coordinating unit as a part of a national program. Such an agency may be helpful in providing data as well as in advising on data collecting.

In concluding this section on the students as a primary factor in curriculum and instructional planning, we emphasize again that a curriculum is planned for a particular group of students for a particular time in their schooling and in a specific social and environmental situation. Hence, the information teachers and other curriculum planners need originates with that particular group of students; moreover, it must treat each student in the group as an individual.

Lawrence Cremin, drawing on Dewey's writings, makes the same point:

Dewey once described the child and the curriculum as two limts which define a single process. "Just as two points define a straight line, so the present standpoint of the child and the facts and truths of the studies define instruction. It is a continuous reconstruction, moving from the child's present experience out into that represented by the organized bodies of truth we call studies." But as Dewey pointed out again and again in his writings, the child is always a particular child with a particular experience, not some abstraction in the curriculum-maker's mind.[3]

SOCIAL AND CULTURAL FACTORS IN PLANNING

Dewey, as quoted previously, considered education to depend on two interacting factors—the learner and the social and cultural milieu in which the education is being provided. The two factors are equally significant and are always present in any learning situation. In fact, it is impossible to plan and carry out an educational program without giving the fullest consideration to both the characteristics of the students to be

[3] Lawrence A. Cremin, "Curriculum-Making in the United States," *Teachers College Record*, 73, 219 (December 1971).

educated and the nature of the society which established the schools. This section will recommend the kinds of data and information about the society that we believe are essential for valid curriculum and instructional planning.

First, however, it is desirable that we analyze the role of a formal school in a society as a guide to the kinds of data that should be collected and the concepts that should be formulated for valid curriculum planning.

The Social Functions of a School

Schools have been established historically by a social group to serve these functions:

> Transmit the culture
> Contribute to the socialization of the young
> Aid in the preservation of the society as a nation
> Contribute to the preparation of the young for adulthood
> Assist in the personal development of the young members of the society.

Obviously these functions are not clear-cut, discrete categories of purposes served by the schools; they intertwine and are complementary, perhaps even reciprocal, aspects of the total process of growing up in a society. But they do constitute major points of emphasis, controlling approaches to curriculum development and program planning and constituting varying patterns of design in the fabric of education. Moreover, educators must recognize that a school must serve adequately and appropriately those functions deemed essential and highly desirable by the citizens who exercise political control over the local school systems by the vote and other means or these persons will force changes in the school's staff, policies, curriculum, and program of instruction.[4]

Recognition of the things the social group wants the schools to do and the nature of this group's control over the schools is essential if educational planning is to be acceptable to the citizens who are in charge. Let us consider briefly these five functions of the school as a starting point in listing the kinds of data, concepts, and information needed.

---

[4] An excellent recent example of this type of political control was the "resignation" of Mark Shedd as superintendent of the Philadelphia Public Schools after the election of a new mayor, one of whose campaign planks was to get rid of Shedd because of the changes he had brought about in the program of the schools. See Peter Binzen, "Philadelphia Politics Invades the Schools," *Saturday Review—Education*, 55 (6), 44–49 (February 5, 1972).

Transmission of the Culture

The schools, particularly since the founding of the Republic, as Bernard Bailyn notes in his essay on the social role of the schools, have had a primary responsibility for transmitting the culture of the society.

He emphasizes that one must think of education "not only as formal pedagogy but as the entire process by which a culture transmits itself across the generations," and one must see "education in its elaborate, intricate involvements with the rest of society, and note its shifting functions, meanings, and purposes."[5] Lawrence Cremin agrees with Bailyn: "I myself am led to the conclusion that the nurture of a common culture remains a central task of American popular education, and that the common school continues to stand as a prime agency for undertaking this task."[6]

Lawrence Kohlberg and Rochelle Mayer, in an excellent essay on the functions of the school, provide this review of cultural transmission as an aim:

> The origins of the cultural transmission ideology are rooted in the classical academic tradition of Western education. Traditional educators believe that their primary task is the transmission to the present generation of bodies of information and of rules or values collected in the past. . . . The important emphasis, however, is not on the sanctity of the past, but on the view that educating consists of transmitting knowledge, skills, and social and moral rules of the culture. Knowledge and rules of the culture may be rapidly changing or they may be static.[7]

Socialization of the Young

The school is a social institution, and, like other social agencies, one of its principal functions is to assist in the socialization of the children of the group so that they will be able to live effectively in the society and to contribute to the advancement of the life of the group. Talcott Parsons, one of the foremost sociologists of our time, analyzes this function:

> the school class . . . is an agency through which individual personalities are trained to be motivationally and technically adequate to the performance

---

[5] Bernard Bailyn, *Education in the Forming of American Society* (Chapel Hill: University of North Carolina Press, 1960), p. 14.

[6] Lawrence A. Cremin, *The Genius of American Education* (Pittsburgh: University of Pittsburgh Press, 1965), p. 75. See also his *American Education: The Colonial Experience, 1607–1783* (New York: Harper & Row, Publishers, 1970).

[7] Lawrence Kohlberg and Rochelle Mayer, "Development as the Aim of Education," *Harvard Educational Review*, 42, 452–453 (November 1972).

of adult roles. . . . The socialization function may be summed up as the development in individuals of the commitments and capacities which are essential prerequisites of their future role-performance. Commitments may be broken down in turn into two components: commitment to the implementation of the broad *values* of society, and commitment to the performance of a specific type of role within the *structure* of society.[8]

Alex Inkeles, also a Harvard sociologist, while accepting Parsons' definition of socialization, holds that the competence to live in a society must take account of the fact that competency must be broadly defined, and, moreover, that requirements change in any given society. Thus he believes that we should direct our attention to the "end-product, the person as he is *after* he has been socialized, rather than the formative process itself."[9] This means, in his opinion, that

The main business of socialization is the training of infants, children, adolescents (and sometimes adults) so that they can ultimately fulfill the social obligations that their society and culture will place on them. . . . And not excluded is the thought that the term "social obligations" includes elaborating and acting effectively in roles not commonly assigned by the given sociocultural system.[10]

Inkeles, therefore, proposes that socialization must develop competencies that will enable the person to fulfill adequately a role at some future date; hence he presents in outline form and later in a long listing the principal components of personality and the "qualities" needed by socially competent persons. He indicates "the *kinds* of personal attributes which I feel a modern industrial society requires in significant quantity of substantial numbers of its citizens. Without most of this array, one is not completely prepared for life in our society, and must sink into some form of dependency or deviance."[11]

Preservation of the Social Order

Any politically organized society seeks to perpetuate itself as a nation. The schools by the very nature of their origin and control as social agencies contribute to this function of national continuity. This is not to say that the schools must or do support the established order of

---

[8] Talcott Parsons, "The School Class as a Social System: Some of Its Functions in American Society," *Harvard Educational Review*, 29, 297–298 (Fall 1959).

[9] Alex Inkeles, "Social Structure and the Socialization of Competence," *Harvard Educational Review*, 36, 265 (Summer 1966).

[10] Inkeles, p. 279.

[11] Inkeles, p. 281.

things or serve as vehicles or handmaidens for those entrenched in power or in control of social and political institutions. In most nations, and certainly in the United States, the role of the school is more subtle than this. This role, as Parsons pointed out, consists of commitments and capacities.

V. O. Key, Jr., the distinguished professor of government at Harvard University, stated that

> all national educational systems indoctrinate the oncoming generation with the basic outlooks and values of the political order . . . elementary and secondary schools mold children into little Americans, little Germans, little Russians . . . the modern educational system conducts a massive operation in transmission of the traditions, learning, and skills necessary to maintain a society.[12]

Robert Hutchins, an eminent spokesman for social preservation, stated the matter eloquently:

> Schools are public because they are dedicated to the maintenance and improvement of what the philosopher Scott Buchanan called the Public Thing, the *res publica*; they are the common schools of the commonwealth, the political community. They may do many things for the young: they may amuse them, comfort them, look after their health, and keep them off the streets. But they are not public schools unless they start their pupils toward an understanding of what it means to be a self-governing citizen of a self-governing political community.[13]

This conservation function is an extension of the socialization function, yet stands in its own right as a distinct obligation of the school. Traditionally, one of the most insidious ways in which the school contributes to the preservation of society is by its role in "manpower allocation," or its classification of persons in terms of future status in the society. Much has been written about this aspect of the school's socialization process.[14] This role, in light of increasing concern throughout our society

---

[12] V. O. Key, Jr., *Public Opinion and American Democracy* (New York: Alfred A. Knopf, 1961), pp. 315–316 *passim*.

[13] Robert M. Hutchins, "The Great Anti-School Campaign," *The Great Ideas Today, 1972* (Chicago: Encyclopedia Britannica, 1972), p. 223.

[14] These studies and reports, among many, are suggested: Parsons; Christopher Jencks and others, *Inequality: A Reassessment of the Effect of Family and Schooling in America* (New York: Basic Books, Inc., 1972); James S. Coleman and others, *Equality of Educational Opportunity* (Washington, D.C.: Government Printing Office, 1966); Colin Greer, *The Great School Legend* (New York: Basic Books, Inc., 1971); Michael B. Katz, *Class, Bureaucracy, and Schools* (New York: Frederick A. Praeger, 1972); Torsten Husèn, *Social Background and Educational Career* (Paris: Centre for Educational Research and Innovation of the Organization for Economic Cooperation and Development, 1973). But for other types of evidence see Godfrey Hodgson, "Do Schools Make a Difference?" *The Atlantic Monthly*, 231, 35–46 (March 1973).

for the individual and his own self-fulfillment and self-development, is increasingly coming under attack. Although by the very nature of the program of schooling, such a role of classifying students in terms of their possible roles in the adult world may not be rejected in the future, certainly, these demands will result in a more humane and democratic basis. Thus the individual will be helped to choose his own role as an adult rather than the choice being dictated by external social, economic, and political factors.

Preparation for Adulthood

A primary purpose of all education is preparation for adulthood. In the transmission of the culture of the society, the socialization of young people, and the development of loyalty to the values and structures of the social group, the school is preparing the student for an adult status in the society. But the school also plays a more explicit part in assisting learners to become competent, effective, and satisfied adults.

A major aspect of this purpose of the school is the teaching of the skills and competencies needed by all citizens. The student must learn to use language, communicate, make mathematical computations, develop skill in social relations, carry out directions, suppress personal desires and interests for the good of a group or firm, control aggressiveness or indifference, and much else.

Specific occupational training is also evident in school programs, particularly those that stress job competencies and employer-employee relations.

In a broader sense, each of the "Cardinal Principles of Education" (see Chapter 4) is an area of adult living for which the school should prepare students—health, command of fundamental processes, worthy home membership, vocation, citizenship, worthy use of leisure, and ethical character. In past years we have seen major projects launched under the auspices of the U.S. Office of Education for life-adjustment education and career education. Recently developed programs on drug education, sex education, driver education, family living, consumer education, and environmental education also are directly pointed to the preparation of the child for adult status in the society.

Development of the Individual

The development of the individual as a person is emerging more strongly than ever as a primary function of the school. All of the previously discussed functions, of course, contribute to the development of the child and the adolescent, and these approaches remain significant aspects of a total program designed for development. In recent years, however, much more attention has been given to this highly important function in and of itself. Such terms as "humane school," "humanistic curriculum," "discovery," "inquiry," "equality," "the school as a community," "commitment," "freeing intelligence," and similar ones characterize the current efforts that are being made to elevate personal development as the aim of education.

This conception of function stems directly from the work of John Dewey, although many other philosophers and psychologists have contributed to its definition. Dewey defined education as "the process of remaking, or reconstituting, experience"; hence "the remaking of experience is just as good at one point as it is at any other. It is not a remaking which is to be finished up at a certain point." In this conception of education "the fundamental significance of the idea of reconstruction is the elimination of the idea of preparation as the essence of an educational process." He continued:

> If remaking of experience is both the process and the aim of education, then the end is an immediate and present one, one which is capable of direct consideration of being directly acted upon, and of direct realization, instead of being set off as a mark clear ahead in the future, toward which the child is to be lured along by making things interesting, or forced by disciplinary stimuli, or else by a mixture of the two, so much of one and so much of the other. The fitness for life which is got through the educative process is fitness for the only life we live, the life of every day.[15]

Kohlberg and Mayer, who provide an excellent analysis of development as the aim of education, state that this ideology rests "on the value postulates of ethical liberalism. This position rejects traditional standards and value-relativism in favor of ethical universals. . . . The liberal school recognizes that ethical principles determine the ends as well as the means of education."[16]

Educators are endeavoring in many ways to implement a philosophy of development as a function of the school, but much remains to be done to develop a school fully dedicated to this aim.

The School as One of Many Social Agencies

In serving these five functions the school is, of course, only one social agency or force contributing to the education of children and youth. The family, unquestionably, is a dominant force in fulfilling all of

[15] Excerpts taken from "Lecture XII, A Formal Definition of Education," in Reginald D. Archambault, ed., *Lectures in the Philosophy of Education, 1899, by John Dewey* (New York: Random House, Inc., 1966), pp. 113–115.

[16] Kohlberg and Mayer, pp. 472–473.

these purposes; the peer group, particularly among adolescents, is a powerful factor in socialization and personal development, as well as in the transmission of values. In today's world the communications media, especially television and motion pictures, must be considered significant forces; other social agencies, such as child- and youth-serving organizations, churches, and voluntary community groups, contribute to the total educational process.

Cremin stated, "I am led to observe that there are other agencies that can—and do—contribute significantly to the common education of the public, and that it is a serious error to discuss the problem without paying heed to the new opportunities they afford."[17] His colleague, John Fischer, President of Teachers College, Columbia University, considered this matter at length:

What is the special function of the school in our society? . . . A more reasonable approach is to assign to the school the systematic development of intellectual, social, and vocational competence and to assign to other agencies the functions they can perform. Such a division of labor is no argument for a narrow or formalized curriculum. The good school is always concerned with the promotion of physical and mental health, with productive and satisfying human relations in a setting of moral and ethical values. Its teaching must be based upon the best that is known about human development and the nature of learning.[18]

Torsten Husèn of the University of Stockholm, a shrewd observer of education in the Western world, has pointed out that

for a long time it has been almost a professional disease among educators to regard school education as though it operated in a social vacuum and to disregard the incompatibilities between school and society. This attitude provides a very efficient defense mechanism against demands for educational change that would bring the educational system into line with changes in society at large. . . .[19]

Thus the debate over the functions of the school, and especially its role alongside the family and community agencies of an educational nature, continues. The point to be emphasized here is that curriculum planners must recognize that the school is only one agency of education, albeit a very important one. To prepare a child for today's complex and

[17] Cremin, *The Genius of American Education*, p. 75.
[18] John Fischer, "Schools Are for Learning," *Saturday Review*, 43, 72 (September 17, 1960).
[19] Husèn, p. 157.

fast-changing world, the schools must deal much more realistically with the total set of social institutions and cultural transmitters than they have in the past. Elsewhere in this book we consider this matter in its proper perspective. Here we list the important kinds of data and information needed about society and its agencies if planning is to be valid and appropriate.

DATA ABOUT SOCIETY

In light of the demands made on the school by society, what kinds of information and data does the curriculum planner need to develop a valid and viable curriculum? Table 7 lists our recommendations.

Table 7
Kinds of Information Needed about the Culture and the Social Group

ITEM	POSSIBLE SOURCES	SUGGESTED USES
1. Values: the fundamental values of the people as a nation; basic tenets of democracy; the essence of our cultural ethos.	Great documents of the American people; writings of scholars, statesmen, interpreters of the American scene; U.S. Supreme Court decisions; literature, drama, essays; writings of journalists and columnists; TV programs that interpret American thought and actions.	Constitute basic elements in program planning, including organizational and administrative arrangements, curriculum, school policies and regulations; nature and character of discipline; plans for desegregation; implementation of concept of equality; selection of staff members; defining goals and objectives.
2. Values of a less basic nature: the mores and traditions of the citizens of the local school district and of subgroups within the community; evidence on pluralism in values; the "counterculture" movement; diverse points of view on morality; evidence of anomie, despair, lack of commitment or faith in American beliefs; factors in alienation of youth.	Opinion polls; community surveys; editorials in local news media; selection of news and "slanting" in local press; city ordinances on liquor, pornography, amusements, and so on; views of political leaders and office holders; activities and views of local civic, patriotic, educational, and political action groups; "ear-to-the-ground" listening; shrewd observations.	Same as above; in addition: providing opportunities for students to express and state views on values, mores, traditions, and so on; student involvement in all aspects of planning; seminars, minicourses, and so on, on current issues and problems; student involvement in governance of school.

ITEM	POSSIBLE SOURCES	SUGGESTED USES
3. Expectations: demands made on the schools; views on purposes, functions, and goals of the schools; approval or disapproval of activities, programs, regulations, policies, practices, courses, teachers, and administrators; political views.	Same as above; in addition: programs and projects of parent-teacher groups; results of local elections; actions taken by school advisory councils; conferences with parents; careful analysis of educational history and developments in recent years.	Same as above; in addition: actions of teachers in relation to community mores and views; programs and activities of parent and student groups; organization of parent advisory councils; desirability of organizing adult study groups; planning and carrying on programs of public information; activities to gain public support for desirable changes and new programs.
4. Political power structure: controllers and molders of public opinion; attitudes of citizens on educational and public issues and matters; attitudes of citizens on political activities of teachers.	Opinion polls; surveys; citizens' advisory groups; PTA plans, programs, and actions; astute observation; sociological analysis, for example, Kimbrough's studies.[a]	Ascertain things community will support; involve key people in planning; nature of campaigns for millage increases and bonds; kinds of programs needed to develop enlightened support for improved schools; "behind-the-scenes" activities for public support of schools.
5. The trends of the times: predictions about future developments in social, political, and economic life of the United States; major problems and issues in national life; world problems and issues.	Census data; publications and reports of planning agencies and government bureaus and commissions; publications of United Nations and UNESCO; commentary of columnists and editors; writings of scholars, research agencies, advocacy groups, and so on; reports of appropriate local, state, national, and international conferences and study groups.	Program planning in terms of future needs and conditions of life; courses and content dealing with future conditions, social needs, and social issues; student seminars; "open classroom" program; development of community school concept; assembly programs and speakers; take active part in "new towns" and the "garden city" movement; planning new types of schools and programs for new sub-communities of the district.
6. Trends, problems, and issues in local	Census data; local surveys; government	Same as above; also efforts by school officials to awaken

[a] See Ralph B. Kimbrough, *Political Power and Educational Decision-Making* (Chicago: Rand-McNally & Company, 1964); see also Herman Zeigler and Wayne Peak, "The Political Functions of the Educational System," *Sociology of Education,* 43, 115–142 (Spring 1970), and their bibliography.

Table 7
Kinds of Information Needed about the Culture and the Social Group (cont.)

ITEM	POSSIBLE SOURCES	SUGGESTED USES
community: prospects for the future of the community; problems of relations with surrounding and nearby communities; attitudes of citizens on community matters, problems, and conditions.	planning and commissions at state and local levels; observation; student investigations; local authorities; laws enacted.	community spirit and to promote community improvements, including the school's program; organize community study and work groups; involve students in community-improvement efforts; desirability of regional pacts or programs.
7. Occupations (see Table 6).	These two types of essential data may be categorized as student data or social group data; we included it as student data, hence see that section.	
8. Family status and conditions (see Table 5).		

Helpful references on the social basis of education in addition to those cited in the footnotes include:

> James B. Macdonald, "Curriculum Development in Relation to Social and Intellectual Systems"; and Harry S. Broudy, "Democratic Values and Educational Goals," in Robert M. McClure, ed., *The Curriculum: Retrospect and Prospect*, 70th Yearbook, Part I, National Society for the Study of Education (Chicago: University of Chicago Press, 1971), pp. 95–112 and 113–152.
> Don Adams, *Schooling and Social Change in Modern America* (New York: David McKay Company, Inc., 1972).
> David A. Goslin, *The School in Contemporary Society* (Glenview, Ill.: Scott, Foresman and Company, 1965).
> Robert E. Herriott and B. J. Hodgkins, *The Environment of Schooling: Formal Education as an Open Social System* (Englewood Cliffs, N.J.: Prentice-Hall, Inc., 1973).

Table 7 suggests an almost overwhelming job for curriculum planners in obtaining data about the society in which the educational process is being undertaken. However, as is clear from the table, a considerable portion of the data, once collected, will be valid for some time, other parts would need to be updated only on occasion, and in some instances additional and new information would be added as it becomes available. The staff in the central administrative offices should collect a great deal of the information and raw data, taking the surveys and polls and assembling research reports, scholarly essays, articles, and books. Analysis and interpretation, however, should be the responsibility of all of those involved in planning—teachers, parents, other citizens, and students.

THE LEARNING PROCESS

The process by which students learn is, of course, a very important consideration in planning. Psychology provides the teacher with the knowledge and understanding of these processes. Changes in behavior and behavioral potential—the act of learning—can be directed and guided by the skillful teacher. This is what the psychology of learning is all about. Table 8 lists the broad types of information needed about the learning process.

As is true for all categories of data discussed in this chapter, the professional literature is extensive. Here we cite a few references that may be especially helpful and that illustrate types of publications that contribute to an understanding of the learning process.

Sidney Strauss, "Learning Theories of Gagné and Piaget: Implications for Curriculum Development," *Teachers College Record*, 74, 81–102 (September 1972). Also has excellent citations to the literature.

Robert M. Gagné, *The Conditions of Learning*, 2d ed. (New York: Holt, Rinehart and Winston, Inc., 1970).

William F. White, *Psychosocial Principles Applied to Classroom Teaching* (New York: McGraw-Hill Book Company, Inc., 1969).

James L. Kuethe, *The Teaching-Learning Process* (Glenview, Ill.: Scott, Foresman and Company, 1968).

"Motivation," Special Issue, *Theory into Practice*, Vol. 9, No. 1 (February 1970); also contains excellent bibliographies.

Ernest R. Hilgard, ed., *Theories of Learning and Instruction*, 63d Yearbook, Part I, National Society for the Study of Education (Chicago: University of Chicago Press, 1964).

Carl E. Thoresen, ed., *Behavior Modification in Education*, 72d Yearbook, Part I, National Society for the Study of Education (Chicago: University of Chicago Press, 1973).

Jerome S. Bruner and others, *Studies in Cognitive Growth* (New York: John Wiley and Sons, Inc., 1966).

Table 8
Kinds of Information Needed about the Learning Process

ITEM	POSSIBLE SOURCES	SUGGESTED USES
1. The nature of learning: definition; process of reconstructing experience into knowledge, generalizations, concepts, values, attitudes; determinants of behavior; possibilities and nature of behavior modification; the process of cognitive development; process of building values; effects of environment on intellectual development.	Professional literature; research studies; publications of USOE R & D centers; case studies of children and youth; shrewd observation of students; consultants; research on effects of early schooling; Piagetian theories.	Basis for curriculum and instructional planning; plans for student involvement in planning and development of learning activities; plans for remedial type programs; assistance for students in goal setting, development of self-concepts and appropriate aspirations; guiding behavior modifications; counseling; standards for evaluation of curriculum and instructional plans.
2. Theories of learning: stimulus-response and behaviorism; cognitive and Gestalt; functionalism.	See above.	Planning drill work, skill-development activities, and recall and continued use of learning; designing instructional modes; use of interactive processes in learning situations.
3. Motivation, drives, needs: definition; basis of; role in behavior and in learning.	See above; also interviews; interest inventories; conferences with parents; anecdotal records.	Planning learning experiences for each student that he or she can cope with and do successfully, yet challenge and stimulate participation; determination of instructional modes.
4. Self-concepts: aspirations, self-esteem; goal setting; evidence of alienation and disillusionment.	As above.	Counseling; planning individualized program of experiences; conferences with parents; involvement in projects and activities; "schools without failure."
5. Readiness: physical basis of; developmental levels.	Appropriate tests; records on school achievement.	Program planning; determination of scope and sequence of curriculum.
6. Transfer of learning: definition; nature of; basis for.	See (1) above.	Modes of teaching; development of higher cognitive processes.

Victor H. Denenberg, *Education of the Infant and Young Child* (New York: Academic Press, Inc., 1970).
Also works by Piaget—see references on page 110.

THE AVAILABILITY AND ORGANIZATION OF KNOWLEDGE

The fourth basic factor to be considered in planning the curriculum concerns the knowledge extant in the social group that may be used in the education of young people at various stages of development, the bases for selecting content for specific units of instruction, and the modes, themes, or centers for organizing such content for use in the classroom. Any curriculum plan by the very nature of schooling must include a consideration of the subject matter that is appropriate for the learning experiences being recommended. Broudy, Smith, and Burnett state well the importance of knowledge as a component of curriculum planning: "His intellectual content—images, meanings, knowledge—and its organization are of utmost importance in an individual's education. Curriculum development has seldom given adequate attention to this point."[20]

In planning, therefore, the curriculum worker must give major consideration to these aspects of content: (1) What subject matter is desirable and appropriate for attaining the goals and achieving the objectives designated in the curriculum plan? (2) How should this body of content be organized for use by the students?

Selection of content and the way in which it is organized for school use lie at the heart of curriculum planning. It will be necessary, therefore, for the educator to have the kinds of information listed in Table 9 concerning the nature and availability of knowledge, the bases for selection, and the modes for its organization.

Although we treat the selection and organization of content extensively in Chapter 5, a few useful references are cited here:

Planning the Curriculum

Arthur R. King, Jr., and John A. Brownell, *The Curriculum and the Disciplines of Knowledge* (New York: John Wiley and Sons, Inc., 1966).

---

[20] Harry S. Broudy, B. Othanel Smith, and Joe R. Burnett, *Democracy and Excellence in American Secondary Education* (Chicago: Rand McNally & Company, 1964), p. 112.

Table 9
**Kinds of Understandings and Information Needed on the Nature
of Knowledge and Its Selection and Organization**

ITEM	POSSIBLE SOURCES	SUGGESTED USES
1. As appropriate knowledge of one's subject field(s) of specialization: basic principles, abstractions, and structures; research methods of the field; methods of inquiry and discovery of knowledge in the field; new developments, trends, and discoveries; forecasts of future developments.	Advanced study, as appropriate, in the field; research assistantship periodically, or time for research; scholarly works on current developments; participation in meetings of learned society.	Selection of content for curriculum and instructional plans; selection of textbooks, reference works, and teaching materials; participation in community and larger meetings of scholars in the field; preparing teaching materials, teaching units, brochures, and books.
2. Criteria and guidelines for selecting appropriate kinds of content: how to select content for achieving particular goals and objectives; how to decide what knowledge is of most worth in a particular unit of study.	Views and recommendations of scholars; principles used in national curriculum projects; examples of other curriculum plans.	Use in curriculum and instructional planning; recommendations in curriculum plans for content; preparing study guides for students; selecting textbooks and teaching materials.
3. Ways in which knowledge may be organized for school use: advantages and disadvantages of each mode for a group of students seeking to achieve desired goals.	Books and articles on curriculum planning; analysis of organization used in national curriculum projects; teachers' manuals and books on methodology of teaching; examples of curriculum plans.	Selecting a design or designs for organization of curriculum and instruction; developing curriculum plans.
4. Criteria for analysis and selection of textbooks and other instructional materials: content included in each and its appropriateness for achieving goals; authenticity; organizational structure; level of difficulty in relation to group for which intended.	Examination of criteria proposed by others; conferences with authors and publishers; advice and counsel of specialists in the area or domain of study and psychologists; reactions of students.	Selecting and purchasing textbooks and instructional materials; using textbooks and instructional materials in teaching situations.

ITEM	POSSIBLE SOURCES	SUGGESTED USES
5. Criteria for determining relevance of content: possibilities of using alternative bodies of content to achieve specified goals.	Use of sociological and psychological principles in determining relevance; opinions of students and parents; expert opinion; tryout of material.	Differentiation of instruction; motivation of students; capitalizing on individual talents.

Hilda Taba, *Curriculum Development: Theory and Practice* (New York: Harcourt Brace Jovanovich, Inc., 1962), especially Chaps. 12, 18, and 21.

Jerome S. Bruner, *The Process of Education* (Cambridge, Mass.: Harvard University Press, 1961).

William T. Lowe, *Structure and the Social Studies* (Ithaca, N.Y.: Cornell University Press, 1969).

Symposium on Educational Research, Phi Delta Kappa, *Education and the Structure of Knowledge* (Chicago: Rand-McNally & Company, 1964).

Use of Knowledge in Teaching

Martin Buber, *Between Man and Man* (New York: The Macmillan Company, 1965).

John R. Scudder, Jr., "Freedom with Authority: A Buber Model for Teaching," *Educational Theory*, 18, 133–142 (Spring 1968).

Israel Scheffler, "Philosophical Models of Teaching," in Israel Scheffler, ed., *Philosophy and Education* (Boston: Allyn and Bacon, Inc., 1966).

THE COMPLEX NATURE OF PLANNING

Thus far in this chapter we have considered the four primary determinants of the curriculum identified in Figure 3, Chapter 1—students, society, the learning process, and knowledge—and listed the major kinds and sources of data needed in planning and then suggested particular aspects of planning in which such data constitute basic input.

All Factors Essential Considerations

It should now be evident that the enormous task of developing a curriculum must be guided by the wisdom, insight, understanding, and beliefs of the teachers and other persons responsible for making instructional decisions. Educational planning obviously involves making choices among many possibilities, and these choices constitute judgments on the part of the planners. All of the data and information collected, often synthesized into concepts, generalizations, and beliefs, help the teacher in making choices. But there is no one-to-one relation between any single set of data and a curriculum decision. All data from the four basic factors must be considered in a proper relation in making such decisions. This is an activity for human beings who have intelligence adequate for the job, vision of what ought to be, imagination in devising alternatives, a high sense of moral and ethical responsibility, and, above all, compassion for children and youth.

Dewey made this point in an early essay, limiting his discussion to the two basic factors he identified—the child and the society:

It is easier to see the conditions in their separateness, to insist upon one at the expense of the other, to make antagonists of them, than to discover a reality to which each belongs. The easy thing is to seize upon something in the nature of the child, or upon something in the developed consciousness of the adult, and insist upon *that* as the key to the whole problem. When this happens a really serious practical problem—that of interaction—is transformed into an unreal, and hence insoluble, theoretic problem.[21]

A Relevant Curriculum

In recent years many educators have agreed with Van Til's argument that the curriculum "should be made more relevant to the lives of the children and youth for whom the curriculum exists. . . . The obvious and sensible thing to do is to replace the irrelevant through changing the content."[22] Beck and others have stated: "There are many serious cases of irrelevance still with us today. They typically rest on one of two bases. Either the teacher does not recognize that the matter is now irrelevant, if it ever was relevant, or he is unwilling to change, discard, or restructure his materials and procedure as relevance demands."[23]

As a result of student demands or in anticipation of such demands many high schools and colleges have introduced new courses, new topics in existing courses, or minicourses that treat new content under the slogan of "relevance." Students have demanded that courses in "Black Studies," "Indian Culture," "The Negro in American Literature," "The War in Vietnam," "Alternatives to the Draft," "Pollution," "Save Our

[21] Dewey, *The Child and the Curriculum*, p. 8.

[22] William Van Til, "The Key Word Is Relevance," *Today's Education*, 58, 14–17 (January 1969).

[23] Carlton E. Beck and others, *Education for Relevance: The Schools and Social Change* (Boston: Houghton Mifflin Company, 1968), p. 238.

Environment,'" "Rock Music," "Drug Abuse," "Sex and Sexuality," and many others dealing with issues of current concern be included in the curriculum. These matters have been considered relevant while Shakespeare's *Hamlet*, the Peloponnesian War, the human bone structure, or quadratic equations have been regarded as irrelevant.

The controversy over what is relevant still rages, and well it should, for it raises a question fundamental to education: What knowledge is of most worth? In curriculum terms the question becomes: How best can the school help each pupil to achieve appropriate and valid goals?

The answer to the question, and hence a definition of what is relevant, requires the teacher and anyone else involved in planning for a particular group of pupils to return to the four basic factors considered thus far in this chapter. There is no other way to build a "relevant" curriculum. As Wagschal has said, "I can't remember ever using the word 'relevant' without adding 'to x.' . . . Relevant to what?"[24] If social demands, socialization of the child, or transmission of the culture of the society are given precedence over other considerations, whatever content is taught may very well be meaningless, boring, or confusing to a student. On the other hand, if the student is permitted to select only those bits and bodies of content which interest him or which he finds meaningful, he may very well lack the capacities and competencies that will enable him to achieve full development as a member of the social group. If content for learning activities is improperly selected, the student may find himself unable to carry on the kinds of adult activities, particularly in an occupation, in which he is greatly interested. But even the best content can, if it is poorly used to carry on learning activities, result in a low level of student interest and understanding.[25]

It is important in planning to remember that the *general* goals of the school, or, if one prefers, the goals of general education, may be attained through a variety of types of activities. Imagine, for example, that the goal is, "To be able to communicate in effective and correct English in oral and written form." Obviously, no prescribed, predeter-

---

[24] Peter H. Wagschal, "On the Irrelevance of Relevance," *Phi Delta Kappan*, 51, 61 (October 1969); see also a brilliant essay with this same point of view by A. Jane Major and Donald B. Cochrane, "Education and Relevance: A Philosophical Analysis of William Glasser," in James J. Jelinek, ed., *Philosophy of Education, 1971–1972* (Tempe, Ariz.: Bureau of Educational Research, Arizona State University, 1972), pp. 131–145. For further testimony on what is or is not "relevant" see Thomas Sowell, *Black Education: Myths and Tragedies* (New York: David McKay Co., Inc. 1972).

[25] On this point see Calvert H. Smith, "Teaching in the Inner City: Six Prerequisites to Success," *Teachers College Record*, 73, 547–558 (May 1972).

mined body of content or of learning activities is postulated for the achievement of this goal. The student could achieve it by writing an essay or giving a talk on "The Contributions of Black Authors to American Literature," "The Physiological Effects of Addictive Drugs," or any subject of interest to him, or by analyzing the style used in *Hamlet*; or by analyzing the meaning of Plato's *The Republic*. Neither the content nor the mode of instruction is prescribed by the goal itself; hence the teacher may very well give students almost free choice of content, allowing them to determine for themselves what is relevant for attaining the goal.

But another consideration enters into planning. Any learning experience may, and usually does, contribute to the achievement of a number of general goals. Add to the goal illustrated above the parallel goal, "To understand what constitutes equality in American life." Now the choice of content for the class in English becomes more complicated. Would an analysis of *Hamlet* or *The Republic* contribute more fully to both goals than a study of "The Student as Nigger" or *To Kill a Mockingbird* by Harper Lee? Would "The Moral Decay of Roman Society" be a better essay topic than "The Women's Liberation Movement"?

In planning learning activities for the achievement of *specific* goals, relevance can be measured by a simpler criterion. These goals often state or clearly imply a body of content. Let us say that such a goal is, "To be able to use logarithms accurately in solving mathematical problems." Obviously, content will be pretty largely determined by the goal itself; however, teaching methods will not be, and here the teacher draws extensively on his knowledge of learning theory. If the goal is, "To know the basic elements of an adequate diet and to be able to explain the contributions of each to good health," again content is somewhat predetermined in broad scope, yet a considerable range of choices of both content and process would be possible in helping students to acquire this knowledge. The English teacher, in endeavoring to develop good communication skills, may encourage a student in homemaking to write a research paper on the subject to fulfill the English assignment, thereby enabling the student to progress in attaining two goals.

Curriculum and instructional planning is indeed a complicated business. And there is much more to achieving relevance than merely introducing a new course or changing the content of an existing one in response to student or adult demands.[26] The basic question remains, "Relevant to what?"

---

[26] For highly regarded philosophical considerations of this whole matter of content selection see R. S. Peters, *Ethics and Education* (Glenview, Ill.: Scott, Foresman and Company, 1967), Chap. 1; and Herbert J. Muller, *In Pursuit of Relevance* (Bloomington, Ind.: Indiana University Press, 1971).

OTHER SIGNIFICANT FACTORS IN PLANNING

At the beginning of this chapter we listed three other types of factors that control curriculum and instructional planning. In actual practice one or more of these factors in combination may dictate specific aspects of the curriculum to an even greater extent than the four primary sources treated previously. They are, nevertheless, secondary in consideration because they themselves are rooted in the four basic factors, and their influence should be fully consistent and in harmony with the data obtained from the primary ones. Moreover, in Chapter 1 we identified some external forces that also influence, and often directly shape, the formulation of curriculum plans. While the external factors considered there have no legal base for compelling a course of action in the schools, those discussed in this section constitute legal authority over curriculum planning, or, in the case of research, support legal actions.

Legal Structures Controlling the Schools

Schools are established under laws enacted by state legislatures and are subject to all of the legal conditions existing as a part of the federal system of government in the United States. Curriculum planning, obviously, must conform to and take place within these legal structures. They exist at three levels of government—local, state, and national—and the schools are subject to controls at each level. Table 10 lists the kinds of information educators need concerning the legal structures that affect the schools.

Schools and Politics

Schools are political institutions, that is, they "relate to government or the conduct of government." All schools, whether public or nonpublic, are subject to political control and direction; they are instruments of the social group, and the group collectively exercises its control through political action. Decisions made by boards of education and the staffs of schools must fall within legal structures that have been politically determined. Those who administer and staff the schools are inevitably engaged in the science or art of political government. It is especially important that curriculum planners recognize fully the political control of schools, for it must be a major consideration in decision-making. It is because they are political institutions that the schools today are being subjected to pressure from all sides. Key notes that "an institution that enjoys the repute for influence held by the schools would scarcely be expected to be permitted by those dominant in the political order to roam freely."[27]

[27] Key p. 316.

Table 10
Kinds of Information Needed about Legal Structures and
Controls over Curriculum Planning

ITEM	POSSIBLE SOURCES	SUGGESTED USES
1. The federal system of government with respect to schools: legal authority to establish schools; controls over education in the federal system.	Constitution of the U.S. and of the state; textbooks on government and political science; Supreme Court decisions.	Determining powers of each level of government from the standpoint of control over curriculum, and the nature of such controls.
2. Constitutional rights of citizens with respect to schools and schooling: rights guaranteed by the Constitution and protected by the Supreme Court; aspects of schooling within jurisdiction of the Court; principles enunciated in Court decisions.	Constitution; Supreme Court decisions; articles on these decisions; books on school law.	Curriculum and instructional practices permitted and prohibited by the Supreme Court in areas of its jurisdiction; taking steps to carry out Court decisions; adhering in all practices to rights of citizens.
3. Role of the federal government: authority for and nature and scope of participation in education; controls and influence exercised over curriculum; existing programs of support and basis of and procedures for obtaining it.	Books on school law; articles on federal programs and laws; copies of specific laws; rules and regulations issued by the federal government for specific program grants; annual and other reports of cognizant federal agencies; newsletters, bulletins, and so on; guides to federal programs.	Curriculum and instructional planning of federally supported programs; applying for and using federal subsidies for specified programs; developing new programs with federal support; advocacy role on federal legislation.
4. Role of the state: constitutional provisions; financing of schools; laws relating to program, curriculum, instruction, evaluation, selection of instructional materials, and so on.	State constitution and statutes on education and schools; appropriation bills.	Legal requirements with respect to planning all educational matters and carrying out programs; advocacy role; planning budgets; holding elections on millage levies, and so on.
5. Role of state department of education: rules and regulations relative to same matters as in (4) above; services	Same as (4) above; also all publications issued by the department; conferences, workshops, institutes	All matters related to curriculum and instructional planning; preparing reports for accreditation; obtaining authorization, if required,

ITEM	POSSIBLE SOURCES	SUGGESTED USES
available to planners; relation to and support of innovations; accreditation standards; research and development funds for local use.	with staff members; visitations with staff members; letters, and so on.	to introduce innovations or experimental programs; applications for special grants; points of advocacy for better activities and programs by department.
6. Role of the board of education: policies, regulations, rules, and requirements relative to curriculum and instruction; budget-making procedures, policies, and priorities; process of budget-making and of setting policy and rules on curriculum matters; degree of freedom and of flexibility in planning granted local building staff and individual teachers; provisions of negotiated contracts with staff on planning matters.	Published policies of board of education; handbooks; notices and newsletters issued by superintendent or board; verbal communications by superintendent.	All matters related to curriculum and instructional planning; procedures and policies followed in selection of instructional materials; use of such materials in controversial units of instruction; determining the authority and roles of a building staff and individual teachers in planning; developing and carrying out a program for planning the curriculum and instruction; advocacy role in arousing citizens for better schools.

Political control of the schools imposes three important obligations on educators:

1. Know the constitution and laws to which the schools are subject and the court decisions that interpret these instruments.

2. Understand the nature of the power structure and views, expectations, and demands of those who exercise power at all levels of government and the judiciary.

3. Determine a proper role for themselves in political activities. In the past the public strongly believed that teachers and administrators should not engage in overt political activity, especially of a partisan nature or that related directly to the operation of the schools. But this is obviously an undesirable, if not impossible, restraint. Who is in a better position to seek quality in U.S. education than those who devote full time to the field? Educators must be advocates for schools; they must endeavor to influence political action, promoting desirable plans and programs and opposing undesirable ones. The situation in recent years

with respect to performance contracting, the voucher system, accountability drives, desegregation, busing to alleviate segregation, providing
equality in financial support for all children, and many other issues
illustrates the necessity for educators, especially those with major responsibilities for planning, to engage in political action.

Resources and Facilities

An important consideration in curriculum and instructional
planning has to do with the resources and facilities available or that may
be made available for school purposes. Of course, what constitutes
resources and facilities must be interpreted broadly and imaginatively,
as is evidenced by the recent movement to "street academies," schools
without walls, and community-centered schools. The kinds of information needed by educators concerning resources are listed in Table 11.

Research Reports and Professional Advice

Information that can help in curriculum planning may be found
in research publications, scholarly reports of commissions, agencies, and
institutes and the views and recommendations of recognized authorities
on education and related areas.

In recent years the federal government has allocated considerable sums of money to support research projects, task force studies, investigations and studies by commissions, and innovations and experiments
in education as well as to disseminate the findings and recommendations
of such undertakings. Nonprofit foundations, state governments, universities, and individuals have also contributed to the large volume of
literature now available to planners.

Special mention will be made of four important sources of
research and scholarly literature supported by the federal government.

Research and development centers have been established under
federal auspices in recent years at a number of leading universities.
These centers carry on specialized research of a sophisticated nature on
designated aspects of education. Usually a center works with cooperating
schools in implementing new programs or new approaches to education
that embody its research findings. Each center issues reports, newsletters,
and similar literature on its activities, and several, for example, the
Wisconsin Research and Development Center for Cognitive Learning,
University of Wisconsin, and the Pittsburgh Learning Research and

Table 11
Kinds of Information Needed about Resources and Facilities for Schooling

ITEM	POSSIBLE SOURCES	SUGGESTED USES
1. The school staff: number, specializations, talents, and interests of those available in a given situation; policies and procedures on teaching load, assignments, and inservice and professional activities.	School personnel records; conferences; staff meetings; records on past experience; school board and administrative policies and regulations	Determining areas of instruction feasible to include in program; planning in-service education programs; determining extra-instructional program; determining possibilities for experimentation and innovations; organizing staff for planning purposes.
2. Other staff members: availability of consultants and special and helping teachers; policies on assignment and use; interest in experimentation and innovation.	Staff meetings; staff activities; conferences and interviews; news-letters from central office.	Planning inservice and professional development program; planning special instructional programs; planning experiments and innovations; advice in selecting instructional materials.
3. Buildings, equipment, and facilities: facilities available in a given situation; policies on their use; policies on alterations; policies and procedures for planning new buildings and renovation of existing ones; policies and practices on use of community facilities; availability of life science areas, and so on.	Records and plates or blueprints; visual inspection; board policies; conferences with responsible administrators; school budget; long-range plans.	Determining feasibility of curriculum and instructional programs; purchasing equipment; planning alterations and renovations; planning new buildings; planning use of community facilities and cooperative programs; planning programs for adults or for evening and part-time programs.
4. Instructional materials: nature and extent of; availability and ease of use; policies and procedures for selection; budget provisions.	School records, lists, and catalogs; adopted budget; school board policies; building inventories.	Recommendations included in curriculum and instructional plans; selecting and purchasing materials; plans and practices for use; planning new programs, courses, and so on.
5. Professional literature: nature and extent; availability; possibilities for additions.	Records; budget; board policies; inspection.	Inservice and professional development programs; resources for use in curriculum and instructional planning.

Development Center, University of Pittsburgh, publish curriculum materials.[28]

Two other types of research and development centers were listed earlier in this chapter: The National Program on Early Childhood Education and the Vocational and Technical Research and Developmental Centers. In addition, the U.S. Office of Education has established two educational policy research centers.[29] The scope and nature of research and development programs have changed somewhat over a period of several years, so educators need to keep informed on new programs as well as on those of existing centers.

The second activity of the federal government of interest here is its sponsorship of the Educational Research Information Center (ERIC), which is concerned with the dissemination aspect of the federal research program in education. The national center publishes monthly, with an annual compilation, an index to educational research and scholarly publications. Entitled *Research in Education*, it is available on a subscription basis from the Government Printing Office. This publication is the best listing in this country of educational research and scholarly kinds of information; it is well indexed by title, subject, and author, and each item is briefly annotated. The U.S. Office of Education makes available for purchase film copies or printouts of each of these reports. Recent issues have included curriculum guides put out by school systems, state education departments, and other agencies, with brief annotations on each.

Moreover, ERIC has established a number of research clearinghouses, each one responsible for a specific area of education. The clearinghouse collects research reports and other useful publications, sees that they are listed in *Research in Education*, and often publishes bulletins that report on developments in its areas. Educators may write directly to each clearinghouse for information about its services and publications.[30]

A third program established by the federal government is a network of educational laboratories.[31] Each laboratory develops its own program, although those activities subsidized by the federal government must be approved by the U.S. Office of Education. Some of the activities

[28] For a brief summary of the program see Herbert J. Klausmeier, "Educational Research: From the R & D Centers into Practice," *Educational Leadership*, 29, 598–601 (April 1972); and National Center for Educational Research and Development, *Educational R & D Programs Conducted by Laboratories and Centers* (Washington, D.C.: Government Printing Office, 1971, Stock No. FS 5.212:12056), pp. 1–6.

[29] National Center for Educational Research and Development, pp. 14–18.

[30] See issues of *Research in Education* for a listing of areas of specialization.

[31] National Center for Educational Research and Development, pp. 7–13.

of particular laboratories are carried on independently and do not receive subsidies. Most of the laboratories now produce materials of various kinds, some of a curricular nature, which may be purchased. All of them are engaged in educational experimentation and trying out new work with the schools of their region in programs and projects.

The fourth activity of the federal government in research and its dissemination is carried on through the National Institute of Education (NIE), established in 1972. In establishing the agency Congress declared that "the federal government has a clear responsibility to provide leadership in the conduct and support of scientific inquiry into the educational process."[32] The act assigned these responsibilities to the NIE:

1. Helping to solve or alleviate the problems of and achieve the objectives of American education
2. Advancing the practice of education as an art, science, and profession
3. Strengthening the scientific and technological foundations of education
4. Building an effective educational research and development system

NIE absorbed under its authority many of the research, development, and dissemination activities previously carried on by the U.S. Office of Education, but it has gradually expanded the scope of such work, and, depending on Congressional support and appropriation, will continue to broaden the educational research activities of the federal government.[33]

In 1971 the federally sponsored research and development centers and the educational laboratories established the Information Office, Council for Educational Development and Research. The Information Office regularly publishes a newsletter, *D & R Report*, which contains brief descriptions of activities and publications of the research and development centers and educational laboratories. It also publishes a *CEDaR Catalog* which lists current programs, projects, and products of the centers and laboratories.[34]

Although *Research in Education* is a rather complete listing of

[32] "Education Amendments of 1972," *Public Law 92–318, 92nd Congress, S. 659* (June 23, 1972), Title III.

[33] For an excellent essay on the history of the development of interest in educational research on the part of the federal government and an analysis of the potentialities of the National Institute of Education, see Donald R. Warren, "The National Institute of Education and School Reform: Questions from the Past," *Intellect* (formerly *School and Society*), 101, 219–224 (January 1973).

[34] Information Office, Council for Educational Development and Research, 775 Lincoln Tower, 1860 Lincoln St., Denver, Colo. 80203.

research, reports, and papers of a scholarly nature, the curriculum planner will want to check professional publications, such as books, magazines, and bulletins, for other information on educational developments, innovations, points of view, issues and problems, and recommendations of insightful people in the field. The usual bibliographic sources may be used to locate pertinent materials.

If one is interested in curriculum guides and related materials prepared by school systems and state departments of education, the Association for Supervision and Curriculum Development annually publishes a list of those that are submitted for exhibit at the annual convention of the Association.[35] In 1973 Xerox University Microfilms launched a "Curriculum Materials Clearinghouse" that disseminates information about curriculum materials and products through four types of publications.

ADDITIONAL SUGGESTIONS FOR FURTHER STUDY

Dreeben, Robert, "The Contribution of Schooling to the Learning of Norms," *Harvard Educational Review,* 37, 211–237 (Spring 1967). Analyzes the social structure of the school, in contrast to the family, and considers the relationship between this structure and the socialization process.

Erickson, Edsel L., Clifford E. Bryan, and Lewis Walker, eds., *Social Change, Conflict and Education.* Columbus, O.: Charles E. Merrill Publishing Company, 1972. A series of readings on the subject of social goals and social controls as factors in determining the program of the schools.

Hauser, Robert M., *Socioeconomic Background and Educational Performance.* Washington, D.C.: American Sociological Association, 1972. Utilizes data from a city school survery to study the relationship of the socioeconomic background of students and their performance in school.

Jackson, Philip W., *Life in Classrooms.* New York: Holt, Rinehart and Winston, Inc., 1968. An excellent study of the nature of the socialization process involved in the "hidden" curriculum of the schools, as well as the ways in which teachers formulate their own goals and objectives, regardless of the official curriculum plans.

Massialas, Byron G., *Education and the Political System.* Reading, Mass.: Addison-Wesley Publishing Company, Inc., 1969. Reports studies of the ways in which the schools socialize the young and provide political instruction. See especially Chapter 3.

Pharis, William L., Lloyd E. Robinson, and John Walden, *Decision Making*

---

[35] *Current Curriculum Materials* (Washington, D.C.: Association for Supervision and Curriculum Development, annually).

and Schools for the 70's, Schools for the 70's series. Washington, D.C.: National Education Association, 1970. Analyzes the decision-making process in schools and considers the legal and extralegal components and the influence of selected factors in planning.

Taba, Hilda, *Curriculum Development: Theory and Practice.* New York: Harcourt Brace Jovanovich, Inc., 1962. Although published some years ago, Part One, "The Foundations for Curriculum Development," is one of the most comprehensive treatments of the factors that shape the curriculum of the schools.

4

DEFINING GOALS
AND OBJECTIVES

Stating the purposes for which a school exists and formulating the goals and objectives of an educational program is a demanding and complex aspect of curriculum planning. Yet it must be done, for the goals of education postulate the nature and character of curriculum and instruction, and all planning should be based on such a definition.

A SCHOOL HAS PURPOSES

A society establishes and supports schools for certain purposes; it seeks to achieve certain ends or attain desired outcomes. Efforts of adults to direct the experiences of young people in a formal institution such as a school constitute preferences for certain human ends and

144

values. Schooling is a moral venture, one that necessitates choosing values among innumerable possibilities. These choices constitute the starting point in curriculum planning.

Deliberate Choices among Possibilities

The founding and operation of a school is itself an expression of a value. The people, acting through their political agencies, express their wish to have the children in their society receive some of their education in a formal school setting. Everything that is done in the school and by the school staff, similarly, embodies a system of values. The curriculum is but an expression of what some person or some agency prefers over some other possibility. John L. Childs, the well-known philosopher of education, has stated the nature of schooling as follows:

A manifestation of preference for certain patterns of living as opposed to others is therefore inherent in every program of deliberate education. Schools always exhibit in their purposes and their programs of study that which the adults of a soceity have come to prize in their experience and most deeply desire to nurture in their own children . . . the making of choices that have to do with the destinies of human beings cannot be eliminated from that directing of experience and learning which is the distinctive function of the school.[1]

Harry S. Broudy, another well-known philosopher of education, in a significant article on the formulation of goals, has pointed out the scope of the choices that may be made:

To state educational objectives is therefore important. However, it becomes a problem because life, like a big country, offers a wide choice of destinations. Educational objectives may be broad, narrow, remote or proximate. They can be stated in terms of overt behavior, character traits, developmental tasks, life-styles, learning products, learning processes, tendencies, dispositions, habits; school outcomes, test results, generic operations; attitudinal syndromes and learning strategies; national security, rates of juvenile and adult delinquency, church attendance, and credit ratings. In short, anything anyone regards as desirable can become an educational objective and, not infrequently, a school objective.[2]

---

[1] John L. Childs, *Education and Morals: An Experimentalist Philosophy of Education* (New York: Appleton-Century-Crofts, 1960), pp. 7–8; on this point see also James B. Macdonald and Dwight Clark, "Critical Value Questions and the Analysis of Objectives and Curricula," in Robert M. W. Travers, ed., *Second Handbook of Research on Teaching* (Chicago: Rand McNally & Company, 1973), pp. 405–412.

[2] Harry S. Broudy, "Philosophical Foundations for Educational Objectives," *Educational Theory*, 20, 4–5 (Winter 1970).

In selecting the basic goals which the school should seek to serve from among the sum total of ends for which people strive the curriculum planner faces this major issue: In the total process of human development what parts or aspects should the school accept responsibility for guiding? Much of the education of the child, as well as of the adult, takes place outside the formal school program. The educator is faced with the all-important decision of just what part the school can and should play in guiding the development of young people. A corollary matter is how the school will correlate its program of schooling with the education of students that has occurred and that will occur continuously outside the school. Broudy has noted:

> The distinction is related to that between education taken in its broad sense and in its narrower sense of schooling or formal instruction. These differences are important not only because the latter is a relatively small part of the former, but also because they are qualitatively different. That is to say, the informal portion of education, in the broad sense of the word, is virtually the same as learning. . . . Formal education, on the other hand, is structured in terms of means and ends. . . . In the broad sense, education goes on almost from cradle to the grave. The skein of factors that enter into it is a tangle that defies complete analysis. This type of learning is not, to any appreciable extent, within our control. . . . For these reasons a life-style, a form of society, a value pattern are not school outcomes, nor can we fully identify and isolate the part that schooling will play in their development. Efforts to establish a tight correlation between school inputs and this sort of result are misguided precisely because the end result is the effect of so many causes over which we have no control, many of which we cannot even clearly identify, and of some of which we are totally unaware.[3]

It is incumbent on the educator to comprehend the nature of human growth and development and to understand the essential characteristics of society as it exists today and as it may become in the foreseeable future. Curriculum planning must center primarily on those aspects of the total process of education for which the school can reasonably and properly accept responsibility.

Teachers Have Purposes

In curriculum planning the role of the teacher in setting goals and objectives for the interactive processes that constitute the school experience of students should be recognized. The teacher is actually the person who is the interpreter, the arbitrator, and the guide in the implementation of the purposes of the school. Any formal statements of purpose

---

[3] Broudy, "Philosophical Foundations for Educational Objectives," p. 13.

must be translated into learning opportunities for students, and the guidance and development of such school experiences is primarily a teacher's responsibility. Much attention is devoted to this matter throughout the book.

The teacher's own value system, his views of the goals to be served by the school program, and his concepts of the nature and meaning of a stated goal, constitute the filter of meaning through which the school's purposes are applied in planning. The teacher's own values, too, are the starting point for his own planning and for his whole approach to presenting learning opportunities in the classroom.

Students Have Purposes

Students have purposes when they engage in learning opportunities provided by the school. The degree of congruence that exists among the purposes of the three parties in the schooling process—the school, the teachers, and the students—is a crucial matter. The overwhelming assumption in schools, historically and currently, is that a high degree of uniformity of purpose exists. In fact, most modes of teaching, including those used recently in performance contracting and in specific skill development, operate overtly on this assumption.

But such a presumption is not justified. Students establish their own purposes, goals, and objectives. It is indeed a highly competent teacher who is able to obtain widespread acceptance of the school's goals and objectives as interpreted and implemented through his own values and goals.

In recent years a number of sociologists and psychologists have pointed out that students, in addition to whatever obeisance they pay to the goals of the teacher and of the school, also are participants in a "hidden curriculum" and a mode of socialization that may be largely or even totally ignored in the official educational program. Many meaningful student experiences are in the realm of this subtle, unacknowledged aspect of the school's efforts to fulfill the functions identified in Chapter 3, and discussed more fully in Chapter 6. The students often formulate their own desired outcomes from these elements of school life without the help or cooperation of teachers or school administrators.

Achieving a high measure of congruence among the goals and purposes of the school as a formal social institution for educating young people, of the teachers who guide the learning experiences of students, and of the students themselves is a desirable basis for building an effective curriculum.

This chapter considers the process of choosing goals and the means by which those who are involved in curriculum planning may approach this important task.

DEFINITION OF TERMS

The terms "purposes," "goals," "aims," and "objectives" all designate intent, or outcomes desired. In general usage they may be used interchangeably, but in curriculum planning some differentiation in meaning is desirable.

Purpose is used here in a broad sense to refer to a desired result; it is the most inclusive of the terms defined here and is used generically to mean the reason for which something exists or is done.

Aim indicates a direct target, thus an effort directed to a specific end. We will not use the term much in discussing purposes, preferring "goals" instead.

General goal means the end, the result, or the achievement toward which effort is directed. The term is used extensively in this chapter to designate the broad, significant outcomes desired from an educational program.

Domain designates a large group of learning opportunities, broad in scope, that are planned to achieve a single set of closely related major educational goals. Domains are categories for classifying major goals; they do not state the purposes of the school but rather the aspects of human development for which goals have been formulated.

Subgoals further define the sets of major goals that constitute domains of the curriculum. They state in more specific terms the nature of the ends sought in the learning opportunities provided within a domain. They are the basic elements in the detailed job of curriculum planning.

Objectives state the specific, overt changes in student behavior that are expected to result from participation in a unit of learning activities. Obviously, they develop more explicitly the general goals and their respective subgoals for the purpose of planning instruction.

A hierarchy of goal definition is thus envisioned.[4] Overarching the entire process is the determination of a system of values derived from the culture of the social group. As Childs has pointed out, all educational planning must be based on a value system.

In this chapter we formulate curriculum goals and gather these into domains which constitute the broad categories of the overall curriculum plan. Subgoals for each general goal are then formulated which further define the nature of a domain. The subgoals are the basis

---

[4] For further consideration of the proposal that purposes be formulated on the basis of a hierarchy of generality see David R. Krathwohl, "Stating Objectives Appropriately for Program, for Curriculum, and Instructional Materials Development," *Journal of Teacher Education*, 16, 83–92 (March 1965); and Norman E. Gronlund, *Stating Behavioral Objectives for Classroom Instruction* (New York: The Macmillan Company, 1970), Chaps. 2 and 3.

for detailed curriculum planning. Finally, objectives that will contribute significantly to the attainment of the subgoals are selected. Instruction is planned and carried forward on the basis of these objectives. Some of these objectives, of course, may not be in written form but may be clearly envisioned in the mind of the teacher, perhaps with some actually being formulated as instruction is underway.

We speak of the *hidden* or *unstudied curriculum* to designate those organizational aspects of school life and the informal, interpersonal relations among the members of the school community that serve unofficially, and often insidiously, the function of socialization. The term is included here because formulation of goals, subgoals, and objectives should take account of this unofficial aspect of the school program as well as of the planned sets of learning opportunities.

WHO SHOULD PARTICIPATE IN THE FORMULATION OF PURPOSES?

Everyone who is directly concerned with the process of education · should participate in some way at some level in determining the goals and objectives of a school. This means that the students themselves, teachers, other staff members of the school, the board of education, citizens of the community, particularly parents of school children, and the governmental bodies that exercise direct control over the school should share in formulating purposes.

We in professional curriculum planning need to heed the advice of Lawrence Cremin, who, in tracing the evolvement of the public schools in America, stated:

I have portrayed the relationship between the educational profession and the lay public as one of inherent strain and tension, in which the public possesses ultimate legal and financial authority. Given this relationship, it seems to me that the profession is obligated, both in its own interest and in the interest of the service it performs, to assist the public in developing an ever more sophisticated body of opinion about education. . . . in the absence of such a dialogue, large segments of the public have had, at best, a limited understanding of the whys and wherefores of popular schooling.[5]

Participants in Goal Definition

Let us comment on who should participate in the formulation of goals and objectives in terms of our hierarchy:

[5] Lawrence A. Cremin, *The Genius of American Education* (New York: Random House, Inc., 1965), pp. 110–112.

1. *Identification of fundamental values and interpretation of student data.* This is done at some level of curriculum planning, although perhaps not always overtly or directly. All of the groups just listed should participate in this aspect of goal definition. It is, after all, the people as a social group that espouse a set of values and beliefs that characterizes American democracy.

Direct involvement, however, may be limited. Some school systems prepare a statement of beliefs as a basis for further planning, but whether written or not, the values, ideals, and beliefs of the people are inevitably the basis for the formulation of general goals, subgoals, and objectives. If a formal statement of beliefs is prepared, representatives of students, parents, and other citizens should participate with teachers in the development of the statement; it should be presented and discussed at open meetings in the community, and it should finally be adopted by the board of education. Some programs for goal definition, such as the California project, cited later, refer to this initial step as "evolving an educational philosophy." In preparing such a statement the kinds of information and data listed in the tables in Chapter 3 should constitute basic sources.

2. *Formulation of general goals and subgoals by domains.* The definition of goals for the school is a professional responsibility, although citizens, scholars, educational leaders, students, statesmen, and competent analysts of the social scene should share in the process.

The whole apparatus for curriculum planning and development, which was treated in detail in Chapter 2, is involved in the definition of goals. As suggested there, system-wide committees may be established, each building may have a curriculum planning committee, committees may be established for each domain and subject field or area of study, or other procedures may be followed. In any instance, the formulation of goals is a major responsibility of such committees.

In the process of planning it is desirable for every committee to include at least two types of nonprofessional persons—lay citizens and students. Other persons may be appointed as full-fledged members of the committee or used in a consultative capacity. These should include scholars in the appropriate subject fields, psychologists, psychiatrists, and specialists in mental health, instructors in teacher-preparation institutions, and, in many instances, observers of the American life. In the prevocational, vocational, and applied fields of study, leaders in the occupation or field may be committee members. Such committees will, of course, draw on the kinds of basic data listed in Chapter 3 and mentioned above. Goal setting without a deep and penetrating analysis of these data would be in complete contradiction to the principles of sound curriculum planning.

In the formulation of general goals and subgoals, the elements of schooling designated as the hidden or unstudied curriculum should be identified and included in goal definition. This is to suggest that much of the "hiddenness" of the socialization process employed by schools be unveiled. Curriculum planners must give as much attention to institutional arrangements, interpersonal relations, social structures, and the social life of the school as they do to the official components of the school program.

The culminating aspect of these efforts to define goals for the school should be a critical examination of those goals that are selected by appropriate members of the staff. The adoption of goals should involve all members of a building staff for any sets of goals unique to that building and all members of the system staff for those affecting the entire school system. Often such discussions may be held in smaller subgroups, with only representatives of these groups coming together for final approval at the system level.

3. *Determination of behavioral objectives for the instructional program.* The final stage in the formulation of purposes for the school is the preparation of lists of behavioral objectives for the instructional program. Obviously, these should be consistent with and contributory to the attainment of the general goals and subgoals previously defined. Inasmuch as these objectives specify the kinds of learning experiences the teacher chooses to develop with a group or with individual students in striving to achieve these goals, the responsibility for their formulation devolves primarily on the teacher who guides the learning activity. In curriculum planning, however, it is common practice for committees of teachers and staff personnel to prepare instructional guides for courses, a cluster of courses, a unified segment of learning opportunities, and, in terms of our recommendation, the domains of the curriculum. In addition to lists of goals for the subject, field, segment, or domain, such guides may contain lists of objectives for each unit of instruction or activity or a comprehensive list in the introductory section.

Committees of professional organizations, textbook writers, and similar groups or individuals often publish lists of recommended goals and objectives. The Center for the Study of Evaluation, a federally funded agency at the University of California at Los Angeles, has established an Instructional Objectives Exchange which uses computerized methods of recording and retrieving behavioral objectives. Teachers may use this exchange to obtain lists of objectives which have been prepared by teachers, committees, and others.

The possibility of making available objectives on a large scale is further illustrated by the Institute for Educational Research, Downers Grove, Illinois, a Title III Project of a number of cooperating schools and agencies. It reported in 1972 that "schools now have available to them 4,595 behavioral objectives and 27,259 test items based on these objectives."

Regardless of who prepares them, it should be recognized that lists of packaged objectives are helpful to teachers and curriculum committees *provided* planners critically consider the validity of the objectives for their particular instructional program. It is essential that a teacher choose objectives that are appropriate for a unit of instruction for a student or group, giving full consideration to all factors that must be taken into account in any specific piece of curriculum planning. Scissors-and-paste methods of planning a curriculum are to be vigorously condemned when items are uncritically used, but utilizing existing materials of all sorts to glean ideas, suggestions, and items that will enhance planning is simply sharing professional skill.

Figure 8 presents in graphic form the steps to be taken in defining the goals and objectives of a school or school system. Details of the procedures and organizational structures and parameters are not shown, but these are important understandings for effective curriculum planning.

Examples of Programs for the Definition of Purposes

The Lincoln, Nebraska, Public Schools carried out an extensive project for the definition of their goals for the 1970s. The statement finally developed by the schools noted that

> goals are implied in the day-to-day decisions of the Board of Education and staff and are expressed in the expectations of the community for its schools. Although goals exist even when not explicitly stated, some regular attention to compiling and upgrading a comprehensive statement of goals lends cohesion and direction to the work of the staff. Such statements are also useful in unifying or giving perspective to the wishes of the community.[6]

A series of workshops in which an estimated 1000 citizens of the community and a large number of the school staff participated was held during the spring, summer, and early fall of 1970. A working document, *The Purposes of Education in American Democracy*, originally published by the Educational Policies Commission,[7] was distributed to both the professional and lay groups at the beginning of their discussions. The

---

[6] Board of Education of Lincoln, Nebraska, "Direction for the 70's," Supplement to the *Sunday Journal and Star*, October 25, 1970, p. 3.

[7] Educational Policies Commission, National Education Association, *The Purposes of Education in American Democracy* (Washington, D.C.: The Association, 1938).

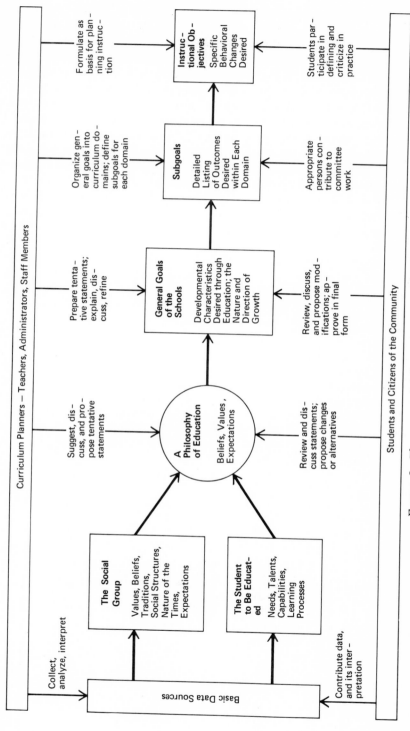

FIGURE 8   The process of defining the purposes of the school.

first set of meetings involved the school staff. A general orientation session for citizens was held in June, but thereafter the participants met in small discussion groups with lay persons as chairmen. A general session for reporting on these discussions concluded the series. All of the recommendations were then considered by the central office staff of the school, under the direction of the director of curriculum, and a final statement of goals was prepared. This was presented to the board of education for discussion and was then adopted in final form. The statement of goals was published as a supplement to the joint Sunday edition of the local newspapers and thus was delivered to over 44,000 homes.

The statement opens with a section entitled "Characteristics of an Educated Person," which presents a broad definition of general goals. Subgoals are then grouped under these headings:

    I—Goals for Students
    II—Goals for Parents
    III—Goals for Staff
    IV—Goals for Community
    V—Goals for Institutions
    VI—Goals for Taxpayers

The official statement adopted by the board states that

a goal is defined as a broad aim, having no real limits, but giving general direction. In this context goals are not to be confused with objectives. Objectives, by contrast, are measurable; are within reasonable limits of attainability; can be achieved within a given time frame; and include in their statement a method of evaluation. Objectives will be developed by the staff after goals have been determined.[8]

During the 1970–1971 school year the curriculum staff developed statements of subgoals for five major instructional fields. In the summer of 1971 public meetings were held to which school personnel and citizens were invited to discuss these sets of goals. But these meetings failed to attract citizens or teachers and participation was very disappointing. Undoubtedly some other type of approach, a better choice of time, or other means need to be used to elicit participation by citizens in aspects of curriculum planning of such a specialized nature. Teachers, curriculum consultants, and other staff members have, subsequently, been involved on a continuing basis in further definitions of goals as actual projects in planning have been undertaken.

The Las Virgenes Unified School District of Calabasas, Califor-

[8] Board of Education of Lincoln, Nebraska, p. 3.

nia, holds a district-wide "goals conference" annually.[9] The district is a rapidly growing one, lying adjacent to Los Angeles, with the attendant problems of bond issues and transportation of school students. Major efforts must be made in this transient community to develop participation in school matters by new residents. A planning committee, composed of representatives of community groups and the school personnel, was established. The purpose of each conference is to provide opportunities for "meaningful dialogue regarding all aspects of the school district." The goals that are proposed by the participants deal more with the operation of the schools and the instructional program than with broad aims for curriculum and instructional planning.

Much activity has been taking place among the schools of California in recent years in the formulation of goals and objectives. Resolutions adopted by the legislature in 1969 and 1970 established a Joint Committee on Educational Goals and Evaluation. This committee was charged with "investigating and recommending to the Legislature the goals of education as developed by local educational agencies, the objectives of educational programs relating to such goals, and an evaluation program."

This mandate stimulated considerable activity in goal definition, with the committee staff sponsoring workshops and issuing guides for the use of school districts in developing statements of goals.[10] Participation by citizens of the community was strongly urged. The Joint Committee prepared principles for the guidance of governing boards and superintendents of local school districts in carrying on the program of goal definition:

1. The governing board and superintendent of schools should jointly propose and initiate the goal setting process as a response to felt needs within the community.

2. Every community member should be invited to participate in the goal setting process.

3. The search for philosophy, goals and objectives relevant for education in the 1970's should be the start of an on-going effort to involve the community in school policy development.

4. The goal setting process should be kept open to all points of view without domination or intimidation by any special interest group.

[9] Robert Boehme and Everett P. Buchanan, "Goals Conference: Dialogue and Direction," *Educational Leadership*, 28, 611–613 (March 1971).

[10] Joint Committee on Educational Goals and Evaluation, *Education for the People*, Vol. I, *Guidelines for Total Community Participation in Forming and Strengthening the Future of Public Elementary and Secondary Education in California*; Vol. II, *A Resource Book for School-Community Decision-Making* (Sacramento: California Legislature, 1972).

5. The purpose of bringing people together is not to dwell on past deficiencies or lay blame, but to evolve a philosophy, identify needs, determine goals, goal indicators, or sub-goals, and program objectives, and to establish priorities.

6. Participants should not expect to have everything their way; they should come seeking a better understanding of the community, its people and problems.

7. A spirit of cooperation and trust should be established among individuals and groups involved in the process.

8. Roles of leadership in school-community planning should be earned rather than based on authority.

9. Individuals and groups who are instrumental to the goal setting process should provide for the open flow of information.

10. The individual school should be the base of operation for bringing people together.

11. In the process of determining philosophy, goals and objectives, opinion must be balanced with fact.

12. The interaction process must begin with the concerns which have high priority for the people involved.

13. The governing board should commit the resources necessary to see the goal setting process through to a satisfactory conclusion: board members should be encouraged to participate in the interaction process, not as board members, but as private citizens.

14. Teachers, administrators and classified employees should honor their responsibility to the community by taking an active part in the goal setting process.

15. A variety of meetings should be held as a part of the goal setting process: mixed groups assist consensus building.

16. Inasmuch as the learning process is recognized as being dynamic and individualistic, any objectives of education that are established should not be so specific or restrictive as to pre-program the learning process for any student.

17. To ensure that the philosophy, goals and objectives of public education continue to be relevant, a recycling process should be designed.

18. The goal setting and planning process should result in observable action.[11]

In Volume II, the Joint Committee published a number of examples of programs developed by school systems in the state for the definition of goals. Procedures for involving citizens are described, and in some instances forms and materials used in carrying on the project are included.

While this project was underway a new California state law, known as the Stull Act, was passed in 1972 which requires every school

[11] Joint Committee on Educational Goals and Evaluation, Vol. 1, pp. 21–26.

district in the state to evaluate the performance of teachers. Such an evaluation, obviously, necessitates the definition of goals and objectives for instruction. It is quite apparent why feverish efforts to define goals have taken place throughout California. Legal action of these kinds may get school staffs, in cooperation with citizens, to prepare statements of goals and objectives, but it is to be hoped that such projects will be carried on throughout the country on a voluntary basis and without legal compulsion or outside pressure from either state or federal authorities.

As a part of these developments in California, Chico State College established the Northern California Program Development Center to assist school districts to "develop educational goals and objectives in a format compatible with current legislation." The Center has prepared handbooks and accompanying sets of work materials for use by the school system in "ranking educational goals in order of their importance" and in developing "program level performance objectives by the professional staff designed to meet the district goals." The recommended procedures involve the citizens of the community in ranking eighteen general goals of education and three or four subgoals for each one in order of relative priority, and then making judgments on how well the district is achieving these goals. Workshops are also conducted to work with teachers in writing performance objectives for the instructional programs that would contribute to the achievement of goals.[12]

Another significant effort to define goals for the schools was carried out by the Cooperative Accountability Project (see Chapter 6). The Project staff collected statements of educational goals from the state departments of education throughout the nation and then compiled them under twelve major classifications:

Basic Learning Area
Cultural Appreciation Area
Self-Realization Area
Citizenship and Political Understanding Area
Human Relations Area
Economic Understanding Area
Physical Environment Area
Mental and Physical Health Area
Creative, Constructive, and Critical Thinking Area
Career Education and Occupational Competence Area

[12] The handbooks, kits of material, and suggested plans for carrying out the program are available from the Center. Moreover, Phi Delta Kappa, a national professional organization, sponsored a nation-wide program to promote the use of this plan of goal development in 1972–1973.

Lifelong Learning Area
Values and Ethics Area[13]

A large number of goals selected from state reports are listed for each area. The booklet is another statement of goals that curriculum planning committees will find useful.

It is worthy of note that none of these programs for goal definition (nor any others we examined but have not cited here) takes account of the hidden or unstudied curriculum. The formal statements do not deal with this aspect of the socialization and peer-development process of schooling. This, in our opinion, constitutes a serious deficiency in curriculum planning efforts throughout the country.

THE SOURCES AND VALIDATION OF GOALS AND OBJECTIVES

A primary and very demanding responsibility of the curriculum worker is to determine the validity, comprehensiveness, and acceptability of the desired outcomes of schooling which are formulated as a part of the planning process. Therefore, we must consider the sources of the educational goals that are formulated before we can discuss these goals and objectives themselves.

The Sources of Goals

Chapter 3 considered in some detail the basic data sources and the kinds of information needed for valid planning. As we have noted, the fundamental factors in educational planning are the students to be educated and the society which establishes and operates a system of schools. These constitute the basic data sources from which we derive the purposes of education.

Some authorities on curriculum planning fail to give adequate recognition to *both* of these data sources and thus formulate an inaccurate and invalid model of the process. Others present an unacceptable explanation of the planning process because, while they may utilize one or both of these data sources, they fail to designate them as the starting points in their models or rationales for curriculum planning.

As was stated in Chapter 1, Ralph Tyler, in developing a guide for curriculum planning in a syllabus he prepared in the late 1930s for a

[13] Cooperative Accountability Project, *Education in Focus: A Collection of State Goals for Public Elementary and Secondary Education* (Denver, Colo.: The Project, 1972).

graduate course at the University of Chicago,[14] identified four fundamental questions which must be answered in developing any curriculum and plan for instruction:

1. What educational purposes should the school seek to attain?
2. What educational experiences can be provided that are likely to attain these purposes?
3. How can these educational experiences be effectively organized?
4. How can we determine whether these purposes are being attained?[15]

To this day, Tyler's pioneer analysis is widely used as *the* model for curriculum planning. Although Tyler did not include in the process itself the sources to be used in defining the purposes of the educational program, he devoted the first section of his syllabus to this matter. He listed and discussed in considerable detail three data sources from which basic information needed for the formulation of objectives should be obtained:

1. Studies of learners themselves as a source of educational objectives
2. Studies of contemporary life outside the school
3. Suggestions about objectives from subject specialists.

These data after being collected should then be subjected to critical analysis and be "screened" by

4. The use of philosophy in selecting objectives
5. The use of a psychology of learning in selecting objectives.[16]

Herbert Kliebard has pointed out the shortcomings of the Tyler scheme, noting particularly that the "last of the three sources turns out to be no source at all but a means of achieving objectives drawn from the other two."[17]

John Goodlad, a highly regarded authority in the field of curriculum planning and, earlier, a student of Tyler's, with the assistance of a colleague at the University of Chicago, Maurice Richter, has published a useful model of a conceptual system for curriculum planning. These

[14] Ralph W. Tyler, *Basic Principles of Curriculum and Instruction* (Chicago: University of Chicago Press, 1950).

[15] Tyler, pp. 1–2.

[16] Tyler, Section II.

[17] Herbert M. Kliebard, "Reappraisal: The Tyler Rationale," *School Review*, 78, 269 (February 1970).

writers state that they "use some of Tyler's concepts, refine others, and add several of our own in attempting to advance the faint but continuing dialogue about curriculum as a field of study."[18] They postulate that "the ultimate starting point for curriculum planning must be a set of values. And, in fact, the most serious difficulty in contemporary curriculum planning appears to be . . . a failure to begin with a set of value premises and to inform various specialists of value decisions already made."[19] They chide Tyler for his failure to start with values:

> Tyler does not propose turning to values first, as we do. Rather, after a tentative list of objectives has been formulated by consulting his three data-sources, they are validated against questions pertaining to the good life in a good society, what knowledge is of most worth, and so on, or against a carefully formulated philosophical system within which answers to such value questions already have been formulated. We propose turning to values as the primary data-source in selecting purposes for the school and as a data-source in making all subsequent curriculum decisions.[20]

But whose values? What are sources of values? All that Goodlad and Richter indicate in their model is reference to and use of what they call "funded knowledge" and "conventional wisdom" as data sources.

Feyereisen, Fiorino, and Nowak in their conceptual system for designing curriculum show three parallel and equal "external variables" —needs of the individual, nature and needs of society, and system of values—and state that these three sets of factors "have been placed above the system and that objectives, and internal variables, are located above the other internal variables."[21] Again, one must ask, whose values? What are the sources of values? How does one validate values?

Validation

This discussion, then, is pointed to an important matter in curriculum planning—how does the curriculum planner, the teacher, or the administrator know whether the goals and objectives defined for curriculum and instruction are valid, that the best possible choices of goals and ends have been made, and that the best educational route has

---

[18] John Goodlad and Maurice N. Richter, Jr., *The Development of a Conceptual System for Dealing with Problems of Curriculum and Instruction* (U.S. Office of Education, Cooperative Research Program, Project No. 454), p. i.

[19] Goodlad and Richter, p. 63.

[20] Goodlad and Richter, p. 27.

[21] Kathryn V. Feyereisen, A. John Fiorino, and Arlene T. Nowak, *Supervision and Curriculum Renewal: A Systems Approach* (New York: Appleton-Century-Crofts, 1970), p. 137.

been selected for the students for whom the curriculum is planned and instruction is carried on?

We emphasize again that educators must obtain as much pertinent data as possible about the young people to be educated, for a curriculum is always planned for students, and about the society that establishes and controls the schools. Then lists of goals and objectives may be formulated that constitute the very best and most astute judgment the planning group can make on the basis of these data. Obviously, there is no one-to-one relation between a specific item of data and a particular goal or objective. Goals or objectives cannot be deduced directly from bits of data. Nor can any computer grind out valid goals, regardless of the sophistication of the programming. Rather, the intelligence, insight, values, attitudes, and beliefs of human beings are the crucial factors in choice making. Wise choices cannot be made without the most complete data obtainable, but judgment must still prevail.

Thus, the curriculum worker engaged in the definition of goals continuously checks the validity of these goals against the basic data obtained from his two sources. He also uses all the results of a broad, continuous program of evaluation of the entire educational program, discussed later in this book, in such an examination and validation of purposes. Curriculum planning must be an ever-continuing cycle of obtaining data, defining objectives, providing learning experiences, evaluating instructional outcomes, reexamining data, and appraising goals in light of all factors.

One further point should be made. A curriculum worker, including a teacher carrying out instruction, may have to discard or to include certain goals or objectives because of legal requirements, court decisions, or state or local regulations. Such a situation does not invalidate otherwise sound purposes; it simply means that the school must operate within a legal structure which in itself is an expression of the values and social expectations of those who control it. If the educator believes that the goals that must be rejected are valid, he should seek to have these goals accepted by those who oppose them. If the goals are not valid in terms of the basic data sources, they should not be included in the school program.

FORMULATING GENERAL GOALS AND DOMAINS

Goals are the basic elements in educational planning. They constitute the structure for building the curriculum. The scope of the entire educational program of the school, the broad design of the curriculum, and the nature of the learning opportunities provided, including courses and various other parts of the program, are embodied in the defined goals of the school.

Goals may be at several levels of generality or specificity, yet they all constitute the building blocks of the total program. The goals may be quite broad, as suggested by the definition Goodlad and Richter give of an educational aim: "a remote end for the guidance of educational activity."[22] The handbook for the California program defines a goal as "a statement of broad direction or intent which is general and timeless and is not concerned with a particular achievement within a specified time period."[23]

David Krathwohl, in proposing a three-tier hierarchy for educational objectives, states that

> at the first and most abstract level are the quite broad and general statements most helpful in the development of programs of instruction, for laying out of types of courses and areas to be covered, and for the general goals toward which several years of education might be aimed or for which an entire unit such as an elementary, junior, or senior high school might strive.[24]

In the sections that follow we consider the steps and processes involved in defining general goals and subgoals. We note how these definitions constitute the guidelines from which the curriculum is constructed, and we describe further the ways in which the curriculum domains are used in planning. These three elements of curriculum development are aspects of the same process of definition, all closely interrelated and all developed as part of the same professional endeavor.

Preparing Statements of General Goals

Curriculum planning groups will find it useful in terms of ongoing activities over the years to first set down in somewhat broad, abstract terms a basic conception of the purpose of the school. Such a declaration clarifies a structure within which all planning should proceed.

We suggest that the first document prepared be a statement of the fundamental purposes of schools—a broad charter that describes the scope and character of schooling. In the preparation of such a declaration the total planning group must seek to answer two basic questions: What essentially are the ideals of American society? and, What are the responsibilities and functions of the school in educating young people to live in this society now and for the rest of their lives?

---

[22] Goodlad and Richter, p. 16.
[23] Joint Committee on Educational Goals and Evaluation, Vol. I, p. 7.
[24] Krathwohl, p. 84.

If a statement of basic values has already been prepared, it will serve to answer the first of these questions. If one has not been prepared, either one may be drawn up as a part of goal definition or an assumption may be made that such basic beliefs will be evident in other documents prepared as a part of curriculum planning. Decisions concerning the primary responsibilities and functions of the school as a social institution are more difficult. Moreover, no final permanent position on the matter should be taken, for the role the school may and usually does play shifts as social conditions and the nature of the times change. But operational decisions must be made, for further curriculum planning embodies fully such decisions.

Some examples of broad, general goals that have been widely used and cited over the years may be informative in determining the nature of the undertaking. Undoubtedly the most famous of all statements on the purposes and nature of schooling is the *Cardinal Principles of Secondary Education* prepared by the Commission on the Reorganization of Secondary Education and published in 1918. Although the work of the Commission was directed particularly at goal definition for secondary schools, the statement is applicable to all levels of formal education and constitutes a point of view worthy of the fullest consideration by all planning groups. The Commission stated that *"education in a democracy, both within and without the school, should develop in each individual the knowledge, interests, ideals, habits, and powers whereby he will find his place and use that place to shape both himself and society toward ever nobler ends."*[25]

The Commission then listed seven areas of daily living which should be covered in the school program and stated the broad goals to be sought in each area:

CARDINAL PRINCIPLES OF SECONDARY EDUCATION

1. Health
The secondary school should therefore provide health instruction, inculcate health habits, organize an effective program of physical activities, regard health needs in planning work and play, and cooperate with home and community in safeguarding and promoting health interests.

2. Command of fundamental processes
The facility that a child of 12 or 14 may acquire in the use of these tools is not sufficient for the needs of modern life.

---

[25] Commission on the Reorganization of Secondary Education, U.S. Office of Education, *Cardinal Principles of Secondary Education* (Washington, D.C.: Government Printing Office, 1918), Bulletin No. 35, p. 9.

3. Worthy home-membership

Worthy home-membership as an objective calls for the development of those qualities that make the individual a worthy member of a family, both contributing to and deriving benefit from that membership.

4. Vocation

Vocational education should equip the individual to secure a livelihood for himself and those dependent on him, to serve society well through his vocation, to maintain the right relationships toward his fellow workers and society, and, as far as possible, to find in that vocation his own best development.

5. Civic education

Civic education should develop in the individual those qualities whereby he will act well his part as a member of neighborhood, town or city, State, and Nation, and give him a basis for understanding international problems.

6. Worthy use of leisure

Education should equip the individual to secure from his leisure the recreation of body, mind, and spirit, and the enrichment and enlargement of his personality.

7. Ethical character

In a democratic society ethical character becomes paramount among the objectives of the secondary school.[26]

Two decades later, the Educational Policies Commission, established by the National Education Association to recommend school policies, published an important statement on the functions of education in U.S. society. The Commission declared that formal education has these basic functions:

> In any realistic definition of education for the United States, therefore, must appear the whole philosophy and practice of democracy. Education cherishes and inculcates its moral values, disseminates knowledge necessary to its functioning, spreads information relevant to its institutions and economy, keeps alive the creative and sustaining spirit without which the letter is dead.[27]

The Educational Policies Commission published two additional reports worthy of citation here as examples of general goals for the schools.

The Purposes of Education in American Democracy, published in 1938, proposed that educational goals be defined in terms of four

---

[26] Commission on the Reorganization of Secondary Education, pp. 11–15.

[27] Educational Policies Commission, National Education Association, *The Unique Function of Education in American Democracy* (Washington, D.C.: The Association, 1937), p. 89.

aspects of human responsibility. The categories and two examples for each one follow:

THE OBJECTIVES OF SELF-REALIZATION

The Inquiring Mind. The educated person has an appetite for learning.
Character. The educated person gives responsible direction to his own life.

THE OBJECTIVES OF HUMAN RELATIONSHIPS

Respect for Humanity. The educated person puts human relationships first.
Democracy in the Home. The educated person maintains democratic family relationships.

THE OBJECTIVES OF ECONOMIC EFFICIENCY

Occupational Efficiency. The educated producer succeeds in his chosen vocation.
Consumer Judgment. The educated consumer develops standards for guiding his expenditures.

THE OBJECTIVES OF CIVIC RESPONSIBILITY

Social Justice. The educated citizen is sensitive to the disparities of human circumstance.
Conservation. The educated citizen has a regard for the nation's resources.[28]

Continuing its efforts to assist educators in planning, in 1944 the Commission proposed a set of what we designate as general goals for secondary schools. The list is entitled "Imperative Educational Needs of Youth." This statement has been used extensively by curriculum planning groups at the secondary school level. In light of its significance and continued use it is quoted here in full:

1. All youth need to develop salable skills and those understandings and attitudes that make the worker an intelligent and productive participant in economic life. To this end, most youth need supervised work experience as well as education in the skills and knowledge of their occupations.

2. All youth need to develop and maintain good health and physical fitness.

[28] Educational Policies Commission, *The Purposes of Education in American Democracy*, pp. 50, 72, 90, and 108.

3. All youth need to understand the rights and duties of the citizens of a democratic society, and to be diligent and competent in the performance of their obligations as members of the community and citizens of the state and nation.

4. All youth need to understand the significance of the family for the individual and society and the conditions conducive to successful family life.

5. All youth need to know how to purchase and use goods and services intelligently, understanding both the values received by the consumer and the economic consequences of their acts.

6. All youth need to understand the methods of science, the influence of science on human life, and the main scientific facts concerning the nature of the world and of man.

7. All youth need opportunities to develop their capacities to appreciate beauty in literature, art, music, and nature.

8. All youth need to be able to use their leisure time well and to budget it wisely, balancing activities that yield satisfactions to the individual with those that are socially useful.

9. All youth need to develop respect for other persons, to grow in their insight into ethical values and principles, and to be able to live and work cooperatively with others.

10. All youth need to grow in their ability to think rationally, to express their thoughts clearly, and to read and listen with understanding.[29]

The Northern California Program Development Center, in its kit of materials prepared in 1971 for aiding local school systems in the definition of goals, proposed eighteen general educational goals. Each one is amplified by the statement of three or four "similar" goals. The general goals are:

To understand and practice the skills of family living
To learn how to be a good manager of time, money, and property
To gain a general education
To develop good character and self-respect
Develop skills in reading, writing, speaking, and listening
To learn about and try to understand the changes that take place in the world
Learn how to examine and use information
Develop a desire for learning now and in the future
Help students develop a pride in their work and a feeling of self-worth
To prepare students to enter the world of work
Practice and understand the ideas of health and safety
To learn how to respect and get along with people who think, act, and dress
    differently

[29] Educational Policies Commission, National Education Association, *Education for All American Youth* (Washington, D.C.: The Association, 1944), pp. 225–226.

Understand and practice democratic ideas and ideals
To learn to respect and get along with people with whom we work and live
To learn how to use leisure time
To learn how to be a good citizen
Develop the ability to make job selections
To help students appreciate the culture and beauty in their world[30]

Many present-day curriculum workers, behavioral psychologists, evaluation specialists, and teachers themselves regard such general statements of goals for the total school program as meaningless, impossible to attain in practice, and useless as a basis for curriculum and instructional planning. The whole movement to state goals and objectives in behavioral terms, as will be considered in a later section, is a vigorous protest against bland definitions of this kind. Other authorities, such as Goodlad and Richter and Krathwohl—already cited—and Eisner, McDonald, Broudy, and others—to be cited later—see such efforts as the starting point, and, in some instances, as the end point of curriculum planning.

In our opinion, the dissatisfaction with general statements of goals stems from the failure of curriculum planners to complete the task of goal definition as it is presented in this chapter. Obviously, further steps must be taken to translate these general goals into specific curriculum goals and instructional objectives. All too often efforts in the past, until the behavioral approaches became widely accepted in the 1960s, ended with lists that read well when suitably printed and framed or distributed in booklet form to teachers and citizens. It was the failure to complete the process of definition that should be criticized, not the products themselves.

Identifying Curriculum Domains

Part of the process of goal definition must be the identification of broad domains of the curriculum as the basis for designing the educational program, further defining subgoals, stating instructional objectives, selecting curriculum content, and planning appropriate instructional modes.

In Chapter 1 the conception of curriculum domains was presented, and in Chapter 5 the use of domains as a basis for designing the curriculum will be considered in detail. Here we relate the determination of appropriate domains to the formulation of general goals and subgoals.

In preparing the general goals of the school, work committees

[30] Northern California Program Development Center, "Goal Card" (Chico, Calif.: The Center, 1971).

can readily begin to organize groups of closely related sets of desired outcomes. Such groupings may center around the activities of human beings, for example, as they grow and develop personally, live together in a social group, work together in sustaining and improving the life of each individual and the group collectively, govern themselves, or rear their children. Other bases for grouping major goals of schooling may also be used.

We propose for the consideration of planning groups four major domains within which general goals and correlative subgoals may be grouped for planning and instructional purposes: personal development, human relations, continued learning skills, and specialization. The rationale for such a classification is given in Chapters 1 and 5.

To assist curriculum planners, we review here some other schemes that have been used to designate the broad areas of the curriculum.

The *Cardinal Principles of Secondary Education*, already cited, listed seven categories of "activities of the individual"; these areas could very well be used as domains for curriculum and instructional planning, although we do not believe that adequate attention is given to the fullest development of the individual learner in terms of his capabilities and to the continuous, lifetime nature of learning itself.

The four categories of purposes delineated by the Educational Policies Commission (see page 165) may be used as the domains for organizing and planning the curriculum and carrying on the instructional program: Self-Realization, Human Relationships, Economic Efficiency, and Civic Responsibility.

Broudy, Smith, and Burnett envision a high school program for general education organized around five basic strands: symbolic studies, basic sciences, developmental studies, aesthetic studies, and molar problems.[31] A complete program of schooling would need to include, in addition, a domain devoted to specialization.

Although they would not constitute our conception of domains for planning programs, the broad fields of study encompassed within the usual school program could be used. Wilhelms, for example, advocates the organization of the curriculum into four "great" streams: science-mathematics, social studies, humanities, and vocational preparation.[32] Craig Wilson, in his plea for an "open access curriculum," stated

[31] Harry S. Broudy, B. Othanel Smith, and Joe R. Burnett, *Democracy and Excellence in American Secondary Education* (Chicago: Rand McNally and Company, 1964), p. 83.

[32] Fred T. Wilhelms, "Some Hunches of a Revolutionary," in Richard Hart and J. Galen Saylor, eds., *Student Unrest: Threat or Promise?* (Washington, D.C.: Association for Supervision and Curriculum Development, 1970), pp. 66–79.

that such a plan "will create large clusters of content, such as the sciences, the arts, and the humanities, as a substitute for proliferation of autonomous lesser courses."[33]

Bruce Joyce's proposal for curriculum domains most closely parallels the conception we present in this book:

> The primary task in selecting an educational mission is to identify the domains through which the program will enter the life of the learner in order to change his responses to living in the world. . . . Although these domains are not mutually exclusive (personal creativity, for example, may be an avenue to improve interpersonal and academic performance), we can use these three categories, the personal, the social, and the academic, to sort out some of the possible functions of education.[34]

We do not intend to be arbitrary or dogmatic about the designation of the domains, although we believe that the inclusion of the domain of specialization is highly desirable in all of these proposals. We recognize, as Joyce does, that there may be some overlapping in the scope and nature of the domains and that programs developed for one domain may —and should—contribute to development in one or more of the others.

We have emphasized that the curriculum domains are not themselves educational goals. They constitute the broad organizing elements of the curriculum plan, comprising a set of closely related major goals and subgoals that provide the basis for developing learning opportunities of all sorts, including subjects and courses, activities, community experiences, independent learning activities, informal types of school programs, and the like.

DEFINING SUBGOALS

A major aspect of goal definition is the determination of subgoals. These are basic elements in curriculum planning, the statements of the outcomes desired that postulate the kinds of learning opportunities that should be provided students. Of course, the subgoals are consistent with the general goals of the school, but they are much more detailed and specific, spelling out the parameters and nature of a domain of the curriculum, and they must be formulated for each aspect of the educational program from nursery school through adult programs.

[33] L. Craig Wilson, *The Open Access Curriculum* (Boston: Allyn and Bacon, Inc., 1971), p. 15.

[34] Bruce R. Joyce, "The Curriculum Worker of the Future," in Robert M. McClure, ed., *The Curriculum: Retrospect and Prospect,* 70th Yearbook, Part I, National Society for the Study of Education (Chicago: University of Chicago Press, 1971), p. 332.

Obviously, this is a job requiring a high level of professional skill and a great deal of effort. The task primarily falls on the educator, but a number of other specialists should be involved rather extensively in the preparation of these subgoals and in planning the content and kinds of learning activities to be provided. Particularly, specialists in the substantive content of a broad area of study, for example, and psychologists, sociologists, philosophers, political scientists, and anthropologists, should participate in these aspects of curriculum planning. Goodlad and Richter have described the role of such specialists:

> Most educational objectives have two component parts: a *behavioral* element and a *substantive element.* . . . it would appear that the category, "subject-matter specialists," constitutes the prime data-source in refining statements of educational aims to the point where they take on the greater clarity and specificity of educational objectives. . . . This presupposes, of course, much wider representation of sub-publics in the initial selection of aims. . . . these specialists are consulted not for purposes of determining the aims that *ought* to be selected . . . but for the purposes of refining aims already selected.[35]

Should Subgoals Be Stated Behaviorally?

Considerable controversy has raged in educational circles in recent years about the extent to which subgoals should be stated in behavioral terms. At one time educational groups were even using such slogans as "Help stamp out nonbehavioral objectives" or "Down with behavioral objectives."[36]

The advocates of behavioristically stated goals and objectives are revolting against broad statements of goals that are so vague that they are meaningless as a basis for planning specific parts of the curriculum or carrying on instruction. Such general listings provide no help to the teacher in determining what content to select, what learning experiences to develop with students, or how to evaluate the outcomes of instruction.

The movement to state goals in behavioral terms is often credited to Tyler, who, directing the evaluation program for the Eight-Year Study of the Progressive Education Association in the 1930s, wrote that "each objective must be defined in terms which clarify the kind of behavior which the course should help to develop among students; that is to say, a statement is needed which explains the meaning of the objective by describing the reactions we can expect of persons who have

---

[35] Goodlad and Richter, pp. 48, 50.

[36] Harry S. Broudy, "Can Research Escape the Dogma of Behavioral Objectives?" *School Review*, 79, 43–55 (November 1970).

reached the objective."[37] Later, in his syllabus, Tyler emphasized this point: "The purpose of a statement of objectives is to indicate the kinds of changes in the student to be brought about so that instruction activities can be planned and developed in a way likely to attain these objectives; that is, to bring about these changes in students."[38]

One of the most comprehensive and helpful efforts to define curriculum goals in terms of changes in behavior or behavioral potential was a project completed by Will French and a group of associates.[39] Although the formulation was specifically designed for the secondary level of schooling, the plan and even the list of goals are appropriate for other levels. French insisted that

two of the first steps toward further improvement in the high school's general education program would seem to be: (1) the acceptance of the idea that its outcomes are best described in terms of behavioral competence, and (2) the development of more explicit statements of some of the principal kinds and levels of behavior which it is reasonable for general education in high school to undertake to achieve.[40]

Although both Tyler and French strongly recommended that goals state the *kinds* of changes the school should seek to achieve through its program, the behavioral goals they proposed, and gave as illustrations, are much broader and more fundamental in nature than the detailed ones recommended more recently by the authors of numerous handbooks or than those available by the thousands on computer tapes.

The Case for Explicit Behavioral Objectives

The arguments advanced for stating goals in terms of behavioral outcomes may be summarized as follows[41]:

[37] Ralph W. Tyler, *Constructing Achievement Tests* (Columbus: Ohio State University, 1934), p. 18.

[38] Tyler, *Basic Principles of Curriculum and Instruction*, p. 29.

[39] Will French and associates, *Behavioral Goals of General Education in High School* (New York: Russell Sage Foundation, 1957).

[40] French and associates, p. 34.

[41] See especially Robert F. Mager, *Preparing Instructional Objectives* (Palo Alto, Calif.: Fearon Publishers, 1962); Robert J. Kibler, Larry L. Barker, and David T. Miles, *Behavioral Objectives and Instruction* (Boston: Allyn and Bacon, Inc., 1970); Gronlund; H. H. McAshan, *Writing Behavioral Objectives* (New York: Harper & Row, Publishers, 1970); Ralph H. Ojemann, "Should Educational Objectives Be Stated in Behavioral Terms?" *Elementary School Journal*, Part I, 68, 223–231 (February 1968), Part II, 69, 229–235 (February 1969), Part III, 70, 271–278 (February 1970); David T. Miles and Roger E. Robinson, "Behavioral Objectives: An Even Closer Look," *Educational Technology*, 11, 39–44 (June 1971); W. James Popham,

1. Since the purpose of instruction is to change behavior in one way or another, the objectives of instruction should state specifically and overtly the "pattern of behavior (performance) we want the learner to be able to demonstrate."[42] Nonbehavioral goals are too gross for planning either the curriculum or instruction. Even if a goal is a broad, long-term one that states a high level of complex functioning of mental activity, for instructional purposes it can and should be broken into component parts which in total make up the complex behavior.

2. Communication among all of those involved in the schooling process is greatly enhanced by the use of behavioral objectives. Gagné has pointed out that

> statements describing instructional objectives have the primary purpose of *communicating*. Assuming that education has the form of an organized system, communication of its intended and actual outcomes is necessary, among and between the designers of instructional materials, the planners of courses and programs, the teachers, the students, and the parents.[43]

3. Behavioral objectives indicate clearly what it is the teacher should do in providing classroom experiences to enable students to achieve a goal. They provide direct, useful guidance to the curriculum planner and the teacher in answering the question, "What should we teach?" Such an objective provides overt, detailed help to the teacher in selecting content, choosing instructional materials and methods, and directing classroom activities. This is the only efficient method of educating young people. "An instructor will function in a fog of his own making until he knows just what he wants his students to be able to do at the end of the instruction."[44] Popham notes that "precise objectives stated in terms of measurable learner behavior makes it definitely easier for the teacher to engage in curricular decisions. The clarity of precisely stated goals permits the teacher to make far more judicious choices regarding what ought to be included in the curriculum."[45]

"Objectives and Instruction," and Howard J. Sullivan, "Objectives, Evaluation, and Improved Learner Achievement," in Robert E. Stake, ed., *Instructional Objectives* (Chicago: Rand McNally and Company, 1969), pp. 32–52 and 65–90; Richard E. Schutz, Robert L. Baker, and Vernon S. Gerlach, *Stating Educational Outcomes* (New York: Van Nostrand Reinhold Company, 1971); Robert L. Baker and Vernon S. Gerlach, *Constructing Objectives of Cognitive Behavior* (New York: Van Nostrand Reinhold Company, 1971); and Daniel Tanner, *Using Behavioral Objectives in the Classroom* (New York: The Macmillan Company, 1972).

[42] Mager, p. 3.

[43] Robert M. Gagné, "Behavioral Objectives? Yes," *Educational Leadership*, 29, 395 (February 1972).

[44] Mager, p. 3.

[45] Popham, "Objectives and Instruction," p. 40.

4. The school becomes a much more efficient institution. Instruction is pointed to clearly defined aims so that all learning experiences may be selected and developed to achieve specified objectives. The student knows from the outset what he is expected to accomplish. The aimless, confused behavior often noticeable in the classroom is eliminated; everything proceeds with a specific purpose. A student can readily note progress in goal attainment; thus directed, purposeful behavior is reinforced. Appropriate practice activities are easily selected, hence there is no wasted effort. Students may readily establish their level of entry behavior and proceed from that level of accomplishment. Schutz, Baker, and Gerlach insist that "the less ambiguity surrounding a statement of an educational outcome, the more cues we have as to the kind of instructional sequence that will prove effective."[46]

5. Behavioral objectives may be differentiated more readily for each student and may be stated for an individual student or for small groups of students at comparable levels of development. This procedure is particularly used in computer-assisted instruction or in individually prescribed learning activities.

6. Behaviorally stated objectives provide the only meaningful basis for evaluating the outcomes of instruction. Learning can be overtly demonstrated in behavior; otherwise it very likely does not exist. Evaluation is readily made, for the objective itself defines what kinds of behavior are to be demonstrated. Evaluating the attainment of a gross objective such as, "To develop an appreciation of good literature" is difficult, especially by the classroom teacher on the spot. In a classroom where instruction is based on such broad goals, the teacher, school authorities, parents, or the students themselves never really know if the school is achieving the outcome which is desired.

Leon Lessinger, an outspoken advocate of stating educational objectives in specific terms, has stated:

General objectives, goals, or purposes serve a useful purpose, but American education suffers no shortage of them. On the other hand, we need more performance criteria that clearly specify the student competency to be displayed, the methods for displaying it, and the standards for judging whether it is sufficient. For example, we can specify that 90 percent of all students should score 90 percent or higher on a given test of reading based on certain materials. Auditors and local officials will discuss, in advance, which tests to use and what numbers are acceptable, but performance criteria, however they are phrased, must always be specific.[47]

[46] Schutz, Baker, and Gerlach, p. 3.
[47] Leon M. Lessinger, *Every Kid a Winner: Accountability in Education* (New York: Simon and Schuster, Inc., 1970), p. 86.

The Case for Broader, Nonexplicit Goals

Many curriculum workers in recent years have opposed the behavioristic approach to defining educational goals, advocating instead a much broader, more flexible, and open-ended type of definition.[48] More significant is the fact that overwhelmingly classroom teachers and many supervisors and other curriculum workers in the schools themselves do not favor a narrow conception of the curriculum. Either they have never fallen in line with the behaviorists, or, if they have used their procedures, have become disillusioned with them and revolted against the movement.

The principal arguments in favor of the broader type of goal statement, and hence the reasons for the rejection of the explicit approach, may be summarized as follows:

1. Human behavior in actuality is much broader in scope and purpose than the sum of specific bits of behavior learned in isolation. Behavioral objectives of the performance type fail to take account of the higher or more complex levels of functioning. The behavioralists presume that nothing is learned if it cannot be evidenced in behavior; in fact, they hold that there are no broad outcomes that cannot be stated in

[48] See the following for arguments favoring broad goal statements: Elliot W. Eisner, "Instructional and Expressive Educational Objectives: Their Formulation and Use in Curriculum," in Stake, pp. 1–31, and "Educational Objectives: Help or Hindrance," *School Review*, 75, 250–266 (Autumn 1967); James B. Macdonald, "Myths about Instruction," *Educational Leadership*, 22, 571–576, 609–617 (May 1965); James B. Macdonald and Bernice J. Wolfson, "A Case against Behavioral Objectives," *Elementary School Journal*, 71, 119–128 (December 1970); Broudy, "Can Research Escape the Dogma of Behavioral Objectives?", "The Philosophical Foundations of Educational Objectives," *Educational Theory*, 20, 3–21 (Winter 1970), and "Can We Define Good Teaching," *Teachers College Record*, 70, 583–592 (April 1969); Herbert M. Kliebard, "Curricular Objectives and Evaluation: A Reassessment," *High School Journal*, 51, 241–247 (March 1968), and "Reappraisal: The Tyler Rationale," *School Review*, 78, 259–272 (February 1970); J. Myron Atkin, "Behavioral Objectives in Curriculum Design: A Cautionary Note," *Science Teacher*, 35, 27–30 (May 1968); James D. Raths, "Teaching without Specific Objectives," *Educational Leadership*, 28, 714–720 (April 1971); Philip Jackson and Elizabeth Belford, "Educational Objectives and the Joys of Teaching," *School Review*, 73, 267–291 (Autumn 1965); Ira S. Steinberg, "Behavioral Definition of Educational Objectives: A Critique," in Lawrence G. Thomas, ed., *Philosophical Redirection of Educational Research*, 71st Yearbook, Part 1, National Society for the Study of Education (Chicago: University of Chicago Press, 1972), pp. 143–163; Ronald T. Hyman, "Means-Ends Reasoning and the Curriculum," *Teachers College Record*, 73, 393–401 (February 1972); and Herbert D. Simons, "Behavioral Objectives: A False Hope for Education," *Elementary School Journal*, 73, 173–181 (January 1973).

testable, overt behaviors. This assumption is denied by educational philosophers and many scholars in various disciplines.[49]

2. Behavioral objectives disregard the broad, interrelated categories of human activity and hence often ignore or even conflict with the long-range, more meaningful outcomes that constitute the general goals of the school. Thus they militate against the development of a program that will enable a student to attain maximum development of his potentialities. The specific, isolated acts of behavior may fall far short of adding up to a well-rounded, complete education. As Robert Glaser pointed out, such bits of behavior constitute training, a necessary and desirable aspect of human development, but fall short of being the total program:

> A distinction must be made between instructional goals and terminal behavior. The goals of education are desirably long range and involve complex human behaviors and aspirations. Specification of these goals involves philosophical and ethical considerations for which the educator must share responsibility as a member of the society.[50]

Asahel Woodruff and Philip Kapfer, in an article in which they endeavor to bring both approaches together into a usable model, point out the problem:

> Behavioral objectives are a powerful tool for making educational goals precise, for identifying relevant media and learning activities, and for knowing when goals have been achieved. The threat potential of behavioral objectives exists in the tendency of some modern behaviorists to limit objectives to overt visible behaviors, thus excluding the important behavioral processes of perception, concept formation, thinking, feeling, synthesizing, creating and so on. The atomistic specification of behavioral objectives also excludes the highly significant decision-making and decision-executing areas of human behavior, which represent the most significant aims of education.[51]

In 1972, James Popham, one of the most vociferous advocates of behaviorally stated objectives, relented enough to state: "*However*, there are some important goals which we have for our children which are

---

[49] See especially Broudy, "The Philosophical Foundations of Educational Objectives," pp. 12–15.

[50] Robert Glaser, *Training Research and Education* (New York: John Wiley & Sons, Inc., 1965), p. 7.

[51] Asahel D. Woodruff and Philip G. Kapfer, "Behavioral Objectives and Humanism in Education: A Question of Specificity," *Educational Technology*, 12, 51 (January 1972).

currently unassessable. To the extent that such goals are extremely meritorious, they are *worth the risk* of our pursuing them if we cannot reliably discern whether they have been accomplished."[52]

Educators working in the areas of the arts and the humanities especially feel that many of the kinds of learning activities which they regard as essential aspects of schooling cannot be stated in precise performance standards or even overt behaviors.

3. The practice of defining classroom activities in terms of specific behaviors severely restricts the scope and significance of instruction, greatly reduces the flexibility and freedom of the teacher and the classroom group, and stifles student initiative, creativeness, and the joy of participating in learning experiences, individually or in the group. Raths insists that

> once it has been decided that all students are to acquire a specific instruction objective, the teacher's task becomes at once difficult and tedious. He must inform his students of the objective to which they are expected to aspire; he must convince them of the relevance of this objective to their lives; he must give students the opportunity to practice the behavior being taught; he must diagnose individual difficulties encountered by members of his group; he must make prescriptions of assignments based on his diagnosis and repeat the cycle again and again. Needless to say, this "method" of instruction has proved itself effective, if not provocative. It is the training paradigm perfected during both World Wars and utilized extensively in the armed forces and in industry to prepare persons for specific responsibilities.[53]

But the schools have a much bigger, more responsible, and more complex task than preparing "Rosy the Riveter," although that, too, is properly a task of some aspects of the school's program.

4. If done according to the rationale of the procedure, the task of preparing performance, behavior-type objectives would be endless. For every bit of activity undertaken in each classroom there should be an objective, and if instruction is to be personalized as it should be, perhaps a different objective for each pupil. A simple contemplation of this aspect of curriculum planning indicates that each teacher would have volumes of behavioral objectives for his classroom program.[54] No teacher has the time, the resources, or the energy to engage in such an enterprise.

[52] W. James Popham, "Must All Objectives Be Behavioral?" *Educational Leadership*, 29, 608 (April 1972).

[53] Raths, p. 715.

[54] George Kneller has estimated that "the high school teacher of 150 students would be handling millions of objectives—conceivably." See his "Behavioral Objectives? No," *Educational Leadership*, 29, 398 (February 1972).

5. Instruction based on the performance paradigm largely destroys the opportunities for students and teacher to engage in choice making, in probing alternative courses of action, in risk-taking activities, in testing out intuitive hunches, and in cooperatively selecting and planning learning activities that are meaningful and significant—in short, in engaging in the sheer joy of just "growing up," of being oneself. Alice Yardley, a noted authority on the British concept of informal education, after visiting many American schools, scolded us in strong language: "You tend to be obsessed by the need to evaluate or test. As soon as you test you have designed a program into which a student must fit. Rather than allow children to be people, you impose upon them behavioral objectives thought up by adults."[55] Raths, in the article cited, lists twelve criteria for selecting activities that will be maximally worthwhile to students, none of which calls for or justifies the use of performance objectives.

6. The specific, overt statement of the behavioral outcome to be sought through a learning activity usually ignores, by the nature of the paradigm, the probability and possibility of concomitant learnings. An experience, particularly an activity, in a school setting, involving usually a teacher and other students, may actually result in a number of "learnings," planned as well as unplanned. For example, a specific goal might be:

upon completion of a novel, the student will relate the novel to his experience in *any one* of the following ways: (1) by discussing why he could or could not identify with any of the characters; (2) by stating what new ideas the author has presented, or what old ideas have been presented in a new perspective for him; (3) by discussing any particular passage or incident which evoked strong feeling in him.[56]

The teacher in this instance would be obligated to guide learning activities in the classroom that presumably will enable each student to attain this objective and demonstrate his achievement in the manner prescribed. But the students individually may also learn other things not stated in the objective. Some seventh graders may come to dislike novels because they were forced to explain how they related to a specific one. Perhaps they just had vague feelings about the novel which they were not able to express. Some who liked the novel may read others by the same author. Others may see themselves as the principal character and

[55] "Briton Assails 'Mold' Concept of American Schools," *New York Times*, Vol. 122, No. 42092 (April 22, 1973).

[56] From Instructional Objectives Exchange, "Language Arts 7–9" (Los Angeles: Center for the Study of Evaluation, 1971).

daydream about ways in which they could have handled the situations described. Learning experiences are complex in most instances and have "side effects." These are ignored in the performance model of instruction. Macdonald's position on this matter is worthy of citation:

> Objectives are heuristic devices which provide initiating sequences which become altered in the flow of instruction. In the final analysis, it could be argued, the teacher in actuality asks a fundamentally different question from "What am I trying to accomplish?" The teacher asks, "What am I going to do?" and out of the doing comes accomplishment.[57]

Robert Stake, a specialist in evaluation, has commented at some length on the matter of goals and objectives in a position paper that merits consideration. The point of view he presents is reflected in this observation:

> Unfortunately, it is not at all a demonstrated fact that teachers teach better when they critically analyze their own teaching behavior. When I look at teachers who seem to be doing a superb job of teaching my advisees and my children, I seldom find evidence that they are conceptualizing their task in behavior-modification language.[58]

A Suggested Approach

The widespread effort in recent years to state goals and objectives behaviorally has contributed greatly to the process of curriculum planning. But in many instances the advocates of this approach have been overzealous in insisting that all goals be stated in an explicit form and that instruction be devoted primarily, if not exclusively, to assisting students achieve tangible evidences of performance capabilities. Our recommendations on the matter of stating goals and objectives follow:

1. The general goals of the school will be stated in broad, abstract terms, but they will nonetheless define the nature and character of the educational program in language that clearly indicates what kinds of growth and development should be fostered by the school and the broad competencies and capabilities students should attain as a result of schooling.

2. Subgoals for each domain, corollary to the general goals, will

---

[57] Macdonald, p. 614.

[58] Robert E. Stake, "Language, Rationality, and Assessment," in Walcott H. Beatty, ed., *Improving Educational Assessment & an Inventory of Measures of Affective Behavior* (Washington, D.C.: Association for Supervision and Curriculum Development, 1969), p. 28. (The position statement, entitled "Educational Objectives: A Position Statement," follows on pp. 28–30.)

be stated in much more explicit terms and will identify specific outcomes in the form of attainments or characteristics of behavior that students should acquire as a result of the school's instructional program. Subgoals will constitute the basis for selecting the whole range of learning opportunities to be provided by the school. Obviously, the curriculum plan will include organized courses or areas of instruction through which many of the subgoals will be realized; other subgoals will be achieved through the noninstructional activities sponsored by the school, community experiences in which students engage, the interactive process among teachers and pupils, the social life of the school, informal small-group activities, individual projects, and the like.

3. Instructional objectives are derived from subgoals. They constitute the basis for selecting the specific learning activities carried on in the school, choosing content for use in the development of the activities, determining appropriate and desirable modes for developing the instructional activities, and evaluating student outcomes.

In our opinion, general goals, subgoals, and instructional objectives need not be stated in the explicit performance form currently being advocated by some educators. The statement of a subgoal or an objective may be explicit when the desired outcome is a skill, such as typing a letter without error, adding a column of figures, or any one of a multitude of such skills taught by the school. Similarly, explicit objectives are desirable when the purpose of instruction is the acquisition of the ability to do something of an overt nature, such as obtaining data or information on a subject from materials in a resource center, preparing a chart that shows the percent of taxes raised by the state government from various sources, or punctuating correctly a collection of words in a passage in a workbook. If the acquisition of factual knowledge on a subject is desired, as much of the instruction in school is designed to do, objectives may be stated overtly, although it should be recognized by teachers that other, concomitant outcomes are likely to result, and that most of such learning opportunities should not end with an accumulation of knowledge but lead to the higher cognitive processes, such as application, analysis, synthesis, and evaluation. Moreover, many of the desired outcomes at these more sophisticated levels of learning may also be stated explicitly, provided the breadth and scope of mental activity of the student is not restricted by such definitions of outcomes.

However, when the desired outcomes are more general, developmental, or complex in nature and need not be demonstrated by specific acts of behavior on the spot, performance-type behavioral objectives are inappropriate and often detrimental to good teaching. For example, the purpose of a unit of instruction may be aimed at the development of attitudes about matters of personal and social concern, or of the ability to generalize from experience, the examination and clarification of beliefs on a matter of social policy, the sheer enjoyment of a painting or musical selection, or the examination and analysis of one's values. In such instances, and in a whole host of other kinds of learning experiences developed in the school setting, performance-type objectives are apt to be restrictive and delimiting. Broad, open-ended statements of goals serve the teacher and students better.

One of the most helpful schemes for preparing subgoals for education is embodied in A Taxonomy of Educational Objectives: The Classification of Educational Goals.[59] This plan proposes three major categories in which educational goals or objectives should be stated— the cognitive, affective, and psychomotor domains. Within each domain subclasses are specified, and these are arranged in a hierarchy beginning with the more specific and concrete types of outcomes and extending to the more complex and abstract ones. The taxonomy is widely used in curriculum planning. It is not a set of goals but rather a procedure for defining goals in a systematic, comprehensive manner. Nor are the three categories to be confused with the curriculum domains; the taxonomy is a guide for formulating subgoals within the domains, assuring an adequate and comprehensive range of the outcomes being sought.

Attention should also be directed to the hierarchical schemes for defining goal areas and stating objectives developed by the Center for the Study of Evaluation at the University of California at Los Angeles. These hierarchies are presented in two sets of charts published by the Center.[60] The charts are a part of the CSE Elementary School Evaluation Kit: Needs Assessment developed by the Center and are designed to "enable a potential user to begin the development of an objectives-based (criterion-referenced) evaluation system in areas where the offerings of standardized tests are poor or inappropriate."

For the elementary school the charts categorize 41 broad goal areas and 104 subgoals. These 104 subgoal areas are further defined in terms of components, and desirable kinds of behavior are listed for each component. The charts for the preschool-kindergarten level list broad,

[59] Benjamin S. Bloom and others, Handbook I: Cognitive Domain (New York: David McKay Company, Inc., 1956); David R. Krathwohl, Benjamin S. Bloom, and Bertram B. Masia, Handbook II: Affective Domain (New York: David McKay Company, Inc., 1964); and Anita J. Harrow, A Taxonomy of the Psychomotor Domain: A Guide for Developing Behavioral Objectives (New York: David McKay Company, Inc., 1972).

[60] Center for the Study of Evaluation, CSE Preschool/Kindergarten Hierarchical Objectives and CSE Elementary School Hierarchical Objectives Charts (Los Angeles: The Center, University of California at Los Angeles, 1973 and 1970).

general goals, but each goal is defined by several objectives. Behavioral objectives for purposes of carrying on instruction and making evaluations would then need to be written for the illustrative behaviors. This whole conception is similar to that of Will French and his group, except that they worked at the high school level and did not identify subject areas or other areas for instruction as does the Center.

INSTRUCTIONAL OBJECTIVES

The third step in determining the purposes for which schooling should be provided is to state the outcomes desired from participation in a specific learning opportunity or group of related opportunities provided by the school. Usually, curriculum literature designates these as instructional objectives. Obviously, instructional objectives stem from the subgoals and constitute statements of outcomes that would contribute fully to the realization of general goals.

Educators have raised two issues with respect to the definition of instructional objectives. First, they are concerned with the form in which the objectives should be stated. Second, they question whether objectives for instruction should be overtly formulated at all.

We have already considered in the previous section arguments for and against stating educational purposes in behavioral terms. The points of view summarized there apply equally well to the formulation of goals or objectives. Hence no further discussion of that matter will be given here, but several additional points are appropriate.

Overt Objectives or Ends-in-View?

The second point raised about instructional objectives by curriculum theorists has to do with the undesirability of defining objectives prior to engagement in the learning activity. Kliebard issues the challenge:

> One wonders whether the long-standing insistence by curriculum theorists that the first step in making a curriculum be the specification of objectives has any merit whatsoever. It is even questionable whether stating objectives at all, when they represent external goals allegedly reached through the manipulation of learning experiences, is a fruitful way to conceive of the process of curriculum planning.[61]

Macdonald, in identifying six myths of instruction, states that

it is difficult to see how meaningful, integrated behavior could result from a formal series of sequential rational decisions. . . . Another view . . . would

[61] Kliebard, "Reappraisal: The Tyler Rationale," pp. 269–270.

state that our objectives are only known to us in any complete sense after the completion of our act of instruction. No matter what we thought we were attempting to do, we can only know what we wanted to accomplish after the fact.[62]

Our reaction to these points of view is that every teacher engaged in instructional activities is seeking some desired outcomes whether these are stated in written form or exist in the mind of the teacher. If a teacher, for example, is directing an activity in which students are adding columns of three-digit numbers, he or she has at least one important behavioral outcome in mind—each student should be able to add the column after suitable instruction. That objective is obvious to anyone—teacher, students, curriculum director, principal, evaluator, parents. However, the teacher, as a member of a planning team, may also have stated in a curriculum guide or instructional plan or have formulated in his mind other objectives that are equally desirable outcomes from such learning experiences in arithmetic. These, doubtless, may not be evident to students as a matter of course, nor perhaps to the other parties involved in the educational undertaking. If a teacher is directing a study of the powers granted each of the three branches of the federal government by the Constitution, an important desired outcome is also evident—to know and to be able to state the powers of each branch of government. But, similarly, other pupil outcomes should be sought in such a unit of work—few or none of which may be evident to the students themselves or to other interested parties, especially evaluators of the schools.

Good instructional practices and meaningful, purposeful learning experiences for students call for a full recognition by the teacher and the students of the significant outcomes that ought to be attained through participation in the planned instructional activity. The students should know what is *expected* of them in the way of learning outcomes—in terms of knowledge, attitudes, concepts, and skills, for example—so that they may engage purposefully and meaningfully in the learning activities that teachers, in light of their recognition of these desired outcomes, are developing with them.

It may not be necessary or even desirable for skillful teachers to set down in a guide or instructional plan all of these objectives in detail, but we suggest that the most important ones be acknowledged by teacher and student and thus become the basis for planning and carrying on learning activities.

This is not to say that some unplanned or unexpected outcomes

[62] Macdonald, pp. 613–614.

will not result; it is hoped that they will occur, especially from heuristically designed sets of learning opportunities. We reject a narrow conception of instruction in which students move mechanically from one class exercise to the next in pursuit of prescribed sets of objectives. The skillful teacher is always flexible and adaptable, quick to take advantage at any time of a learning situation which offers worthwhile experiences for the participants, but always assessing the value of the activity in light of a clearly identified set of desired outcomes.

The Needs-Assessment Approach

A procedure for defining the purposes of a school program came into use in the early 1970s—in fact, it was forced on the schools by the federal government if they sought certain kinds of support. Title I of the Elementary and Secondary Education Act of 1965, and subsequent amendments, provided federal support for approved school programs for educationally deprived children. In regulations for administration of the Act, local educational agencies had to meet a requirement which stated: "The project for which an application for a grant is made by a local educational agency should be designed to meet the special educational needs of those educationally deprived children who have the greatest need for assistance."[63]

Similarly, the regulations for the administration of Title III of the Act prescribed the following:

Assessment of educational needs. The State plan shall identify the critical educational needs of the State as a whole and the critical educational needs of the various geographic areas and population groups within the State, and shall describe the process by which such needs were identified. This process shall be based upon the use of objective criteria and measurements and shall include procedures for collecting, analyzing, and validating relevant data and translating such data into determinations of critical educational needs.[64]

The Manual for administration of the Act spells out the approach in more detail:

Educational needs assessment is a technique for identifying those educational objectives which most need to be accomplished in a given instructional situation. The concept of educational needs assessment provides for

---

[63] U.S. Office of Education, *Financial Assistance to Meet the Educational Needs of Educationally Deprived Children: Regulations* (Washington, D.C.: Government Printing Office, 1969), p. 11.

[64] "Title 45—Public Welfare, Chapter I—Office of Education, Department of Health, Education and Welfare," *Federal Register*, 37, 24076 (November 11, 1972).

(a) the identifying of a desired learner outcome and (b) the ascertaining of the learner's current status with respect to the outcome. The educational needs constitute the difference between the current status and the desired status. The assessing of educational needs should be learner-oriented, focusing on the behavioral needs of children in the cognitive, affective and psychomotor domains. Such needs assessment is essential to making any significant improvement in educational outcomes and should be carefully planned and implemented with both short and long range objectives.[65]

Inasmuch as the states have avidly sought federal funds available under the Elementary and Secondary Education Act, they set about in 1972 to implement the needs-assessment project, periodically updating the data. Local school systems and other educational agencies eligible for funds, likewise, have had to make such assessments to meet state requirements.

The U.S. Office of Education does not specify the nature or form of the basic list of "desired learner outcomes." It offers some suggestions for defining them, however, and lists the *CSE Hierarchical Objectives Charts*, mentioned earlier, as an example of a structural breakdown for establishing goals. What this entire program does do is to insist that state school systems formulate a set of goals and objectives and then plan the special and supplementary programs eligible for support from federal funds to serve the educational needs that have not been adequately met in existing school programs. Similarly, the state has made the same requirement of local school agencies.

There is complete freedom on the part of school systems to establish the kinds of goals and objectives discussed in this chapter and to base such definitions on the kinds of data recommended in Chapter 3. The Manual states that "the entire range of student achievement in all areas of learning should be included in the assessment of student needs."[66] However, in carrying out the project the Manual also specifies that "the assessment strategy should include both long and short range goals and objectives that are behavioral, measurable, and representative of cognitive, affective, and psychomotor domains."[67] It is the execution of the needs-assessment program in state and local systems that raises the same issues considered in this chapter.

An important point is to note that these federal regulations, and legislation like the Stull Act in California, have compelled schools throughout the nation to define their purposes in a meaningful manner.

[65] U.S. Office of Education, *State Plan Administrator's Manual, ESEA, Title III* (Washington, D.C.: The Office, 1971), p. 20.

[66] U.S. Office of Education, *State Plan Administrator's Manual*, p. 21.

[67] U.S. Office of Education, *State Plan Administrator's Manual*, pp. 21–22.

EXAMPLES OF GOAL DEFINITION

In concluding this chapter we recommend some useful lists of goals and objectives. It is not our purpose to define the purposes of the school but rather to explain and recommend procedures and principles for formulating them. The sources we list here contain the kinds of statements that illustrate the approaches advocated throughout this book. Of course, lists of these kinds are not to be accepted willy-nilly; they are cited as examples of what curriculum groups may wish to do in their planning efforts.

General Goals

We believe that the formulation of general goals and the selection of curriculum domains should proceed together. Hence a committee may start with a tentative list of the broad aspects of schooling and then decide on general goals that state the desired nature of growth and development in each category, refining and revising both statements as work progresses.

On this basis, we suggest the following as desirable sources of help in establishing the domains:

> *Cardinal Principles of Secondary Education* (equally pertinent for education at all maturity levels).
> *The Purposes of Education in American Democracy.*
> "Chart of the Directions and Areas of Growth Toward Maturity," in Will French and associates, *Behavioral Goals of General Education in High School*, pp. 88–89.
> *Taxonomy of Educational Objectives, Handbook I, Cognitive Domain; Handbook II, Affective Domain.*
> *CSE Hierarchical Objectives Charts* (41 broad goal areas).

Lists of what we designate as general goals may be found in each of the above publications. We especially recommend the basic statement for each of twelve boxes of the French chart (items numbered 1.1, 1.2, 1.3, 1.4, 2.1, 2.2, 2.3, 2.4, 3.1, 3.2, 3.3, and 3.4, pages 92–198).

The "Imperative Educational Needs of Youth," prepared by the Educational Policies Committee and cited previously in this chapter, may also be useful in defining general goals

An important source for recommendations about the purposes and program of the school that would greatly contribute to the thinking of a curriculum planning committee in defining general goals are the two volumes containing the reports of the various forums and work groups of the 1970 White House Conference on Children and the White House Conference on Youth held in March 1971 (see Chapter 3 for more detailed information).

Subgoals and Instructional Objectives

Often publications with lists of curriculum and instructional goals do not distinguish between what we have designated as subgoals and as instructional objectives, or they develop both kinds of statements as a unit. Hence, the two types will be treated together here.

An excellent source of subgoals and objectives is the French report.[68] For each of the twelve designated goal areas, the book lists a great number of subgoals, with illustrative behaviors which constitute in fact instructional objectives (the extent of the list is shown by the fact that it extends for 123 pages).

A somewhat comparable report for the elementary school, although we emphasize that French's goals are appropriate for that level also, was prepared by Nolan Kearney. It is entitled *Elementary School Objectives* (New York: Russell Sage Foundation, 1953). It presents instructional objectives classified in nine categories that constitute aspects of living.

Most available sets of subgoals and objectives are prepared for subject fields. Such lists may be useful to committees that work on those types of curriculum plans. Unfortunately, few lists are available for other kinds of learning opportunities, such as community experiences, noninstructional activities, interactive relations of teachers and students, and the like, except as these activities stem from and relate directly to a course offering. Hence, curriculum committees will largely need to start from scratch in preparing subgoals and objectives for programs of this kind.

Sets of subgoals and objectives that have been distributed widely are those prepared for the National Assessment of Educational Progress.[69] The sets have been prepared for ten subject areas: citizenship (also a revised set), writing, science (also a revised set), reading, literature, mathematics, music, social studies, art, and career and occupational development. The booklets may be ordered from the NAEP Office, 1860 Lincoln Street, Denver, Colorado 80203.

Many handbooks and other publications are issued by a number of professional organizations concerned with curriculum and teaching in

[68] This publication is out of print, but it could be made available by reproducing, with permission, a copy obtainable at a library or repository.

[69] See Chapter 7.

a subject field. Most teachers are aware of such publications for their area of specialization. Examples are Arnold Lazarus and Rozanne Knudson, *Selected Objectives for the English Language Arts, Grades 7–12* (Boston: Houghton Mifflin Company, 1967); Albert F. Eiss and Mary Blatt Harbeck, *Behavioral Objectives in the Affective Domain* (Washington, D.C.: National Science Teachers Association, 1969); Rebecca M. Valette and Renee S. Disick, *Modern Language Performance Objectives and Individualization* (New York: Harcourt Brace Jovanovich, Inc., 1973); Donovan A. Johnson, "Behavioral Objectives for Mathematics," *School Science and Mathematics*, 71, 109–115 (February 1971); and School Mathematics Study Group, "Minimum Goals for Mathematics Education," *Newsletter*, No. 38, August 1972.

A very useful guide and source of help in writing subgoals and objectives for subject fields is the *Handbook on Formative and Summative Evaluation of Student Learning* by Bloom, Hastings, and Madaus, cited earlier in this chapter. It contains a chapter on each of eleven subject fields and includes suggestions for use of a two-dimensional chart in defining objectives.

Another useful kind of source is the curriculum guides prepared by other school systems, state departments of education, national curriculum planning groups, and other agencies concerned with curriculum development. A guide to these curriculum bulletins and materials is the annual booklet issued by the Association for Supervision and Curriculum Development, *Curriculum Materials*. It is usually issued in March.

As stated earlier, the Instructional Objectives Exchange, Box 24095, Los Angeles 90024, collects lists of instructional objectives from anyone interested in cooperating and then assembles them into sets according to subject field and in some instances grade level. These sets may be purchased.

Also, the Center for the Study of Evaluation, the parent agency for the Exchange, publishes the *CSE Hierarchical Objectives Charts* (cited on page 180), which provide extensive guides for stating subgoals and objectives. The various handbooks cited elsewhere in this chapter often contain a number of examples of objectives as well as instructions for writing them.

The formulation of the aims, goals, and objectives of the school is a very demanding, time-consuming, and, sometimes, frustrating job; yet it is an essential aspect of curriculum planning, a major factor in determining the quality of the program. These definitions may range from an overt, specific act of behavior to a broad, fundamental statement of a concept of humanism. The quality of living and being for all children and youth in U.S. schools is at stake in these efforts.

ADDITIONAL SUGGESTIONS FOR
FURTHER STUDY

Kapfer, Mariam B., ed., *Behavioral Objectives in Curriculum Development*. Englewood Cliffs, N.J.: Educational Technology Publications, 1971. An extensive collection of readings on the whole matter of behavioral objectives. This volume brings together many important articles on this movement in curriculum planning.

Macdonald, James B., "Curriculum Development in Relation to Social and Intellectual Systems," and Harry S. Broudy, "Democratic Values and Educational Goals," in Robert M. McClure, ed., *The Curriculum: Retrospect and Prospect*, 70th Yearbook, Part I, National Society for the Study of Education. Chicago: University of Chicago Press, 1971, Chapters 5 and 6. Two authorities on curriculum planning provide basic considerations for goal definition.

Mager, Robert F., *Goal Analysis*. Belmont, Calif.: Fearon Publishers, 1972. Mager recognizes the importance of intangible goals, but suggests five steps by which they may be "tangibilitated."

Maxwell, John C., and Anthony Tovatt, *On Writing Behavioral Objectives for English*. Urbana, Ill.: National Council of Teachers of English, 1970. An excellent series of articles on the reasons for using objectives, their formulation, and their use in instruction. The lead essay presents in dialogue arguments for and against the statement of objectives behaviorally.

Price, Roy A., "Goals for the Social Studies," in Dorothy McClure Fraser, ed., *Social Studies Curriculum Development: Prospects and Problems*, 39th Yearbook, National Council for the Social Studies. Washington, D.C.: The Council, 1969, pp. 33–64. An excellent chapter on the formulation of goals and objectives. Although directed to the social studies, it is helpful in recommending procedures, suggesting form, and giving examples.

"What Are Schools For?" A Symposium by Robert L. Ebel, Theodore Brameld, Joseph Junell, and T. Robert Bassett, *Phi Delta Kappan*, 54, 3–17 (September 1972). Four points of view that clarify problems and issues in defining the goals of the school.

Wight, Albert R., "Beyond Behavioral Objectives," *Educational Technology*, 12, 9–14 (July 1972). Discusses the deficiencies of behavioral objectives and proposes the separation of objectives and measurement as a solution to the problem.

5

SELECTING APPROPRIATE CURRICULUM DESIGNS

Each theory of curriculum that we have identified so far involves some concept of curriculum design. Indeed, design is the element that distinguishes one curriculum theory from another. By design is meant a particular shape, framework, or pattern of learning opportunities; thus, for any particular population, the scope and types of learning opportunities identify a curriculum design. Since the opportunities are not all provided at once, and since they lack the permanent structure of a building or the texture and color of a dress, the design is not so rapidly visualized. Yet when one observes a group of students closely following a textbook or syllabus in a subject field, it is apparent that the curriculum design is at least for this time and place a subject-focused one; if the same group is observed vigorously pursuing a discussion of happenings in their school community, it is apparent that more than one theory of design is operative in their curriculum plan. That is, alternative designs are used even in the same curriculum plan.

The purpose of this chapter is to present the concept of curriculum design, to describe various designs, and to relate designing to the total process of curriculum planning.

CURRICULUM THEORY AND CURRICULUM DESIGN

Curriculum theory and curriculum design are almost inextricably related. The theorist's notion as to the nature of design and his own reasoning as to what is appropriate design are at the core of his theory. Earlier we described three major curriculum concepts that differed from our view of the curriculum as a plan: (1) the curriculum as subjects and subject matter; (2) the curriculum as experiences; and (3) the curriculum as objectives.

The first two of these concepts and the theories supporting them, in particular, reflect contrasting designs. Although the concept of the curriculum as objectives permits alternative designs, some extensions of this concept into a performance-based curriculum make relatively narrowly defined objectives the scope and pattern of the curriculum plan.

Indeed, the preoccupation of some curriculum theorists with a single principle or focus may be partially responsible for the confusion in curriculum theory. In 1962 Taba scored the tendency of designs "to center their rationale in some single criterion or principle":

> This tendency to rationalize a curriculum pattern in terms of a single principle, at least in theoretical statements, while overlooking the relevance of other equally important considerations is in effect a gross oversimplification which has many undesirable consequences. One is a kind of myopia in developing and implementing curriculum designs. The patterns for the scope and sequence appropriate for social studies have been discussed as if they were equally appropriate for all subjects. The designs which have been tested only on the elementary level have been extended into high school without testing their appropriateness on that level.[1]

We believe that a curriculum design does involve the selection of a single designing principle. The fallacy lies in the assumption that the single principle—the discipline or some other—can and should be applied to the entire curriculum. As Taba indicated, the adherence to a single design eliminates learning opportunities which cannot be so designed.

[1]Hilda Taba, *Curriculum Development: Theory and Practice* (New York: Harcourt Brace Jovanovich, Inc., 1962), pp. 414–415.

Our position is that curriculum planners should design whatever learning opportunities are most appropriate for the domains and objectives; in other words, design should follow function rather than vice versa, and consequently a comprehensive curriculum plan may utilize more than one design. Any curriculum theory which posits a single design as appropriate to the total array of learning opportunities a school can provide deserves such criticism at Taba's.

CURRICULUM DOMAINS AND DESIGNS

In this book we view curriculum as a system that moves from goals into curriculum domains, with the total curriculum plan including curriculum design, implementation, and evaluation (see Figure 3, page 23). The relation between curriculum domains and design is explained in this section.

Gap between Goals and Design

The gap that exists in many schools between broad goals of the curriculum and its design(s) results from too ready adoption of single-principle designs in which objectives are imbedded that may bear little relation to school goals as determined at another level. Indeed, persons at other levels in the school may not even be consulted by the committees or teaching groups who ultimately settle on the curriculum design and its plan for implementation. As Taba put it:

> the lack of relationship among objectives, the content outline, and the evaluation program has often been noted. Objectives tend to be more ambitious than the provisions for learning experience warrant. Evidently, the conceptual framework of the newer curriculum designs does not provide adequately for moving from objectives to content or the instructional pattern and from both to the methods and the manner of evaluation.[2]

Goodlad and Klein's firsthand study of primary classrooms led them to conclude that "a sense of direction or priorities for each individual school" was lacking, with classroom programs being "remarkably similar from school to school, regardless of location and local realities"; in fact, they concluded that there was a "notable absence of total staff or small group dialogue about education in general or school plans and prospects."[3]

[2] Taba, p. 417.

[3] John I. Goodlad, M. Frances Klein, and associates, *Behind the Classroom Door* (Worthington, O.: Charles A. Jones Publishing Company, 1970), pp. 78–79.

Charles Silberman's study of the schools, culminating in his popular *Crisis in the Classroom*, led him to conclude that "mindlessness" was the central problem and to recommend a continuing "infusion" of purpose.[4]

The Concept of Curriculum Domains

We have included in our models of curriculum planning the concept of curriculum domains. The *domain*, in this theory of curriculum planning, is created and defined by a set of broad educational goals. For example, if the curriculum has as one central goal the development by each student of more effective human relations, there needs to be a broad grouping of learning opportunities which the planners view as contributing to the achievement of effective human relations. The curriculum planners identify these opportunities and suggest ways and means of initiating and/or evaluating them. In this process one or more designs are selected to give these learning opportunities greater relatedness and cohesion. The variety of opportunities even within a single domain may be such that more than one design is needed. For example, much content in the social studies area may be relevant to the human relations domain for a particular school and population, and the most appropriate design for this may be a subject one. But other opportunities considered relevant may be in the social life of the school, and for classifying these the planners may prefer a needs and interests design. That is, a single set of goals defines a broad categorization of learning opportunities we define as a domain but *not* a single design that patterns all of these opportunities into one mold.

As already observed, the weaknesses of traditional designing efforts and the theories to which they relate lie in the assumption that a curriculum plan should have a single design. Thus past curriculum practice has tended to try to fit all curriculum innovations into the traditional subject mold, with its attendant sequential expectations, including a grading system, mastery and achievement levels, and even credits and hourly schedules. In using this approach the goals get bypassed, for learning opportunities needed to achieve some broad goals do not fit into these molds. The situation Taba described over a decade ago has become even more chaotic in today's schools, in which goals are changing and efforts are being made to introduce new learning opportunities but without modifying curriculum design:

Decisions leading to changes in curriculum organization have been made largely by pressure, by hunches, or in terms of expediency instead of being

[4] Charles E. Silberman, *Crisis in the Classroom* (New York: Random House, Inc., 1970), p. 11.

based on clear-cut theoretical considerations or tested knowledge. The scope of the curriculum has been extended vastly without an adequate consideration of the consequences of this extension on sequence or cumulative learning. The order in which subjects are taught has been shifted. All this has been done without fundamental reconsideration of the assumptions underlying the classical curriculum. The result has been to make the curriculum, especially that of the high school, an unmanageable, overcrowded hodgepodge, an atomistic cafeteria table of offerings, and to play havoc with whatever sequence the traditional subjects represented and achieved.[5]

We view the designing of a curriculum somewhat as we do the planning of a building. Each part (floor, wing, and so on) has a particular function—it is a "domain"—and its features are selected to serve this function. Even within a wing there may be subfunctions, requiring different designs of furnishings and decoration. The designs are also chosen to create particular effect(s) the architect and decorator believe are appropriate to the functions of the building and to the people who use it. Similarly, a curriculum domain serves a particular set of goals, and the learning opportunities contained in it are relevant to these goals. Further, the learning opportunities are grouped and shaped so as to create the particular design(s) the planners believe are appropriate to the goals and to the population. The population served by the curriculum domain tends to change more rapidly than the occupants of the building, and the learning opportunities and their designs may need much more frequent change than the furnishings of the offices, suites, apartments, or other components of the building. Unfortunately, curriculum designs and opportunities tend to become fixed and to become as inappropriate for successive populations as would the old furnishings for new types of building domains and new occupants with different ideas as to the functions of their quarters.

STEPS IN CURRICULUM DESIGNING

As presented in this book the curriculum planning process involves four principal phases:

1. Setting major goals (and domains) through basic data analysis
2. Designing curriculum domains, each related to one major set of goals
3. Anticipating curriculum implementation (instruction)
4. Planning curriculum evaluation.

[5] Taba, pp. 383–384.

Our concern here is with the second phase, designing, and we now consider the process in detail. Our treatment assumes the prior selection of major goals and domains, as described above.

Step One—Considering Basic Factors
Relating to the Domain

Much as the curriculum planners may have consulted data about social aims and needs, learners and the learning processes, and knowledge requirements, they will need to focus on specific data relevant to a domain and population when these are known. For example, assume that the faculty of a middle school has identified as *one* of its major goals assisting each of its students to explore and identify special interests that can become bases for continued and successful learning and living. Immediately such questions as the following are raised: What special interests do our students already have? What other interests are appropriate and feasible for such a population? Of present and possible interests, are any unacceptable in this community? Of present and possible interests, which have carry-over effect into future academic-, career-, or leisure-oriented activities? Of present and possible interests, which are possible for development within our school and community? Consideration of these types of questions is essential to further planning within this particular domain.

Step Two—Identifying Subgoals of the Domain

The hierarchy of goals and objectives was fully explained in Chapter 4. Designing requires goal setting on a second level. It involves moving from the broad goal of a domain to subgoals that are hypothesized as achievable for a particular population and within the potentials of the domain. Subgoals need not be narrowly stated; they may be open-ended statements of desired outcomes broadly defined.

For example, we can easily assume that any elementary school faculty would set as one broad goal helping its students to attain skills of continued learning. Within the learning skills domain subgoals would be set relating to skills of reading, listening, questioning, organizing information, and others. The more specific the data the faculty has consulted regarding the current status of student learning skills, the more specific subgoals become.

Or, for another example, a high school faculty might place high priority on the major goal of developing skills of independent, self-directed learning. Its study of the nature of such learning activity and its analysis of the needs of the students in this area would lead to subgoals relating to independent study practices, motivation for independent learning, selection of curriculum options, self-evaluation patterns, and others.

Step Three—Identifying Possible Types of Learning Opportunities

The third step in curriculum designing is a blend of visionary brainstorming and realistic appraisal of actual possibilities. For example, the middle school faculty seeking to develop a special interests domain has to reconcile all of its dreaming, perhaps augmented by the hopes of the students themselves, with activities that are actually possible given the personnel and facilities of the school and community. The limitations may be far less than those usually operating if the faculty includes the possibilities of community facilities, public media, and community resource people.

At this stage some tentative classification is helpful both to extend the listing of opportunities and to lead toward the selection of designs. Thus one type of learning opportunity would be that of short-term exploratory courses in such areas as arts and crafts, industrial arts, music, art, and foreign languages. Another might be mini-courses related to fields of social studies and language arts: short-term arrangements supplementing basic instruction in these fields that would focus on political parties, local history, individual historical events or movements, dramatic productions, literary types or pieces, and other interests. Another type of learning opportunity would be independent study projects for students with special interests in any subject field, that is, individual projects growing out of but not required in regular group instruction. Still another type of learning opportunity, perhaps the most common, would be special activities organized for and largely by students and related to any of a very wide range of possibilities, from acrobatics to xylophones.

Similarly, in any domain this step involves identification of a few organizing centers or learning opportunities, a trial classification of these, usually according to the way in which they are provided, an extension of types that seem to persist in discussion and planning, and the ultimate development of agreed-upon, possible opportunities classified tentatively as a basis for relating them to design principles.

Step Four—Settling on Appropriate Curriculum Designs

With the domain determined, subgoals tentatively set, and possible types of learning opportunities explored, the planning group is ready for the step that is given major attention here: considering and selecting design alternatives.

A high school curriculum council seeking to develop an area or domain of specialization would undoubtedly list many subgoals relating to a wide spectrum of specialized interests to be served and advanced by the high school curriculum. If the group is or becomes knowledgeable about alternative curriculum designs, it is unlikely to settle on any one design focus for the very wide range of specialization opportunities. Instead, it might categorize opportunities into several designs.

An expected area of specialization for many students would be preparation for further study after high school in one or more subject areas. Advanced offerings in English, foreign languages, mathematics, science, and social studies would be made available for these students, and the disciplines/subjects design theories would define the scope and sequence of these opportunities.

As their area of specialization many students might choose the expressive arts. Here there is no specific design principle more applicable than the one we later describe as individual needs and interests. Although music, for example, includes systematic and sequential instruction for specific musical performance, individual interests and needs would determine the grouping and to some extent the scope and sequence of learning opportunities. Similarly, effective programs in other specialties within the arts field also seem much more appropriately planned by a needs and interests principle than by other designs.

Some high school students would specialize in skills training for occupations they can enter after high school, and for them specific vocational training would be made available. This specific training is appropriately designed in accordance with the principle we designate below as "specific competencies."

Still other specialization programs may be developed by other design principles. Thus, the specialization domain, embracing many types of specialized interests and related learning opportunities, also requires several curriculum designs. Other domains, for example, the human relations one, may also involve more than one design. The domain of continued learning skills seems clearly to match in purpose and scope the design principle we describe as learning processes.

It should be emphasized that a planning group may well set domains other than the four we have illustrated, but the matching of domains and designs is a process requiring the steps described above as well as a knowledge of alternative designs. Without such steps and such knowledge, designing is lacking or inadequate, as is generally the case when all learning opportunities are reduced to so-called subjects and designed according to the traditional subject design with its attendant textbooks, homework, examinations, and credit units.

Step Five—Preparing Tentative Design Specifications

Step five is a refinement of Step four. At the latter point the designing group makes a trial listing of types of learning opportunities— study units, skills sequences, activity groupings, subjects or courses, mini-courses, community experiences, independent studies, and so forth—as a basis for selecting design principles. Once the designs have been selected, learning opportunities are more deliberately planned. Thus a plan for the domain of human relations might include at least two major designs, disciplines/subjects and social activities and problems. In the first category would be placed specific subject matter related to the human relations goal—history of the movements in the world and in the United States to advance human relations and the conditions of human life; concepts in sociology, political science, economics, and other social sciences; and other subject matter. The design specifications would indicate organizing centers for this content and possible instructional organizations such as interdisciplinary units, mini-courses, and semester- or year-long courses.

In the second category, social problems and processes, the designing group might very well place many learning opportunities frequently classified as "activities": student government, homeroom, community services, student forums, civic participation, human relations councils, and others. The tentative answers to these questions for each such opportunity are the basic ones in all design specifications:

1. For what learners?
2. For which subgoals or objectives of the domain?
3. What types of learning experiences?
4. Roles of participants: learners, teachers, others?
5. What time and space dimensions?
6. Criteria for assessment?

Step Six—Identifying Implementation Requirements

With tentative decisions made regarding the questions just listed, the designers can identify requirements for implementation. Imagine that a middle school planning group has designed a series of teaching units around the subject matter of human relations movements and events and has planned for these units to be developed for two teams of 120 students each. Implementation requirements would include arranging for the appropriate team teachers or leaders, especially in social studies and language arts, to prepare the detailed unit plans, deciding on a physical setting for large-group instruction, and ordering any special materials.

Implementation requirements for some designs can be more demanding. For example, a design in the personal development domain might include systematic instruction in sex education, drug abuse, or other sensitive areas. For this, implementation may well require advance communication with parents, approval of appropriate community groups

and agencies, and enlistment of special professional assistance in instruction. Or the social activities design for learning opportunities through
civic participation would likely require considerable advance spadework
in the community to identify and screen possible opportunities in government agencies, civic associations, and other organizations.

DESIGNS FOCUSED ON SPECIFIC COMPETENCIES

We now consider particular curriculum designs. As we view the
various design possibilities, the most narrow or limited ones are those
that focus on specific competencies. It matters little whether the competencies are stated in terms of the activity analysis procedures of the
1920s, the related job analysis used in vocational education for many
years, or the competency- or performance-based curriculum and instructional plans widely promoted in the early 1970s. In describing these and
the other designs included in subsequent sections of this chapter we will
deal with their characteristic features, the arguments or case for them,
and their applications, both actual and potential, and limitations.

Characteristic Features

The performance-based objectives and curriculum plans advocated in part as a phase of the accountability movement of the 1970s
seem distinctly related to many earlier curriculum theories and practices
that also emphasized performance. Obviously, all curriculum plans anticipate some type of eventual performance on the part of the learner, but
the design we are describing assumes a direct relation among objective,
learning activity, and performance. Other designs assume a much less
direct relation among these components, and to some extent they anticipate that the learner's ultimate behavior will be the outgrowth of many
learning experiences through which he fashions his own performance
objectives and standards. In a competency-based design, the desired
performances are stipulated as behavioral or performance objectives or
competencies, learning activities are planned to achieve each objective,
and the learner's performance is checked as a basis for his moving from
one objective to another. Thus, in typing instruction the learner must
demonstrate his knowledge of the keyboard before he moves to mastery
of particular typing forms. In golf he learns and shows how to grip the
club before he learns and shows how to make particular strokes with it.
In social studies he learns how to read a map and demonstrates this competency before he learns about and demonstrates his knowledge of
particular geographic locations and relations. Thus, a design based on

specific competencies is characterized by specific, sequential, and demonstrable learnings of the tasks, activities, or skills which constitute the acts to be learned and performed by students.

The Case for Designs Focused on Specific Competencies

The earliest published justification of a competency-based curriculum design appeared in 1918 in Bobbitt's *The Curriculum*. In this and a related volume (1924) describing the Los Angeles curriculum program, Bobbitt argued for an activity analysis approach to curriculum planning. His theory, he said, was "simple":

> The word *curriculum* is Latin for a *race-course*, or the *race* itself —a place of deeds, or a series of deeds. As applied to education, it is that *series of things which children and youth must do and experience* by way of developing abilities to do the things well that make up the affairs of adult life; and to be in all respects what adults should be.[6]

In further developing this theory Bobbitt distinguished between "directed" and "undirected" training experience. He proposed that the curriculum aim at objectives not attained by undirected training and that "the curriculum of the directed training is to be discovered in the shortcomings of individuals after they have had all that can be done in the undirected training."[7] Bobbitt recognized that his activity analysis procedures would be more easily applied in "spelling, grammar, and other subjects that result in objective performance, such as pronunciation, drawing, music, computation, etc.," but argued that it was equally valid in its application to all other fields, including "civic, moral, vocational, sanitational, recreational, and parental education"[8]:

> Only as we agree upon *what ought to be* in each of these difficult fields, can we know at what the training should aim. Only as we list the errors and shortcomings of human performance in each of the fields can we know what to include and to emphasize in the directed curriculum of the schools.

To Bobbitt the case for a curriculum based on activity analysis and leading to performance was basically that of the lack of relevance, in more recent terminology, of past curriculum practice to present human needs and the resultant deficiencies in human affairs. By focusing educa-

[6] Franklin Bobbitt, *The Curriculum* (Boston: Houghton Mifflin Company, 1918), p. 42.

[7] Bobbitt, *The Curriculum*, p. 45.

[8] Bobbitt, *The Curriculum*, pp. 51–52.

tion on the "shortcomings of children and men" the schools can discharge new and needed functions, he argued.[9] Bobbitt's report of curriculum development in Los Angeles presented a classification of hundreds of objectives by subject fields; however, he cautioned against starting with the subjects in this description of the process of defining abilities.[10] Thus to Bobbitt the essential step in designing was the development of objectives by analysis of human needs and deficiencies of undirected training; this step, he felt, would give the schools proper focus:

> The comprehensive working list of abilities should be put into printed form. This makes them definite. It prevents their becoming confused and changed through processes of discussion. It enables all concerned to have the same things before them and the same things in mind at once. It enables one to see the entire range of abilities as he considers any one of them or any group of them. It assists in seeing each in relation to all. It prevents losing sight of any one of them. It assists in providing a broad common ground of understanding for all concerned.[11]

More detail on activity analysis was presented by W. W. Charters in his 1923 publication, *Curriculum Construction*, which Bobbitt cited frequently in his book of the following year as the source to follow in the analysis process. Charters' own statement as to the weakness of curriculum planning is the familiar criticism of the gap between educational aims and the selection and teaching of subject matter; in fact, it is the rationale for our own use some fifty years later of curriculum domains as a classification scheme:

> While writers on the curriculum have begun with the statement of aim, none has been able to derive a curriculum logically from his statement of aim. In every case he has made an arbitrary mental leap from the *aim* to the *subject matter*, without providing us with adequate principles such as would bridge the gap—without presenting steps which irresistibly lead us from aim to selection of materials.[12]

Charters proposed that the curriculum should be derived from both "ideals" and "activities": "Activities are not carried on without ideals to govern, and ideals will not operate except through activities." Activity

[9] Bobbitt, *The Curriculum*, p. iv.

[10] Franklin Bobbitt, *How To Make a Curriculum* (Boston: Houghton Mifflin Company, 1924), pp. 39–40.

[11] Bobbitt, *How To Make a Curriculum*, p. 37.

[12] W. W. Charters, *Curriculum Construction* (New York: The Macmillan Company, 1923), pp. 6–7.

analysis was regarded by Charters as an extension of job analysis, which, he suggested, could be done through at least four methods: (1) introspection, (2) interviewing, (3) working on the job, and (4) questionnaires. He also described the "difficulty analysis" Bobbitt had cited and summarized the importance of the whole process in these words:

> In determining the activities upon which instruction is to be given, analysis is necessary. This may be done by the use of job analysis in certain types of situation, or by setting up control elements in informational analysis. Difficulty analysis indicates the duties and information upon which special emphasis must be laid in the curriculum. Without such analysis we are entirely at a loss to know how to proceed in building the curriculum.[13]

Charters' "rules for curriculum construction" gave major emphasis to the definition of objectives, ideals, and activities.[14] Thus, Charters and Bobbitt some fifty years ago were arguing for a designing process that would give priority in curriculum planning to analytical procedures focused on teaching students to perform the activities and demonstrate the ideals determined by analysis of human needs and activities as significant for direct training. In this way, they reasoned, the curriculum would be more relevant, more attainable, and more efficient.

Undoubtedly, these early curriculum theorists substantially influenced processes of curriculum development by their emphasis on specific objectives and on analytical procedures for defining them. They placed objectives before subject matter and called for a curriculum plan which would be built around specific life activities of adults. Their theories did not include a detailed plan for relating instruction to each activity or objective, although they clearly anticipated a close relation.[15] It was over four decades later that a movement toward the use of behavioral objectives linked objectives, instruction, and performance in a narrower sense than Bobbitt and Charters had advocated. The behavioral objectives movement is discussed in Chapter 4, and here we merely note the use of this approach in a competency-based curriculum design. This use is exemplified in a definition and model by two leading advocates, Popham and Baker. They define the curriculum as "all the planned learning outcomes for which the school is responsible" and also as "the desired consequences of instruction," and state that "using tests as measures of outcomes might better exemplify *what* is the curriculum than a list of

---

[13] Charters, p. 40.
[14] Charters, p. 102.
[15] See Bobbitt, *How To Make a Curriculum*, pp. 44–45.

texts or materials used in instruction."[16] They recommend the Tyler rationale for the identification of objectives and describe the subsequent step in curriculum design as "the precise description of the final set of objectives in operational terms."[17] Popham and Baker also admit the possibility of objectives that are not stated behaviorally, although the use of these in the design is unclear:

> It is our position that the teacher should try to state goals operationally for all those that he is *seriously trying to accomplish.* However, it seems foolhardy to select objectives and evaluate teaching proficiency on the basis of very low probability ventures such as promoting the pupil's "personality integration." One way to deal with this problem is to distinguish clearly between those goals for which you will accept *instructional responsibility* and those areas over which you would like to exert some influence, while recognizing that other factors, factors over which you have no control, are playing more important roles. Your operational instructional objectives should usually include some in the affective domain, but only for those attitudes and tendencies that are measurable and potentially modifiable in the classroom.[18]

Once the objectives have been so specifically determined, curriculum designing in this model involves these steps: (1) ordering the objectives and sub-objectives and placing them in a time frame; and (2) selecting instructional activities to promote the attainment of the objectives within the time period. Preassessment, instruction ("classroom transactions"), and evaluation follow. For evaluation Popham and Baker recommend "criterion-referenced tests," which are "tests designed exclusively to measure the objectives taught." Such tests of the performance of students, they note, "can be used to make valid judgments regarding the performance of the teacher, generally in terms of the previously established class minimal level of student performance."[19]

Obviously, there are major differences between the specific-competencies design of Bobbitt and Charters in the 1920s and those of its proponents a half century later, of whom Popham is probably the most articulate and prolific writer. In both sets of theories, however, much emphasis is placed on the definition of objectives as the first step in curriculum development; indeed, this emphasis characterizes most curriculum

[16] W. James Popham and Eva L. Baker, *Systematic Instruction* (Englewood Cliffs, N.J.: Prentice-Hall, Inc., 1970), p. 48.

[17] Popham and Baker, pp. 59–60.

[18] Popham and Baker, pp. 60–61.

[19] Popham and Baker, pp. 130–131.

design theories proposed in the fifty years between Bobbitt's and Popham's writings. A characteristic more unique to these two theorists is their insistence that the objectives should be focused on what the learner is to learn *to do*, not on what he is to study or to experience or even to know. But Bobbitt and Charters envisioned performance in far more general terms than do competency-based curriculum protagonists of today. Furthermore, the former seemingly viewed their objectives, though pointed to performance, as more general guidelines for instruction; Popham's design relates the classroom transaction and the criterion-referenced test to specific objectives so that the quality of teaching and learning can be assessed in terms of the objectives sought. Thus, the case for the behavioral objectives design, with its performance standards and tests, includes the argument that both student and teacher performance can be effectively determined by this model.

A somewhat specialized aspect of the competency-based design theories is the job analysis procedure, which we see as tending to include characteristic features of both of the theories we have just described. Indeed, Charters applied the technique of job analysis to curriculum development in general and reported in his 1923 publication many applications in diverse fields. Bobbitt's and Charters' activity analysis procedures simply extended the analysis of a vocational job to the analysis of adult activities in general as a basis for determining curriculum needs and objectives. But job analysis as a specific basis for curriculum planning in vocational education continued to be employed after the activity analyses in the 1920s and 1930s of adult activities in general became less popular approaches to curriculum development.

In its narrowest use, job analysis involves specification of the basic skills of a trade or occupation and development of specific training activities for the skills in a sequential arrangement. Although most vocational education programs have been broadened over the years since job analysis was introduced, there remains a strong core of specific job training. Its nature and justification were described in the following terms by Haskew and Tumlin:

> Content which is dominantly oriented toward performance . . . may be derived from modern analysis of the dynamics of job-evolution and worker-progression, rather than from stilted job descriptions. It may focus on life-off-the-job as well as life-on-the-job. But, the prime criteria proposed for selection are (a) the performance ability essential to success, as judged by the employer and by the employee himself, and (b) the knowledge, understanding, and ability necessary to the worker's continued progress and adequacy in a dynamic occupational world. These criteria almost dictate

considerable reliance upon practice as the means for acquiring the content selected, since actual performance is the referent.[20]

Obviously, all workers must learn the skills of their trade. To the extent that the school trains its students for particular jobs, a job analysis basis for specific job training is essential. This curriculum design contributes efficiently to the development of job competency. Motivation on the basis of job aspirations is high in this phase of the curriculum, and it contributes to the development of talents and capabilities not fully provided for in other curriculum designs. Furthermore, specific job training utilizes to the fullest the maxim that learning results from experience, and the more meaningful and significant the experience, the more is learned.

Applications and Limitations

A competency-based approach to curriculum development has been used at some time in some way in virtually every curriculum area. What teacher has not dreamed of teaching his students to perform as he would have them with some simple formula of training to intervene between objective and learned performance? One of us recalls trying to teach citizenship attitudes and behaviors by a system of merits and demerits for observed behavior; indeed, most military training and some other types have long used such systems. But performance can be contrived and falsified, especially when it becomes a basis for marks and rewards and punishment; in the affective domain and even in many cognitive areas one soon encounters fallacies and insurmountable difficulties in shaping one-to-one matches of specific competencies and learning experiences.

As we see it, and as we noted earlier in our discussion of behavioral objectives, competency-based curriculum plans have much utility for some objectives but are futile for others. Specifically, these designs have maximum utility in the learning skills and specialized training domains of the curriculum. The failure of many adults to exercise adequately skills of continued learning through critical reading, listening, and discussion is evidence of past failures on the part of the schools to develop the skills and the will to continue learning. Much of this failure is due, we believe, to norm-referenced group instruction—or perhaps even a lack of instruction—in major learning skills, all of which may be

[20] Lawrence D. Haskew and Inez Wallace Tumlin, "Vocational Education in the Curriculum of the Common School," in Melvin L. Barlow, ed., *Vocational Education,* Sixty-fourth Yearbook, National Society for the Study of Education, Part I (Chicago: University of Chicago Press, 1965), p. 77.

traced to a lack of adequate curriculum planning for skills instruction. In this domain clearly focused, sequential instruction based on specification of objectives, diagnosis of skills status and difficulties, and individualized instruction, with adequate posttesting and recycling, is highly logical. The design must, of course, include many measures for ensuring the learner's interest in using each skill for purposes important to him.

Similarly, many specialized interests require a type of competency or job analysis with specific designs of learning opportunities fashioned toward desired performance. In terms of usual curriculum areas, we see such commonly available opportunities as those in the arts, foreign languages, and vocational and technical education as having a definite emphasis on specific competencies once the general education and exploration of interest phases have yielded defined interests for specialized training in art, music, dramatics, journalism, proficiency in a language, or training for a particular job. Furthermore, most of the school's extrainstructional learning opportunities—athletics, photography, community service or work roles, for example—involve specific training which focuses on performance objectives. And in-depth specialization for continued study in any discipline may involve learning the processes and procedure of the discipline to a high level of competence as a mathematician, scientist, or social scientist, for example.

But we do not see specific competencies as the basis of curriculum designs for most learning opportunities in the curriculum domains of personal development and human relations. A possible exception is in health, physical, and safety education where some competencies such as those of routine care of the body, physical exercise, and driver education may be developed on a performance basis with due attention to individual differences and attitudes. But in these domains there is heavy emphasis on affective objectives and on human interaction, and for these we consider other designs far more appropriate.

DESIGNS FOCUSED ON DISCIPLINES/SUBJECTS

We have noted that the dominant concept of the curriculum, historically and currently, is that of school subjects taught by teachers and learned by students. Correspondingly, the dominant curriculum design is that of a curriculum framework of subjects, usually but not necessarily derived from the major disciplines of knowledge, with the framework reflecting design decisions as to specific subjects and their scope and sequence. Attention is now given to the characteristic features of this familiar design, the case for it, and its applications and limitations.

Characteristic Features

The most characteristic and comprehensive feature of the subject design is the relative orderliness of this pattern. The curriculum plan appears neatly divided into subjects, which themselves frequently are subdivided into divisions corresponding to school grades and even marking and reporting periods. The Carnegie unit system entrenched the subject design and a related schedule in the high school with the original definition (1909) of a unit of credit as the study of a subject in high school for one period a day throughout the school year. Even before such a curriculum accounting system was developed, the subject design was regularized to facilitate the expansion of schooling for America's expanding population. The educational historian Lawrence A. Cremin credits the efforts during the 1870s of a St. Louis school superintendent, William Torrey Harris, to define the curriculum as the beginning of the modern curriculum movement. Cremin interprets Harris' theory of education and the curriculum as holding the curriculum responsible for making the accumulated wisdom of the race "economically and systematically available" and describes Harris' "analytical paradigm" as embracing the following components:

> There is the learner, self-active and self-willed by virtue of his humanity and thus self-propelled into the educative process; there is the course of study, organized by responsible adults with appropriate concern for priority, sequence, and scope; there are materials of instruction which particularize the course of study; there is the teacher who encourages and mediates the process of instruction; there are the examinations which appraise it; and there is the organizational structure within which it proceeds and within which large numbers of individuals are enabled simultaneously to enjoy its benefits.[21]

This, Cremin writes, set forth "all the pieces . . . for the game of curriculum-making that would be played over the next half-century"; indeed, Cremin further shows, as we will review later, the marked similarity between Harris' efforts at curriculum reform in the 1870s and those of other reformers in the 1950s and 1960s.

A more significant type of orderliness characterizes the disciplines/subject design, however, than these somewhat mechanical aspects. This is the inherent principle or structure of a discipline. The structure of a discipline is the set of fundamental generalizations that bind a field of knowledge into a unity, organize this body of knowledge into a cohesive whole, fix the limits of investigation and inclusion of knowledge for

[21] Lawrence A. Cremin, "Curriculum-Making in the United States," *Teachers College Record*, 73, 210 (December 1971).

the discipline itself, and provide the basis for discovering what else exists within the field. Thus, each of the traditional school subjects such as mathematics, chemistry, and physics, which are well-ordered disciplines, has its own distinct design, and the school curriculum planner has only to determine what of this design to use, and when and how. But the structure of other subjects created for practical and important purposes is very unclear, if not completely lacking.

Hence with the subject design there is a confusion as to what is a subject and what internal logic there is in the design. At least three usages of the term "subject" confuse the disciplines/subject design principle of internal order. First, in the selection of a particular phase of a discipline for school study such distortion can occur as to make invalid the usual structure of the discipline. For example, various efforts to select and simplify aspects of mathematics and physical science, respectively, into so-called practical or general mathematics and consumer or practical chemistry necessitate the creation of special scope and sequence plans for these courses. Second, the widespread practice, especially in the elementary school curriculum, of encompassing materials from more than one basic discipline, for example, incorporating history and anthropology into social studies, has also necessitated special designing of some order of the content. Third, in many cases the established disciplines do not offer students opportunities to learn to deal with problems of living, and new organizations of content that are basically extradisciplinary or perhaps interdisciplinary have been created and classified as subjects. Business education, character education, driver education, drug education, environmental education, family life education, homemaking education, health education, industrial arts education, physical education, and safety education are just a few of the many invented subjects.

Thus, while the established disciplines and the subjects clearly derived from them have an order or structure which marks their designs, many so-called subjects have no inherent design, and their planning may well use any of the other design principles we are considering. In practice, these latter subjects may be so diverse and their design of such varied quality as to make the total design appear confused and shapeless when the same schedule and instructional organization are used for all curriculum elements from algebra to office machines or from athletics to zoology.

The Case for the Disciplines/Subjects Design

Curriculum publications have long been replete with arguments for and against a curriculum organization based on subjects. One of the most persistent and perhaps the most influential argument has been that of educational convenience; that is, since knowledge is organized into disciplines which can be used or adapted as school subjects, the easiest way to set a school curriculum, the argument says, is to use these subjects, providing a matching instructional organization and student progress system. Selecting and teaching subject matter and testing student knowledge thereof is the process, and it is argued that this can be readily implemented by knowledgeable teachers, organization into classes, and written tests. This argument of convenience assumes that schools, colleges, teachers, parents, and citizens in general are geared to the subject-centered curriculum and support wholeheartedly this organizational plan. In effect, the argument is for maintaining the status quo because it is simpler to do so; we cannot accept this view. The case has to rest on the relative values of the subject design.

The values of the design are derived from the important role of knowledge in the curriculum. Here there can be no real quarrel, for there would indeed be no curriculum if there were no content, no knowledge to use as the substance of experience. The kinds and amounts of knowledge and its availability for school use are major determinants of the curriculum. Since knowledge is organized into disciplines, it follows logically that the disciplines are primary sources of curriculum content. The strongest advocate of a disciplines design goes further and makes the disciplines synonymous with the curriculum. In their well-developed curriculum theory King and Brownell summarized their position as follows:

> We have defined the school as a microcosm of the world of intellect. The curriculum in the disciplines is the heart of such a school. The curricular function is paramount. The nondiscipline curriculum—straightforward occupational, social, and personal training—should not under any circumstances replace an element of the liberal curriculum for any student.[22]

Although outspoken in their theory as to the primacy of the disciplines, King and Brownell were envisioning a plan for the continuing development of the disciplines and in no way assuming a static content. Indeed, the curriculum theorists who argue for disciplines/subjects designs generally assume a continuing process of changing knowledge and changing subject matter in the curriculum. Their case emphasizes the fact that the disciplines and correspondingly the school subjects have an internal structure to which new knowledge can be added and from which obsolescent knowledge can be dropped. The bodies of subject matter, they believe, best help the learner to test out information, to answer questions, to inquire, to reconstruct his own knowledge and use it—in short, to develop his intellectual powers.

[22] Arthur R. King, Jr., and John A. Brownell, *The Curriculum and the Disciplines of Knowledge* (New York: John Wiley & Sons, Inc., 1966), p. 119.

The disciplines/subjects designers generally assume that there is a body of knowledge that constitutes the curriculum and that the task of designing involves decisions as to what phases and organizations of knowledge are to be taught to whom, and when and how. Thus Henry Clinton Morrison, whose Morrisonian unit curriculum and instructional system greatly influenced high school curriculum planning from the 1920s into the 1950s and even later, described the curriculum as "constant and universal." Thus "the content of Education is at bottom the same the world over, and the framework upon which that content is hung, namely, the Curriculum, is the same in essentials. The *pedagogical problems* arise in the fields of programming and of teaching."[23] In *The Curriculum of the Common School* he identified major phases of twelve "universal institutions" (language, mathematics, graphics, science, religion, morality and moral institutions, art, civics, politics, commerce, industry, and health) that he considered to be "the curriculum of the common school," or as he further defined it, "the content of the general education of the common man."

In *A Functional Curriculum for Youth*, published a decade after Morrison's book, William B. Featherstone also upheld the role of the subjects and emphasized the necessity of selecting and programming appropriate content, noting that "the practical problem of how to program a curriculum so that the essential contents—essential for general education—of all necessary subjects can be taught effectively has become increasingly difficult to solve satisfactorily."[24] He argued for a selection of content to be based on the "functions" of the curriculum and proposed a curriculum plan not unlike our own concept of "domains." The four functions Featherstone outlined are integration, supplementation, exploration, and specialization; this view involved a different conception of the functions of the subjects and their solution, but not their abandonment:

Efforts to devise a suitable curriculum by vitalizing the conventional subjects, reshuffling them into new patterns, or amalgamating them into broad fields do not seem promising. It is probably not necessary to scrap the entire conventional curriculum, but it is apparent that an improved conception of the structure and functions of the curriculum is needed before one can decide what parts of the old curriculum can be salvaged and for what purpose.[25]

[23] Henry Clinton Morrison, *The Curriculum of the Common School* (Chicago: University of Chicago Press, 1940), p. 5.

[24] William B. Featherstone, *A Functional Curriculum for Youth* (New York: American Book Company, 1950), p. 112.

[25] Featherstone, p. 133.

In fact, Featherstone's theory justified existing subjects and called for new ones to serve the specialization function.[26]

Writing almost two decades after Featherstone, Alpren also emphasized the role of educational functions in curriculum development, but embraced the intellectual function as the priority one, taking a position then on the disciplines/subjects approach similar to that of King and Brownell.[27]

This emphasis on the intellectual component of the curriculum was clearly stimulated by the post-Sputnik emphasis on mathematics and the sciences beginning in the late 1950s. This reappraisal of the contributions of education to the defense posture of the United States as it faced competition with Russia in space technology brought about an infusion of federal dollars into curriculum development through the National Defense Education Act, the National Science Foundation, and later federal acts and appropriations. The new phenomena in curriculum development were the national curriculum projects, hundreds of which were established beginning in the late 1950s, with many still continuing in the 1970s. We cited in Chapter 2 the formula for curriculum planning and improvement in these projects described by Zacharias, the original director of the Physical Science Study Committee, and White.[28] The questions they saw as determining the subject matter of a unit were: "First, what is it desired that the student learn from the unit? Second, what selection of material and what ordering of that material will make it most probable that he will indeed learn?"[29] The basic intents of the projects were described by Jerome Bruner in his widely cited report of the 1959 Woods Hole Conference of project directors, in which he advanced the case for teaching the structure of the subjects:

> the curriculum of a subject should be determined by the most fundamental understanding that can be achieved of the underlying principles that give structure to that subject. . . . Organizing facts in terms of principles and ideas from which they may be inferred is the only known way of reducing the quick rate of loss of human memory.[30]

Emphasis on structure, he wrote, would help each student to achieve his

---

[26] Featherstone, p. 143.

[27] Morton Alpren, ed., *The Subject Curriculum, Grades K–12* (Columbus, O.: Charles E. Merrill Books, Inc., 1967), p. 38.

[28] See Jerrold R. Zacharias and Stephen White, "The Requirements for Major Curriculum Revision," in Robert W. Heath, ed., *New Curricula* (New York: Harper & Row, Publishers, 1964).

[29] Zacharias and White, p. 71.

[30] Jerome S. Bruner, *The Process of Education* (Cambridge, Mass.: Harvard University Press, 1960), pp. 31–32.

"optimum intellectual development"[31] and provide "a general picture in terms of which the relations between things encountered earlier and later are made as clear as possible."[32]

Thus, proponents of the disciplines/subjects design have going for them the undeniably strong argument that knowledge is of necessity at the base of the curriculum. Knowledge is organized into disciplines, and school subjects organized out of these disciplines can be the skeleton of the curriculum. Whether the ultimate organization presents the subjects through Morrison's "institutions," Featherstone's "functions," our "domains," or through "new" subject organizations, it is still basically a disciplines/subjects design focused on the intellectual development of the learner.

Applications and Limitations

The utilization of the disciplines/subjects design is well known and has been described at various points in this chapter. To summarize these references, we suggest two generalizations: (1) knowledge from the disciplines as reflected in the organization of school subjects has been and remains the dominant design of curriculum planning; (2) many curriculum elements called subjects have been created to meet curriculum needs that are not matched by disciplinary content and have tended to confuse curriculum design with the program of studies. Our further discussion of the limitations of the subject design will build upon these two points.

First, the tendency in curriculum development to create "subjects" that have no real basis in organized disciplines reveals the inadequacy of the subject design used alone. Most of the other designs we consider in this chapter are ways of achieving curriculum goals other than through the acquisition of existing knowledge as organized in disciplines and academic subjects. But such factors as accrediting standards, graduation and college entrance requirements, elementary school time allotments, and secondary school schedules have recognized subjects as the curriculum, so that whatever has been added, however unrelated it might be to the traditional disciplines, has been classified as a subject. Once so classified, the subject has tended to become fixed and the curriculum that much more inflexible. In his classic satire on the curriculum, Harold Benjamin (alias J. Abner Peddiwell) put in the mouth of the old men of the tribe the traditional argument for the established fundamentals (here "the saber-tooth curriculum"):

---

[31] Bruner, *The Process of Education*, pp. 9–10.
[32] Bruner, *The Process of Education*, pp. 11–12.

With all the intricate details of fish-grabbing, horse-clubbing, and tiger-scaring—the standard cultural subjects—the school curriculum is too crowded now. We can't add these fads and frills of net-making, antelope-snaring, and—of all things—bear-killing. . . . You must know that there are some eternal verities, and the saber-tooth curriculum is one of them.[33]

Other limitations of the subjects due to the schools' tendency to fix them inflexibly and separately have occasioned many criticisms and limitations. For example, Beauchamp's review of curriculum design theories noted the absence of adequate plans for relating the subjects as taught to particular students day by day.[34]

The national projects, however much they helped to discard obsolete material and introduce new subject matter, did not basically change the curriculum design; in fact, Cremin likened the Zacharias model of project development to the Harris one of nearly a century earlier, noting that:

Seeking to rid himself of the pedagogical preoccupations of the Progressive Era by avoiding the literature of education, Zacharias ended up by accepting the paradigm of curriculum-making that had prevailed for three-quarters of a century. And in avoiding the literature, he and others like him inevitably impoverished the character of educational discussion. Insistently eschewing the past, the curriculum reformers of the fifties and sixties eventually became its captives. . . .[35]

A leading scientist who was instrumental in the development of the Biological Sciences Curriculum Study, Bentley Glass, noted the needs for continuing revision of subjects and for continuing education of teachers in them if the subject design is maintained:

During the past decade we have seen, in the United States, the development of numerous curriculum studies, first revitalizing the secondary school teaching of physics, mathematics, chemistry, biology, and earth sciences, and later extended to elementary school science and mathematics. . . . Yet one must recognize, sadly, that very few of the teachers now in our schools are prepared to take any new curriculum and utilize it well. Often their enthusiasm outruns their knowledge and their current skill. Moreover, the new curricula, which must at best be regarded as no more than a few steps in the right direction, must be continuously revised to keep pace with

[33] J. Abner Peddiwell, *The Saber-Tooth Curriculum* (New York: McGraw-Hill Book Company, 1939), pp. 41–44.

[34] George A. Beauchamp, *Curriculum Theory*, 2d ed. (Wilmette, Ill.: The Kaag Press, 1968), p. 104.

[35] Cremin, "Curriculum-Making in the United States," p. 216.

the advances of science and the development of fresh human problems. Hence, the teachers must be trained not once, but many times over, throughout their professional lives.[36]

Furthermore, the "new" subject matter, with its emphasis on inquiry and problem-solving, frequently has been introduced in inflexible school organizations poorly adapted to achieving such goals.[37] Eisner's review of the curriculum reform movement noted the student resistance to academic prescriptions:

> The emphasis on the academic discipline and on discipline-generated problems in contrast to problems generated from the interests of the student as person and as citizen is now being brought into question as students are becoming more vocal and less willing to accept the educational prescriptions of academics and school-board members a generation or more older than they.[38]

Probably the chief limitation of the subjects design, however well planned and implemented, is the lack of direct relation of the organized subject matter to the problems and interests of the learner. Hollis Caswell stated in 1946 that "the conventional curriculum framework is the greatest single obstacle to the development of a program in the high school which provides the necessary assistance to youth in achieving in actual living the various developmental tasks which our society demands."[39] Two decades later the schools were still being criticized for the same reason, but it remained for the student uprisings in colleges and universities in the late 1960s and their counterparts in high schools to focus curriculum improvement once again on the matter of relevancy. Jerome Bruner, who had led curriculum theory to a renewed emphasis on the subjects, in 1971 expressed "doubts as to whether the conventional models, the forms of our knowledge, are appropriate to our purposes in our times," reflecting that "perhaps new requirements of action were proving the inadequacy of our models as they have emerged historically."[40] In an address at the 1971 Annual Conference of the Asso-

---

[36] From pages 49–50 of *The Timely and the Timeless: The Interrelationships of Science, Education, and Society,* by Bentley Glass. © by Basic Books, Inc., Publishers, N.Y.

[37] See Elliot W. Eisner, ed., *Confronting Curriculum Reform* (Boston: Little, Brown and Company, 1971), for a commentary on these inconsistencies.

[38] Eisner, pp. 9–10.

[39] Hollis L. Caswell, "Curriculum Proposals for the Future," in Hollis L. Caswell, ed., *The American High School,* Eighth Yearbook of the John Dewey Society (New York: Harper & Brothers, 1946), p. 140.

[40] Jerome S. Bruner, *The Relevance of Education,* Anita Gil, ed. (New York: W. W. Norton & Company, Inc., 1971), p. xii.

ciation for Supervision and Curriculum Development, he called for a moratorium or de-emphasis on structure of the subjects in favor of attention to more urgent problems:

> If I had my choice now, in terms of a curriculum project for the seventies, it would be to find the means whereby we could bring society back to its sense of values and priorities in life. I believe I would be quite satisfied to declare, if not a moratorium, then something of a de-emphasis on matters that have to do with the structure of history, the structure of physics, the nature of mathematical consistency, and deal with curriculum rather in the context of the problems that face us. We might better concern ourselves with how these problems can be solved, not just by practical action, but by putting knowledge, wherever we find it and in whatever form we find it, to work in these massive tasks. We might put vocation and intention back into process of education, much more firmly than we had it there before.
>
> A decade later, we realize that *Process of Education* was the beginning of a revolution, and one cannot yet know how far it will go. Reform of the curriculum is not enough. Reform of the school is probably not enough. The issue is one of man's capacity for creating a culture, society, and technology that not only feed him but keep him caring and belonging.[41]

DESIGNS FOCUSED ON SOCIAL ACTIVITIES AND PROBLEMS

Each curriculum design tends to reflect a position regarding the relative emphasis given to the major determinants of the curriculum. Thus the subject design emphasizes the role of organized knowledge. We turn now to the designs which emphasize society.

Characteristic Features

The socially focused designs exhibit more diversity than the performance-based and disciplines/subjects ones we have discussed. We include three design theories within this category: (1) the social functions or areas of social living or persistent life situation approaches that are based on the belief that the curriculum design should follow the persistent functions, areas, or life situations in man's existence as a social being; (2) the theory that the curriculum should be organized around

[41] Jerome S. Bruner, "The Process of Education Reconsidered," in Robert R. Leeper, ed., *Dare To Care/Dare To Act* (Washington, D.C.: Association for Supervision and Curriculum Development, National Education Association, 1971), pp. 29–30.

aspects or problems of community life—the community school concept; and (3) the social action or reconstruction theories that hold the improvement of society through direct involvement of the schools and their students to be a major goal or even the primary goal of the curriculum. The common denominator of these theories is a curriculum design that features social activities and/or problems rather than subjects or objectives or other organizing elements. The core curriculum is sometimes classified as a curriculum design and may have a dominantly social emphasis; we prefer to treat it as an application of usually more than one design.

Thus a curriculum design based on social activities or functions exhibits an organizational pattern derived from studies of group life. Caswell, who directed numerous state curriculum programs in the 1930s that utilized this design, and his colleague Doak S. Campbell explained the concept in their 1935 publication, *Curriculum Development*:

> Studies of group life show that there are certain major centers about which the activities of individuals and the plans and problems of the group tend to cluster. These centers, which may be referred to as social functions, tend to persist and to be common for all organized groups. . . . Since these centers or social functions represent points about which real life activities tend to gather and organize, it is considered reasonable that a curriculum which is concerned with guiding children into effective participation in the activities of real life may appropriately use these social functions as points for emphasis and orientation in outlining the curriculum.[42]

The Virginia state course of study developed through this procedure used the following list of major functions of social living:

> Protection and conservation of life, property, and natural resources
> Production of goods and services and distribution of the returns of production
> Consumption of goods and services
> Communication and transportation of goods and people
> Recreation
> Expression of aesthetic impulses
> Expression of religious impulses
> Education
> Extension of freedom
> Integration of the individual
> Exploration

A design based on community activities or problems might employ a similar list but use only those functions and aspects thereof

---

[42] Hollis L. Caswell and Doak S. Campbell, *Curriculum Development* (New York: American Book Company, 1935), p. 173.

that are significant in the community concerned. Seay, for example, classified the "problems of people" basic to the program of the community school as those of food, clothing, shelter, recreation, health, citizenship, morality and religion, and work.[43]

The social reconstruction theory has been less fully developed as a curriculum design than as an educational philosophy. However, recent and present educational reformers insist on building social action into the curriculum. Mario D. Fantini has listed a set of objectives dealing with "the political socialization—the citizenship of the student" and has described the nature of a program to develop these objectives:

> In order to develop skills in social action, the learners must be given opportunities in real life situations. Roles are learned from participation in reality contexts. This means that students would be working with poverty agencies, early childhood units, governmental institutions, hospitals, old age homes, etc. By relating to these clinical environments, students would acquire both the language and the behaviors necessary to deal with current social problems. The school would help the student conceptualize social realities and assist him in the process of developing alternative approaches to improving the environment of all people.[44]

In all of the designs described in this section the organizing element is a strand or cluster of social activities and/or problems. In the broader design of social functions these elements are somewhat universal and timeless; in the community school the selection criterion is local significance; in the social action program the criterion becomes problem areas or "realities" in which students can participate effectively.

These designs may be primarily criteria for the selection of subject matter and learning opportunities. In his description of the community school Krug noted that there was "nothing in the way of commitment to any type of curriculum" and that "a community-school program of classroom studies may be developed in a variety of curriculum patterns."[45] Caswell's use of the social functions design in the various programs he directed was primarily to define the scope of the curriculum. He suggested three analyses—the major social functions; forces influencing these; and the interests, needs, and abilities of children by level—that

[43] Maurice F. Seay, "The Community School: New Meaning for an Old Term," in Nelson B. Henry, ed., *The Community School*, Fifty-second Yearbook, Part II, National Society for the Study of Education (Chicago: University of Chicago Press, 1953), pp. 3–4.

[44] Mario D. Fantini, *The Reform of Urban Schools*, Schools for the 70's Preliminary Series (Washington, D.C.: National Education Association, 1970), p. 45.

[45] Edward Krug, "The Program of the Community School," in Henry, pp. 97–98.

would create a "core" for the curriculum.[46] The further development of the social activities design by Florence B. Stratemeyer and her associates employed the concept of "persistent life situations" in a curriculum in which:

> the *content* and *organization* of learning experiences are determined by the experiences of learners as they deal with everyday concerns and the persistent life situations which are a part of them (these situations of everyday living take the place of "subjects" and the varied other ways of focusing the curriculum).[47]

In summary, the socially centered curriculum designs have as their central element a focus on social activities and/or problems, and these define the scope of the curriculum or a major portion of it. These activities and problems may be the centers around which instruction is organized or they may serve primarily as criteria for the selection of content within the subject or other organizational unit.

The Case for Designs Focused on Social Activities and Problems

There are two primary arguments for socially centered curriculum designs: (1) they can directly contribute to the needs of society for continuing improvement; and (2) they are relevant to student needs and concerns and are therefore of great significance and interest to students. For example, Caswell and Campbell justified the social functions procedure on the assumption that "the activities of children in school should be organized in such a way as to carry over with the greatest ease to life situations."[48] Stratemeyer and her collaborators claimed for the persistent life situations concept that it would aid balanced development, continuity, depth of learning, economy of time, wise selection of content, and varied experience.[49]

As to the aims of the community school earlier in this century, Seay wrote of "the power of education when put to work to improve community living" and stated that the community school would result in "an improvement in the living conditions and standards of the community" and "the development of the appropriate skills, values and con-

---

[46] Caswell and Campbell, p. 177.

[47] Florence B. Stratemeyer, Hamden L. Forkner, Margaret G. McKim, and A. Harry Passow, *Developing a Curriculum for Modern Living*, 2d ed. (New York: Teachers College Press, 1957), pp. 116–117.

[48] Caswell and Campbell, p. 173.

[49] See Stratemeyer and others, pp. 121–140.

cepts, to the end that individuals will function more effectively in all their independent and co-operative undertakings."[50] More recently the community school idea has been broadened to "the community as a classroom" and "school without walls" concepts, which retain the claims of the earlier community-centered school. A 1971 publication began with the relevance argument: "For many children the community and the classroom are two different, unrelated worlds. Perhaps these two worlds can become one if the community is used effectively and extensively as a learning laboratory."[51] The Parkway Program in Philadelphia is generally credited with sparking the movement in urban centers toward school programs that use community facilities on a massive scale with very minimal central school facilities (therefore, the term "school without walls"); Parkway's first director, John Bremer, emphasized "the city" as a major aspect of the curriculum:

> Every student must come to know the city, the complex of places, processes, and people with which he lives. He must know it for what it is, understand it in terms of what he can do, and respect it for what it could be. He must know it, respect it, and revere it simply because he is about to change it— not do it violence, not destroy it, but change it—that is, transform it in terms of the principles of its being into what, potentially, it already is. Since the Parkway Program has the city as its curriculum, it must have the city as its campus. This is the educational reason for the school without walls. To learn about the city, to let it become familiar, to see it as the earthly counterpart of the City of God, can be accomplished only in the city; only academics suppose that this is learned in a course called Urban Dwelling 1 followed by Urban Dwelling 2.[52]

Social action through the school curriculum seems to us directly related to the educational philosophy of reconstructionism, as far removed as that philosophy is from the other socially focused designs we have considered. That is, while the social activities and community-centered approaches aim toward social improvement, they do not call on the schools to lead in social action and reform movements as does reconstructionism. According to Pratte's interpretation of the works of the leading spokesman for this philosophy, Theodore Brameld, it has not resulted in a curriculum design but only in a point of view.[53] But designs

[50] Seay, p. 11.

[51] Martha Irwin and Wilma Russell, *The Community Is the Classroom* (Midland, Mich.: Pendell Publishing Company, 1971), p. 3.

[52] John Bremer and Michael von Moschzisker, *The School Without Walls: Philadelphia's Parkway Program* (New York: Holt, Rinehart and Winston, Inc., 1971), pp. 46–47.

[53] Richard Pratte, *Contemporary Theories of Education* (Scranton, Pa.: Intext Educational Publishers, 1971), p. 236.

are suggested in recent interpretations of a social action curriculum. Fantini and Weinstein argued, for example, that "the present social context makes the reconstructionist point of view more relevant than ever" and that "skills development in the social action process is mandatory for keeping a democratic society healthy, vital, and growing." Accordingly, they proposed "a spiral of social action projects."[54] They described an eighth-grade project which involved the students in a local election and another project resulting in improvement of the school cafeteria and concluded: "We recommend not only decision-making and power-experience, but also the focus of learning on constructive utilization of power through a social action curriculum—that is, of course, if we really want an active citizen rather than merely a talkative one."[55]

Those who advocate a social action approach in the extreme would do away entirely with schools as we know them. Ivan Illich in *Dechooling Society* and Everett Reimer in *School Is Dead* propose a complete educational revolution. It is doubtful whether such notions could be acceptable to either school personnel or even parents, since Reimer writes that "perhaps the most important single thing that individuals can do" to revolutionize the social system is "to take back their responsibility for the education of their children."[56] These views may not affect the curriculum at all, but they do grow out of the problems of people worldwide, and conceivably social action curriculums could lead to study and action which would eliminate schools as we have them. Illich's proposed alternatives of "networks" (See Chapter 2) may be suggestive of other curriculum designs for education.[57]

Applications and Limitations

The social-centered design has had wide application, although we know of no schools in which it is the sole focus of the curriculum. Instead, social-centered designs affect the selection of subject matter in subject-organized programs or the choice of activities in less structured programs. For example, interdisciplinary units of work in elementary and middle schools are frequently chosen because of their relation to social

---

[54] Mario D. Fantini and Gerald Weinstein, *Toward a Contact Curriculum* (New York: Anti-Defamation League of B'Nai B'rith, n.d.), pp. 30–31.

[55] Fantini and Weinstein, p. 33.

[56] Everett Reimer, *School Is Dead: Alternatives to Education* (New York: Doubleday & Company, Inc., 1971), p. 194.

[57] See Ivan Illich, "Education Without School: How It Can Be Done," Daniel U. Levine and Robert J. Havighurst, eds., *Farewell to Schools???* Contemporary Educational Issues, National Society for the Study of Education (Worthington, O.: Charles A. Jones Publishing Company, 1971), and criticisms of this proposal by other authors. Also see Ivan Illich, *Deschooling Society* (New York: Harper & Row, 1971) for Illich's full analysis and proposals.

functions, activities, or persistent life situations. The core programs of middle, junior high, and high schools are frequently based on analysis of social problems. Vars described structured core programs as "categories of human experience that embrace both the personal problems, interests, and needs of students and the problems confronting contemporary society."[58] A quarter of a century earlier the influential *Education for All American Youth* recommended a "common learnings" core for high schools and junior colleges that would include six areas, four of which emphasized social problems:

1. Civic responsibility and competence
2. Understanding of the operation of the economic system and of the human relations involved therein
3. Family relationships
4. Intelligent action as consumers
5. Appreciation of beauty
6. Proficiency in the use of language.[59]

Similarly, the social activities/problems design is widely used in interdisciplinary courses in colleges; for example, Vars cited several problem-centered interdisciplinary courses offered at Livingston College, Rutgers University: "Life in the Cities," "Problems in Population and Environment," "Ethnic Groups in America," "The Formation and Justification of Beliefs and Attitudes," "Some Contemporary Moral Issues and Contemporary Youth Movements."[60] In pointing toward further development of core programs, Vars stated that "a carefully selected set of problem areas, supported by well-developed resource units, appears to be the best way to provide the necessary degree of structure for a problem-centered program."[61]

The social-centered design is also followed within the social studies as a basis for organizing units of work at all levels. Indeed, entire courses in secondary and higher education are built around major social functions, particularly in the areas of economics, political science, and sociology.

---

[58] Gordon F. Vars, "A Contemporary View of the Core Curriculum," in Gordon F. Vars, ed., *Common Learnings: Core and Interdisciplinary Team Approaches* (Scranton, Pa.: International Textbook Company, 1969), p. 8.

[59] Educational Policies Commission, *Education for All American Youth* (Washington, D.C.: National Education Association, 1944), pp. 249–250.

[60] Gordon F. Vars, "Curriculum in Secondary Schools and Colleges," in James R. Squire, ed., *A New Look at Progressive Education* (Washington, D.C.: Association for Supervision and Curriculum Development, 1972), p. 242.

[61] Vars, "Curriculum in Secondary Schools and Colleges," p. 248.

The limitations of the social-centered design are indicated by its use generally for only a portion of the curriculum. Even at Parkway, with its emphasis on the social problems of urban life, tutorials in basic skills, experiences in the arts, and learning opportunities other than those unique to the city are used. And even the social action educational revolutionists recognize the importance of specific learning opportunities for individual competence in learning skills and specialized interests and occupations.

But this design theory is highly applicable to some curriculum domains, especially to the one we designate as human relations. Study and experience in persistent social activities and problems, hopefully organized directly around these to ensure consideration and student involvement, seem mandatory educational components if young people are to have happy, successful, and constructive relations with their fellows in the multifaceted human organization we call society.

DESIGNS FOCUSED ON PROCESS SKILLS

Although less clearly defined than other designs, a focus on process skills has been advocated, especially in recent publications, by various theorists and is utilized, perhaps less widely than it is advocated, in some curriculum plans. We do not consider skills in general as process skills; most skills taught in such areas as music, physical education, driver education, and vocational courses are clearly competencies of the type envisioned in our specific competencies design. The process focus is most frequently advocated in terms of learning processes, although some design theorists would use the process approach of inquiry and problem-solving instead of fixed content (however structured), for the entire curriculum plan or some major aspect of the plan.

Characteristic Features

A process focus is more characteristic of instructional methodology than of curriculum design, and it is difficult to separate instructional processes and curriculum organizing centers of a process type. Thus problem-solving procedures may be the method used within an instructional program organized around the learning process of problem-solving; the procedure can also be used in a program organized around the traditional subjects or around social problems. Hence we consider the curriculum design to be one focused on process skills only when the latter are clearly defined as organizing centers for the curriculum plan. A social studies component of the curriculum plan is considered to reflect a process design only when the basic pattern of social studies is set by processes not unique to this field and for which various types of content can be selected from more than one field. The design may be considered a process one when the process of problem-solving, for example, dictates the selection of content in social studies and other subjects.

Process designs were used in various national curriculum projects in the 1960s. For example, *Science—A Process Approach* organizes science in the elementary school around such processes as observing, classifying, interpreting, and experimenting, with materials drawn from the various sciences to develop these processes. An authority on social studies curriculum development has stated that "the emphasis on process as content may be the most significant aspect of the search for relevancy in selecting content for the social studies program," noting that "content becomes a vehicle for developing process goals, such as the learners' ability to engage in rational decision-making."[62]

An earlier usage of the "social-process approach" in the social studies, which was recommended in a report of the Commission on the Social Studies in the 1930s, conforms more to the social activities and problems design than to the process skills focus we are now identifying; note the definition of "social processes" in the 1936 report: "there run through human living recognizable processes which have significance throughout the length and breadth of human history . . . human activities can be grouped in terms of classification of basic social processes, valid for particular purposes."[63]

The clearest statement available on the learning processes design is Parker and Rubin's *Process as Content*; what they were "after," they wrote, was "an expanded preoccupation with the processes embodied in the phenomenon of human living."[64] They contrasted content and process:

> The crux of the assumed contradiction between content and process lies in the difference between passive and active approaches to learning. . . .
>
> Where the stress is upon process, the assimilation of knowledge is not derogated, but greater importance is attached to the methods of its acquisition and to its subsequent utilization. Therefore, a discrimination must be made between knowing something and knowing what it is good for. Knowledge becomes the vehicle rather than the destination.[65]

[62] Dorothy Fraser, "A Painful Search for New Relevancy," *Nation's Schools*, 84, 35 (July 1969).

[63] Leon C. Marshall and Rachel Marshall Goetz, *Curriculum Making in the Social Studies*, Report of the Commission on the Social Studies, Part VIII (New York: Charles Scribner's Sons, 1936), pp. 13–14.

[64] J. Cecil Parker and Louis J. Rubin, *Process as Content: Curriculum Design and the Application of Knowledge* (Chicago: Rand McNally & Company, 1966), p. 11.

[65] Parker and Rubin, p. 2.

Parker and Rubin did not outline a single model of a curriculum design; indeed, they called for research and development to produce designs. They did, however, describe three models as beginning points, two of which could be fitted into existing designs and the third of which made learning processes the bases of curriculum organization. They built into the latter model "intake," "manipulative," and "applicative" operations: "The learning situation, at least as we conceive of it, consists of three interacting operations; the learner must take in data; he must manipulate it; and he must apply it."[66] They recommended using these guidelines in the selection of curriculum opportunities:

> First, some forms of knowledge have general applicability whereas others do not; to the extent that it is possible, the curriculum should be restricted to that which does.
> Second, processes which have a broad usefulness to be the primary, rather than the subsidiary benefit of content, should be used. They are not only to be regarded as a means to an end, but both as means and ends. In what may by now be an overly trite observation, the work of moment and the distinguished achievements of our society are performed by men conspicuous by the intellectual processes they muster to their cause.
> Third, exposing the learner to a variety of processes will not serve our purpose. He must suffer more than mere exposure. He must grasp the nature of the process and grasp how it got that way; he must know where it has been used in the past and where it might be used in the future; and he must know how to use it in diverse contexts, to modify it as circumstances demand, to fit it to his purpose, and to assess its results.[67]

Two other relatively recent statements of curriculum design theory would make problem-solving a major component of the curriculum, but one that is developed systematically as only one phase of the design. Broudy, Smith, and Burnett proposed for secondary education five "basic strands": symbolic studies, basic sciences, developmental studies, aesthetic studies or exemplars, and problem-solving strategies (molar problems). They clarified the relation of the latter category to conventional problem-solving as follows:

> Let it be reiterated that this kind of "course" or activity is not to be confused with problems studied in chemistry, physics, or mathematics. Nor is it to be identified with the familiar project or core approach, a device that takes the place of studying the several subject matters directly, separately, and systematically. There is a place in the curriculum for both of these problem-solving activities; the study of the basic sciences certainly uses

---

[66] Parker and Rubin, p. 62.
[67] Parker and Rubin, p. 13.

the first, while the developmental studies utilize the second. In the molar problem-solving course, however, the school outcome is not knowledge primarily, or even habituation in the use of the scientific method as such. On the contrary, the school outcomes, which in this instance approximate very closely the life outcomes corresponding to them, are the habits of deliberation, the skills of using diverse interpretive frames, and the practice of the attitudes needed for group thinking and decision.[68]

They envisioned such molar problem-solving as taking place in the latter years of the secondary school and viewed its development as "a fairly long transaction each year with two or three social problems of the magnitude of juvenile delinquency, disarmament, the problems of economic democracy, and the like."[69] They regarded this component of the curriculum design as "the integrative experience par excellence of the whole schooling process. It should reveal something about how well the other strands of the curriculum have been taught for it is a small sample of how schooling should be used in life."[70]

A contrasting position is reflected in Wilson's "open access" curriculum. He classified knowledge as being of three types: fact, contested truth, and open exploration. His curriculum design would *not* make the accumulation of fact prerequisite to exploration or problem-solving; indeed, this sequence, he wrote, has been a major weakness of earlier curriculum designs.[71] Wilson's design would create large clusters of content, such as the sciences, the arts, and the humanities, define each of these to include his three types of knowledge and learning processes, and "define multiple entry points to each large body of content, beginning in several cases with the outer (exploratory) area and proceeding toward the more certain knowledge at the center."[72]

Some curriculum design theories focus on valuing processes. In 1963 Kimball Wiles proposed four curriculum domains—analysis of experiences and values, acquisition of fundamental skills, exploration of the cultural heritage, and specialization and creativity—and suggested the following design for the first of these, values analysis:

In the school, each pupil will spend six hours a week in an Analysis Group. With ten other pupils of his own age and a skilled teacher-counselor he will discuss any problem of ethics, social concern, out-of-school experi-

[68] Harry S. Broudy, B. Othanel Smith, and Joe R. Burnett, *Democracy and Excellence in American Secondary Education* (Chicago: Rand McNally & Company, 1964), p. 242.

[69] Broudy, Smith, and Burnett, p. 241.

[70] Broudy, Smith, and Burnett, p. 243.

[71] L. Craig Wilson, *The Open Access Curriculum* (Boston: Allyn and Bacon, Inc., 1971), p. 12.

[72] Wilson, p. 16.

ence, or implication of knowledge encountered in other classes. No curriculum content will be established in advance for the Analysis Groups. The exploration of questions, ideas, or values advanced by group members will constitute the primary type of experience.

The purpose of the Analysis Group will be to help each pupil discover meaning, to develop increased commitment to a set of values, and to offer opportunity to examine the conflicts among the many sets of values and viewpoints held by members of the society.[73]

Unfortunately, Wiles was killed in an automobile accident in 1968, before he could know how accurate the following prophecy had been:

In the late sixties, it will begin to be recognized that unless citizens have values they accept, understand, and can apply, the social structure will disintegrate until authoritarian controls are applied. To counter the danger of collapse of the democratic way of life, the school will be assigned the task of making as sure that each child develops a set of values as it does that he is able to read.[74]

A somewhat similar purpose is served in the elementary school by the classroom meeting advocated by William Glasser:

There are three types of classroom meetings: the *social–problem-solving* meeting, concerned with the students' social behavior in school; the *open-ended* meeting, concerned with intellectually important subjects; and the *educational-diagnostic* meeting, concerned with how well the students understand the concepts of the curriculum.[75]

Raths, Harmin, and Simon have developed a theory of values and a methodology of valuing, with teaching strategies which focus on three basic processes: choosing, prizing, and acting. Full utilization of their teaching strategies would make the valuing process a significant curriculum component.[76]

The most comprehensive process-centered curriculum design is that of Louise Berman, who sees as the aim of education the development of "process-oriented" persons, or "persons who are able to handle themselves and the situations of which they are a part with adequacy and

[73] Kimball Wiles, *The Changing Curriculum of the American High School* (Englewood Cliffs, N.J.: Prentice-Hall, Inc., 1963), p. 301.

[74] Wiles, p. 302.

[75] William Glasser, M.D., *Schools Without Failure* (New York: Harper & Row, Publishers, 1969), p. 122.

[76] See Louis E. Raths, Merrill Harmin, and Sidney B. Simon, *Values and Teaching: Working with Values in the Classroom* (Columbus, O.: Charles E. Merrill Publishing Company, 1966).

ease. Such persons are the contributors to as well as the recipients of society's resources."[77] She described in detail eight process skills: perceiving, communicating, loving, decision-making, knowing, organizing, creating, and valuing. Berman described six curriculum designs, not espousing a particular one, and the process skills involved in each. Three of these designs maintained a subject organization and the other three an organization based on her proposed processes.

A somewhat similar view of the purpose of schooling and the focus of the curriculum was given in the 1969 Yearbook of the Association for Supervision and Curriculum Development. In an article by Edward J. Meade, Jr., "life skills" were identified as "powers of analysis, characterological flexibility, self-starting creativity in the use of off-work time, a built-in preference and facility for democratic interpersonal relations, and the ability to remain an individual in a mass society."[78] The Yearbook offered no curriculum design; as the chairman and editor wrote, yearbooks "are designed more as messages outlining the state of the union than as handbooks on procedure."[79]

In summary, there is *no* single curriculum design and set of characteristic features that incorporate all of the theories we have identified as focusing on process skills. One group of theories places major emphasis on learning processes, whether as curriculum organizing centers themselves or as criteria for selecting content and instructional arrangements from other designs. Some design theories give problem-solving activities a separate and significant role. Others focus on valuing processes as a major component of the curriculum design. One theory views process skills more generally and as so significant as to permeate the subject design or even to replace it. The common element in these design theories is their emphasis on processes as more dynamic curriculum elements than more fixed structures of knowledge; their diversity is in their definitions of processes and in the extent to which the processes constitute organizing centers in the curriculum plan.

The Case for Designs Focused on Process Skills

Each of the curriculum designs that focuses on process skills is based on one or more of the following arguments:

[77] Louise M. Berman, *New Priorities in the Curriculum* (Columbus, O.: Charles E. Merrill Publishing Company, 1968), p. 10.

[78] Edward J. Meade, Jr., "The Changing Society and Its Schools," in Louis J. Rubin, ed., *Life Skills in School and Society*, 1969 Yearbook of the Association for Supervision and Curriculum Development, National Education Association (Washington, D.C.: The Association, 1969), p. 50.

[79] Louis J. Rubin, "Epilogue: The Skills We Need," in Rubin, p. 156.

1. Since the most significant goal of schooling is the development of lifelong learning skills and interests, curriculum plans should make these skills and interests central.

2. The curriculum should be planned and organized so as to have maximum carry-over into life processes and skills; greater carry-over is likely when the curriculum design directly reflects these processes and skills.

3. The process of valuing and other processes having a high affective element can be taught as well as essentially cognitive skills; the former should be as well represented in the curriculum as the latter. Since these arguments were reflected in the sources already cited, only one additional illustration of each is presented here.

One of the most eloquent and prolific spokesmen for the lifelong-learning focus is John W. Gardner, who has served education as head of the Carnegie Foundation and as U.S. Commissioner of Health, Education and Welfare. He has emphasized the notion of education for self-renewal as follows:

> We are moving away from teaching things that readily become outmoded, and toward things that will have the greatest long-term effect on the young person's capacity to understand and perform. Increasing emphasis is being given to instruction in methods of analysis and modes of attack on problems. In many subjects, this means more attention to basic principles, less to applications of immediate "practical" use. In all subjects it means teaching habits of mind that will be useful in new situations—curiosity, open-mindedness, objectivity, respect for evidence and the capacity to think critically.[80]

The argument of carry-over to relevance has been used in connection with most curriculum designs that depart from traditional ones, and it is the main argument of the process versus—or as—content approach. For example, the Philadelphia Affective Education Project was described as "a 'process' curriculum, in which students can use their energies to accomplish something tangible."[81]

Arthur W. Combs, a perceptual psychologist, has argued cogently for a curriculum which would give greater attention to affective content:

[80] John W. Gardner, *Self-Renewal: The Individual and the Innovative Society* (New York: Harper & Row, Publishers, 1963), pp. 22–23.

[81] See Mark R. Shedd, Norman A. Newberg, and Richard H. De Lone, "Yesterday's Curriculum/Today's World: Time To Reinvent the Wheel," in Robert M. McClure, ed., *The Curriculum: Retrospect and Prospect*, Seventieth Yearbook, Part I, National Society for the Study of Education (Chicago: University of Chicago Press, 1971).

If we would prepare youth properly for the human world they must live in and for the human problems they must solve, the curriculum of our schools must provide students opportunities to explore human questions. Vital questions of values, beliefs, feelings, emotions and human interrelationships in all forms must be integral parts of the curriculum. To achieve this end, it is not enough that we simply teach the humanities. Instruction in English, social studies, art, music, and drama is not enough. Humanism and the humanities are by no means synonymous. As a matter of fact, such subjects are often taught in the most inhuman fashion. It is a fascinating thing that the human qualities of love, compassion, concern, caring, responsibility, honor, indignation, and the like are largely left to accident in our schools.[82]

Applications and Limitations

The theory of process skills is being applied in a variety of curriculum plans, usually not as a total design but embracing significant portions of the program. For example, most laboratory schools and laboratory approaches or methods have given major attention to the acquisition of process skills. The use of the term "laboratory school" was explained by John Dewey in connection with the one he opened at the University of Chicago in 1896:

Thus the name Laboratory *School* (originally suggested by Ella Flagg Young) gives a key to the work of the school. A laboratory is, as the word implies, a place for activity, for work, for the constructive carrying on of an occupation and in the case of education the occupation must be inclusive of all fundamental human values. A laboratory also implies directive ideas, leading hypotheses that, as they are applied, lead to new understandings.[83]

Some seventy years later Robert Schaefer, Dean of Teachers College, Columbia University, argued for a somewhat but not wholly different conception of a laboratory school—the school as a center of inquiry.[84] Thus both the school Dewey established and the one Schaefer envisioned

---

[82] Arthur W. Combs, "An Educational Imperative: The Human Dimension," in Mary-Margaret Scobey and Grace Graham, eds., *To Nurture Humaneness: Commitment for the '70's*, 1970 Yearbook, Association for Supervision and Curriculum Development, National Education Association (Washington, D.C.: The Association, 1970), p. 181.

[83] Quoted in Katherine Camp Mayhew and Anna Camp Edwards, *The Dewey School* (New York: D. Appleton-Century Company, 1936; reprinted by Atherton Press, 1966), p. 7.

[84] See Robert J. Schaefer, *The School as a Center of Inquiry*, John Dewey Society Lecture Number Nine (New York: Harper & Row, Publishers, 1967).

emphasized process as content, and to us this emphasis is characteristic of laboratory patterns of education. We consider today's so-called open classroom also illustrative, although such classrooms could be characteristic of most curriculum designs and are especially relevant to the needs and interests design we consider next.

Process skills are also emphasized in most plans of group guidance. For example, our conceptions of the middle school home-base group, comparable to Wiles' analysis groups and Glasser's classroom meetings cited earlier, is somewhat descriptive of various home-base advisory groupings in operation in emergent middle schools:

[issues] arising almost daily in the lives of middle school children are treated in various ways in the home-base group. Total group discussions may at times be desirable, usually preceded by an analysis of the issue through pupil or teacher presentation, a film or other aid, or the services of resource persons. Small groups within the home-base group may be formed to analyze each issue, with resultant total group consideration of alternative positions. Committees functioning on a continuing basis may bring periodic reports to the total group. The essential points are that issues which are real to the students be identified and considered, that alternative positions be fully explored, and that the consequences of preferred positions be clearly understood.[85]

The College Entrance Examination Board has developed a series of publications for use in a "Decision-Making Program" for junior high school students that is illustrative of the interest in group guidance and problem-solving activities.

The focus on process is also somewhat characteristic of curriculum, instructional, and organizational efforts to implement the continuum notion of education, or continuous progress education. If Shane and Anderson's prediction of a "gradual transformation of education from its present loosely articulated segments into a seamless continuum which, in time, might well extend, literally, from the womb to advanced old age"[86] is correct, and we rather agree with it, curriculum design will have to focus on skills and processes which are themselves continuous rather than on discrete, one-time learnings.

We ourselves hope for more fully developed design theories for process skills and for practices that implement these theories. So far the

[85] William M. Alexander and others, *The Emergent Middle School*, 2d ed. (New York: Holt, Rinehart and Winston, Inc., 1969), p. 67.

[86] Robert H. Anderson and Harold G. Shane, "Implications of Early Childhood Education for Lifelong Learning," in Ira J. Gordon, ed., *Early Childhood Education*, Seventy-first Yearbook, Part II, National Society for the Study of Education (Chicago: University of Chicago Press, 1972), p. 388.

theories have tended to focus on only a portion of the curriculum plan, and most of them lack specificity. We see the learning process designs as matching closely, and therefore most appropriate to, the curriculum domain of continued learning skills. The proposals for valuing and other affective processes have much promise for the personal development domain.

DESIGNS FOCUSED ON INDIVIDUAL NEEDS AND INTERESTS

The movement away from the traditional curriculum of school subjects has usually been toward a program that emphasizes the interests and needs of students. This approach was used in the eighteenth century by Rousseau in the education of Emile, by Pestalozzi early in the next century in Switzerland, and to an extent by Dewey in his laboratory school in 1896–1904. During the present century, each of the designs we have considered other than the subjects one has moved toward the child. Now we turn to theories that more directly use learner needs and interests as a design base. Variously called child-centered, experience-centered, and progressive education and, more recently, open, alternative, and humanistic education, all of these twentieth-century efforts reflect, we believe, the influence of Dewey. In *Experience and Education* Dewey included such key statements as these: "a coherent *theory* of experience, affording positive direction to selection and organization of appropriate educational methods and materials, is required by the attempt to give new direction to the work of the schools"; and "it is a cardinal principle of education that the beginning of instruction shall be made with the experience learners already have; that this experience and the capacities that have been developed during its course provide the starting point for all further learning."[87] Some of the child-centered activity programs developed by Dewey's followers lacked the attention to substantive material and continuity of child growth and development advocated by Dewey, and current emphasis on student-centered programs does not always acknowledge the Dewey philosophy or such similar models as those described in John and Evelyn Dewey's *Schools of Tomorrow* (1915). But Dewey's influence on the movement to incorporate more student-serving learning opportunities into the curriculum has been very great, and it may be argued that more recent models have

---

[87] John Dewey, *Experience and Education* (New York: The Macmillan Company, 1938), pp. 21 and 88.

advanced but little, if any, from Dewey's at the turn of the century. In fact, Charles Silberman's recent review of American education noted this comparison between "schools of tomorrow" as reported in 1960 by Morse and as by the Deweys forty-five years earlier:

> most of Morse's schools of tomorrow look strangely like the schools of yesterday and today. Compared to the schools described in the volume whose title Morse borrowed, John and Evelyn Dewey's *Schools of Tomorrow*, first published in 1915, Morse's schools are remarkably conventional; for the most part, what are hailed as new methods of organization, new technologies, and new concepts of the role of the teacher turn out, on examination, to be more gimmickry and packaging than substantive change.[88]

Perhaps the lag in utilization of the learner-centered focus has resulted from a tendency on the part of curriculum planners to interpret the needs and interests design as one based on *common* needs and interests of learners rather than on those of the particular population to be served. Reflected in curriculum plans, this interpretation could, and sometimes did, become the rationale for teaching what had been taught before or for implementing some other design that did not involve the study of children's needs and interests. Research in this area in recent years, however, has made it possible for curriculum planners to develop a better base for student-centered designs. Modern learning theory and widespread dissatisfaction of students and their parents with traditional practice are moving curriculum and instruction toward designs that focus on genuine student needs and interests. We will examine these applications in a subsequent section.

Characteristic Features

A curriculum design focused on individual needs and interests has these characteristic features, we believe:

1. The curriculum plan is based on a knowledge of learners' needs and interests in general and involves diagnosis of the specific needs and interests of the population served by the plan.

2. The curriculum plan is highly flexible, with built-in provisions for development and modification to conform to the needs and interests of particular learners and with many options available to the learners. In fact, the learner may develop his own curriculum plan in some designs, but with guidance in selecting options and in planning.

3. The learner is consulted and instructed individually at appropriate points in the curriculum and instructional process.

[88] Silberman, p. 160.

The Dewey School at the University of Chicago, which was in operation from 1896 to 1904, as described by Mayhew and Edwards in *The Dewey School* and by other authors,[89] seems to have illustrated all of these features. In theory and practice this school aimed at the progressive growth of children toward responsible participation in present and future social life. Hines wrote that "the school was not primarily child-centered or subject-centered, it was community-centered."[90] However, he presented it as a first and exemplary illustration of the children's "interests and needs emphasis in progressive education" and extolled its accomplishments.[91]

The "project method" was advocated by William Heard Kilpatrick, a leading interpreter of Dewey, and was the subject of a much cited study by Ellsworth Collings in McDonald County, Missouri. Kilpatrick's introduction to Collings' report of his study explained the needs and interests rationale.[92] Collings described the curriculum design of the experimental school as follows:

> The above program of studies represents four types of child projects—Play, Excursion, Story, and Hand—experimentally determined on the basis of affording boys and girls opportunity to realize their own purposes during the operation of the Experimental School. Play Projects represent those experiences in which the purpose is to engage in such group activities as games, folk dancing, dramatization, or social parties. Excursion Projects involve purposeful study of problems connected with environments and activities of people. Story Projects include purposes to enjoy the story in its various forms—oral, song, picture, phonograph, or piano. Hand Projects represent purposes to express ideas in concrete form—to make a rabbit trap, to prepare cocoa for the school luncheon, or to grow cantaloupes.[93]

Collings' description of the experimental school curriculum included some details of several projects and long lists of others under each type.

Rugg and Shumaker in 1928 described many examples of the new educational program and attempted to evaluate the child-centered

[89] See Harold Rugg, *Foundations of Modern Education* (Yonkers, N.Y.: World Book Company, 1947); Lawrence Cremin, *The Transformation of the School* (New York: Alfred A. Knopf, 1961); and Vynce A. Hines, "Progressivism in Practice," in Squire.

[90] Hines, p. 122.

[91] Hines, pp. 137–138.

[92] William Heard Kilpatrick, "Introduction," in Ellsworth Collings, *An Experiment with a Project Curriculum* (New York: The Macmillan Company, 1923), pp. xvii–xviii.

[93] Collings, p. 48.

movement. Some characteristic features of the programs, diverse as they were, are indicated in this paragraph:

> These programs are also interesting from the standpoint of their diversity. One school makes use of "central themes" around which the whole work of a school year is developed. Similarly another school gives each grade a practical "job" for which it is responsible and through which it may attain educative experiences; e.g., managing the school store, the school bank, the fruit shop. Some schools organize the work of a grade so that all the child's undertakings shall contribute to this centralizing year-long activity. Others permit a variety of smaller units to develop, alongside the main unit. Still other schools permit each grade to develop a series of small, relatively unrelated units. In some cases these are developed in succession; in others they are developed simultaneously.[94]

The authors also commented on the participation of learners in the life of the school, noting that "the school's organization is not a full-fledged system to which the pupil must conform."[95]

A 1953 publication, *A Public School for Tomorrow*, described the Matthew F. Maury School in Richmond, Virginia. This description, also introduced by Kilpatrick, reported on eighteen years of experience in trying "to provide for every child, whatever his ability, the kind of environment that will bring growth upward and outward toward self-enhancement."[96] The chapter headings indicate the scope of the curriculum:

> We Plan Our Living
> We Play, We Eat, We Rest
> We Listen, We Talk, We Read, We Write
> We Need Music Every Day
> We Use Art in Our Search for Beauty
> We Deal with Quantity and Space
> We Explore Our Universe
> We Seek To Live Well with Others
> We Work To Be at One with Our Community

But no specific units, grade placements, and time allotments were given, since the Maury design was one for planning rather than a fixed plan.[97]

[94] Harold Rugg and Ann Shumaker, *The Child-Centered School: An Appraisal of the New Education* (Yonkers, N.Y.: World Book Company, 1928), p. 91.

[95] Rugg and Shumaker, p. 96.

[96] Marion Nesbitt, *A Public School for Tomorrow* (New York: Harper & Brothers, 1953), p. 101.

[97] Nesbitt, pp. 21–22.

Two other child-centered schools have been the subjects of more recent books. Summerhill, in England, has received much attention in educational literature. This school is perhaps a prototype of some recently established "free" and other alternative schools in the United States. Its director, A. S. Neill, stated that it was started *"to make the school fit the child*—instead of making the child fit the school" and was based on faith in "the goodness of the child."[98] A decade after Neill's book was published fifteen authors contributed to *Summerhill: For and Against* some widely varying opinions about the school's philosophy and program. We find Fred Hechinger's opening comment a fair appraisal of the Summerhill idea:

> Summerhill is not a school but a religion. That is why one can be intrigued by it—can even admire it—without being converted to it. To derive benefits from it for one's children requires religious faith in the efficacy of its myths. As with every religion, faith distilled into fanaticisms can be dangerous. But there is so much essential goodness of intent and spirit in Summerhill that its doctrine may—in modified form—be most beneficial to ordinary parents who send their children to a variety of ordinary schools.[99]

Certainly Summerhill is an extreme application of the needs and interests design, lacking as it does the balance of freedom and guided options available in most child-centered schools of the past.

In *The School in Rose Valley* Grace Rotzel relates the development over thirty-six years of a school founded by parents in Pennsylvania in 1929. The author, who was the first principal of the school, reported that "as the school's staff worked together on curriculum in the exciting first years, we also studied child development, so that we could perceive the stages of child growth and provide a balance of freedom and restraint that would encourage inner discipline."[100] As to curriculum design, she noted:

> Our curriculum evolved from the basic concepts the teachers agreed were important to this school and for these children; structure would depend partly on teachers and partly on children. We determined the major areas and expected to help the children choose from these areas what they were to work on, and how.[101]

Thus, these child-centered schools, primarily elementary schools,

[98] A. S. Neill, *Summerhill: A Radical Approach to Child Rearing* (New York: Hart Publishing Company, Inc., 1960), p. 4.

[99] Fred M. Hechinger in *Summerhill: For and Against* (New York: Hart Publishing Company, Inc., 1970), p. 35.

[100] Grace Rotzel, *The School in Rose Valley* (Baltimore, Md.: The Johns Hopkins Press, 1971), p. 2.

[101] Rotzel, pp. 130–131.

have typically exhibited the features listed at the beginning of this section, although some descriptions are somewhat vague as to how learners' needs and interests are identified and how learners are guided in their choice making. Current efforts toward curriculum individualization, especially in middle and high schools and in post-high school education, may be more completely designed in terms of these features. Before turning to these efforts we should review (see Chapter 2) the movement toward various types of "free" and "alternative" schools.

The common denominator of these various schools, many of them unidentifiable and many of them temporary, has been that they are "free" of, or "alternative" to, public schools and are typically organized by parents, teachers, or even students because of dissatisfaction with public schools. However, in the 1970s some public school systems created their own alternative schools or subsystems, so that this common denominator is not wholly inclusive. As we noted in Chapter 2, Jonathan Kozol's book, *Free Schools*, deals primarily with only one type of school.[102] Kozol's free schools are concerned with the needs and interests of their students, but many of these needs are those of the entire ghetto community, and the educational program is decidedly realistic.[103] The chief generalization we can make about the curriculum design of the several varieties of free and other alternative schools is that one could find some such schools with as traditional designs as the most traditional public school and others as free and unstructured as Summerhill. Their relation to the needs and interests design stems primarily from the origin of these schools: they are generally created to meet some needs and interests of particular students which the founders see as being unmet in conventional public schools.

Turning now to other approaches to curriculum individualization, we find that probably the most common approach to meeting the needs and interests of learners has been the categorical grouping of students for special programs believed by the planners to match the needs and interests of the students concerned. Ability and other forms of homogeneous grouping at all levels, curriculum tracks in the high school, multiple curricula in colleges and universities, and the electives system itself in secondary and higher education have been widely provided as approaches to individualizing curriculum. Efforts of this kind are also represented by a multiplicity of programs for such special groups as the academically talented, the disadvantaged, dropouts (actual and potential), the gifted, the mentally handicapped, minority, cultural, and ethnic

---

[102] See Jonathan Kozol, *Free Schools* (Boston: Houghton Mifflin Company, 1972).
[103] See, for example, the description of one unidentified school in Kozol, p. 74.

groups, the physically handicapped, the socially and emotionally mal-adjusted, underachievers, and others. These various programs have generally included curriculum plans that focus on the needs and interests of learners within the categories, our first characteristic feature of the needs and interests design. But these approaches have not necessarily had the flexibility and student involvement in planning that we also consider characteristic.

The predominant use of the needs and interests design in cur-riculum planning is in the provision of *options* for individual students. For example, the emergent middle schools provide many special-interest activities, exploratory courses, and other experiences aimed at giving each student opportunities to explore and deepen his own interests. The system of elective courses in high schools and colleges, plus the wide range of activities open to students, is currently being expanded by the offering of mini-courses planned with students to fit special needs and interests. Don Glines' description of the Wilson Campus School at Mankato State College, Minnesota, illustrates the complete utilization of the option principle:

> Further, part of the Wilson program calls for options. Courses can be mini or maxi. Pupils can go duck hunting whenever they want during the year, work, sleep, stay at home, and generally "do their thing" as long as it does not hurt others. The opportunity for options is available to students K–12. We believe that humaneness involves choice of teachers, choice of courses, daily schedules, optional attendance, freedom of dress, and indi-vidualized evaluation (no report cards), as examples of some of the changes toward a humane school. . . .
>
> The schedule is a daily smorgasbord schedule. The student selects as much as is needed or desirable, when it is needed, for as long as it is needed. . . . Each day a new schedule is developed for students to select the opportunities which they desire to pursue. They may go home for part of the day, if that best suits their needs.[104]

Currently the movement in higher education toward "open uni-versity" arrangements and continuing education in general illustrates the options feature of the needs and interests design. Peter F. Drucker argues for continuing education which assumes "that the more experience in life and work people have, the more eager they will be to learn and the more capable they will be of learning."[105] Also related to the options concept is Drucker's suggestion regarding the curriculum:

[104] Don Glines, "Implementing a Humane School," *Educational Leadership*, 28, 187–189 (November 1970).

[105] Peter F. Drucker, *The Age of Discontinuity* (London: William Heinemann, Ltd., 1969), p. 302.

The twin problems of adolescence and drop-outs indicate that we will have to learn to build school curricula that serve the individual, that is, school curricula composed of standard units that can be put together to serve individual needs, to satisfy individual aspirations, and to conform to the one fact we really know about growing up: that no two people ever grow up exactly alike.[106]

Curriculum plans emphasizing the options concept can and generally do have the three features of a needs and interests design: (1) the options are based on knowledge of learner characteristics; (2) scheduling and other arrangements facilitate ready selection and choice of options, with counseling services available to help students; and (3) students are actively involved in planning and evaluating the options in general and for themselves in particular.

The Case for the Needs and Interests Design

Our study of the theory and practice of the needs and interests design suggests three major arguments for it: (1) learning opportunities based on needs and interests are more relevant to the learners; (2) the needs and interests design involves a high degree of motivation and therefore success of the learner; and (3) achievement of the individual's potential is facilitated by this design.

The validity of the first argument is obvious; that is, if the learning opportunity is truly chosen because of the individual's needs and interests, it surely must relate to them. As to the second argument, the reasoning is similar, but it must be noted that motivation is a highly internalized matter and that learners are not necessarily motivated for a learning opportunity planned externally.[107] Dewey had emphasized the importance of building on the "natural learning" of the child, explaining the curriculum of his laboratory school as based on this motivation principle.[108] Many years later the same principle was developed by Crary; describing the "natural learner" as "tireless," he wrote:

Too often the school slanders its pupils. It judges them lazy, weary or inattentive; it acts as though these were natural characteristics of learners. On the contrary, these are protective poses of people who are unwilling to

[106] Drucker, p. 309.

[107] See L. Thomas Hopkins, *Interaction: The Democratic Process* (Boston: D. C. Heath & Company, 1941), for the insistence of one strong advocate of the experience curriculum that the learner's "real felt needs" be basic.

[108] Quoted in Mayhew and Edwards, p. 33.

invest themselves in adventures not their own. When the school helps students to discover the mountains they want to climb it also discovers their energies and capacities.[109]

As to the third argument, facilitating the achievement of the individual's potential, this is the argument for all plans and strategies of individualization, including some categorical arrangements such as multiple tracks that we consider fallacious. Which curriculum designs focused on individual needs and interests represent the best approach has not been demonstrated, but certainly there is much evidence from research and observation that diagnosis of individual student needs and interests and provision for them are essential in good education. We accept Harold Benjamin's argument which is charmingly presented as that of Old Man Coyote: "Old Man Coyote insists that the boy whose mathematical, linguistic, geographical, or other peaks of ability are built to great heights will have his valleys of ability in other areas pulled up towards his peaks until the sum of his achievements will be far above the minimum essentials ever set by plodding plainsmen."[110]

Applications and Limitations

We have already cited many applications of the needs and interests design. Here we point only to a few that seem of particular significance for the future. In doing so, we should also note that the chief limitation of this design is its possible neglect of social goals. If the needs and interests principle is fully utilized, especially as excluding learning opportunities not based on learners' "felt" needs, there is no assurance of learners becoming equipped to participate effectively in social activities, particularly those of adulthood involved in work and citizenship. Hence we see the needs and interests design as especially appropriate for the personal development domain and for some aspects of the continued learning skills and specialization ones, but not for the human relations domain.

As to future applications, we suspect that the establishment of so-called free and other alternative forms of schooling will continue, although it seems probable that these may increasingly be developed within rather than without public school systems. It is even conceivable that Illich's "networks" concept may be developed under public auspices,

[109] Ryland W. Crary, *Humanizing the School: Curriculum Development and Theory* (New York: Alfred A. Knopf, 1969), p. 114.

[110] Harold Benjamin, *The Cultivation of Idiosyncrasy*, Inglis Lecture, 1949 (Cambridge, Mass.: Harvard University Press, 1949), p. 19.

with computerized management. "Open" universities and schools may also be expected to utilize the needs and interests design in offering a great variety of student-requested programs.

An especially attractive application is the "open classroom," combining the best of earlier progressive education, the English "informal" schools, and modern technology. An example of such an application in Philadelphia included learning centers, math laboratories, instructional materials centers, intensive learning centers, open-space schools, the Parkway Program, and reading skills centers.[111] It seems predictable that such open-classroom plans involving guided exploration and participation in planned learning environments and opportunities will become more common at the elementary, middle, and high school levels and in nongraded school organizations.

Independent study, which is both a curriculum option and an instructional strategy—indeed both a means and an end (independent learning)—seems to us to be an especially useful application of the needs and interests design. It is largely an individually motivated and a guided learning activity:

> *Independent study* is considered by us to be learning activity largely motivated by the learner's own aims to learn and largely rewarded in terms of its intrinsic values. Such activity as carried on under the auspices of secondary schools is somewhat independent of the class or other group organization dominant in past and present secondary school organizational practices, and it utilizes the services of teachers and other professional personnel primarily as resources for the learner.[112]

Although many usages of the term are misapplications,[113] many schools, colleges, and universities do have planned guidance of a wide variety of independent study opportunities conforming to the needs and interests principle.

It is the needs and interests principle rather than a particular design which has most influence and applicability. Within each of the other designs—including subjects/disciplines—points arrive in planning curriculum and instruction at which decisions must be made regarding each student's program and progress. To the extent that consideration is

---

[111] See I. Ezra Staples, "The 'Open-Space' Plan in Education," *Educational Leadership*, 28, 458–463 (February 1971).

[112] William M. Alexander, Vynce A. Hines, and associates, *Independent Study in Secondary School* (New York: Holt, Rinehart and Winston, Inc., 1967), p. 12.

[113] See William M. Alexander and William I. Burke, "Independent Study in Secondary Schools," *Interchange*, 3, 102–113 (Numbers 2–3, 1972).

given to the individual student's needs and interests in these decisions, the principle is utilized. We ourselves believe that such utilization is an essential phase of the curriculum planning needed now and hereafter.

EMERGENT DESIGNS

We have considered in some detail five sets of curriculum design theories. Each of these, we believe, has been sufficiently described in theoretical works and applied in practice to be classified as a curriculum design, despite the considerable variations in theories and practices within each category. Additionally, there is always the possibility of other categories taking shape.

For example, in the early 1970s several dissatisfactions with existing school programs and education in general were expressed in arguments against "dehumanizing" practices and for more "humanistic" or "humane" education.[114] Although these terms and the emphasis on human values and affective outcomes are certainly appealing, we have not been able to locate in such sources any consensus as to curriculum design or, in fact, any unique proposal of sufficient detail to be comparable to the other design theories. Indeed, so far it is clearer as to what "humanistic" education is against than what it is for! Hence we see this literature as placing a needed emphasis in the needs and interests design on affective, human relations goals and have made our prior references to it in relation to the needs and interests design. But we do foresee the possibility of further exploration, theorizing, and designing efforts resulting in a more complete and unique "humanistic design."

Additionally, there are always current concerns in society and education that are expressed as curriculum demands and proposals and that may thus eventually emerge as curriculum designs. Thus the specific competencies design today reflects the great concern for improved educational results; the social activities designs grew out of social unrest and problems in the 1930s; the needs and interests design has been stimulated intermittently by such diverse forces as the scientific movement in education, the move toward universal secondary education, and the student unrest of the late 1960s. Currently American society is plagued by drug abuse, environmental pollution, population crises, crises in international affairs, inflation, and many other problems. For each of these there are

---

[114] See, for example, Gerald Weinstein and Mario D. Fantini, *Toward Humanistic Education: A Curriculum of Affect* (New York: Frederick A. Praeger, Inc., 1970); 1970 Yearbook, Association for Supervision and Curriculum Development, *To Nurture Humaneness*; and Crary.

formulas as to what the schools should do to solve or alleviate the problem: drug abuse education, environmental education, population and sex education, international education, economic education, and so forth. Any of these "formulas" may become a "subject" in the curriculum—indeed some already have—or a new and pervasive emphasis that becomes in time a curriculum design.

SELECTING APPROPRIATE CURRICULUM DESIGNS: GUIDELINES

No one curriculum design can be adequate for the total curriculum plan of a school serving the varied population and the multiple goals our schools generally serve. Instead, we see the curriculum planners as properly selecting, even developing, appropriate designs for particular curriculum goals, domains, and learning opportunities. Inevitably designing is an area of decision-making to be shared by those immediately responsible for the curriculum plan of a particular school.

It is therefore essential that curriculum planners be knowledgeable about curriculum designs and the designing process. Without some understanding of past and current efforts to develop designs more appropriate to the goals and domains of the school curriculum, planners continue to repeat the mistakes they have made in the past. They need to recognize many so-called innovations as renovations and to be able to at least turn to the sources which have described and evaluated these. They need to identify the backgrounds of a new theory formulation and find the elements of it that have not been previously tested as well as those that have been. Thus a major justification for the study of curriculum design theories as presented in this chapter is to aid the curriculum planner in adding to his own store of knowledge to help him understand, classify, and evaluate curriculum design theories and proposals.

But curriculum planners cannot confine their designing efforts to reflection about past and present. The planners must also fit appropriate designs to their particular goals and domains. Design gives a curriculum plan a framework for its organization, implementation, and evaluation. It constitutes an order, however flexible and changing, for the organization of sets of learning opportunities. Thus, with goals established and domains tentatively organized around sets of goals, planners must identify the learning opportunities appropriate to their goals, domains, and populations and anticipate them in detail through a process of fitting opportunities and design principles together in a promising framework. As the planners engage in this process, they may find in the five groups of design theories we have considered adequate designs and design principles, or they may need to try to create some new designs or to combine several tested principles into some new constellation that becomes a design. The important guideline, we believe, is for the planners to go through the designing process in a systematic fashion. We suggested early in this chapter these steps:

1. Consider basic factors about a particular population relating to each curriculum domain for which curriculum planning is in process
2. Identify subgoals of each set of broad goals and related learning opportunities constituting a domain
3. Identify possible types of learning opportunities appropriate to each domain and its subgoals
4. For each domain settle on one or more appropriate curriculum designs (more than one design is usually needed for even one domain)
5. Prepare tentative design specifications (that is, the more detailed fit of design and learning opportunities)
6. Identify implementation requirements—that is, know what must be done in advance of instruction to implement the planned design.

In this chapter we have given detailed consideration to the characteristic features, cases for, and applications and limitations of five general designs. Each design is really a classification of design theories that focus on the same organizing principle or at least on very closely related organizing principles. We believe that curriculum planners need to be cognizant of these five design possibilities, and of the multiple patterns each entails, in order to make intelligent decisions about their own plans.

In closing this chapter we emphasize again these two guidelines in the use of available design theories and designs:

1. Use whatever designs are appropriate for *the entire curriculum plan*, remembering that the widespread attempt to use the subjects/disciplines design to cover all goals and domains has been primarily responsible for the gap between goals and practice. The gap has been most acute because of the tendency to design the program of studies and neglect the other, sometimes more important, phases of the curriculum—activities, services, the so-called hidden curriculum, and others. We introduced the concept of domain to embrace all of these learning opportunities, and we have attempted to include all of them in illustrating and analyzing the various types of designs and steps in designing. Once again we call attention to the necessity of a curriculum plan designed to give

optimum exposure of *all* learning opportunities the school should and can provide.

2. Move as carefully and rapidly as possible to *test out chosen designs*. Selection or development of an appropriate design for a series of learning opportunities related to some curriculum domain and a set of its subgoals is an important step toward an effective curriculum plan, but this step is primarily that of giving order to the plan. It is in the translation of that order into practice through wise planning and execution of the implementation phase—instruction, in its broadest sense— that the plan is really tested.

ADDITIONAL SUGGESTIONS FOR FURTHER STUDY

Burns, Richard W., and Gary D. Brooks, eds., *Curriculum Design in a Changing Society*. Englewood Cliffs, N.J.: Educational Technology Publications, 1972. Essays on various aspects, problems, and foci of curriculum design, with an epilogue by John Goodlad.

Cole, Henry P., *Process Education: The New Direction for Elementary–Secondary Schools*. Englewood Cliffs, N.J.: Educational Technology Publications, 1972. A more definitive and systematic presentation of the process design theory than most writings on this subject. Includes analysis of roles and steps in implementation.

Drumheller, Sidney J., *Handbook of Curriculum Design for Individualized Instruction*. Englewood Cliffs, N.J.: Educational Technology Publications, 1971. A complex model for designing and developing curriculum materials from rigorously defined behavioral objectives.

Frazier, Alexander, *Open Schools for Children*. Washington, D.C.: Association for Supervision and Curriculum Development, 1972. Explores the relations of open space, open structure, and open curriculum. Part 4 examines various proposals for the elementary curriculum and offers guidelines for "opening up curriculum."

Glines, Don, *Creating Humane Schools: Expanded Supplementary Edition*. Mankato, Minn.: Campus Publishers, 1972. Describes many innovative practices used in the Wilson Campus School, Mankato State University.

Heath, Douglas H., *Humanizing Schools*. New York: Hayden Book Company, Inc., 1971. Describes youth alienation and states the author's beliefs as to "a consensus about educational goals and changes needed to implement them."

Hyman, Ronald T., *Approaches in Curriculum*. Englewood Cliffs, N.J.: Prentice-Hall, Inc., 1973. Eleven selections from the writings of curriculum theorists, including Dewey, Kilpatrick, Stratemeyer, Hand, King and Brownell, Bellack, Berman, and others.

Krug, Mark M., *What Will Be Taught—The Next Decade*. Itasca, Ill.: F. E. Peacock Publishers, Inc., 1972. Contributors assess the present situation, indicate possible future trends, and evaluate the directions in English, visual (art) education, science, foreign languages, mathematics, social studies, and teacher education.

Purpel, David E., and Maurice Belanger, eds., *Curriculum and the Cultural Revolution*. Berkeley, Calif.: McCutchan Publishing Corporation, 1972. The introduction states briefly the humanistic curriculum theory of the editors, and this theory is further developed in various essays, especially in Part Four, "The Development of Self-Awareness and Personal Growth."

"The School as a Community," *Theory Into Practice*, 11, 1–72 (entire issue, February 1972). Various articles examine the concept of the school as a community organized and operated as a participatory democracy.

"Whatever Happened to Curriculum Content Revision?" *Educational Leadership*, 30, 587–590, 596–627 (April 1973). Nine articles on the theme of this issue provide information and perspective on current curriculum development, especially regarding social studies, science, mathematics, humanities, and reading.

Wilhelms, Fred T., *What Should the Schools Teach?* Phi Delta Kappa Fastbacks, No. 13. Bloomington, Ind.: Phi Delta Kappa Educational Foundation, 1972. Emphasizes four categories of the curriculum: offering a career education, living with the great technology, developing effective citizenship, and promoting personal fulfillment.

6

PLANNING CURRICULUM IMPLEMENTATION: INSTRUCTION

The purpose of all curriculum planning is to provide opportunities for an individual student or a group of students to benefit
maximally from participation in selected learning activities. As the students partake of learning opportunities, whether these are planned by
the teacher or improvised on the spot by the teacher or student(s) or
both, such participation becomes a learning experience which results in
personal growth. This is the process of instruction.

Instruction is thus the implementation of the curriculum plan,
usually, but not necessarily, involving teaching in the sense of student-
teacher interaction in a school setting. There would be no reason for
developing curriculum plans if there were no instruction. Curriculum
plans, by their very nature, are simply efforts to guide and direct in one
way or another the nature and character of the learning opportunities in

which students participate. All curriculum planning is for naught unless it influences and shapes the things which students do under the auspices of the school. Obviously, the planner must see instruction and teaching as the summation of his efforts. In this chapter we will consider instructional planning as the next step in curriculum development.

STARTING POINTS IN INSTRUCTIONAL PLANNING

In planning instruction the teacher, a team of teachers, or the school staff begins with the essential kinds of data listed in Chapter 3 and whatever formal curriculum plans have been made or are made available by the school system or the school. These types of curriculum plans were described in Chapter 2, and their designs in Chapter 5. For review and a point of reference here we list the types of curriculum guides usually made available in U.S. schools:

1. *The purposes of the school.* In one form or another the school system should have prepared statements on the goals and subgoals which it seeks to serve. The formulation of these purposes was described in Chapter 4.

2. *An officially adopted textbook, or even sets of textbooks or a packaged instructional system.* These guides and their use in curriculum planning were described in Chapter 2. The significance of the textbook or sets of instructional materials as an instructional plan is not to be minimized. Kirst and Walker, in reviewing the status of curriculum policy making, stated:

> The bald fact is that most teaching in our schools is and must be from a textbook or other curriculum package. We do not trust teachers to write their own materials, we do not give them the time or money, and we insist on standardization. So long as this is true, the suppliers of teaching materials will have a potentially powerful effect on the curriculum.[1]

3. *A curriculum guide.* As explained in Chapter 2, curriculum guides may range from being broad sets of recommendations for teaching a subject to detailed plans which list goals and objectives for a field of study, a course, or a segment of instruction; content to be used; recommended teaching resources; learning opportunities that may be provided; and evaluative methods. The traditional course of study for a

---

[1] Michael W. Kirst and Decker F. Walker, "An Analysis of Curriculum Policy-Making," *Review of Educational Research*, 41, 492 (December 1971).

school subject is still the most common form of prepared guides of this type.

4. *Curriculum materials of a limited scope.* In addition to or in place of the more formal, often comprehensive, curriculum guides, many school systems or individual schools prepare or obtain from other sources bulletins, brochures, pamphlets, and similar aids for planning instruction. These may constitute resource units, suggested teaching resources on a subject, suggestions for developing a topic of study with students, lists of recommended community resources, booklets listing goals and objectives for an area of study, or other materials of value to teachers. Descriptions of practice are also frequently published.

5. *Informal work plans.* A team of teachers or a departmental staff in high school, for example, may set down in written form decisions and recommendations made by the group for instruction in a particular field of study or in a topic or unit of work.

6. *A set of self-instructional materials.* Individualized learning packets for individually guided education, study and work guides for computerized instruction, and the like, will also be available to teachers in schools using these modes of instruction.

7. *Professional materials.* Books, magazines, pamphlets, brochures, leaflets, newsletters, video tapes, films, unit sets of training materials, and similar aids are available in great numbers from professional organizations, publishing firms, and other educational agencies.

8. *A plan for no, or little, prestructured plans.* In some instances the school abandons all forms of formal, published, or written curriculum plans and adheres to a policy of permitting—or requiring through necessity—teachers to be completely or largely free of the necessity to use predetermined types of learning activities in the classroom.

THE NATURE OF INSTRUCTIONAL PLANNING

With one or more types of curriculum plans available in most school situations as a starting point for planning instructional activities, the next questions are, who should participate in instructional planning and what should be the nature of these plans?

Who Should Participate?

In Chapter 2 we considered in detail the persons, groups, and agencies who participate in curriculum planning. Here we focus on those who should contribute in important ways to instructional planning:

1. The teacher or a teaching team that is responsible for guid-

ing the development of learning opportunities in a school situation. It is inconceivable that a teacher could work with a group of students or even an individual student in an interactive process of instruction without some planning having been done beforehand.

2. Student(s) who participate in the learning activities. Whether the students are invited to participate in a formal or recognized manner, they play a significant role in the development of the activities, and, hence, in planning them as they develop. We have urged throughout this book that students be included in a challenging manner in all aspects of formal planning, and this recommendation is especially appropriate at the instructional level. Cooperative planning of instruction by teacher and students, as it was then designated, was one of the most laudable features of the "progressive" schools of the 1930s and 1940s. It still is a part of planning in many schools, especially in the "informal" or "open classroom" programs in elementary schools, in the humanities, social studies, and practical arts programs in secondary schools, and in the newer types of alternative programs. The impact of national curriculum projects in science and mathematics, however, has often militated against student participation in planning in these subjects except as an aspect of independent study.

3. Curriculum consultants. The curriculum consultant of a school or school district, including the principal when he acts in this role, should participate in instructional planning. The nature and extent of involvement will depend, of course, on the staff situation. Such professionals can be exceedingly helpful when new curriculum plans, especially those for innovative programs, are implemented. Examples include the work of consultants in developing instruction in the "new math," in introducing the Hilda Taba program in social studies, or in helping to shape an individually guided program in reading.

Some producers of the new curriculum plans will not permit their use, by purchase of the materials, in school systems until consultants and often the teachers themselves have participated in a special training program sponsored by the producer.

Mention should also be made of the use as consultants of qualified persons outside the school system, such as scholars in a discipline, specialists in an area of instruction from colleges and universities, state departments of education, and educational agencies, and producers of instructional materials.

We emphasize again the tremendous responsibility residing in the office of the director of curriculum in guiding and directing all phases of the curriculum planning process, not the least of which is planning instruction. Teachers, of course, are primarily responsible for planning instruction, but the best schooling for children and youth will come about only through the combined efforts of an entire staff, with enlightened leadership from those in key positions.

Types of Instructional Plans

Just as do curriculum guides, instructional plans vary greatly in nature, comprehensiveness, and character. They may be classified as follows:

1. Inclusion in curriculum guides. Often a curriculum guide or other kinds of prepared curriculum plans, such as resource units or teachers' manuals, contain plans for carrying on instruction. In fact, this is the most common kind of formal written planning for instruction. Such guides contain recommendations on objectives, content, teaching resources to be used, learning activities appropriate for use with students, teaching methods and procedures, and methods of evaluating outcomes.

2. Formal guides for instruction. If recommendations for instruction are not included in the curriculum guide, then an additional guide for instruction may be prepared. It would include the kinds of suggestions listed above.

3. Informal written plans. These may vary from a rather complete set of objectives and recommendations on content, teaching methods, and learning activities prepared by a teacher or a team for developing a unit of learning activities—such as map study in sixth grade social studies, the foreign policy of the United States since World War II, a study of our neighborhood in grade 2—to notes the teacher writes for himself.

4. Daily lesson plans. Often a teacher or team prepares a plan for the day's activities of a class group, noting things to do, ideas for developing a unit of work, materials to use, topics for discussion, and other ideas.

5. Unwritten plans. Every teacher, even if a guide of the type listed above is available, and especially so if one is not, has in mind plans for carrying on instruction. It seems reasonable to assume that actually such ideas in the mind of the teacher characterize much of the instructional planning in schools today in a supplementary manner or as the only plan.

We recommend that written instructional plans be developed by teachers, that they be cumulative in nature from year to year, with work notes of all kinds and added suggestions for learning activities and teaching procedures, and that lists of new teaching resources be added continuously as such ideas come to the teacher. In addition, a teacher, on a day-by-day basis, will wish to use his own ideas concerning procedures and methods for carrying on instruction. This is not to sanction shoddy work in the classroom, indifference, boresomeness, or any of the other faults students vehemently protest in their "underground" manner or openly and that have been vigorously condemned by shrewd observers, concerned parents, and educational leaders everywhere. Rather, it is to emphasize the professionalism of teaching and to plead for an imaginative, visionary, highly competent teacher in every interactive situation involving students.

Characteristics of Instructional Plans

In whatever form they are prepared, good instructional plans should:

1. Enable a teacher or team to exercise a great deal of choice, day by day as well as over the long term, in developing learning opportunities with students. The plans should encourage teachers to be highly flexible in working with students and to use their own imaginations, competencies, and biases in developing the instructional program.

2. Explain overtly and explicitly ways to use a number of instructional modes appropriate for developing a unit of work or a series of units within a course or unified segment of instruction.

3. If prepared for a corps of teachers whose preparation and teaching experience may vary widely, such as social studies teachers in middle schools, contain illustrations of how to use the more heuristically oriented methods or list references to available professional literature on such instructional modes.

4. Suggest ways in which a teacher or team may involve students in planning the development of a unit of work.

5. Suggest ways in which available staff members or members of a team, particularly aides, paraprofessional staff, and student teachers, may contribute significantly in carrying on the teaching situation.

6. Illustrate how feedback from evaluations of students' activities and accomplishments may be used to revise or modify further activities.

A CATALOG OF INSTRUCTIONAL MODES: STRUCTURED CLASS SITUATIONS

In assisting educators in the total job of curriculum planning, we list and describe briefly in this section and the following one the principal instructional modes that may be used in carrying on learning activities with students in a school situation. We believe such an analysis will be helpful, for the best and most appropriate implementation of a curriculum plan depends on what occurs in schools in the interactive process among teachers and students.

In presenting such a list, we emphasize that instruction, as illustrated in Figure 3 in Chapter 1, is one of the three basic aspects of a curriculum plan. Hence, we are still dealing here with curriculum planning, not teaching methods, although, of course, methods of teaching constitute a significant part of the instructional process.

In the analysis attention is centered principally on the degree of what Piaget designates as "passivity" or "activity," the nature of groupings, and the extent of individualization and personalization of the instruction. This section will analyze modes generally used in the more formal situation of a class, as we commonly use that term in educational circles; the second section will treat instruction in nonstructured situations; and the third section will examine learning opportunities and experiences in relation to the unstudied, hidden, or unofficial "curriculum."

In presenting these descriptions of instructional modes, the reader is urged to study the excellent analysis of models of the teaching process presented by Nuthall and Snook in one of the significant contributions to educational literature, the *Second Handbook of Research on Teaching*. They identify three distinct models of teaching:

> The *behavior-control or behavior-modification model*. . . . it might be called the stimulus-response view of teaching, and it incorporates within its boundaries the theoretical residue of the programmed instruction movement and the present claims of behavior-modification advocates.
>
> The *discovery-learning* model incorporates those views of teaching which place greatest emphasis on the self-directed activity of the student. It might be seen as the contemporary successor to the authoritarian democratic model, but incorporates some of the present-day concern for creativity. . . . it finds some of its strongest proponents in the recent curriculum reform movements.
>
> The *rational* model owes a lot of its impetus to the recent application of analytic philosophy to educational issues. . . . Central to this model is the claim that teaching must be concerned with rationality and that the practice of teaching must be influenced by the logic of argument and justification.[2]

These models serve well as the framework within which to analyze what we choose to call the modes of the instructional process

[2] Graham Nuthall and Ivan Snook, "Contemporary Models of Teaching," in Robert M. W. Travers, ed., *Second Handbook of Research on Teaching* (Chicago: Rand McNally and Company, 1973), p. 49.

itself. The reader may readily identify some modes with a particular model described by Nuthall and Snook, but it should be recognized that any particular teaching strategy may have elements of more than one of the models, being eclectic in application rather than restricted to one form of teaching.

Lecture and Verbal Presentation Modes[3]

The traditional transmission-of-knowledge modes are familiar to everyone.

Major characteristics: Talk, address, or other type of verbal presentation to students by a teacher, guest speaker, or panel.

Groupings: Any size class, but usually from 20–25 to 200–300 students. Primarily used with students in middle, junior high, or high school and with students in general education courses at the postsecondary school level.

Student activity: Highly passive, reception and, hopefully, assimilation of information, note taking, listening; perhaps some viewing as a supplement; answering a test.

Teacher activity: Speaking, reading, often some illustrating visually.

Teaching resources: Often only the teacher; perhaps a chalkboard, a model, transparencies, or other visual or auditory aids.

Uses and value: Creating interest in a topic or subject; transmitting knowledge to students; presenting students new information or explanations of events or things, interpretations, and generalizations; helping students to clarify and gain a better understanding of a subject, topic, matter, or event; organizing and systematizing knowledge; reading or reciting poems, dramas, essays, and similar types of literature or performing a dance, musical selection, gymnastic acts, and the like; providing opportunity for other persons (guests or staff) to present information, views, or explanations or descriptions of events, phenomena, or issues. Although these particular modes are used to implement all five types of curriculum designs presented in Chapter 5, they loom especially large in the disciplines/subjects organization.

Drawbacks and defects: The opposite of the uses and values cited below for those modes involving a large measure of student activity and involvement.

---

[3] Useful references on these modes include Ronald T. Hyman, *Ways of Teaching* (Philadelphia: J. B. Lippincott Company, 1970), Part Three; Kenneth H. Hoover, *Learning and Teaching in the Secondary School*, 2d ed. (Boston: Allyn and Bacon, Inc., 1968), Chap. 14; and David P. Ausubel, *Educational Psychology: A Cognitive View* (New York: Holt, Rinehart and Winston, Inc., 1968).

Discussion—Questioning Modes[4]

Often the traditional recitation method of teaching and a somewhat broader mode of participation that may be labeled as discussion are intermingled with the lecture mode in secondary schools today; these methods are also widely used at the elementary school level. A wide range of interactive processes could be subsumed under this title, but we will reserve for later treatment the more participative group methods widely used by teachers today. Clear-cut categories are hard to identify, but here we are considering the more traditional modes of the recitation format.

Major characteristics: Questions and answers over assigned material or related topics; discourse among members of the class and the teacher, largely on the topics under study but sometimes consideration of other matters introduced by the teacher or class members; working or presenting solutions to assigned problems, such as in mathematics and the sciences.

Groupings: Usually the traditionally sized classes—20–35 students. Used extensively at all levels of schooling.

Student activity: Varies greatly among members of the class and from time to time, depending on the topic or subject. Some members of the class are quite passive most of the time. Teacher-pupil interaction quite structured, except for occasional diversions to other matters.

Teacher activity: Teacher very much dominates the classroom situation; often quite structured; usually talks a large portion of the time; may show film or use audio materials as supplement to recitation and discussion.

Teaching resources: Usually only the teacher; perhaps use of open textbook or other printed materials; chalkboard used for recording items; occasional use of visual or auditory materials.

Uses and value: Transmitting knowledge to students; assisting them in organizing knowledge and developing concepts and generalizations; testing students' achievement of objectives; identifying students interested in the subject and those with special ability; motivating students to carry out the assignment; answering students' questions; clarifying understanding; showing how to solve a problem or do something; giving students opportunities to participate in an interactive process;

---

[4] References on these modes include William C. Nutting, *Designing Classroom Spontaneity* (Englewood Cliffs, N.J.: Prentice-Hall, Inc., 1973); Hyman, Part Two; Hoover, Chaps. 6, 11, and 15; Jean D. Grambs, John C. Carr, and Robert M. Fitch, *Modern Methods in Secondary Education*, 3d ed. (New York: Holt, Rinehart and Winston, Inc., 1970), Chap. 10. Books on curriculum and teaching for a subject field usually have lengthy treatments of these modes.

improving students' ability to speak on a subject, to organize thoughts, and to communicate effectively; identifying difficulties in achieving objectives and helping students overcome them. These kinds of instructional methods may be used in carrying out any of the five types of designs, but they predominate in the disciplines/subjects one.

Drawbacks and defects: Much too often is a regurgitative process with little real thought or reasoning apparent; too much teacher talk; may not expand knowledge or add to stock of information; may be too punitive in approach rather than developmental; students not involved actively learn little from the lesson; often quite boring to students; low level of student participation of the kinds described in some modes.

Practice and Drill Modes[5]

Modes that rely on practice are, of course, used extensively when the purpose of instruction is to enable students to acquire a skill or a proficiency in doing some overt act. Often it is intermingled with recitation and discussion methods, such as in courses in foreign languages, mathematics, music, and art and in athletic programs of all kinds.

Major characteristics: Repeated performance of a learning act until a desired level of skill to do the act correctly is attained or the teacher and student settle for a lesser level of competency; the performance may be verbal, as in music, speaking a foreign language, and speech correction and therapy, written, as in mathematics, spelling, and shorthand, or manual, as in shop, art, athletics and physical education, and typing.

Groupings: May be done in unison or by one or more individual members of a class of any size or by individuals in laboratories, teaching or resource centers, study halls, libraries, or audiovisual centers or at home. Used with students at all levels of the common schools and for appropriate courses at higher levels.

Student activity: Complete student involvement with performance of overt acts; some witnessing of demonstration of the act or listening to explanation of what to do. May involve use of a machine, such as a

---

[5] Helpful references on these modes include many books on educational psychology (sections on drill, practice, memorization, retention, and so on). See especially Robert M. Gagné, *The Conditions of Learning*, 2d ed. (New York: Holt, Rinehart and Winston, Inc., 1970), Chap. 9, and his "Military Training and Principles of Learning," *American Psychologist*, 17, 83–91 (February 1962); Herbert J. Klausmeier and Richard E. Ripple, *Learning and Human Abilities*, 3d ed. (New York: Harper & Row, Publishers, 1971), Chaps. 13 and 16; E. A. Bilodeau and Ina McD. Bilodeau, eds., *Principles of Skill Acquisition* (New York: Academic Press, Inc., 1969); Hoover, Chap. 20; Grambs, Carr, and Fitch, Chap. 11.

programmed teaching machine, a computer, or a machine necessary to the operation.

Teacher activity: Explaining the nature of the act verbally, visually, or both; demonstrating proper ways of doing the act; explaining to students, usually individually, errors in performance and showing how to correct them; supervising students during practice periods; observing students in performance, such as athletic games, musical events, and sports exhibitions, and noting success as basis for further teaching and practice; evaluating performance, skills, and competencies.

Teaching resources: Models, equipment, chalkboard, films, video tapes, recordings, machines, tools, materials needed for the performance, computers, teaching machines, communication systems.

Uses and value: To develop a desirable skill to perform an act or to acquire a proficiency, especially one that may be habituated; to continue to repeat an act, to make something or to write or say something verbally until it is fully understood; to accomplish something overtly that provides a student with a competency or sense of satisfaction, especially if it motivates further participation in learning activities; to develop an understanding of the principles underlying the operation of a machine, a tool, or object used in the performance of the skill; to be able to judge the quality of such an object; to individualize instruction, especially through use of teaching machines, computers, and audiovisual equipment. This set of instructional modes is especially appropriate for a curriculum designed to develop specific competencies, although other methods of implementation would also be used for that design.

Drawbacks and defects: If overused, stultifying and boring, especially to students who readily learn such skills; often teachers fail to teach the principles underlying the skill or to develop concepts and understandings that extend the kinds of learning outcomes possible; failure to individualize instruction in learning skills, thus wasting the time of many students; so much time spent on skills that other goals of learning are seriously neglected.

Viewing, Listening, Answering Modes[6]

Every teacher today uses, to some extent at least, "educational technology" in carrying on instruction. It is an instructional mode in its own right, but is also used as a part of the instructional process in almost

[6] The professional literature on the use of audio and visual teaching resources and all other kinds of technological processes involving machines and equipment for viewing, listening, and utilizing is very extensive. Here we cite a few selected references on the psychological bases for use of these instruments and on the use of them in teaching from the standpoint of methodology. See Klausmeier and Ripple, Chap. 5;

all other modes, even lecturing and recitation. Here we will analyze the use of instructional materials, machines, and equipment on the basis of their use as such, including use in conjunction with other modes or as the sole or principal mode. Formal laboratory work will be treated later.

Major characteristics: Use of printed material for reading and study by students individually or in small groups; use of materials for viewing and/or listening; use of materials or models for observing; use of materials solely for listening; personally observing existing events, conditions, materials, processes, and habitats; using a machine to present questions or problems and elicit answers or solutions; handling materials and using them in learning size, weight, color discrimination, and the like.

Groups: Regular-sized classes to large groups; many instances of individual use of materials, equipment, or machines; some small-group use. Used at all school levels, including higher education.

Student activity: Ranges from very passive, as may be true in viewing television or film or listening to tapes or recordings, to very active, as in using teaching machines or equipment for practice, making a tape or recording, handling objects to be sorted or used for some purpose, or making field trips to observe and study actual things or situations. Passivity versus activity varies exceedingly according to kind of resource used and the purpose in using it.

Teacher activity: Varies considerably, also, although usually the teacher does not dominate the learning activity itself. Arranges for use of equipment and materials, if necessary; plans showings, listenings, or observations; often explains or may demonstrate use of what students should do, see, or listen for; helps individual students who may have trouble in using equipment properly or in selecting or preparing correct answer; evaluates student competencies, especially in programmed learning activities.

Teaching resources: Printed—books, pamphlets, magazines, newspapers, workbooks, manuals, encyclopedias, atlases; visual, often with listening—motion pictures, slides, filmstrips, videotapes, television, flat pictures, charts, graphs, maps, globes, chalkboard, models, exhibits, specimens; auditory—recordings, tapes, radio; observing actual things—

Grambs, Carr, and Fitch, Chap. 6; Hoover, Chap. 25; Bryce B. Hudgins, *The Instructional Process* (Chicago: Rand McNally and Company, 1971), Chap. 9; Marvin D. Alcorn, James S. Kinder, and Jim R. Schunert, *Better Teaching in Secondary Schools*, 3d ed. (New York: Holt, Rinehart and Winston, Inc., 1970), Chaps. 9–11. Bibliographies and citations in these books list many other good references; planners should be aware of the opportunity to view and evaluate all sorts of learning materials at the Educational Facilities Center, 223 North Michigan Avenue, Chicago.

field trips of all sorts; manipulative—objects for handling, sorting, and using; instructional machines—teaching machines, computers, electronically equipped teaching laboratories, such as for instruction in languages, reading skills, typing, and shorthand.

Uses and Values: Educational technology contributes tremendously to teaching if used wisely and appropriately; some types are especially helpful in providing individual instruction; useful in providing remedial or catch-up work; especially useful in concept development among disadvantaged children; those that require active participation by students may be highly valuable in motivating student activity; provides very meaningful experiences in developing the senses and concepts among the youngest children. Used in the implementation of all types of curriculum design.

Drawbacks and defects: May be improperly or inappropriately used by teachers and hence ineffective in contributing to goals; teachers may overuse to the neglect of other desirable teaching modes.

Problem-Solving, Heuristic, and Discovery Modes[7]

In this category of teaching methods we will consider projects, case studies, research activities, problem-solving, the widely recommended approach in recent years designated as the discovery method, and a more general set of student-interactive processes simply labeled as heuristic.

The Stanford Center describes the more sophisticated use of the methods, labeled by them as heuristic, in this manner:

[7] References that provide additional analyses and help include Byron G. Massialas and Jack Zevin, *Creative Encounters in the Classroom: Teaching and Learning through Discovery* (New York: John Wiley & Sons, Inc., 1967); Harold Morine, *Discovery: A Challenge to Teachers* (Englewood Cliffs, N.J.: Prentice-Hall, Inc., 1973); Gagné, Chap. 8; Klausmeier and Ripple, Chap. 12; Hoover, Chap. 9; Hudgins, Chap. 7; Hyman, Chaps. 3 and 14; Louis E. Raths and others, *Teaching for Thinking: Theory and Application* (Columbus, O.: Charles E. Merrill Publishing Company, 1967); Jean Fair and Fannie Shaftel, eds., *Effective Thinking in the Social Studies*, Thirty-seventh Yearbook, National Council for the Social Studies (Washington, D.C.: The Council, 1967); Lawrence E. Metcalf, ed., *Values Education: Rationale, Strategies, and Procedures*, Forty-first Yearbook, National Council for the Social Studies (Washington, D.C.: The Council, 1971); Albert R. Wight, "Participative Education and the Inevitable Revolution," *Journal of Creative Behavior*, 4, 234–282 (Fall 1970); Jerome S. Bruner, "The Act of Discovery," *Harvard Educational Review*, 31, 21–32 (Winter 1961). The Stanford Center for Research and Development in Teaching in recent years has been doing excellent work in analyzing and preparing models and plans for a broad category of processes they label heuristic; see Richard E. Snow, ed., "A Symposium on Heuristic Teaching: A Report of Addresses at a Conference," available as ERIC Document No. 046893 (December 1970). Presumably, additional reports and other publications will be available from time to time.

Heuristic teaching refers to styles of teaching which emphasize the development of self-initiated and self-directed pupil learning; which stress the pupil's discovering rather than absorbing knowledge; which place the student in the role of the inquirer; which aim at heightening the relevance of school to the pupil's life; which are concerned with the emotional and social development of the pupil as well as with his cognitive growth.[8]

Major characteristics: Students, with various degrees of teacher supervision, engage in the processes of problem-solving and rational thinking as delineated in the major analyses of such processes; investigation of problems, issues, and conditions; preparation of research reports based on empirical data or analysis of the literature; surveys of actual situations with conclusions and recommendations; extensive discussion; use of reference works and current literature.

Groupings: Usually not larger than a normal class (22–35 students); often small-group and committee activity; individual study and investigation. Used primarily in upper elementary, middle, or junior high school, and at high school levels, but many aspects used at an introductory level with younger children. Often is the primary method used in specialized courses at the postsecondary school level, such as seminars, research programs, and tutorials.

Student activity: Extensive student activity—reading, discussing, collecting information and data; making surveys and conducting interviews; preparing reports; making oral reports to class; conducting experiments; cooperative planning—often students themselves determine matters they will investigate or study and the activities in which they will engage in such study.

Teacher activity: Guides the activities of the class through discussion, advice, counseling, conference, or instructions, written or oral; while responsible, subordinates self in the planning, work, and activities of the members of the group; cooperative planning with students; advises and guides the work of students participating in independent study programs; evaluates the activities of each member of the group in terms of goal attainment.

Teacher resources: Any appropriate ones; much viewing and listening, observing, and interviewing by students, collectively or individually; books, reports, and similar library resources especially useful.

Uses and values: Acquire and refine system of values; develop cognitive knowledge; develop ability to be self-directive in continued

[8] Snow, p. 9.

learning; develop sensitivity to important social, political, and economic problems and issues in the society; motivate students to engage in learning experiences that significantly contribute to general goals of education; acquire methods of rational thinking and desire to use them in solving problems; develop interest in engaging in challenging learning activities; communication skills. The best set of modes for implementing designs organized on the basis of social activities and problems, process skills, and individual needs and interests, but also used in other designs.

Drawbacks and defects: May be more time-consuming for results obtained, especially in cognitive development; difficulties in involving some students in a meaningful way, especially the culturally disadvantaged, slow learners, or the alienated; problems in reducing dominance of the very verbal, the highly opinionated, or the advocate of a cause; requires a great deal of teacher time in planning and in directing activities of committees and individuals if outcomes are to be high.

Laboratory and Inquiry Modes[9]

A distinction is made here among those methods that involve direct work in a laboratory on a regular basis or utilize an actual situation and those just considered in the previous section as problem-solving or discovery methods. We acknowledge that the line of demarcation between problem-solving and inquiry methods may not be sharp in practice. Laboratory work, especially in the sciences, is a traditional and extensively used method of instruction, but in recent years the nature of such activities has changed considerably in most schools, with much greater attention being given to the use of the methodologies of scientists and to inquiry as a mode of learning.

[9] Many of the references listed for the previous section are applicable for these modes. Specific references include John T. Mallan and Richard Hersh, *No G.O.D.s* (Giver of Direction) *in the Classroom,* 3 vols. (Philadelphia: W. B. Saunders Company, 1972); James L. Hill, "Building and Using Inquiry Models in the Teaching of Geography," in Phillip Bacon, ed., *Focus on Geography: Key Concepts and Teaching Strategies,* Fortieth Yearbook, National Council for the Social Studies (Washington, D.C.: The Council, 1970), Chap. 12; series of articles on the Mid-Continent Regional Educational Laboratory–Biological Sciences Curriculum Study, "Inquiry Objectives in the Teaching of Biology," *American Biology Teacher,* 32, 474–479 and 544–554 (November and December 1970), and the basic document on the program, Richard M. Bingman, *Inquiry Objectives in the Teaching of Biology* (Kansas City, Mo.: Mid-Continent Regional Educational Laboratory, 1969); Norval Scott, "The Strategy of Inquiry and Styles of Categorization," *Journal of Research in Science Teaching,* Vol. 4, No. 2, pp. 143–154 (1966); Hoover, Chap. 17; William D. Romey, *Inquiry Techniques for Teaching Science* (Englewood Cliffs, N.J.: Prentice-Hall, Inc., 1968).

Major characteristics: Students engage in experimentation in a laboratory, designing and carrying out original (for them) projects using scientific-inquiry methods; often, however, students follow a manual or guide which may vary from a broad form to a highly structured "recipe" form in carrying out the projects; investigations of actual phenomena or situations, involving data collecting, hypothesizing, and drawing conclusions. Inquiry in the social sciences follows much the same methodology as discovery methods, but emphasis is on investigations, data collecting, and drawing conclusions.

Groupings: No more than class-size group of 20–35; often small groups or an individual, especially as aspect of independent study. Upper grade through graduate and professional schools.

Student activity: Direct and extensive activity in carrying on laboratory projects, original research, and investigations; discussion among students involved in common or similar projects; preparing written reports and often extensive research papers.

Teacher activity: Assigns laboratory activities or investigations; counsels students on projects they may undertake; supervises activities of students; advises them on techniques, methods of research or investigation, and preparing conclusions and a report. Counsels and supervises students on independent study projects. Evaluates and grades report.

Teaching resources: Laboratory fully equipped for area of study; films, tapes, videotapes, TV; models, cutaways, charts, manuals; actual objects being studied, such as in biology and other sciences; official records in public offices; citizens of the community; instruments needed to collect data outside the school.

Uses and values: Cognitive knowledge; attitudes; values; skills in rational thinking; motivation to continue study in the field of investigation; concern for the future of man and his world; skills in handling equipment, often very sensitive or delicate; developing an interest in science or social research; prepare interested students for advanced study. Characterizes implementation of the disciplines/subjects design, especially in the sciences, visual arts, music, practical arts, and technology of various kinds, but also useful in other types of designs as appropriate.

Drawbacks and defects: Too often laboratory work is routine or a highly structured activity of little real value to the student; high costs for adequate laboratories excellently equipped; too few teachers have competency or desire to guide and challenge students with high level of talent; restrictions on field trips or class activities outside the school campus.

Modes to Develop Creativeness[10]

The modes already analyzed may all contribute to the development of an ability to be creative or to the enhancement of the creativeness of students. But the development of creativeness in those instructional processes except in the use of discovery or inquiry methods is quite incidental or peripheral and is not the principal end sought in the learning activity. Here we will analyze instructional methods designed primarily to develop the creative talents of the participants, but we remind the reader that the methods of instruction designated as discovery and inquiry, when used imaginatively, also are creative in mode.

Major characteristics: Creation of things, such as sculpture, visual arts, music, motion pictures, telecasts, photographs, drama, dance form, fashion design, literature, a machine, plans for material objects (buildings, parks, and so on) or an important project or undertaking (conservation of energy sources) that constitute original work by the student; preparing solutions other than those listed or taught in class for a mathematical problem or social issue of some complexity; devising a better way of performing a complex operation or process.

Groupings: Not more than the traditional class size of 20–35, but the act of creation is individual; often much of the work is done individually in laboratory, studio, library, learning center, or the home. Used at all levels of schooling, also in colleges, institutes, technical schools, and universities.

Student activity: Complete involvement when engaged in creative activities; the output is the student's unique creation.

Teacher activity: Quite limited—encouraging, stimulating, advising, counseling, supervising, suggesting, explaining, demonstrating; proposing projects for interested students; evaluating product; continuously endeavoring to identify students with potentialities for creative work; judging a student's work or activity.

Teaching resources: Anything appropriate to the project; school should have ample resources for a wide variety of projects.

Uses and value: Development of potentialities and talents;

[10] References include Klausmeier and Ripple, pp. 448–474; Joe L. Frost and G. Thomas Rowland, *Curricula for the Seventies: Early Childhood through Early Adolescence* (Boston: Houghton Mifflin Company, 1969), Chap 6; E. Paul Torrance, *Encouraging Creativity in the Classroom* (Dubuque, Iowa: William C. Brown Company, Publishers, 1970); E. Paul Torrance and R. E. Myers, *Creative Learning and Teaching* (New York: Dodd, Mead Company, 1970); and Gary A. Davis and Joseph A. Scott, *Training Creative Thinking* (New York: Holt, Rinehart and Winston, Inc. 1971).

development of feeling of accomplishment, of success; appreciation of beauty in every form of nature and life; development of standards of quality for types of endeavors in which interested; arousal of high interest in the school's or institution's program; development of ability to be self-directive; encouragement of interests for lifelong endeavors; attainment of a sense of well-being and a high measure of self-satisfaction; acquisition of competencies for advanced study and/or career in a field. Should be an aspect of instruction in all types of curriculum design, but especially desirable in implementation of the individual needs and interests and the process-skills designs.

Drawbacks and defects: Difficulty in identifying talents of all students; problems in getting uninterested, alienated, or resentful students to engage in creative endeavors; requires considerable time on part of staff to offer widespread opportunities for so many individuals and demands space and materials often not available; too many teachers unprepared to identify and work with talented students.

Role Playing, Simulation, and Games[11]

Much of classroom instruction is carried on in a contrived learning situation, but some teachers use an overt type of contrivance in games, simulated situations, and role playing. This mode of instruction introduces an element of reality in the carrying out of a unit of learning experience that often is more effective in achieving student outcomes than talking about a situation.

Major characteristics: Carrying out an imaginary situation in which students assume the roles, as they conceive them, of persons actually engaged in such a situation in real life; engaging in behavior that is presumed to replicate what designated people often do in real life; select-

[11] Useful references include The Kentucky Group, "Gaining a Perspective on Simulation and Gaming," *Bulletin*, National Association of Secondary School Principals, 57, 43–49 (February 1973); F. L. Goodman, "Gaming and Simulation," in Robert M. W. Travers, ed., *Second Handbook of Research on Teaching* (Chicago: Rand McNally and Company, 1973), pp. 926–939; Sarane S. Boocock and E. O. Schild, eds., *Simulation Games in Learning* (Beverly Hills, Calif.: Sage Publications, Inc., 1968), particularly their appendixes; Angus M. Gunn, "Educational Simulations in School Geography," in Bacon, Chap. 13; Hoover, Chap. 8; Hyman, Part IV; Richard E. Barton, *A Primer on Simulation and Gaming* (Englewood Cliffs, N.J.: Prentice-Hall, Inc., 1970); Alice K. Gordon, *Games for Growth: Educational Games in the Classroom* (Chicago: Science Research Associates, 1970); and Cheryl Charle and Ronald Stadsklev, eds., *Learning with Games: Analysis of Social Studies Educational Games and Simulations* (Boulder, Colo.: Social Science Education Consortium, Inc., 1972).

ing a real-life situation and then engaging in behavior that the participants believe should have taken place or describing what they think
should have been done; engaging in a game in which a contest among
adversaries occurs; interpreting through one's own actions what he or she
assumes was or would be the actual behavior or course of action of a
person in a similar real-life situation.

Groupings: Small groups or committees of a class; remainder of
the class witness the event. Used with all age groups on a proper level of
maturity, but most often in secondary schools and higher institutions.

Student activity: Complete involvement of those chosen to participate; passive on the part of remainder of class, except as they discuss
the event.

Teacher activity: Choosing or guiding the choice of the contrived situation; supervising the action; leading a discussion afterwards.

Teaching resources: Usually few needed, but sometimes a film,
slide, photograph, or videotape for the portrayal of the lifelike situation;
the materials for the game itself.

Uses and value: Develop values and attitudes; understand the
feelings, emotions, and prejudices of other people; develop insight and
understanding of basic principles and concepts, as in geography or psychology; develop a skill to do something, as speaking on a subject;
stimulate interest and provide variety in classroom activities. Especially
useful in the process-skills type of curriculum plan, but may be used in
any design.

Drawbacks and defects: Difficult to portray feelings or conduct
of a real-life situation; possibility of offending some students; may force
a student to take a position or act opposite to what he himself believes;
quite time-consuming; often does not really clarify a situation or adequately identify points of view.

A CATALOG OF INSTRUCTIONAL MODES:
FREE-FORM AND NONCLASS SITUATIONS

In the modern school a considerable portion of the learning
opportunities provided students occur outside of the formal classroom
program. They may be carried on in a place known as a classroom, but
the activities and procedures are not formally structured, although they
are planned, that is, planned to be free form or unstructured. Other
such opportunities are provided in nonclassroom situations, as will be
indicated.

Play, Handling, Manipulating, Acting

This mode characterizes a considerable portion of instructional activities in the early childhood years—nursery school, kindergarten, and early grades.

Major characteristics: Playing with toys, blocks, devices, equipment of a more complicated nature; playing group games of an interactive type; singing, dancing, imitating; manipulating articles or discriminating or judging among them as to color, size, weight, and shape; solving puzzles; making articles; acting out a story or event.

Groupings: Varies from a single person engaging in an activity to a normal-sized class group of 20–30; much small-group (1–5 persons) activity.

Student activity: Complete involvement of participants; may be some watching when others engage in the activity.

Teacher activity: May choose the activity, but much opportunity for choice by a child; supervising activity; leading, if desirable; showing how to do the game or manipulate the materials.

Teaching resources: All sorts of games, materials, toys, devices, and objects; records or tapes for dances and games; materials for making things.

Uses and values: Develop physical dexterity; develop sense of color, size, weight, shape; develop discrimination; obtain participation of students, especially reluctant ones, in group activities; develop sense of independence and self-reliance; socialization, concern for others, sharing, cooperation.

Drawbacks and defects: Cost of equipment, materials, and supplies; may be overemphasized in terms of other kinds of opportunities.

Telling

A considerable portion of young children's school activities are devoted to a telling type of experience. On the one hand the teacher tells the children stories, talks about events, reads them stories and factual material, or has them listen to recordings and tapes. The children, in turn, tell about themselves, their experiences, their families, their interests, and happenings.

Such learning activities provide excellent opportunities for socialization, for developing an understanding of people, their problems, their daily lives, and parent-child relationships. They contribute to a development of self-confidence and self-assurance, unless a child, for some reason, has an unpleasant or embarrassing experience.

School-Activities Program

What is often designated as the extracurricular activities program of a school we term extrainstructional activities. These are an important part of the school's efforts to implement its curriculum plans. Instructional planning, by all means, should devote considerable attention to these activities so that they contribute maximally in terms of time and effort devoted to them to the realization of the goals of the school.

Major characteristics: Wide range of activities available, especially in secondary schools; usually of five types—activities that extend and enrich class instruction, service activities for the school or community, school-development activities, athletics, and activities for personal development; high degree of flexibility in carrying on the activity and freedom to choose among many feasible endeavors; informality; much personal interaction with other participants.

Groupings: Many involve small number of students, perhaps 5–25, except athletics; considerable individual or small-committee work. In elementary school often blended with class activities, so that amount of extraclass time is limited. Athletics often conducted quite differently than other types of activities.

Student activity: Extensive—actually should be almost entirely student planned, directed, and carried out; student officers usually elected.

Teacher activity: Serve as sponsor, but in athletics, music, and journalism direct the practice and performance; advise and counsel the group; represent the administration in setting and enforcing rules and limits of the activity; serve as a resource of ideas and plans for the activities of the group.

Teaching resources: Any equipment, materials, and supplies needed to carry on the activity.

Uses and values: Contributes significantly to the attainment of school goals, especially those in the affective domain, but in class-related groups also to the cognitive goals; develops talents and potentialities of participating students; fosters interest in an area of study, significant both for the present program and for later specialization; may enable student to obtain scholarship to a higher institution, as in athletics, music, or a subject field; may enhance opportunity for admission to a higher institution; contributes to public interest in the school, and, perhaps, support in financial matters; contributes to student morale, enjoyment, and interest.

Drawbacks and defects: Often real contributions to educational goals are quite limited due to inept leadership and sponsorship, wrong emphasis, and poor choice of activities; sponsors inclined to usurp leadership responsibilities and dictate or play too large a role in selecting and carrying on activities; many students do not participate or only in a very limited way, hence little benefit from an important part of the school program; expense to both the students and the school; often not the best choice of priorities; detracts attention and decreases involvement of parents and other citizens in other aspects of the school program; similarly, students may become too involved in activities to devote desirable levels of energy and involvement to the class program.

Independent Learning and Self-Instructional Modes[12]

Students study, in the traditional sense of that term and much of it on an individual basis, in all modes of instruction. Any learning is always an individual matter regardless of the nature of teaching. But here we single out for consideration what has become a very important dimension of schooling and a readily identified process of instruction in recent years, especially in the secondary school. Traditionally, independent study is a major aspect of instruction in higher institutions.

The term "independent study" was used originally to designate a particular kind of instructional process and it has remained in the vernacular in that sense as an instructional method. We are not including here any method of individualizing instruction, but rather what Jourard defines as the "embodiment and implementation of imaginative fascination"[13] and Macdonald as self-selection—"student choice of activity as well as independent pursuit of tasks."[14]

Major characteristics: Student proposes to proper member of the staff a study project, investigation, research, or production of something which he or she will carry on largely independently of other class work or in lieu of class work in a course; if approved, carries out the activity

[12] William M. Alexander, Vynce Hines, and associates, *Independent Study in Secondary Schools* (New York: Holt, Rinehart and Winston, Inc., 1967); Hoover, Chaps. 16 and 18; Gerald T. Gleason, ed., *The Theory and Nature of Independent Learning* (Scranton, Pa.: International Textbook Company, 1967); B. Frank Brown, *Education by Appointment: New Approaches to Independent Study* (West Nyack, N.Y.: Parker Publishing Company, 1968); Gaynor Petrequin, *Individualizing Learning through Modular-Flexible Programming* (New York: McGraw-Hill Book Company, Inc., 1968).

[13] Sidney M. Jourard, "Fascination: A Phenomenological Perspective on Independent Learning," in Gleason, p. 85.

[14] James B. Macdonald, "Independent Learning: The Theme of the Conference," in Gleason, p. 2.

under supervision of the staff member; may be the pursuit of a formal correspondence course carried on under the supervision of the school.

Groupings: Individual. Usually restricted to high school and postsecondary school students, but increasingly available to middle school students.

Student activity: Complete involvement—must plan, obtain approval for, and carry out project, usually with minimum of supervision and direction.

Teacher activity: Stimulate qualified students to participate; advise and counsel on possible projects; grant approval if appropriate; supervise student as desirable; evaluate completed project.

Teaching resources: Any appropriate ones, especially learning resources in libraries, laboratories, studios, and shops.

Uses and values: High level of cognitive and affective development; develop competency in a specific field of study at a high level; develop self-directiveness and ability to further own learning; enable particular students to develop a specialized talent or capability; prepare a student for advanced study in a field. Should be used in the carrying out of any type of curriculum design.

Drawbacks and defects: Inclination to use independent study possibilities for routine class work of little real challenge; homework under another name; difficulty of maintaining student interest in a project over a long period of time; lack of facilities to accommodate all qualified students; student specializes too early in his education, neglecting other general goals.

Community Activities

Throughout this book we have emphasized the desirability of a program of community-centered experiences for students, especially those enrolled in the middle and high schools. This aspect of the curriculum should loom large in instructional planning. In fact, community experiences should not and cannot be carried out unless there is a fully developed plan that states objectives for the entire program as well as each segment, the kinds of opportunities which will be made available for students, the conditions under which they will participate, the nature of supervision and control, and the responsibilities and obligations of the students participating. These community experiences, in turn, provide some of the most important opportunities provided in the entire instructional program.

Major characteristics: Student participation in the work and activities of governmental agencies, social service and welfare agencies, civic organizations and programs, churches and synagogues, child-care centers, health clinics, nursing and convalescent homes, home-service programs, and similar service organizations, agencies, or groups; work in businesses, offices of professional persons, factories, construction firms, industrial firms on a nonpaying basis; participate on a paid basis in work-experience programs established by the school in cooperation with firms; participate in various types of campaigns, such as appeals for funds for community agencies, political campaigns, civic improvement programs, celebrations, and special events; engage in human development program, often on a one-to-one basis.

Groupings: Individual or small groups; usually at high school level, but some possibilities should be available for younger students.

Student activity: Complete involvement on a personal basis.

Teacher activity: Sponsor individuals or small groups; plan the program, ascertaining opportunities available; supervise students in their work.

Teaching resources: The facilities and people of the entire community.

Uses and values: Contributes significantly to attainment of goals of the school, especially in the affective domain; assists students in making career choices; develops good work habits; contributes to an understanding of the community—problems, future developments, needs, desirability as a place to live; develops leadership, self-assurance, self-discipline, and ingenuity; contributes to motivation for school work.

Drawbacks and defects: Great difficulty in obtaining enough opportunities in community service for all students; extra cost and expense to the student; requires additional staff to provide supervision and administration, hence question of priorities in budget making; problem of safety and security; difficult to administer in terms of student schedules, other nonclass activities, bus schedules, lunch periods, outside-of-school duties; resistance of many taxpayers, parents, and employers of the community; opposition or lack of cooperation by employees in cooperating firms, offices, and agencies.

Services Provided by the School

The services provided students contribute also to the attainment of goals and should be recognized as a part of the instructional program. The principal contributions to instructional objectives are made by the school counseling and guidance service, health services, and services for exceptional children in need of special provisions. These services not only contribute to the personal development of the individual but directly provide learning opportunities for the student. Again, the staff persons in charge of these services should engage in the same kinds of planning as those guiding classroom instruction—define desired student outcomes as objectives, plan learning opportunities that will enable students to achieve these objectives, and evaluate the quality of the service in terms of these objectives.

INSTRUCTION AND THE HIDDEN OR UNSTUDIED "CURRICULUM"

In Chapter 4 we defined what some educational sociologists designate as the hidden or unstudied "curriculum" and noted that students in school have purposes and objectives that may not be fully congruent with those of the school or the teacher. Moreover, they also set purposes for themselves that are usually unrecognized by the school officially or teachers in interacting with students in classroom or non-classroom situations. Yet it is apparent to shrewd observers of student behavior in school and the few researchers who have studied the situation that this "unofficial curriculum" is an important aspect of the student's schooling. We will examine the matter as a part of the instructional program—that is, as an aspect of curriculum implementation.

Nature of the Unofficial Instructional Program

Three kinds of unofficial sets of learning situations may be identified: the managerial and organizational apparatus and arrangements of the school; the sociology of the school, that is, the social climate and processes of group living and the interactions among the school family; and the images and situation-sets of students with regard to teachers and the school as an institution, and of teachers and administrators with regard to the students.

By and large, the unstudied "curriculum," more appropriately designated as the unofficial instructional program of the school, is primarily concerned with the socialization function of the school, and, hence, directly or indirectly with preparation for adulthood (see Chapter 3). Robert Dreeben, now at the University of Chicago, in a sociological analysis of schooling, brilliantly argues

that schools, through their structural arrangements and the behavior patterns of teachers, provide pupils with certain experiences largely unavailable in other social settings, and that these experiences, by virtue of their peculiar characteristics, represent conditions conducive to the acquisition of norms. . . . pupils learn the norms of independence, achievement, universalism, and specificity as outcomes of the schooling process.[15]

At another point in his study, he elaborates on the question of "what is learned in school" in this unstudied aspect of the program:

Pupils learn to accept principles of conduct, or social norms, and to act according to them. Implicit in this contention are the following assumptions: (1) Tasks, constraints, and opportunities available within social settings vary with the structural properties of those settings; (2) individuals who participate in those tasks, constraints, and opportunities derive principles of conduct (norms) based on their experiences in coping with them; and (3) the content of the principles varies with the setting.[16]

Lawrence Kohlberg, an educational sociologist of Harvard, takes the same position on the importance and effects of the hidden "curriculum" on the socialization of students: "What is the essential nature of the hidden curriculum as a vehicle of moral growth? Our viewpoint accepts as inevitable the crowds, the praise, and the power which the school inevitably contains."[17] Philip Jackson, in his study of some important characteristics of a classroom, points out the nature of the socialization process and the significance of the hidden curriculum:

As he learns to live in school our student learns to subjugate his own desires to the will of the teacher and to subdue his own actions in the interest of the common good. He learns to be passive and to acquiesce to the network of rules, regulations, and routines in which he is embedded. He learns to tolerate petty frustrations and accept plans and policies of higher authorities, even when their rationale is unexplained and their meaning unclear.[18]

Aspects of the Unofficial Learning Opportunities

The three major types of the hidden or unstudied "curriculum" are intertwined, all being part of a philosophy of schooling that pervades any particular school. For purposes of discussion we will consider each briefly, yet acknowledging their interrelatedness.

[15] Robert Dreeben, *On What Is Learned in School* (Reading, Mass.: Addison-Wesley Publishing Company, Inc., 1968), p. 84.

[16] Dreeben, p. 44. In an interesting and illuminating report of a research study Sara Lawrence Lightfoot describes the process by which the hidden curriculum contributes to the socialization role of the school. See her "Politics and Reasoning: Through the Eyes of Teachers and Children," *Harvard Educational Review*, 43, 197–244 (May 1973).

[17] Lawrence Kohlberg, "The Moral Atmosphere of the School," in Norman V. Overly, ed., *The Unstudied Curriculum* (Washington, D.C.: Association for Supervision and Curriculum Development, 1970), p. 120.

[18] Philip W. Jackson, *Life in the Classroom* (New York: Holt, Rinehart and Winston, Inc., 1968), p. 36.

The administrative bureaucracy of the school often with its massive sets of rules, regulations, procedures, and managerial arrangements is a very significant element of the hidden "curriculum." Many sociologists regard these aspects of the schooling process as a primary factor in the socialization of the child and the adolescent. Easily identifiable elements of this nature are the whole classification system employed in school (school grades, groupings, attendance areas, vertical organization of school levels, promotion practices, eligibility for activities); evaluation methods (tests, grading and marking, honor rolls, achievement awards); rules for order (movement of students, attendance, toilet use, class seating arrangements, up and down staircases); sanctions and methods of punishment (scolding, ridicule, detention, suspension, dismissal, isolation, denial of privileges, chores); limitation and control of individual and group action (closed campus, censorship of publications, programs, presentations, and the like, selection of outside speakers, activities of clubs, student body committees, social affairs, behavior at school athletic events); and the authoritarianism of school officials and staff.

The social climate of the school is less readily characterized by overt actions, yet it too is a pervasive factor in schooling. A number of studies present evidence on its importance.[19] In planning instruction, teachers should take cognizance of this whole set of informal arrangements and the nature of the interpersonal relationships that exist among and between students and the faculty. The peer-mediated culture, especially in the upper levels of schooling, is a significant factor in the education of the young. Francis A. J. Ianni of Teachers College, Columbia University, points out that

(1) two distinct peer-mediated social systems exist—one for the adult . . . and one for the child, (2) the values and behaviors particular to each of these systems are to some extent generation and role bound, (3) there are in every high school at least two sets of values and norms and so at least two implicit codes of behavior, and (4) the dissonance between the two is at the heart of the failure of our high schools.[20]

[19] See especially Charles E. Bidwell, "The Social Psychology of Teaching," in Robert M. W. Travers, ed., *Second Handbook of Research on Teaching* (Chicago: Rand McNally and Company, 1973), pp. 413–449 and the research studies and other literature cited; also, Patricia Minuchin and others, *The Psychological Impact of School Experience* (New York: Basic Books, Inc., 1969); also, James S. Coleman, *The Adolescent Society* (New York: The Free Press, Inc., 1961); and Talcott Parsons, "The School Class as a Social System: Some of Its Functions in American Society," *Harvard Educational Review*, 29, 297–318 (Fall 1959).

[20] "An Anthropological View of High Schools: A Case Study," *T. C. Today*, 38, 1 (December, 1971).

One of the most serious concerns of many educators today is the impact of the school climate and the socializing processes of the school on students from culturally disadvantaged and/or impoverished homes. Commenting on this situation Bidwell points out the role of the teacher in ameliorating this aspect of a hidden "curriculum":

> I believe that a view of teaching as personal influence indicates one set of process of potential power to reduce differential chances for educational attainments that are linked to social origins. I have tried to show how certain social organizational conditions common to American schools make it difficult for teachers to become objects of student respect and sources of positive personal influence upon the formation of students' intellective values and attitudes. . . . If one is convinced that educational equality demands more than equal access, then he may do well to explore in detail those conditions in the social organization of schools that will strengthen or weaken teaching as a personal influence.[21]

Kohlberg adds: "We believe what matters in the hidden curriculum is the moral character and ideology of the teachers and principal as these are translated into a working social atmosphere which influences that atmosphere of children."[22]

Another aspect of the hidden "curriculum" is the images held by students, parents, and citizens generally of the school as an institution and of teachers as teachers. Rather than constituting a separate factor, such images are in large part an element of the other two factors. Yet, these images themselves serve invidiously to perpetuate the undesirable aspects of a hidden "curriculum." George Gerbner, Dean of the Annenberg School of Communications, University of Pennsylvania, writes that "my examination of the evidence suggests that teachers, schools, and scholars project a synthetic cultural image that helps to explain—and determine—the ambivalent functions and paradoxical fortunes of the educational enterprise in American society."[23] He then examines the images of schools and teachers created by the media in this country and considers the symbolic function of such images on schools.

We all know too well the images created by Ichabod Crane, "Our Miss Brooks," "Goodbye, Mr. Chips," "Mr. Peepers," and many more caricatures of school masters and teachers, and the images of the school especially portrayed by sports writers, television shows, movies,

[21] Bidwell, "The Social Psychology of Teaching," p. 442.

[22] Kohlberg, "The Moral Atmosphere of the School," p. 120.

[23] George Gerbner, "Teacher Image and the Hidden Curriculum," *The American Scholar*, 42, 66 (Winter 1972–1973).

novels, and all forms of communications. The impact of such images on the attitudes of students and parents toward teachers and the school is a significant factor in the effectiveness of the school, especially in terms of the moral influence and commitments which Bidwell and Kohlberg advocate so strongly.

What does this brief excursion into the realm of the unofficial instructional program imply for curriculum planning and instruction?

1. The existence, nature, and effect of this unofficial, unstudied aspect of the total program of schooling should be fully acknowledged and understood by administrators, teachers, students, parents, and citizens.

Increasingly significant research and scholarly writings on the matter, citations to some of which have been made, should be examined by educators in graduate studies, institutes, workshops, and staff meetings. Parents and students should be involved in these programs of study.

2. A school staff, with students and parents as participants, should examine in depth the nature and character of the unstudied "curriculum" of their school.

3. Any formal efforts in planning should give attention to the whole matter of the unstudied "curriculum." This is especially desirable in defining goals and subgoals in the affective domain; plans for implementing any curriculum plan should take account of learning opportunities, planned or informally developed, that contribute significantly to the socialization process, especially with respect to moral and character development.

Included in such programs of planning should be a deliberate examination of the organizational structure, administrative arrangements, and policies, rules, regulations, and procedures for the management of the school.

4. Human relationhips are a significant aspect of the hidden "curriculum"; the school staff, with students and parents, should examine the nature and character of these interactive processes, giving special attention to such matters as social class distinctions, cliques, favoritism and rejection, discrimination, and the like. Bidwell, particularly, points out conditions that affect the personal influence of the teacher in the teacher-student dyads.[24]

In essence, the hidden nature of the unstudied "curriculum" should be brought out in the open, be fully examined and evaluated, and then be deliberately made a part of a program of socialization and moral development. Kohlberg summarizes: "The transformation of the hidden

[24] Bidwell, "The Social Psychology of Teaching," pp. 417–429.

curriculum into a moral atmosphere is not a matter of one or another educational technique or ideology or means, but a matter of the moral energy of the educator, of his communicated belief that his school or classroom has a human purpose."[25]

BASES FOR SELECTING INSTRUCTIONAL MODES

Within this wide array of instructional methods—with many variations within a mode possible—teachers face a major professional responsibility in selecting the mode or modes appropriate for implementing an entire instructional program of a school or educational institution. All of the broad types of modes described in the previous sections have merit for accomplishing appropriate purposes; hence all should, and probably will, be used even by an individual teacher and certainly by a staff of teachers in a building during a relatively short period of time. Just as we stated in Chapter 5 that it is desirable, even necessary, to use a number of methods of organizing the curriculum according to the purposes being served at a particular time for a specific group of students, so it is in the selection of instructional modes. A variety of instructional methods is postulated for implementing something as broad and complex as a curriculum plan for the education of children, youth, and young adults. In this section some important guides for the selection of instructional methods will be presented.

Goals and Objectives Being Sought

The first consideration in planning instruction is the purposes for which instruction is being undertaken. The objectives postulated for a course, activity, or unit of work—formulated to contribute maximally to the general goals of the school—should be a primary factor in planning. A general goal often may be attained by a wide range of routes, that is, units of work and teaching methods, but specific objectives for instruction once determined often narrow the choices considerably.

Maximize Opportunities to Achieve Goals

An important consideration in planning instruction is to provide the richest opportunities feasible for achieving goals. Two facets of this aspect of selecting instructional modes are apparent: any particular unit of instruction should be selected and planned so as to contribute maximally to the attainment of specified goals and corollary objectives; but,

---

[25] Kohlberg, "The Moral Atmosphere of the School," p. 121.

concomitant outcomes that may be realized should also be a factor in planning.

To illustrate these points, let us assume a general goal of one of the curriculum domains is: "To express ideas in speech, writing, or in some artistic form with increasing clarity and correctness." A multitude of instructional activities may be used to assist the student in achieving this goal. Hence a teacher or planning team in stating objectives and planning a unit of work, say at the upper elementary school level, that will contribute to the realization of this goal may choose among such activities as "writes a social letter that is correct in form and clear in expression," "speaks before the class in a pleasing manner and voice without being overcome by embarrassment or experiencing undue strain," "chooses the correct word, punctuation, or phrase for blank spaces in sentences in a workbook," or "uses correctly words in a list in sentences, referring to a dictionary if uncertain about the meaning," and so on.

What particular learning activity should be chosen? Additional factors to be considered follow, but here we suggest that it be one that enables students to achieve the goal and, at the same time, promises to provide the most in desirable concomitant learnings. Perhaps in the above list the suggestion of writing a letter may hold such a promise. The boy or girl may write his grandmother to tell her about something he or she did recently. Perhaps, then, the concomitant is enhancement of friendship or of love.

Selecting instructional modes for achieving objectives in the first category of the Bloom taxonomy in the cognitive domain, "knowledge," is quite different from choosing modes that would be appropriate for the fifth category, "synthesis." In the affective domain choices would be more open-ended and less restricted by the purposes being served. However, it should be fully recognized that a choice of modes is available in any instance. Hence, the goals and objectives being sought are directive but not definitive or decisive in planning teaching methods.

Moreover, in planning instruction for the realization of goals, teachers should take account of the effects of the hidden curriculum, as discussed earlier, on the attainment or failure to attain goals. It often will be possible to enhance the contribution of this unofficial aspect of schooling, or, on the other hand, to counteract or eliminate what could be deterrents to goal achievement.

Principles of Learning.

The theories and principles of learning, listed in Chapter 3 as an important data source for curriculum planning, should be drawn upon extensively in selecting modes of instruction. Too often teachers rely on operant conditioning as the psychological base for teaching, neglecting the theories and principles enunciated by Piaget, Carl Rogers, McVicker Hunt, Arthur Combs, Jerome Bruner, Erik Erikson, David Ausubel, Robert Gagné, David McClelland, Robert White, and others.

In spite of all that has been written and advocated by specialists in teaching methodology and psychologists, a rather severe indictment of teaching was made by Frederick McDonald, a well-known psychologist himself, in the first annual report of the Stanford Center for Research and Development in Teaching:

> Teaching style is probably the most static aspect of schooling. Teachers teach today in much the same way as they have for generations. The basic style is didactic, with the teacher dispensing information to passive pupils. At regular intervals, the teacher examines the children upon how much of this information they have absorbed and retained. It is the teacher who asks questions, rarely the pupil. The structure of the answers is predetermined by the context in which the questions are formulated; only infrequently does a child's schooling permit him to discover problems.[26]

Psychologists and educators alike recognize the difficulty in translating psychological principles into practice, but much greater efforts to do so are apparent in recent years. The aspects of psychology that have the most to contribute to instructional planning are the nature of cognitive development, motivation, reinforcement, conceptualization, the development of attitudes and values, and the nature and growth of motor abilities and skills. The concept of basic human needs (Maslow, Prescott, Glasser, Erikson) is also important in planning instruction.

Individual Learning Styles

An increasing amount of significant research in the past few years points out that the interactive process between an individual student and the teacher is a very important factor in determining the nature and quality of learning and development that results from instruction. Bloom, for example, insists that

> some researchers have taken the position that it is the *teaching*, not the teacher, that is the key to the learning of students, that is, it is not what teachers are *like* but what they *do* in interacting with their students in the classroom that determines what students learn and how they feel about the learning and about themselves.[27]

[26] Stanford Center for Research and Development in Teaching, "Second Annual Report" (Palo Alto, Calif.: The Center, April 1968, available as ERIC Document No. 024642), p. 146.

[27] Benjamin S. Bloom, "Innocence in Education," *School Review*, 80, 340 (May 1972).

In a very significant investigation of this whole matter of aptitude-treatment interaction (ATI) Lee Cronbach and Richard Snow not only have analyzed and summarized a large body of research on the subject but report some original investigations of their own.[28] Their principal purpose was: "Assume that a certain set of outcomes from an educational program is desired. In what manner do the characteristics of learners affect the extent to which they attain the outcomes from each of the treatments that might be considered?"[29]

Based on their studies, they believe that the most effective learning takes place when the interactive process (teaching) is one that is best suited to the individual student in terms of his learning style. A learning environment that is "optimal for one person is not optimal for another." The educational environment must be matched with the individual. "Adaptation to the individual," they state, "has never been systematic because no one has known the principles that govern the matching of learner and instructional environment."[30] Hence, they plead for a large body of research that will at least begin to establish tested rules for making adaptations to individual learners that are derived from theory. They hope for "a true education that employs unique means whenever the child's distinctive development makes traditional methods ineffective for him."[31]

They believe that much of our effort in recent years to provide compensatory education for disadvantaged students, including Head Start and the like, and much of the so-called remedial training in schools are ineffective and largely wasted because such programs have treated children en masse rather than providing personalized instruction based on each child's learning style. The ATI is the wrong kind. Yet they conclude their entire study by acknowledging that much more research is needed before really valid principles on ATI can be established.

The ultimate aim of such efforts, as stated by Cronbach and Snow, is to enable teachers to plan better instructional programs:

> The long-range requirement is for an understanding of the factors that cause a pupil to respond to one instructional plan rather than another. These plans should differ in more than the amount of time devoted to specific drills. The range of instructional procedures open to the educator is enormous—individual projects, workbooks, teacher-monitored problem-solving, group

[28] Lee J. Cronbach and Richard E. Snow, "Individual Differences in Learning Ability as a Function of Instructional Variables" (Palo Alto, Calif.: Stanford Center for Research and Development in Teaching, March 1969, available as ERIC Document No. 029001).

[29] Cronbach and Snow, p. 6.

[30] Cronbach and Snow, p. 13.

[31] Cronbach and Snow, p. 11.

projects, discussion, etc. etc. The development of new media greatly extends the range of methods and also extends the capability of the school to administer flexible and diversified programs. There is no reason to assume that an eclectic mixture of all methods will serve all kinds of pupils, or that the choice of methods is a function of subject matter alone. On the contrary, there must be some kinds of pupils who respond best to group discussions, and others who do much better by themselves. The same is to be said of all the parameters of instruction: level of reading and other kinds of comprehension required by the presentation, sternness or permissiveness of supervision, degree to which competition is introduced, etc.[32]

Another significant body of literature on this matter of teacher effectiveness with different children is contained in a recent report issued by the U.S. Office of Education.[33] In a painstaking analysis of research Michelson states that

the concept that teacher resourceness differs by type of child I call "teacher specificity." Since different students will respond differently to different styles, attitudes, activities, language, strictness, etc., these properties of teacher activities should be investigated and directed to teachers who need them.[34]

A third highly significant study adds weight to this basic consideration in the planning of instruction. The prestigious Rand Corporation, widely used by government agencies to make studies for use in formulating public policy, released in late 1971 a report that should be a handbook for all decision-makers in the schools.[35] The study covers a range of topics on the effectiveness of the schools in educating children and youth, but at this point we refer to a conclusion about teaching styles:

There is some weak evidence that the impact of an educational practice may be conditional on other aspects of the situation. Simply stated, this hypothesis argues that teacher, student, instructional method, and, perhaps, other aspects of the educational process interact with each other. Thus, a teacher

[32] Cronbach and Snow, p. 177.

[33] *Do Teachers Make a Difference? A Report of Research on Pupil Achievement* (Washington, D.C.: Government Printing Office, 1970, Catalog No. HE 5.258:58042).

[34] Stephan Michelson, "The Association of Teacher Resourceness with Children's Characteristics" in *Do Teachers Make a Difference?*, pp. 150–151.

[35] Harvey A. Averch and others, *How Effective Is Schooling? A Critical Review and Synthesis of Research Findings*, Final Report to the President's Commission on School Finance (Santa Monica, Calif.: The Rand Corporation, December 1971, available from the Government Printing Office, Washington, D.C., Catalog No. Pr 37.8:Sch 6/Sch. 6/2).

who works well (is effective) with one type of student using one method might be ineffective when working with another student having different characteristics, or when using another method. The effectiveness of a teacher, or method, or whatever, varies from one situation to another.[36]

The authors summarize the research supporting this conclusion in a section of the report, citing a number of studies.[37]

Self-Fulfilling Prophecies and Educational Stratification

Closely related to the matter of aptitude-treatment interaction as a basis for planning instruction is that of teacher expectations. Teachers and other educators became greatly interested in this factor following the publication of a revealing investigation by Robert Rosenthal and Lenore Jacobson.[38] Later, Rosenthal cited other research on the subject and reaffirmed his conclusions.[39] However, reviews of their work by psychologists raised serious questions about the validity of the study, and Elashoff and Snow, with Rosenthal and Jacobson's permission and using much of their raw data, prepared a thorough reanalysis of the research.[40] They conclude that most of the Rosenthal-Jacobson conclusions are invalid, except for some relating to pupils in grades 1 and 2, and in this instance they did not confirm or reject the conclusions but felt that further studies needed to be made.

Nevertheless, these studies have aroused great interest in the possibility of a strong relation between teacher expectations and the methods of instruction used by teachers. Stated in terms of classroom practice, the question is whether teachers who because of previous test data about a pupil's abilities or capabilities to perform in the classroom —whether they regard him or her as a high achiever or a low achiever— markedly influence the ways in which the teacher will work with the pupil, both with regard to the interactive process and the substantive content of instruction.

[36] Averch and others, p. xii.

[37] Averch and others, pp. 50–92.

[38] Robert Rosenthal and Lenore Jacobson, *Pygmalion in the Classroom: Teacher Expectation and Pupils' Intellectual Development* (New York: Holt, Rinehart and Winston, Inc., 1968).

[39] Robert Rosenthal, "Teacher Expectation and Pupil Learning," in Overly, pp. 53–84.

[40] Janet D. Elashoff and Richard E. Snow, *A Case Study in Statistical Inference: Reconsideration of the Rosenthal-Jacobson Data on Teacher Expectancy,* Technical Report No. 15, Stanford Center for Research and Development in Teaching (Palo Alto, Calif.: The Center, December 1970, available as ERIC Document No. 046892); also published in a revised version as *Pygmalion Reconsidered,* Contemporary Educational Issues Series (Worthington, O.: Charles A. Jones Publishing Company, 1972).

Whether Rosenthal and Jacobson, and other researchers on the subject of the self-fulfilling prophecy, have established valid findings from their investigations or not does not belie the fact that teachers' interactive processes with students and the kinds of curriculum and instructional differentiations made in school on the basis of test results, previous academic records, the cultural, economic, and social status of the family, personal prejudices, and personal likes and dislikes with respect to the characteristics of an individual pupil do occur.

Another aspect of this matter is the establishment of "remedial" programs of instruction and so-called compensatory education by schools. It is not the adaptation of instruction to individual differences on the basis of learning styles, achievement rates, or levels of achievement that is the issue, for the entire educational program must be personalized to the maximum degree possible, but the issues are the methods used to assess abilities and potentialities of the students and the kinds and qualities of learning activities provided students assigned or enrolled in such instructional programs.

There are those, including eminent psychologists, who believe that children differ innately in their learning abilities and processes, ranging from a low level of associative, or rote, learning to the higher levels of conceptualization.[41] On the basis of these sharp differences that are postulated to exist among children, educational processes should also be differentiated. Jensen, for example, states blandly that "I am reasonably convinced that all the basic scholastic skills can be learned by children with normal Level I learning ability [associative level], provided the instructional techniques do not make g (i.e., Level II) [conceptual ability] the *sine qua non* of being able to learn."[42] Thus he clearly calls for a two-stream system of education—one stream for Level I-type children and another for the "superior," Level II children. But he has a sop for the Level I group: "But schools must also be able to find ways of utilizing other strengths in children whose major strength is not of the cognitive variety."[43]

In contrast, Cronbach and Snow, in what must surely be one of the most significant research documents appearing in recent years, state the issue and take their stand:

This raises questions of educational and social policy, as well as of psychological theory and instructional tactics. Unless the rote instruction carries the

[41] Arthur R. Jensen, "How Much Can We Boost IQ and Scholastic Achievement?" *Harvard Educational Review*, 39, 1–123 (Winter 1969).

[42] Jensen, p. 117.

[43] Jensen, p. 117.

pupil towards the true educational goals of the common school program, it cannot be defended as a proper application of ATI [Aptitude-Treatment Interaction]. To teach some children those skills that can be learned by rote and deprive them of concepts that cannot is not effective education.[44]

Certainly no truly professional educator will ever be willing to condemn children on the basis of contrived tests, observation, or past attainments to a "Jensen," Level I-type of educational program. This simply is not a humane, democratic, or valid way to plan an instructional program. Different procedures and methods will need to be used with different students for the attainment of educational goals, but regardless of his abilities and learning styles these efforts to personalize instruction should never deny a student the whole range of opportunities for the fullest measure of development of his unique potentialities.

Thought must turn to an education that is not merely remedial in the narrow "training" sense, but to a true education that employs unique means wherever the child's distincitve development makes traditional methods ineffective for him. The seriousness of this matter depends on the stage of development of a nation.[45]

Continued tenacity on the part of teachers in holding to traditional concepts of stratification and postulated correlative methods of teaching, or even to a more humane effort to rely on an inaccurate intuitiveness, cannot be accepted as a basis for instruction in the 1970s. B. F. Skinner stated the requirement for the future: "We need to find practices which permit all teachers to teach well and under which all students learn as efficiently as their talents permit."[46]

The only acceptable prophecy that should be self-fulfilling among teachers today is that every child has precious talents and potentialities that should be developed to the utmost. The school's responsibility is to contribute in every way feasible to his or her self-realization.

Feasibility of Teaching Teams

Instructional planning may be considerably different and alter the selection of instructional modes in schools that use teams of teachers. A team-teaching plan augurs well for better instruction in a number of ways, but it may also become a scheme that aggravates stolid modes of teaching. The latter result of a team is evidenced in many high schools

---

[44] Cronbach and Snow, p. 191.

[45] Cronbach and Snow, p. 11.

[46] B. F. Skinner, "Teaching Science in High School—What Is Wrong?" *Science,* 159, 705 (February 1968).

that systematically schedule large group classes and in elementary schools that select team members primarily to teach a subject specialty.

On the positive side, a team could provide various styles of student-teacher interaction that would enhance a more desirable match between student and teacher; it would enable the team to provide a broader range of learning activities for a group of students, thus contributing to more personalized instruction. A selected subgroup of students could engage in a set of learning activities planned by the team specifically to meet an educational need they have in common, and then they could return to the larger group for setting up new groupings to serve other needs and interests. Such an arrangement is one way of reducing the need for special remedial classes.

A primary advantage of a team that genuinely functions as a planning group is the sharing of know-how, insight, and competencies. Two heads are better than one in planning the educational opportunities to be provided a particular group of students.

Facilities, Equipment, and Resources

Instructional planning, unfortunately, is often circumscribed by the facilities available, the equipment and teaching resources that may be used, and the administrative organization and structure of the school. The relation is evident in the use of educational technology, laboratories, shops, gymnasiums, outdoor or other life science centers, camps, and the like. Similarly, the use of games is restricted to those available or that can be contrived by teachers; field trips and community experiences, at least to some extent, are dependent on the availability of transportation. Creative work in some areas is limited by available materials; inquiry and discovery requires adequate library and other types of learning resources.

The whole administrative arrangements and structure also influence instructional planning. For example, if the time schedule is a rigid one set up in tightly prescribed blocks, independent study of the kind described above may be more difficult to arrange; if students are not permitted to work in laboratories or shops unless a teacher is present to supervise, inquiry and creative work may be curtailed; if students in secondary schools are rigidly scheduled in traditional classes for 25–28 of 30 available weekly periods, independent study, small-group work, use of learning resources on an individual basis, and similar student participation in self-learning is more difficult to arrange.

With respect to instructional planning, teachers should be as imaginative and resourceful as possible in a given situation in using modes that involve students in a highly active role. Most observers point out that teachers can involve students much more than they do regardless of the restrictive factors considered above. Examples of how schools in both England and this country have been able to develop their programs of informal education in the most conventional and restricted settings point the way. In addition, teachers, individually and collectively, should be fully involved in budget-making and the selection and purchase of equipment, supplies, books, teaching materials, and the like. And, of course, teachers should be extensively involved in planning new buildings and renovations of existing buildings.

ACCOUNTABILITY

Teachers, administrators, and others employed to provide educational programs for children and youth have always been accountable to the citizens for the quality of their work. Socrates was put to death as a result of his accounting. And the earliest schoolmaster on record in this country, one Philemon Pormont, was accountable to the citizens of the Massachusetts Bay Colony who employed him in 1635 "to become schoolmaster for the teaching and nurturing of children with us." In recent years accountability by the schools has been a matter prompting legislation in some states, school board policy in some communities, and public discussion by newspaper editors, taxpayers, groups, parents, and citizens generally.

Inasmuch as instruction is the implementation of curriculum plans and a whole host of decisions by policy-makers, the outcomes of instruction constitute the starting point in an accounting of results. The concluding section of this chapter will, therefore, give consideration to the matter of accountability in education.

The term "accountability" itself denotes the meaning of the concept—someone "having to report, explain, or justify"[47] to someone else, obviously in authority over the individual. Thus accountability is a master-servant, employer-employee, voter-office holder, citizens-public servant, taxpayer-government, contractee-contractor relation, that is, one party answering to another party. Its use in educational management and planning circles means that those employed to operate the schools must report, explain, or justify what they do to persons superior to them, not only within the system itself but to the legal authorities vested with control of the school—a board of education, a state department of education, a state legislature, and, in certain respects (see Chapter 1), agen-

[47] *Random House Dictionary of the English Language* (New York: Random House, Inc., 1966), p. 10.

cies of the federal government. Accountability must involve assessment, appraisal, and evaluation, whichever is appropriate.

The blue-ribbon President's Commission on School Finance put it well: "If education is to compete successfully with these other functions [of government], its proponents must be able to demonstrate that whatever funds are provided are achieving the desired results.[48] Marvin C. Alkin, Director of the Center for the Study of Evaluation, restricts the term as used in schools today drastically—"Accountability is a negotiated relationship in which the participants agree in advance to accept specified rewards and costs on the basis of evaluation findings as to the attainment of specified ends."[49]

Leon Lessinger, who takes an extreme position in support of the movement, states that "accountability means that the members of the public as well as school officials will be able to compare the costs of producing certain benefits in various ways."[50] In fact, Lessinger calls his own plan for making schools accountable "educational engineering" and writes in terms of "development capital" and "management support." The product in his instance is not nuts and bolts but "kids" who can perform assigned tasks. Obviously, the current movement is part and parcel of the whole systems approach to educational planning, with great emphasis on results, costs of producing these results, and alternative possibilities weighed on the basis of costs. Lessinger insists that "essentially we judge a school, or ought to judge it, by whether its students gain certain skills and knowledge that can be measured against some set of standards or judgments, and by the cost of producing these gains."[51]

Murray Wax, a cultural anthropologist, has made an analogy that seems tragically apt: "If I had to use a particular imagery for the analysis of most programs of accountability with regard to schools, I would say that the appropriate image is that of a *factory*—the mass production factory."[52]

Dennis Gooler has given the most common sense definition in light of the present situations: "Educational accountability is concerned with determining how *well* the school is doing what it does, *and* whether

[48] President's Commission on School Finance, *Schools, People, and Money: The Need for Educational Reform*, Final Report (Washington, D.C.: Government Printing Office, 1972), p. 58.

[49] Marvin C. Alkin, "Accountability Defined," *The Journal of Educational Evaluation: Evaluation Comment*, Vol. 3, No. 3 (May 1972), p. 2.

[50] Leon M. Lessinger, *Every Kid a Winner: Accountability in Education* (New York: Simon and Schuster, Inc., 1970), p. 32.

[51] Lessinger, p. 8.

[52] Murray L. Wax, "How Should Schools Be Held Accountable?" *Urban Review*, 5, 11 (January 1972).

it is doing those things it should."[53] But Robert Nash and Russell Agne, another anthropologist and a science educator, have offered a scathing analysis of the current movements in accountability:

> The accountability movement is generating an ethos among educators that must not go unchallenged. This ethos—whose governing principles are based on a technological-economic world-view—is distinguished by its frenzied insistence of the large-scale transportation of attitudes and practices from the world of business, engineering, and science to the world of education. One result of this slavish dependence on the beliefs and procedures of other fields has been to reduce the total educational endeavor to a tired litany of achievement, performance, and production characterized by the blank torpor of systems analysis, technological engineering, quality control, and replicability.[54]

Elements in Accountability

These are the three broad aspects of accountability as applied to schools: (1) decide for what should the schools be held accountable; (2) obtain evidence on the extent to which these postulated obligations have been fulfilled; (3) judge in terms of some standards whether the program of the school for fulfilling its responsibilities is acceptable, or, as an alternative, whether the stated responsibilities should be redefined. Inasmuch as we treat evaluation as an aspect of the curriculum planning process in Chapter 7, only a brief discussion of the current movement of accountability as it relates to instructional planning will be included here.

For What Should the Schools Be Accountable?

In principle a school should be accountable for all of the purposes for which it was established by the citizens. While this seems to be common sense and the only acceptable answer to the question, in practice views on the scope of accountability range all the way from those who would hold the school accountable only for the behavioral objectives which may be measured in quantifiable terms to those that wish to include the myriad of functions and purposes which properly are assigned schools in the assessment. This difference in point of view is the basis of a bitter controversy among educators, and, to some extent, the public as it has become involved in the movement. In Chapter 4 we considered these differences, and that is the same issue at stake in accountability.

[53] Dennis L. Gooler, "Some Uneasy Inquiries into Accountability," in Leon M. Lessinger and Ralph W. Tyler, eds., Accountability in Education (Worthington, O.: Charles A. Jones Publishing Company, 1971), p. 54.
[54] Robert J. Nash and Russell M. Agne, "The Ethos of Accountability—A Critique," Teachers College Record, 73, 357 (February 1972).

Sampling of these positions on the scope of accountability illustrate the issue.

The President's Commission stated that

> Educators are expected to perform functions which impart to students the knowledge of basic skills such as reading, writing, and arithmetic, and they can, and should, be held accountable for their ability to teach those skills. In addition to basic skills, they must try to develop for students a desire to learn; a socially acceptable set of values and attitudes; and an ability to relate to others. These latter student attributes are not easily measured.[55]

The narrowest, most limited view of accountability calls only for a measure of instruction on the basis of behavioral outcomes. Lessinger stated this position: "When a program in the schools is well engineered, it will require educational planners to specify, in measurable terms, what they are trying to accomplish."[56] And one federal official, responsible for administering laws that require at least some kind of accounting for results obtained from federal grants, said that "our goals must be stated in quantifiable terms. Broad, sweeping, and idealistic generalities will not do if we seek to measure ends and those means that may influence ends. . . . Educational goals, stated in a quantifiable language, will provide the end we seek to attain."[57]

The advocates of quantifiable objectives or performance specifications recognize, of course, that there are other kinds of outcomes desired from the school experience. Bell continued: "Although some goals in education will be difficult to quantify and respected authorities will differ on some priorities, there exists, it seems to me, a general consensus about many desired outcomes. This is represented in many almost universally accepted curricula found in schools across the nation."[58] Lessinger takes the same position, recognizing that the schools do have many broad goals that are difficult to state objectively, but he insists, nevertheless, that we proceed to obtain data on those things that can be measured, believing that these aspects of the school program will comprise much of the curriculum and will constitute valid judgments about the school's total effectiveness. If it is effective in teaching basic skills and other com-

---

[55] President's Commission on School Finance, p. 58.

[56] Lessinger, *Every Kid a Winner: Accountability in Education*, p. 13.

[57] Terrel H. Bell, "The Means and Ends of Accountability," in John H. Fischer, chairman, *Proceedings of the Conferences on Educational Accountability* (Princeton, N.J.: Educational Testing Service, 1971), p. C–3.

[58] Bell, p. C–3.

petencies, he insists that it will likely be effective in teaching attitudes, meanings, self-concepts, desires, and the like—and vice versa.

This narrow type of accountability is closely related to and often associated with performance contracting, in which a contractor, often a private business firm but sometimes a teacher or staff of teachers, makes a contract with the board of education to instruct designated students so as to achieve prescribed levels of performance on specified behavioral objectives.

It should be emphasized that advocates of this limited kind of accountability do not repudiate or decry other functions and goals of the school, but only wish to establish this degree of accountability. Their point of view is that every child, except a few very exceptional ones, should acquire the basic skills of reading, writing, and arithmetic and essential knowledge for citizenship responsibilities and that the school must be held responsible for achieving such ends. Thus, accountability can clearly be specified in behavioral objectives, and results are definitively measured by appropriate tests. The educators themselves, the board of education, and the public can then judge whether the schools have done this job.

Another point of view on the scope of accountability differs sharply from the concept of behavioral objectives-performance standards measurement of quantifiable outcomes. H. Thomas James, President of the Spencer Foundation, has taken a determined stand on the matter:

> We have been notably unsuccessful as a society in this century in stating our aims of education. To face the prospect of being driven by circumstances, created as casually as by acceptance of the concept of accountability, to set trivial goals for our educational institutions, is appalling. A quite contrary course seems indicated, rather to dare to set our goals to fit our broadest perception of the scope of the human condition, and to challenge our model-builders to reach toward them, and to be critical of their failures to reach them.[59]

In an important essay on the subject of accountability, Arthur Combs recognized the significance of the movement but pointed out the serious deficiencies of the behavioral objectives approach for obtaining the output data. He proposed a much broader definition of what schools should be accountable for: "A truly comprehensive approach to account-

---

[59] H. Thomas James, "Public Expectations," in Fischer, *Proceedings of the Conferences on Educational Accountability*, p. H–8.

ability must take into consideration all aspects affecting the outcomes of schooling, using each for what it can contribute to the total picture, with full recognition that all are related and all are required."[60] He acknowledges the place behavioral statements of objectives have in planning and in evaluation, being useful for defining outcomes in skills and cognitive knowledge, but he insists that "they do not lend themselves well to more general objectives."

Combs believes that the overarching function of the school is to contribute to the development of intelligent persons who behave in an intelligent manner. Furthermore, intelligent behavior is based on "(a) the provision of new information or experience, and (b) the personal discovery by the learner of its personal meaning for him."[61] The schools must be held accountable for both of these aspects of education. Goals and objectives for instruction to fulfill the first responsibility may be stated behaviorally, and measured accordingly, but that is only a small part of instruction, and thus accountableness. Far more significant is the fostering of personal meaning and all that Combs endeavors to convey by that term; thus providing evidence for an accounting is a far different matter than testing performance on an objective test.

The most inclusive concept of accountability holds that the school should provide evidence of how well it is fulfilling the total set of purposes and functions for which it has accepted responsibility; this is, how well is it enabling every child, youth, and young adult in the community to achieve the general goals of education. Anything that contributes to the attainment of goals is encompassed within the scope of accountability: administrative policies and regulations; management processes; staff; parent-school relations; the goals for the school themselves, including the allocation of priorities and resources among curriculum domains; the total instructional program and process, including extrainstructional activities, services, the institutional climate, and the evaluation program; learning resources; and community experiences.

John Fischer has said about this whole matter of accountability:

But whether we speak as professionals or for the public, we had better remind ourselves that it is not yet possible to measure precisely everything that is important in education. Many of the qualities that made schools attractive to discerning parents and beneficial to children remain beyond the reach of available instruments. . . . In my view it would be grossly mis-

[60] Arthur W. Combs, *Educational Accountability: Beyond Behavioral Objectives* (Washington, D.C.: Association for Supervision and Curriculum Development, 1972), p. 2.

[61] Combs, p. 21.

leading to suggest that schools can be either soundly constructive or honestly accountable without a deep and continuing concern for their comprehensive institutional character. The cultivation of those qualities depends upon wise and farsighted combinations of policy, professional practice and personal commitment.[62]

Robert E. Stake of the Center for Instructional Research and Curriculum Evaluation, University of Illinois, strongly condemns most recent efforts to force an accountability plan on the schools:

Most state accountability proposals call for more uniform standards across the state, greater prespecification of objectives, more careful analysis of learning sequences, and better testing of student performance. These plans are doomed. What they bring is more bureaucracy, more subterfuge, and more constraints on student opportunities to learn. The newly enacted school accountability laws will not succeed in improving the quality of education for any group of learners.[63]

But, writes Stake, there are ways in which schools may properly be accountable:

Each school should confirm, and periodically reconfirm, its commitment to provide (a) high-quality teaching in the academic areas; (b) opportunities for experience that leads to social and intellectual maturity, personal responsibility, and human sensitivity; and (c) accommodation to the individual needs and aspirations of students and their parents.[64]

Accounting Evidence

The kinds of evidence that should be used to determine the degree to which a school has fulfilled its purposes will depend on what is being assessed. If a school wishes to determine if its use of Title I funds allocated by the federal government under the amended Elementary and Secondary Education Act has produced desirable results in educating disadvantaged children, it will obtain evidence of some kind in terms of the purposes of the special programs established with those funds. If a school wishes to provide evidence on how well it is developing intelligent behavior among its high school students, very different kinds of data and information will be needed.

Accounting for outcomes of instruction stated as behavioral

[62] John H. Fischer, "To Hold Ourselves Accountable," *Perspectives on Education,* Vol. 5, No. 3 (Summer 1972), pp. 4–6.

[63] Robert E. Stake, "School Accountability Laws," *The Journal of Educational Evaluation: Evaluation Comment,* 4, 1 (February 1973).

[64]   Stake, p. 2.

objectives or performance standards will be rendered usually in the form of test data stated in terms of norm- or criterion-referenced scores. An excerpt from a performance contract between the Dorsett Educational Systems, Inc., and the Texarkana, Arkansas, School System illustrates accounting of this extreme type:

> In consideration for services rendered, Dorsett will be compensated on the basis of actual student performance. . . . The student performance differential is determined by subtracting the entering grade-level achievement in math and reading from the exit level. Entry status and exit status are based on the SRA and ITBS tests as weighted.[65]

The Stull Bill, adopted by the state of California in July 1971, provides for the "evaluation and assessment of the performance of certificated personnel within each school district of the state." Each school district is required to

> adopt specific evaluation and assessment guidelines which shall include but not necessarily be limited . . . to (a) the establishment of standards of expected student progress in each area of study and of techniques for the assessment of that progress, (b) assessment of certificated personnel competence as it relates to the established standards. . . .[66]

It is indeed interesting to observe the ways in which California school districts have endeavored to carry out this act of accountability and the kinds of evidence being submitted to teachers on their performance.

As will be pointed out in Chapter 7, many kinds of data and information will be necessary if a proper and adequate accounting is to be made of all educational goals and other functions of the school. No additional treatment of such an evaluation need be made here, except to point out the necessity of including all important kinds of input—antecedent conditions, transactions, and the like.

It is evident that when a school makes public a report on its efforts to fulfill the obligations of accountability, the document should state fully the scope, limitations, and nature of the evidence. It should clearly show just what portion of the school's sets of goals and objectives, and of the program carried out to fulfill these goals, has been assessed.

---

[65] Lessinger, p. 212; for another example of performance contracting see Nolan Estes and Donald R. Waldrip, "Their Lives and Our Careers: Accountability as a Fair Trade in Education," in Fischer, *Proceedings of the Conferences on Educational Accountability*, pp. D–1 through 9.

[66] Assembly Bill 293 (Chapter 361, Sections 13403–13489, Education Code).

A report might, for example, cover only achievement in reading, as measured by a specified test, for grades 4 through 6 or just for pupils classified in grade 7. Results should be interpreted in terms of antecedent conditions, time allotments, instructional materials available, and similar pertinent information. The report should call attention to the limited scope of the test—what it measures, and what it does not measure, that, nevertheless, are important objectives of the reading program. A news release on the number of semifinalists among high school seniors on the National Merit Scholarship program is hardly a valid accounting of the program of that high school.

Standards for Judging

The third aspect of accountability is to judge whether the outputs are acceptable. As with every aspect of evaluation, this is a difficult matter to handle, especially in those types of accounting that consider costs—a very proper part of the procedure, in light of priorities. But how can a teacher, an educator, a school board member, or a citizen determine whether it is better to spend, say, $30 a pupil a year to carry on a special elementary school remedial reading program, to spend $22 a pupil a year to make available instructional television programs for all students in the school, not to do either of these but to hire another teacher so that foreign language instruction may be provided, or not to do any of these things and thus save the money? Similarly, should a remedial reading program be discontinued because the pupils participating in it gained only 0.80 of a grade on a standard reading test during the year, or should a school in which the students tested on the average to be seven to fifteen months below grade norms in mathematical skills be allocated enough money to install a new program of individualized instruction in mathematics?

On the other hand, should an individualized packet-prepared program for teaching high school biology be enthusiastically approved and continued because the evidence shows that 88 percent of the class completed all of the assigned packets by satisfactorily passing unit tests for each packet, but no evidence has been presented on the students' interest in and concern about environmental conditions in the community, region, and nation? When a millage increase vote fails on a school election, what specific programs should be eliminated in budget reduction— all kindergartens, intercollegiate athletics, instrumental music in the middle schools, or driver education, or should the staff be reduced accordingly, with all teachers being assigned larger classes and bigger loads? This is accountability, as the term is now commonly used, in action.

Obviously, all of these decisions are judgmental in nature. The issue is the kinds of evaluative data used in making the decision. Accountability that is based on hearsay, prejudice, incomplete or invalid data, a false or incomplete picture of feasible alternatives, erroneous conclusions, or deliberate withholding or failure to obtain essential evidence is vicious in its impact on schooling.[67]

In being accountable, and all educators and all schools as institutions are, goals and objectives must be valid, inclusive, and attainable, the proper kinds of evidence must be obtained, and judgments need to be based on a critical examination of the evidence in terms of feasible alternatives. It is an exceedingly complex and difficult undertaking in educational planning.

State legislatures, state departments of education, local boards of education, and the U.S. Congress are busily engaged in various kinds of accountability programs. So widespread is the movement that seven state departments of education—Colorado, Florida, Maryland, Michigan, Minnesota, Oregon, and Wisconsin—joined together in April 1972 to establish, with federal support, the Cooperative Accountability Project. The purpose of the Project, as stated by the operations board, is to serve the critical needs of the seven participating states in carrying on accountability programs, and then to help all states. It has been engaged in the development of "an accountability system that will serve as a model for State Education Agencies." The system was developed by the Project staff in cooperation with the seven state education departments, the U.S. Office of Education, and consultants in accountability and evaluation.

Some of the early work of the staff was to publish a compilation of goals developed by state agencies, laws passed by the various states on the subject of accountability and assessment, and a bibliography of state publications on these matters.[68]

Such efforts are in line with the recommendations of the President's Commission on School Finance:

The Commission recommends that state governments establish statewide evaluation systems to measure the effectiveness of educational programs.

[67] For an especially good discussion of these matters see J. Wayne Wrightstone, Thomas P. Hogan, and Muriel M. Abbott, *Accountability in Education and Associated Measurement Problems*, Test Service Notebook 33 (New York: Harcourt Brace Jovanovich, Inc., no date).

[68] Cooperative Accountability Project, *Legislation by the States: Accountability and Assessment in Education*, 1972; *Education in Focus: A Collection of State Goals for Elementary and Secondary Education*, 1972; *Bibliography of the State Educational Accountability Repository*, 1972; *Characteristics of and Models for State Accountability Legislation*; and untitled brochures (1362 Lincoln St., Denver, Colo. 80203: The Project).

These systems should include improved techniques for measuring progress and achievement in school as well as the ability of secondary school graduates to perform effectively in productive jobs or succeed in schools of higher education.[69]

The then U.S. Commissioner of Education, Sidney Marland, forecast in 1972 that

Indeed, within our time—perhaps within the next ten years—there could well be a nationwide accounting process or institution which would act like a certified public accountant in business, objectively assessing the success and failure of our schools and reporting the findings to the public. This agency would find ways to assess both the structure and the content of the educational process.[70]

The sweep of the accountability movement in recent years is also illustrated by developments in New York State. Governor Nelson Rockefeller in mid-April 1973 submitted to the legislature a proposal to establish in his own office (and independent of the State Board of Regents) an "inspector general of education," officially designated as "an office of education performance review." The office would be empowered to "investigate, with subpoena powers, the cost, quality and effectiveness of elementary and secondary education." The news article announcing the governor's action stated that "Mr. Rockefeller portrays himself as the restive captive of a fat, lazy educational establishment that is more inclined to call for millions of additional dollars than to examine the efficiency of its current expenditures."[71] Is that really an acceptable image of the schools and their respective staffs at this point in educational history?

Nevertheless, on the basis of a broad, sound approach, efforts to hold the schools accountable to their governing bodies and citizens is a movement that should be supported. Teachers, administrators, and other school personnel should insist that the accounting be all inclusive in terms of the accepted functions and purposes of the school, or that an accounting on a narrow segment of the total program be correctly accepted by those in authority and the public as only applying to that portion of the program, but in no way accounting for other portions. They should also demand that the evidence used in determining acceptability of the total program, or the segment, be as valid as it is possible to

[69] The President's Commission on School Finance, p. 58.

[70] Sidney Marland, "Accountability in Education," *Teachers College Record*, 73, 344 (February 1972).

[71] *New York Times*, April 22, 1973, p. 50. On July 1, 1973, Governor Rockefeller established the Office of Education Performance Review (see *New York Times*, Vol. 122, No. 42, 162, July 1, 1973, p. 27).

obtain, that it take account of antecedent conditions that affect outcomes, and that the standards for judging merit be appropriate and proper.

A broad analogy may be taken from the business world, in which accountability also is required. RCA Corporation, on entering the computer field in the early days of its development, lost a large amount of money over a number of years in that part of its business. It "accounted" to the stockholders, reporting these facts, but holding out hope that it could in due time make it profitable. But this hope was not realized, and the board of directors, on advice of the officers of the corporation, discontinued the manufacture of computers, writing off a loss of millions of dollars in their financial statement. This ill-fated undertaking had no bearing on the effectiveness of other parts of the huge company, and RCA products in other lines were widely bought and used with satisfaction. Similarly, a school system may determine through a soundly conceived evaluation program that its program for preparing auto mechanics at an entering level of skill is not effective and that acceptable returns on the expenditures are not being realized in comparison to other programs. The district officials may (1) revamp the program, (2) eliminate the program, or (3) continue to offer an inadequate, unacceptable program, ignoring the findings of the evaluation. Accountability is simply an effort to face such matters squarely and openly and make decisions on a rational basis. After all, RCA tried for years to put the computer division on a profitable basis, and the stockholders did not dismiss the board; the other divisions of the company were performing satisfactorily in terms of the accounts rendered.

From the standpoint of instructional planning, the accountability movement encourages those involved in planning, particularly teachers, to be realistic concerning the goals and objectives they set for specific instructional programs and for the school in general. Accountability also encourages planners to be imaginative in developing instructional opportunities so that all students may achieve the goals and objectives set for them within the limits of their capabilities and to obtain, in cooperation with professional evaluators, the most valid evidence possible on the extent to which these objectives are being realized.

Donald D. Woodington, a state commissioner of education, wrote as follows of the accountability movement:

I believe accountability, properly understood and well implemented, is a gift to parents and children, taxpayers, legislators, and educators. I think education can account for itself. In the accounting, it can develop proofs and insights to point the way to improved education.[72]

[72] Donald D. Woodington, "Accountability from the Viewpoint of a State Commissioner of Education," *Phi Delta Kappan*, 54, 95 (October 1972).

But his concept of being "well implemented" is the basic point to the whole matter:

> It is in this progression that education becomes truly accountable: *establishing goals, setting specific objectives, devising programs to meet the objectives, carrying out the programs, measuring their degree of success, comparing costs and performance under alternate programs, revising and trying again.*[73]

This is what curriculum planning as presented in this book is all about.

ADDITIONAL SUGGESTIONS FOR FURTHER STUDY

Broudy, Harry S., and John R. Palmer, *Exemplars of Teaching Method.* Chicago: Rand McNally and Company, 1965. An interesting and helpful analysis of teaching methods used by the great figures of the past, from the Sophists and Socrates to William Heard Kilpatrick.

Cusick, Philip A., *Inside High School: The Student's World.* New York: Holt, Rinehart and Winston, Inc., 1973. A description of the daily activities of some students in a relatively large senior high school, with particular reference to their adjustment to the hidden "curriculum" of the school.

Glasser, William, *The Effect of School Failure on the Life of a Child.* Washington, D.C.: National Association of Elementary School Principals, 1971. The writings and innovative work of William Glasser are well known. In this booklet he discusses the adverse effects of failure on children and what schools must do to eliminate it.

Hosford, P. L., *An Instructional Theory: A Beginning.* Englewood Cliffs, N.J.: Prentice-Hall, Inc., 1973. Models for the instructional process; relates the preparation of curriculum materials to teaching.

Popham, W. James, and Eva L. Baker, *Systematic Instruction.* Englewood Cliffs, N.J.: Prentice-Hall, Inc., 1970. One of the "handbook" types of publications that provide suggestions, models, and plans for planning and carrying on instruction.

Rist, Ray C., "Student Social Class and Teacher Expectations: The Self-Fulfilling Prophecy in Ghetto Education," *Harvard Educational Review,* 40, 411–450 (August 1970). A report of a study of "the manner in which 'inequalities imposed on children' become manifest within an urban ghetto school and the resultant differential experience for children."

Sciara, Frank J., and Richard K. Jantz, eds., *Accountability in American Education.* Boston: Allyn and Bacon, Inc., 1972. A book of readings that includes

[73] Woodington, p. 95.

a large number of articles on accountability, evaluation, assessment, performance contracting, and related developments.

Wight, Albert R., "Participative Education and the Inevitable Revolution," *Journal of Creative Behavior*, 4, 234–282 (Fall 1970). A well developed proposal for involving students in planning and carrying on their instructional program. Models and summaries are included. A challenging article.

Wynne, Edward, *The Politics of School Accountability*. Berkeley, Calif.: McCutchan Publishing Corporation, 1972. An outstanding study of the whole accountability movement, tracing it back a hundred years. His proposals for being accountable are in harmony with the views of progressive educators, and his methods of providing information and data sound.

7

EVALUATING
CURRICULUM
PLANS

Planning the evaluation of the curriculum and instruction, as was stated in Chapter 1 and shown in the model (Fig. 4), is essential. Evaluation is implied in the very process of planning, for it is the act of placing a value on something, of determining its merits. Inasmuch as planning of any kind constitutes making choices among alternatives, obviously, evaluation of some kind and at some level of sophistication occurs. Hence evaluation is as old as formal education itself. The accountability movement, discussed in Chapter 6, is evidence of increased interest on the part of both legal authorities and citizens in assessing the work of the schools. And certainly this interest is justified, for it is the social group that establishes schools and thus exercises control over the educational experiences of young people.

THE NATURE OF EVALUATION

Although evaluation has only one basic *goal*—the determination of the worth or value of something—it has many *roles*.[1] Appraisal of the outcomes of student learning in all of their ramifications is an example of one role. This type of evaluation is familiar to most teachers and administrators; it is accomplished through testing, measuring, and assessing pupil achievements, diagnosing individual progress, and comparing results with norms and scores of other members of the class or age group.

Another significant function of evaluation is determining the value of the curriculum itself. Is the curriculum fulfilling the purposes for which it was designed? Are the purposes themselves valid? Is the curriculum appropriate for the particular group of students with whom it is being used? Are the instructional modes selected the best choices in light of the goals sought? Is the content the best that may be selected? Are the materials recommended for instructional purposes appropriate and the best available for the purposes envisioned? This is the role of evaluation to be treated in the present chapter.

A third major role of evaluation in schools is to judge the merits of all the administrative and managerial arrangements and practices and the structures within which the school itself operates. These aspects of the school establishment are important determinants of curriculum and instruction, but this type of evaluation is beyond the scope of this book; references cited in this chapter provide assistance in making such evaluations.

Formative and Summative Evaluation

Another way of looking at curriculum evaluation is in terms of the timing of the evaluation, the ways in which it is made and the instruments used, and the purpose for which the results are used. Scriven has introduced into the literature of evaluation in recent years the concept of formative and summative evaluation.[2] Bloom, Hastings, and Madaus, in a useful handbook on evaluation, pick up Scriven's distinction and use it extensively in their treatment of the subject.[3]

---

[1] For a definitive treatment of this point, see Michael Scriven, "The Methodology of Evaluation," in Robert E. Stake, ed., *Perspectives of Curriculum Evaluation*, AERA Monograph Series on Curriculum Evaluation (Chicago: Rand McNally & Company, 1967), pp. 40–43.

[2] Scriven, pp. 40–43.

[3] Benjamin S. Bloom, J. Thomas Hastings, and George F. Madaus, *Handbook on Formative and Summative Evaluation of Student Learning* (New York: McGraw-Hill Book Company, Inc., 1971), especially Chaps. 4–6.

Formative evaluation is concerned with the curriculum and instruction in and of themselves. Its purpose is to contribute to the improvement of the educational program. It should be an integral part of the planning process, although no final decisions should be made until feedback from summative evaluation is also available. *Summative* evaluation measures the effectiveness of the curriculum plan and of instruction carried out in accordance with the plan. It is primarily concerned with what happened to learners as a result of instruction; formative evaluation is concerned with the merits of the plan itself. Obviously, the two roles are interwoven; the distinction has to do largely with the timing of the evaluation and the uses made of it.

In formative evaluation the decision-maker subjects the plan to critical scrutiny and appraisal. Evaluations of this type vary in scope, from, for example, an analysis of plans formulated by the U.S. Office of Education for a program of "career education" or of materials produced by a major national curriculum planning project, such as the Biological Sciences Curriculum Study, to the selection of a new textbook for reading instruction in the primary grades, the development of a new course in humanities in the local high school, or the preparation of a teacher's list of behavioral objectives for a course in general shop. In all of these instances someone, on the basis of some kind of evidence, information, hunch, or tradition, makes decisions that determine what should be included in instruction. The purpose of formative evaluation is to assist such decision-makers in reaching rational and valid decisions.

In summative evaluation, we measure the results of instruction, presumably carried out according to a plan, either the plan previously developed as a part of the planning process or one improvised by the teacher on the spot. This type of evaluation is often based on tests of all sorts, pupil reaction to the instruction, teachers' views concerning the effectiveness of instruction, follow-up studies of students who have participated in a program of instruction, parents' reactions, employer ratings of graduates, reports from college examination bureaus, and similar types of evidence of varying degrees of validity.[4]

It should be evident, however, that any line of distinction between the two types of evaluation is rather nebulous. Certainly, summative evaluation, as described here and in Bloom, Hastings, and Madaus, also contributes highly significant data for revising curriculum plans, formulating new ones, adding or dropping courses of instruction, selecting new content, revising goals and objectives, and the like. The

---

[4] Bloom, Hastings, and Madaus amply illustrate and treat in detail both types of evaluation.

difference lies more in the purposes for which evaluation is used and when it is used than in methodology, analytical techniques, and the like. Nevertheless, Scriven's classification has emphasized the importance of using evaluative processes as a part of planning itself.

The Dawning of a New Day in Evaluation

Since the late 1960s specialists in curriculum evaluation have been doing much soul-searching. One of these specialists, Richard Anderson, stated "if evaluation is a science at all, it is a sick science. As evaluators we have patronized, threatened, and insulted our clients and the people whose programs we have evaluated. Our results, when not trivial, have often been unverifiable, irrelevant, or just plain wrong."[5]

Within the past few years a new emphasis on evaluation, with leadership being provided by a new group of competent, vigorous professionals, has been evident, with the result that new approaches, methods, analytical procedures, and conceptions of the place and role of evaluation are being developed. Evaluation, perhaps at long last, is fulfilling much more effectively its rightful place as a major factor in the process of curriculum and instructional planning. Part of this new emphasis is due to the insistence of the federal government that programs and projects for which it provides funds be evaluated. This requirement is spelled out, for example, in the provisions of the Elementary and Secondary Education Act of 1965 and subsequent amendments, the Vocational Education Act and its later amendments of 1963 and 1968, and the Education Professions Development Act of 1967. Some of this focus is also due to the demands of citizens, legislatures, Congress, students (the clients), and professional educators for accountability. In California, for example, the Stull Act, passed in 1971, requires a "uniform system of evaluation and assessment of the performance of certified personnel within each school district." The Cooperative Accountability Project, previously described, illustrates the importance of the new emphasis on evaluation and appraisal in the schools.

The first great leap forward in the process of evaluation came with the work of Ralph Tyler in the 1930s in conjunction with his evaluation of the program of the Eight-Year Study of the Progressive Education Association. Tyler defined education as changes in behavior; hence evaluation consisted of the measurement of the extent to which such changes had taken place consistent with the previously defined objectives of the educational program being evaluated. This means that, as in all curriculum planning, one starts with a definition of goals and objectives

[5] Richard Anderson, "A Review of *Educational Evaluation and Decision Making* by Daniel L. Stufflebeam and others," *Harvard Educational Review*, 41, 587 (November 1971).

to be sought through schooling; instruction then seeks to bring about these changes in students; evaluation determines whether the desired changes have taken place.[6]

Evaluation in the Tyler model was largely summative, relying on testing, grading, classifying, marking, and measuring students' achievements. This was, and still is, the day of the standardized test, teacher-made objective tests, college entrance examinations, performance standards, percentile ranks, and all of the rest. All too frequently this is about the only kind of formalized evaluation that takes place—even to this day. Little or no effort is made to determine why a unit of educational activities, a program, or an aspect of schooling is offered. Still less attention is given to determining the effectiveness of a program or its appropriateness in meeting the particular needs of the learners for whom it has been planned.

Gene Glass, a leader of the effort to formulate new approaches to evaluation, has critically examined three models of curriculum evaluation—including the Tyler model—and has rejected them all, providing his own model instead. Robert E. Stake, also a recognized authority on evaluation, and cited extensively in this chapter, has also criticized the Tyler model, which he labels as "preordinate evaluation." He pleads for what he designates as "responsive evaluation," which is oriented to "what people do naturally in evaluating things. They observe and react."[7]

Wittrock and Wiley, in advocating new purposes, and hence, new models for evaluation, state the position:

> In the past, evaluation studies have not often been part of instructional research designed to contribute to knowledge and judgments about teaching and learning. If evaluational studies are to contribute further knowledge about instruction, we believe that new research approaches and designs are needed.[8]

A New Definition of Evaluation

These conceptions of new roles and purposes of evaluation call for a new definition and a new methodology of evaluation. To give

---

[6] This rationale is spelled out in a later publication of Tyler's, *Basic Principles of Curriculum and Instruction: Syllabus for Education 305* (Chicago: University of Chicago Press, 1950). Also see Bloom, Hastings, and Madaus, pp. 24–28, for a present-day critical analysis of this approach.

[7] Gene V. Glass, "The Growth of Evaluation Methodology" (mimeographed monograph available from the author, University of Colorado, Boulder, Colo.); Robert E. Stake, "Responsive Evaluation" (unpublished paper, dated February 22, 1973).

[8] M. C. Wittrock and D. E. Wiley, *The Evaluation of Instruction: Issues and Problems* (New York: Holt, Rinehart and Winston, Inc., 1970), p. vii.

greater emphasis to this marked shift in roles and purposes, first let us quote Tyler's statement emerging from his work in the 1930s:

> The process of evaluation is essentially the process of determining to what extent the educational objectives are actually being realized by the program of curriculum and instruction. However, since educational objectives are essentially changes in human beings, that is, the objectives aimed at are to produce desirable changes in the behavior patterns of the student, then evaluation is the process for determining the degree to which these changes in behavior are actually taking place.[9]

The best definition of the new conception of evaluation, we believe, is the one stated by Stufflebeam and his committee in their definitive work: "Educational evaluation is the process of delineating, obtaining, and providing useful information for judging decision alternatives."[10] Cronbach, in a pioneering effort to explain the new concept of evaluation, stated that evaluation may be defined "as the *collection and use of information to make decisions about an educational program*."[11]

The Nature of the Evaluative Process

The steps and the processes involved in making evaluations for use in educational planning may be stated in several ways. The treatment in Chapters 6 and 7 of the book by Stufflebeam and his committee, "Evaluation Methodology" and "Evaluation Types and a Model for Evaluation," is exceptionally clear and extensive, and we recommend this presentation and the models depicted as a basis for planning evaluative programs.[12]

Their work chart of the steps in evaluation is shown in Figure 9. Each of the three major aspects of the process—delineating information needs, obtaining information, and providing information—is further analyzed by them in considerable detail with system work models. Here we draw on the presentation to summarize our analysis of the steps to be taken in the process of evaluation:

> 1. The determination of what is to be evaluated; for what kinds of decisions is evaluative data needed?

[9] Tyler, *Basic Principles of Curriculum and Instruction*, p. 69.

[10] Phi Delta Kappa National Study Committee on Evaluation, Daniel Stufflebeam, chairman, *Educational Evaluation and Decision Making* (Itasca, Ill.: F. E. Peacock Publishers, Inc., 1971), p. 40. Hereafter cited as Stufflebeam.

[11] Lee J. Cronbach, "Course Improvement through Evaluation," *Teachers College Record*, 64, 672 (May 1963).

[12] Stufflebeam, pp. 139–239.

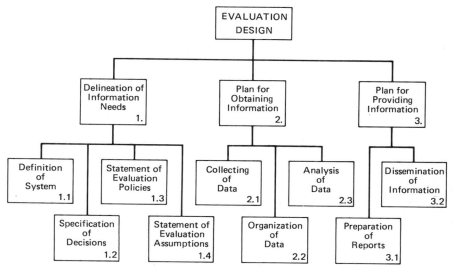

FIGURE 9 Work breakdown for generalized approach to evaluation design. (*From Phi Delta Kappa National Study Committee on Evaluation, Daniel Stufflebeam, chm., Educational Evaluation and Decision Making, 1971, p. 156*)

2. The kinds of data needed in making these decisions
3. The collection of these data
4. Defining criteria for determining the quality of the matter being evaluated
5. Analysis of the data in terms of these criteria
6. Providing information for decision-makers.

Note especially that decision-making is not a part of the evaluative process itself. Evaluation provides the knowledge needed for decision-making, and decision-making involves making choices among alternatives. Of course, often—perhaps usually—the evaluator will make or certainly indicate a preference for a particular decision, but that is going beyond his role of evaluator and becoming a judge. The point of view of the Phi Delta Kappa Committee on this matter is that

> The entire purpose of evaluation . . . is to service the decision-making act— to identify the decision question that calls forth an answer; to identify alternative answers (decision alternatives) that might be given in response; to identify and refine the criteria (values) to be used in choosing among available decision alternatives; to identify, collect, and report information differentiating the decision alternatives; and, finally, to determine whether the chosen alternative did meet expectations for it.[13]

[13] Stufflebeam, p. 43.

EVALUATION MODELS

In a book on curriculum planning, such as this one which treats the whole process of defining goals, designing the curriculum, implementing the curriculum plans, and evaluating curriculum and instruction,. it is not feasible to treat the processes and techniques of evaluation in detail. We will present and consider briefly three models that we believe constitute at the present time the best approaches to evaluation, list references and sources of information that will be helpful to evaluators, and then consider the scope and nature of curriculum evaluation, including the evaluation of instruction, drawing on these models for processes.

The three models are Robert Stake's Congruence–Contingency Model[14]; the evaluation methodology and model presented by the Phi Delta Kappa National Study Committee on Evaluation, of which Daniel Stufflebeam was chairman, and whose name we will use to identify the model[15]; and the Discrepancy Evaluation Model, developed by Malcolm Provus for the Pittsburgh Schools.[16] In light of the great interest now developing in a broad type of evaluation of curriculum and instruction, other models are being used throughout the country and more undoubtedly will be developed. In addition, a number of agencies are providing instruments, technical services, theoretical considerations, and points of view that are also very helpful in planning and carrying on evaluation.[17]

The Stake Congruence–Contingency Model

Figures 10 and 11 depict the Stake model. As Stake explains in the two sources cited, the rows in the first column of Figure 10 list categories of information or other data that an evaluator will need to collect: antecedents—"any condition existing prior to teaching and learning which

[14] Robert E. Stake, "Language, Rationality, and Assessment," in Walcott H. Beatty, ed., *Improving Educational Assessment and An Inventory of Measures of Affective Behavior* (Washington, D.C.: Association for Supervision and Curriculum Development, 1969). See also Robert E. Stake, "The Countenance of Educational Evaluation," *Teachers College Record*, 68, 523–540 (April 1967).

[15] Stufflebeam.

[16] Malcolm Provus, *Discrepancy Evaluation for Educational Program Improvement and Assessment* (Berkeley, Calif.: McCutchan Publishing Corporation, 1971).

[17] Among such agencies are the Center for the Study of Evaluation, University of California at Los Angeles; National Assessment of Educational Progress, Denver, Colo.; Laboratory of Educational Research, University of Colorado, Boulder; Instructional Appraisal Services, Ithaca, N.Y.; and the producers and publishers of tests and measuring instruments; the work by Bloom, Hastings, and Madaus is also a very useful guide.

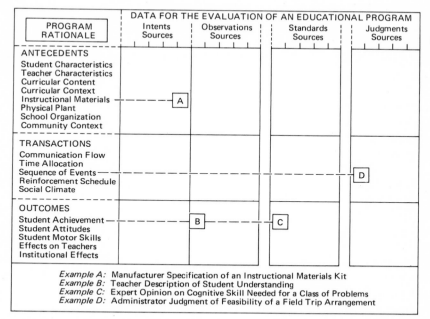

DATA FOR THE EVALUATION OF AN EDUCATIONAL PROGRAM				
PROGRAM RATIONALE	Intents Sources	Observations Sources	Standards Sources	Judgments Sources
ANTECEDENTS Student Characteristics Teacher Characteristics Curricular Content Curricular Context Instructional Materials Physical Plant School Organization Community Context	A			
TRANSACTIONS Communication Flow Time Allocation Sequence of Events Reinforcement Schedule Social Climate				D
OUTCOMES Student Achievement Student Attitudes Student Motor Skills Effects on Teachers Institutional Effects		B	C	

Example A: Manufacturer Specification of an Instructional Materials Kit
Example B: Teacher Description of Student Understanding
Example C: Expert Opinion on Cognitive Skill Needed for a Class of Problems
Example D: Administrator Judgment of Feasibility of a Field Trip Arrangement

FIGURE 10   Robert E. Stake's congruence-contingency model for educational evaluation: "Illustration of Data Possibly Representative of the Contents of Four Cells of the Matrices for a Given Educational Program." (*From Stake, "Language, Rationality, and Assessment," in Walcott H. Beatty, ed.,* Improving Educational Assessment and An Inventory of Measures of Affective Behavior, *1969, p. 16*)

may relate to outcomes"; transactions—"the countless encounters of students with teacher, student with student, author with reader, parent with counselor—the succession of engagements which comprise the process of education"; and outcomes—"abilities, achievements, attitudes, and aspirations of students resulting from an educational experience."

Data may be entered in each of the 12 cells for whatever items are under consideration in the antecedents, transactions, and outcomes. "Intents" are the "intended student outcomes," the goals and objectives; "observations" are the descriptive data—direct observations, test results, biographical data sheets, interviews, checklists, opinionnaires, follow-up reports, and the like. "Standards" are statements of what experts (teachers, administrators, scholars, spokesmen for society, students themselves, and parents) believe should happen in the situation and, as Stake points out, what does happen in similar situations in other schools—"benchmarks of

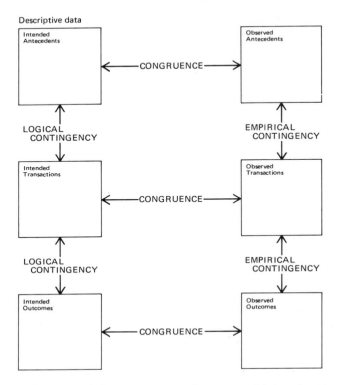

Descriptive data

FIGURE 11   Robert E. Stake's congruence-contingency model for educational evaluation: "A Representation of the Processing of Descriptive Data." (*From Stake, "Language, Rationality, and Assessment," p. 20*)

performance having widespread reference value." Stake insists that "standards vary from student to student, from instructor to instructor, and from reference group to reference group. . . . Part of the responsibility of evaluation is to make known which standards are held by whom."

Furthermore, Stake makes a comment of great significance in curriculum evaluation:

Informal evaluation tends to leave criteria unspecified. Formal evaluation is more specific. But it seems the more careful the evaluation, the fewer the criteria; and the more carefully the criteria are specified, the less the concern given to standards of acceptability. It is a great misfortune that the best trained evaluators have been looking at education with a microscope rather than a panoramic view finder.[18]

[18] Stake, "The Countenance of Educational Evaluation," p. 536.

Judgments, in the Stake model, are the values placed on the program or whatever is being judged. They are "how people feel about aspects of the situation."

The process of evaluation is depicted in Figure 11. This is a method of handling descriptive data, such as would be gathered for columns 1 and 2 of Figure 10. Congruence would be an identical match between what is intended and what is observed. Usually evaluation studies examine only the congruence between intended and observed outcomes, but Stake insists that one can judge the merits of a curriculum plan only if antecedents and transactions are also investigated. Congruence indicates only the degree of match, not the validity or value of the outcomes.

Contingencies are "relationships among the variables." An examination of contingencies is an effort to determine the "whys of the outcomes"—the particular set of antecedent conditions and the set of transactions that produce particular outcomes. What kinds of learning environments, what kinds of teaching methods and classroom procedures, what kinds of school arrangements and structures are casually related to the outcomes? These are the kinds of data or other information needed to make curriculum and instructional decisions.

We believe the Stake model provides a great deal of help in evaluating curriculum plans. The sample tables of contents of the report of an actual program evaluation and of a proposed report for a project and of a work breakdown for that report indicate the scope and methodology of the Stake model.[19]

The Phi Delta Kappa Committee Model

The procedures, or "work breakdown," in the Phi Delta Kappa Committee model were presented in Figure 9. In Figure 12 the model itself is shown. Inasmuch as the methodology and the basic approach are comparable to Stake's recommendations, only brief explanations will be added here.

The Committee believes that four types of evaluation are necessary in education: (1) context evaluation, which contributes to the definition of objectives; (2) input evaluation, which is necessary for decision-making on matters of design; (3) process evaluation, which guides decision-making on operations; and (4) product evaluation, which provides data for judging attainments, and, hence, for revision, termination, or continuation. The ways in which these types of evaluation fit into the process of decision-making and operation are illustrated

[19] Stufflebeam, pp. 201–205.

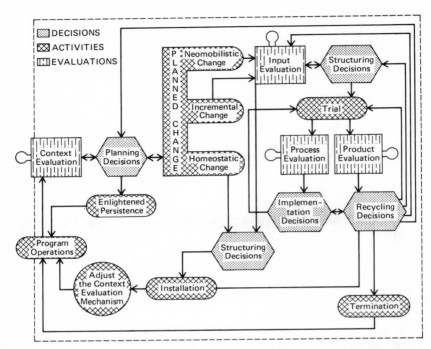

FIGURE 12   The Phi Delta Kappa National Study Committee's model: "An Evaluation Model." (*From Stufflebeam, chm.*, Educational Evaluation and Decision Making, *p. 236*)

in the model. The nature and character of each of these types of evaluation are explained rather fully in Chapter 7 of the Committee's publication.

Provus' Discrepancy Evaluation Model

Provus states that "program evaluation is the process of (1) defining program standards; (2) determining whether a discrepancy exists between some aspect of program performance and the standards governing that aspect of the program; and (3) using discrepancy information either to change performance or to change program standards."[20] In his model, Provus regards four major developmental stages and four steps in each of the three content categories essential for the evaluation of an ongoing, single program. The fifth step, Program Comparison and Cost-Benefit

[20] Provus, p. 183.

Analysis, is an optional one, suggesting the possibility of comparing programs and defining the cost benefit of each in the total program.

Stages	Content		
	Input	Process	Output
1. Design 2. Installation 3. Process 4. Product 5. Program Comparison	Design Adequacy Installation Fidelity Process Adjustment Product Assessment Cost–Benefit Analysis		

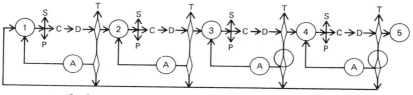

S - Standard
P - Program performance
C - Comparison
D - Discrepancy information

A - To change program
     performance or standards
T - To terminate program

The flow chart above illustrates Provus' process of evaluating an ongoing program. The evaluator starts with an ongoing program (step 1) in which standards (S) have been established as a part of the design process in initiating the program. Appropriate evidence is obtained on performance (P), and this is compared (C) with the standard. Any discrepancy (D) is then evident. Discrepancy information always leads to a decision to either go on to the next stage, recycle the stage after there. has been a change in the program's standards or operations, recycle to the first stage, or terminate the project. Provus describes additional information gathered in successive stages of evaluating a project or program. All of these stages should be completed before any cost-benefit analysis is made.

It should be especially noted that Provus' model necessitates an evaluation of the goals and objectives themselves, something not many of the plans require as a part of the evaluation process. This occurs when program-performance data do not match standards. Provus points out that such a discrepancy requires the program planner either to revise the program's standards, modify the program, or discard the whole thing; if no significant discrepancy is found, the staff moves on to the next stage in the cycle until the whole program is acceptable and valid or has been discarded as undesirable.

Provus claims that his plan may be used to make evaluations of ongoing programs, programs in the planning stage, or programs still being developed and tried out. He describes the use of the model in the Pittsburgh Public Schools, where he served as director of evaluation. He also recommends its use on a state-wide basis and describes the steps and procedures in such a project, and also for evaluating programs and projects sponsored and subsidized by a federal bureau.

ASPECTS OF CURRICULUM EVALUATION

Inasmuch as the program of a school is comprehensive and multifaceted, its evaluation will also be necessarily so. Figure 13 illustrates the scope and nature of curriculum evaluation. It is an overview of the remainder of the chapter and will serve as a guide to the treatment of each part of the evaluation process. It comprehends both formative and summative types of evaluations and also Stake's concept of "preordinate" and "responsive" evaluations. As the figure shows, each aspect of evaluation is interrelated with other aspects; not only does the evaluator draw information and data obtained from other phases of the total program in making judgments about a particular segment, but that aspect contributes information and data in turn to other categories.

EVALUATION OF GOALS, SUBGOALS, AND OBJECTIVES

All plans for schooling—the total program, the curriculum, instruction, and evaluation—should be based on a definition of the purposes for which the school is established. Hence, the first step in curriculum evaluation is determining whether these stated purposes are valid, appropriate, attainable, and acceptable. In terms of our discussion of purposes in Chapter 4, this means that the curriculum evaluator will provide information on the validity of the general goals, the subgoals, the curriculum domains, and instructional objectives.

Messick supports this point of view strongly:

> All appraisal . . . is relative to stated goals, and the concern is with how well the program achieves its intended objectives. In addition, however, we should inquire to what extent the objectives are worth achieving and, in general, should endeavor to include in the evaluation process provisions for evaluating the value judgments, especially the goals.[21]

[21] Samuel Messick, "The Criterion Problem in the Evaluation of Instruction: Assessing Possible, Not Just Intended, Outcomes," in Wittrock and Wiley, pp. 186–187.

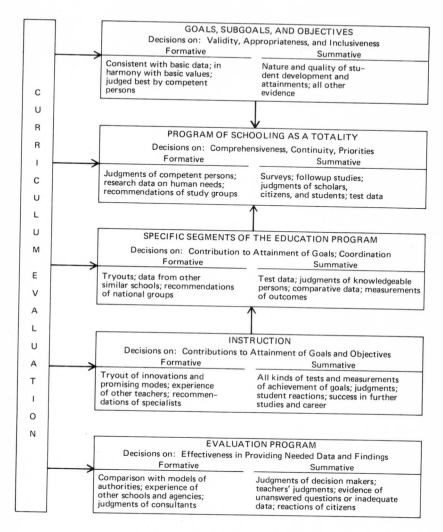

FIGURE 13   The scope and nature of curriculum evaluation.

How does one evaluate the purposes of the school? At the outset, it should be recognized that this is an exceedingly difficult kind of
evaluation to make. The process includes these steps:

1. Analyze as validly and competently as one possibly can the data
obtained from the basic sources listed in Chapter 3.

2. State a philosophy of education.
3. Collect together the views and judgments about the purposes of the school of competent persons.
4. Determine through the total evaluation program the congruence between goals and student achievement and other outcomes.
5. Obtain judgments of competent persons on implications of these tests of congruence.
6. Present the evidence to decision-makers.

The decision-makers then must determine whether the stated goals, subgoals, domains, and objectives are valid or should be revised, extended, or rejected. Tyler, in his widely cited and acclaimed handbook on curriculum planning, supports this approach:

> It is certainly true that in the final analysis objectives are matters of choice, and they must therefore be the considered value judgment of those responsible for the school. A comprehensive philosophy of education is necessary to guide in making these judgments. And, in addition, certain kinds of information and knowledge provide a more intelligent basis for applying the philosophy in making decisions about objectives. If these facts are available to those making decisions, the probability is increased that judgments about objectives will be wise and that the school goals will have greater significance and greater validity.[22]

Bloom and his associates also advocate much this same approach to the evaluation of goals and objectives. They point out that there are two kinds of decisions about objectives—what is possible and what is desirable. They state that

> A more difficult problem in determining objectives is what is *desirable*. This is a value problem which can be helped by the use of evidence but not answered by evidence alone. What is desirable for particular students and groups of students is in part dependent on their present characteristics and their goals and aspirations for the future. . . . If education is really to be developed, objectives must be selected which maximize the range of possible developments. . . .
> Some help in determining the appropriate range of objectives for groups of students may be found in the study of existing society. . . .
> Another source of decision on the desirability of particular objectives is the educational philosophy of the teachers and the school.[23]

Popham, already identified as a leading advocate of the use of behaviorally stated goals in curriculum planning, insists that "if a *goal-*

---

[22] Tyler, *Basic Principles of Curriculum and Instruction*, p. 3.
[23] Bloom, Hastings, and Madaus, pp. 11–12.

based evaluation strategy is used, then the evaluator should be certain to make an assessment of the worth of the original objectives and carefully search for unanticipated side effects of instruction not encompassed by the original goal statements."[24] Note Popham's use of "if," for he recognizes in his more recent writings that some instruction may proceed without defining behavioral objectives, and, citing Scriven, that evaluation of instruction could be *"goal-free evaluation,"* by which is meant that the outside or independent evaluator probably should not be restricted or biased in his collection of data and determination of the outcomes of instruction by acceptance of the planner's or teacher's predetermined goals and objectives. Such an evaluator should "attend to the outcomes of an instructional sequence without any consideration whatsoever of what was intended by the instructional planners."

Although many of the most useful books on evaluation ignore the matter of assessing the goals and objectives themselves, some help is currently available in the literature. Bloom, Hastings, and Madaus include a brief section in their handbook entitled "Evaluating Objectives."[25] It offers specific suggestions and cites two studies that attempted to make such appraisals. Stufflebeam and his committee include a short chapter on this matter.[26] Hulda Grobman, who was associated with the Biological Sciences Curriculum Study for some years, has provided two useful publications on curriculum evaluation.[27] In each book she describes and discusses the formulation of goals and objectives from the standpoint of project development, but also gives some attention to their validation.

The National Assessment of Educational Progress (see pages 339–342 for information on this project) has prepared lengthy sets of what we designate as subgoals. They have used the opinion and judgment of various groups of people in preparing and validating their lists. First, knowledgeable persons in a field prepared preliminary lists; these were then submitted to panels of interested persons, comprised of lay citizens, educators, and scholars, for review and revision. Later, in preparing for a second round of assessment, professional organizations of educators working in a field of study also participated in a revision of the goals.

The California projects in goal definition, cited in Chapter 4,

---

[24] W. James Popham, "Objectives '72," *Phi Delta Kappan*, 53, 435 (March 1972).

[25] Bloom, Hastings, and Madaus, pp. 260–262.

[26] Stufflebeam, Chap. 4.

[27] Hulda Grobman, *Evaluation Activities of Curriculum Projects: A Starting Point*, AERA Monograph Series on Curriculum Evaluation, Robert E. Stake, ed. (Chicago: Rand McNally & Company, 1968); and *Developmental Curriculum Projects: Decision Points and Processes* (Itasca, Ill.: F. E. Peacock Publishers, Inc., 1970).

have developed plans for extensive review and subsequent determination of priorities among approved goals by citizens.[28] However, it should be pointed out that the lists prepared in advance for citizen review in these programs have not been validated by any process other than the judgments of those preparing them, drawing on widely accepted statements available in the literature.

The role of the scholar in a discipline or field of study in defining, and then in validating, goals is an important one, but, we emphasize, not the sole determinant. When educators prepare goals for the subject offerings included in the curriculum domains, as, of course, they do, then the recommendations and views of specialists in the field should be carefully weighed. If feasible, the planner ought to obtain the recommendations of a number of specialists, including some who teach or have taught in the elementary and secondary schools. Learned societies and professional organizations often publish monographs, position papers, and/or lists of recommended goals for particular fields of study that are helpful in validating goals.

A further step, and a crucial one, in determining the validity of goals is to use the results of summative evaluations—the measurement of student outcomes—as feedback data (as shown in our original model, Figure 3). The evaluator analyzes the congruence, as Stake uses that term, or discrepancies, as Provus states in his model, between outcomes and goals. Stake insists in all of his writings that antecedent conditions must be taken into account in any evaluation, and that especially would be true in evaluating goals; the Biological Sciences Curriculum Study also differentiates between "intended" treatment and "actual" treatment and notes the importance of taking both into account in evaluation of objectives.

Taking these conditions into account, the evaluator—the planner would be involved here, too—must analyze congruency or discrepancy and recommend that either the program, the curriculum plan, or whatever is being evaluated be continued in its present form, which is tacit approval of the goals and objectives, the goals be revised in light of these data, or the program be revised so as to better serve the ends sought.

At this final stage of decision-making the views and judgments of competent people, including parents, citizens, students, and experts in the area of instruction, should be obtained. These persons should assist

[28] Joint Committee on Educational Goals and Evaluation, *Education for the People*, Vols. I and II (Sacramento: California Legislature, 1972); "Goal cards" and kit of materials, Northern California Program Development Center (Chico, Calif.: The Center, Chico State College, 1972).

in setting the criteria for judgment. Was what was intended appropriate and sound or are changes in goals desirable? Was what was actually done in seeking to achieve the goals a proper test of the goals? Thus goals are approved, at least for the time being, or revised.

Figure 14, although published by the Center for the Advanced Study of Educational Administration to illustrate their system of program planning and evaluation (see next section), illustrates how the evaluation of goals—labeled desired outputs in the figure—may be made through the process of congruence or discrepancy techniques. Recall, however, that this is not the only method to be used in evaluating goals.

In summary, to evaluate a set of goals, subgoals, or objectives the evaluator subjects them logically to an examination of their appropriateness in light of all of the data that have been collected from primary sources; utilizes the opinions and recommendations of scholars, specialists in curriculum planning, teachers, parents, spokesmen for society at large, and students; makes a logical analysis of antecedent conditions that may affect the choice of goals; and then makes a judgment on the validity of the ends sought for a particular group of students in a particular situation. As summative evaluation of the program under consideration proceeds and moves to conclusions, congruences or discrepancies are analyzed, and in light of such evaluations the goals, subgoals, or objectives are reexamined.

In all candor, however, it must be acknowledged that a considerable degree of uncertainty exists in efforts to evaluate educational goals. The accumulation of many kinds of evidence, extending over years or decades, may be necessary before one may feel reasonably confident

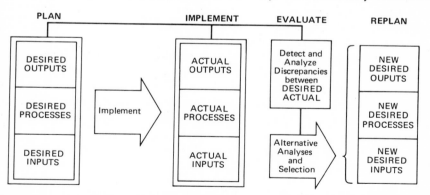

FIGURE 14   The SPECS model for program planning and evaluation. (*From Center for the Advanced Study of Educational Administration*, CASEA Progress Reports, *August 1972*)

in the goals selected for schools. Sociological, anthropological, historical, and comparative data among schools, states, and nations are essential sources in setting standards and making choices of goals.

EVALUATION OF THE TOTAL EDUCATIONAL PROGRAM OF THE SCHOOL

The second aspect of a full-scale program of curriculum evaluation is the assessment of the total set of educational opportunities offered by the school or school system, whichever level is being evaluated. Encompassed in such an evaluative program would be these phases of schooling:

The complete program of the school system: including such things as the school offerings at each age level, from prekindergarten children to senior citizens; provisions for out-of-school educational opportunities; special provisions for persons with exceptional needs; opportunities provided outside the regular school-day program, such as summer programs, evening programs, camping, instruction by television and radio, and self-study programs.

The program of the individual school or school agency: these same aspects of the program, as relevant to the individual situation.

Coordination with community agencies: included in program evaluation should be evidence on the school's relations with other agencies of the community in planning and providing a total program of educational opportunities for the people of the community. One important item of this nature is the coordination and relations between the school and law-enforcement and correctional agencies, public welfare agencies, and health and mental health clinics.

Often it is difficult to obtain valid and reliable evidence that will be adequate for purposes of assessing a total educational program. But educators must make decisions based on such information, and thus it behooves professional evaluators to provide them with the best data possible. As in the previous section, we will not provide a set of plans and procedures for making these kinds of evaluations, but rather will describe some methods now being used as well as consider problems and issues.

Planning-Programming-Budgeting System

It is appropriate at this point to consider a widely publicized systems approach to the evaluation of the total educational program of a school. In the latter part of the 1960s a systems model called the Plan-ing-Programming-Budgeting System (PPBS) came into vogue and has had some limited use in school systems.[29]

California has had a state-wide program for the introduction and use of PPBS. In 1967 it officially established the Advisory Commission on School District Budgeting and Accounting. Its functions were to recommend to the state board of education "procedures for implementing program budgeting and accounting for school districts" and to serve as an advisory group to the department in the development of the system.[30] The Commission prepared an extensive manual for use by the districts in implementing PPBS.[31] During the five years of its existence (the legislature abolished it as of March 4, 1972) the Commission sponsored many workshops on the use of the plan, set up pilot districts for implementing PPBS, and identified 23 county unit centers to assist local districts in developing the management system. But the state board refused to order the use of PPBS, and local districts are not compelled to adhere to this kind of management system of decision-making on curriculum matters.

The Center for the Advanced Study of Educational Administration at the University of Oregon published this comment on PPBS:

> Unfortunately, most efforts to develop PPB systems have been, at best, marginally successful, particularly those designed for schools. Several reasons can be suggested. Sometimes, the systems have been inadequately conceptualized. Other times, they have been operationally reduced to a set of sophisticated budgeting and accounting procedures.[32]

Inasmuch as a major revision of the PPB system has been developed by the Center, we will consider that plan as constituting a better

[29] These books and articles provide descriptions of the system and its use: Stephen J. Knezevich, *Program Budgeting (PPBS): A Resource Allocation Decision System for Education* (Berkeley, Calif.: McCutchan Publishing Corporation, 1973); Harry J. Hartley, *Educational Planning-Programming-Budgeting: A Systems Approach* (Englewood Cliffs, N.J.: Prentice-Hall, Inc., 1968); Robert F. Alioto, *Operational PPBS for Education: A Practical Approach to Effective Decision-Making* (New York: Harper & Row, Publishers, 1971); C. Edwin Brewin, Jr., Roger L. Sisson, and Benjamin H. Renshaw, *Educational-Planning-Programming-Budgeting System* (New York: John Wiley & Sons, Inc., 1971); "Systems Techniques in Educational Planning and Management," special issue, *Educational Technology*, Vol. 12, No. 2 (February 1972); Center for Vocational and Technical Education, *Budgeting Systems for Educators,* Leadership Series Nos. 18 and 19 (Columbus, O.: The Center, 1969).

[30] Advisory Commission on School District Budgeting and Accounting, *Final Report* (Sacramento: The Commission, May 1972), p. 1.

[31] *Educational Planning and Evaluation Guide for California School Districts*, 3d preliminary edition, 1972.

[32] Center for the Advanced Study of Educational Administration, *CASEA Progress Report*, August 1971, p. 1. See also William A. Jenkins and Greg O. Lehman, "Nine Pitfalls of PPBS," *School Management*, 16, 2 (January 1972).

version of a systems approach to program evaluation and planning. This model is designated as the School Planning and Evaluation Communication System (SPECS).[33]

The SPECS model "is designed to focus upon identifiable activities within an organization and to provide a planning strategy for using data about each activity to make future decisions regarding its operation." Furthermore, "the starting point in SPECS is outcomes—changes in the performance of youngsters and organizations—and all else in the planning process flows naturally from the effort to clearly define *desired* outcomes and meaningfully assess actual outcomes."[34]

The system is really made up of three subsystems:

(1) a community-based goal definition subsystem; (2) a professionally-based program planning and evaluation subsystem and (3) a mediating or policy-making subsystem that is designed to monitor and achieve the best possible match between the district's goal hierarchy or "intellectual programs" and the *desired* and *actual* outcomes of its on-going activities or "operating programs."[35]

The components of the system are illustrated in Figure 15.

The model differs from the traditional planning and evaluation one, as explained by the Center:

Rather than adopting the usual, unitary flow of decision making from broad goals to objectives and then to programs and activities, we proposed that goal definition by a school district's community and program planning and evaluation by its professional staff be viewed as two distinct and separate clusters of activity in the district. Furthermore, we proposed that the critical responsibility of a school district's board of education and its administrative staff—its policy making and management component, so to speak—be that of monitoring and mediating the best possible match between the district's community-defined goals and the desired and actual outcomes of its many on-going programs and activities.[36]

We believe that recognition of these two separate aspects of planning and evaluation is realistic and sound. Unfortunately, however, the SPECS model does not include a crucial aspect of evaluation. It

[33] Center for the Advanced Study of Educational Administration, *School Planning and Evaluation Communication System* (SPECS). Published by and training in its use provided by General Learning Corporation, Washington, D.C.

[34] *CASEA Progress Report*, 1971.

[35] *CASEA Progress Report*, August 1972, p. 4.

[36] *CASEA Progress Report*, 1972, p. 2.

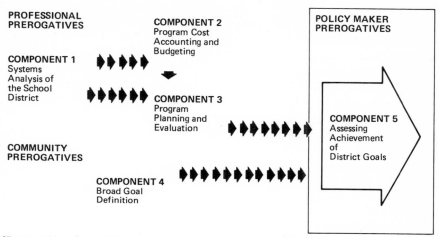

FIGURE 15   The SPECS Organizational Systems Design. (*From* CASEA Progress Reports, *August 1972*)

makes no provision for the validation of the goals established for the program beyond whatever steps are taken by the people of the community in the process of goal definition.

Component 5 in the SPECS model comprehends the whole program of curriculum evaluation as is treated in this chapter. Hence, any school system using a version of the PPBS will necessarily engage in evaluation in some form. Schools should turn to one or more of the three models presented earlier or develop some other procedure. PPBS is directed particularly to the matter of priorities, emphasizing costs and budgeting for various aspects of the total educational program as a part of decision-making; otherwise it introduces no new element in the evaluation process itself. The system may be used to make an assessment of the entire program of a school system or of any segment of it.

Evaluation by Accreditation

Probably the most extensively used educational evaluation procedure has been accreditation. The University of Michigan originated the method in 1871 by inviting high schools of that state to seek University approval of their academic programs. The graduates of the schools that were approved would then be admitted to the University without examination. Late in the nineteenth century voluntary regional accrediting associations for high schools were organized. Standards were set as a basis for membership, a practice that represented, in crude form at least, an appraisal system. In the past these two kinds of accreditation have always exercised a tremendous influence on high school programs throughout the country, shaping decision-making on curriculum matters more significantly than all other factors except legal requirements. In recent decades, however, accreditation of high schools by universities has been virtually eliminated.

State departments of education have been a third agency exercising accreditation power over schools, and at the present time they constitute the primary factor in this form of program appraisal, for most of them are legally bound to make such evaluations. Schools systems must meet accreditation standards set by these departments or suffer severe penalties, which can be as serious as disestablishment or loss of state financial support.

Even though accreditation in any form must be recognized as evaluative in nature, the three types we have considered fall far short of complying with present-day concepts or fulfilling the requirements of the models presented earlier.[37] Two efforts to improve the nature and quality of the evaluations should be noted briefly.

In 1971, the Colorado state department of education announced a plan for "accreditation by contract." The procedure enables a school district to set standards individually for judging its educational program. The district, through studies, determines the educational needs of its students, proposes a program to serve these needs, and then carries it out. Upon approval the proposed program becomes the contract with the state department of education, and accreditation is based on the success of the district in fulfilling its educational "contract."[38]

The National Study of Secondary School Evaluation, originated in 1933, represents an attempt by five voluntary, regional accrediting associations to provide a comprehensive basis on which to accredit high schools. A set of "evaluative criteria"[39] was developed and tried out on an experimental basis. In 1940 the first set of criteria was published. It has been revised every ten years thereafter, with the current edition, the fourth, being copyrighted in 1969. The criteria for eighteen subject fields and for these nine aspects of the secondary school—school and community, philosophy and objectives, student-activities program, educational media services, guidance services, school facilities, school staff and administration, individual staff members, and summary of the self-evaluation—are available in booklet form.

---

[37] See Glass for an excellent review and analysis of accreditation as an evaluative procedure.

[38] Colorado Department of Education, *A School Improvement Process: Accreditation by Contract* (Denver: The Department, 1971).

[39] National Study of Secondary School Evaluation, *Evaluative Criteria*, 1st edition 1940, later ones each ten years thereafter (Washington, D.C.: The Study).

To be accredited, the regional associations require each high school in their respective region—and in more recent years each junior high school, for which the criteria are modified—to evaluate itself, using the criteria. Usually a committee composed of staff members and in some instances a few parents and students conducts the study for each of the 27 aspects. The committee enters its ratings for specific items in a special booklet, along with comments and recommendations concerning the particular field or aspect of schooling. Occasionally test data on achievement may be available, and surveys of opinions of students and/or parents may be made. Follow-up studies may also be used in some instances.

The accrediting associations require that a "visiting committee" then spend one or more days—often three—in the school to make its judgments about the program. Such committees may comprise from 5 to 10 members up to 100 or more. In the latter instance, there usually is a small subcommittee for each of the 27 areas. The visiting committee prepares a report which comments on the evaluations prepared by the school's committee and presents its recommendations, if any, for improvement of each area of the school's program. The regional association determines on the basis of all of this material whether the school is to be accredited. A number of state departments of education use the same set of criteria and the same procedures for state accreditation. The regional associations require schools seeking renewal of their accreditation to repeat this process of self-study and visiting committee every seven years.

The effect of the "evaluative criteria" and such an accreditation program on the total program of a secondary school is often great. Anyone who has participated in the process knows the impact of such an evaluation on a school.[40] Changes in curriculum, instruction, guidance services, availability and use of instructional materials, the extrainstructional program, and, in fact, any area evaluated are easy to identify.

Stake has made these observations on the use of the "evaluative criteria" in the secondary schools:

Its great value may be a catalyst, hastening the maturity of a developing curriculum. However, it can be of only limited value in *evaluating*, for it guides neither the measurement nor the interpretation of measurement. By intent, it deals with criteria (what variables to consider) and leaves the matter of standards (what ratings to consider as meritorious) to the conjecture of the individual observer.[41]

[40] For research evidence on this subject see Vynce A. Hines and William M. Alexander, "High School Self-Evaluations and Curriculum Change," Final Report, Project No. 3130 (Washington, D.C.: Bureau of Research, Office of Education, 1967).
[41] Stake, "The Countenance of Educational Evaluation," p. 535.

Glass concludes his excellent analysis of the "accreditation model" on much the same note:

Evaluation will not enhance the *value* of an educational program if it demands conformity to standards which themselves cannot be demonstrated to lead to valued goals. . . . The genetic flaw in the Accreditation model will probably never be corrected; thus it will not grow into the fully useful methodology of evaluation that is needed.[42]

As crude as accreditation may be in most instances, whether done under the auspices of a state department of education, a regional accrediting association, or a university, it nevertheless represents an effort to appraise the total program of an individual school or, in the instance of state accreditation, an entire school system. Actually, in many schools it is the only continuing effort to make at least some assessment of the total educational program. The accreditation reports made by the outside group have contributed to curriculum decision-making and planning, often in a significant manner.

The whole question of the merit of the evaluation, as both Stake and Glass have emphasized, hinges on the validity of the standards used by the evaluators—often their own judgments—the kinds of data collected for making judgments, and the competency of the judges in terms of their conception of the goals of a school or school system. It should also be noted that Stake, six years after his comments quoted above, in advocating what he designates as "responsive evaluation," strongly recommended that citizens' committees be established as part of a program of school accountability and that such committee(s) make a public report at least annually. "Guides for such visitation should be made available" (the very thing the "Evaluative Criteria" provide). Moreover, he recommended that "judgment of the quality of instruction should be provided by professional educators from within and outside the school. (Accreditation self-study procedures sometimes work well for this purpose.)"[43] Stake's acceptance of judgments and observations of competent persons is evidence of a trend away from the "ordinate" type of data to a much broader base for the evaluation of school programs, especially when it is done as part of a planned program of accountability.

Undoubtedly, accreditation, especially by state agencies, will continue to be a major factor in decision-making on curriculum matters;

[42] Glass, p. 27.
[43] Robert E. Stake, "School Accountability Laws," *The Journal of Educational Evaluation: Evaluation Comment*, 4, 2 (February 1973).

hence, it behooves those responsible for the program to upgrade the methods and procedures used, drawing on present knowledge of the evaluative process.

Appraisal by Surveys and Studies

Formal school surveys have long been used as a means of evaluating an educational program. Widely used in the 1920s and 1930s, their popularity has waned since World War II. A few significant ones in recent years serve well as examples of this procedure for appraising a school program.[44] In some instances the studies have been state-wide, constituting an effort to appraise the educational program of a whole school system without examining individual school programs.

Traditionally the school survey was as broad in scope as the present-day programs that use the "evaluative criteria," although it usually constituted a more intensive investigation of many aspects of the total program and used highly regarded specialists in curriculum and planning for each area of study in making judgments about the program. However, seldom were goals for a specific school situation stated, and the antecedent conditions or context input—essential ingredients in evaluation in the models cited—were largely ignored or scantily investigated.

Many school systems over the years have used citizens' studies to involve the people of the community and the members of the school staff in an assessment of the program of the schools. Staff members of colleges of education often serve as consultants or directors of these projects. A study guide or handbook for data collection is prepared. Opinionnaires, follow-up studies, studies of community occupational patterns, and other data-collecting projects may be a part of the undertaking. Usually some publication is produced that reports the findings and recommendations of the group. State-wide study projects of this kind were carried on in years past in a number of states, including Texas, Georgia, Arkansas, and Kansas. State studies are usually directed more to planning the structure of schools, school financing, and the scope of a school program than evaluating the present program.

Task forces and study commissions have been used for many years as a method of appraising some specific aspect of the schools, such as school finance, provisions for meeting the educational needs of particular groups of children and youth, governance of the schools, and the like, and recommending courses of action. Usually these commissions

---

[44] A. Harry Passow, study director, *Toward Creating a Model Urban System: A Study of the Washington, D.C. Public Schools* (New York: Teachers College Press, 1967); Robert J. Havighurst, *The Public Schools of Chicago* (Chicago: Chicago Board of Education, 1964).

are concerned with schooling at the state or national level. Examples of recent studies of this kind are the *Report of the New York State Commission on the Quality, Cost, and Financing of Elementary and Secondary Education* (the Fleischmann Commission),[45] publications of the National Educational Finance Project,[46] and the California State Department of Education Task Force on Early Childhood Education.[47] Again, such studies are usually concerned with analyzing the school programs which fall within the purview of the study and with recommending future directions.

Perhaps these kinds of surveys, studies, investigations, and appraisals would not be acknowledged by the professional as full-fledged evaluations, just as Stake and Glass did not accept accreditation as an adequate form of assessment, but it is quite evident that such groups are recommending that certain decisions be made and that specific steps be taken to improve programs. If not acknowledged as true evaluation studies, they are certainly aspects of such a study, usually contributing significant data and judgments for a more inclusive program of evaluation. The principal questions from an evaluator's standpoint are these: Have the values, assumptions, and points of view about schooling of the members of the study group been identified? If so, or as implied from the report, are they valid in the judgment of other competent persons? What standards for judging quality were used or implied? Are they valid? Were valid and appropriate data obtained? To what kinds of systematic treatments have the data and the observations been subjected? What evidence is there that the committee was competent to judge the quality of the program(s) under examination?

Too often in recent years decisions on the need for and effectiveness of existing programs have not utilized research and the writings of scholars on the nature of human growth and development and on the role of the schools in guiding the process. This is especially seen in some of the evaluations made of Head Start and other provisions for early schooling, day-care centers, nursery school programs for ameliorating the effects of deprivation and disadvantageousness, and, in fact, many phases of schooling.

In establishing standards for judging a community's provisions for schooling, the most authoritative works and research on the whole matter of human growth and development from birth to death should be fully utilized. Knowledge in these areas is accumulating rapidly, and

[45] Published in three volumes by The Viking Press, New York, 1973.

[46] Available from the project office, University of Florida, Gainesville, 1971.

[47] Available from the state department of education, Sacramento, 1971.

anyone who evaluates programs or makes decisions concerning education should turn to such sources for the judgments of experts. The references cited in Chapter 3 are useful, especially the reports of the 1970 White House Conference on Children and the 1971 one on Youth. Similarly, reports prepared for the 1971 White House Conference on Aging provide useful bases for setting standards.

In the next section the evaluation of specific aspects or segments of the curriculum will be treated; obviously, such program evaluations contribute fully and are necessary to the process of assessing the total educational program of a school. Figure 13 portrays this relation. Formative evaluation of a school program makes use of the findings from the same basic data that are gathered as a part of the planning process itself, but in addition data and recommendations from other competent sources are used. In summative evaluation additional data are collected from a number of sources, as shown in the figure, which, in turn, make use of data available from the evaluation of instruction.

EVALUATING SPECIFIC ASPECTS OF THE CURRICULUM

The ongoing, continuing evaluation of the numerous segments of the curriculum of a school is one of the major responsibilities of the evaluator. Such evaluations are essential in the process of planning. Actually, the curriculum planner and the curriculum evaluator should work closely together in the development and improvement of the educational program of a school; in many situations the same person may serve in both capacities alternately.

Although a part of program evaluation, evaluation of the numerous aspects or segments of curriculum is a major undertaking, broad in scope and encompassing the many kinds of learning opportunities provided by the school. Thus evaluation of the curriculum as a plan for providing sets of learning opportunities must include evaluation of the plan for organizing curriculum domains, the design or designs of the curriculum for each domain, as these are explained in Chapter 5, courses offered, other kinds or sets of learning opportunities provided, extrainstructional activities sponsored, services provided students, community experiences under the direction of the school, and the kinds of informal relations that characterize the school climate. The three evaluation models presented earlier in this chapter serve well in curriculum evaluation.

Steps in Evaluating Segments of the Curriculum

The guide for planning evaluations of unitary segments of the curriculum is the set of subgoals formulated within the general goals for a curriculum domain. However, as Scriven points out in his plea for goal-free evaluation, an evaluator, especially one external to the instructional situation itself, must look at the actual effects of a program of instruction, including the intended outcomes as stated in the goals or objectives, and also "side effects"—outcomes in addition to or in place of those anticipated in planning the program or segment of the curriculum. To judge the merits of a product or effects of a program, an evaluator does not discard goals, but rather establishes standards for outcomes that should result from such instruction, product, or program that are free of the restricting influence of the predetermined goals, so that actual outcomes are judged as to validity, appropriateness, and essentiality.[48]

Cronbach, in an article that has become almost a charter for the broader uses of evaluation, set the basic consideration in course, program, or project evaluation:

> Course evaluation should ascertain what changes a course produces and should identify aspects of the course that need revision. The outcomes observed should include general outcomes ranging far beyond the content of the curriculum itself—attitudes, career choices, general understandings and intellectual powers, and aptitude for further learning in the field.[49]

Similarly, Glass, in commenting on the roles of evaluation, stated that "the goal of evaluation must always be to provide an answer to an all-important question: Does the program under observation have greater value than its competitors or sufficient value of itself that it should be maintained?"[50]

Thus, while summative evaluation of the curriculum necessarily includes conclusions on the extent to which the goals established for a course, segment, or set of opportunities were attained by the students, it should also include "goal-free evaluation." That is, it should seek to

---

[48] On the matter of goal-free evaluation, including Scriven's point of view and responses by other specialists, see "Pros and Cons about Goal-Free Evaluation, *The Journal of Educational Evaluation: Evaluation Comment,* special issue, Vol. 3, No. 2 (December 1972). For another approach to the use of goals and objectives in evaluation examine the "domain-referenced curriculum evaluation" technique explained in Wells Hively and others, *Domain-Referenced Curriculum Evaluation: A Technical Handbook and a Case Study from the Minnemast Project,* CSE Monograph Series in Evaluation (Los Angeles: Center for the Study of Evaluation, 1973).

[49] Cronbach, p. 683.

[50] Glass, p. 32.

determine to what extent a particular segment of the curriculum is contributing to the education of a particular group of students. On the basis of such findings by the evaluation, the curriculum planner is in a position, for example, to decide whether a course in Latin is a better choice for a particular group of students at a particular point in their schooling than, say, a course in French, auto mechanics, or American Indian culture. Or, as an alternative question, does the segment serve the educational needs of a group of students sufficiently to be included in the curriculum? Thus the evaluator makes a contribution to determining priorities, developing cost analyses, and introducing accountability.

The second aspect of program evaluation is the determination of what Stake calls antecedents and what Stufflebeam and his associates label context input. The Provus model would take account of conditions affecting the program in the item labeled standards. In the Biological Sciences Curiculum Study model, presented in Figure 16, "actual treatment" takes account of antecedents and contingencies.

The third step is the collection of data on the outcomes of the program or segment. Here Cronbach early pointed out that there are many "methods for examining pupil performance, and pupil attainment is not the only basis for appraising a course." He recommends "systematic observation, process studies, proficiency measures, attitude measures, and follow-up studies."[51] Stake's model calls for a wide range of data in each of his three categories. With respect to outcomes, he lists student achievement, attitudes and motor skills, effects on teachers, and institutional effects. In a further discussion of the use of various kinds of data, he especially emphasizes the necessity of utilizing judgments; he makes numerous recommendations for obtaining judgment data and for using such data in evaluation.[52] Nevertheless, he states that

> personal value-commitments, educational aims, goals, objectives, priorities, perceived norms, and standards—in one form of expression or another—are judgment data. . . . Compared to many educational-research data, judgment data are messy. They seem particularly susceptible to the obtrusiveness of formal evaluation.[53]

He chides evaluators by saying that "often an evaluator reports gain-score data with decimal precision and no data at all on the suitability of the instructional goals."[54]

[51] Cronbach, pp. 677 and 678.
[52] Robert E. Stake, "Objectives, Priorities, and Other Judgment Data," *Review of Educational Research*, 40, 181–212 (April 1970).
[53] Stake, "Objectives, Priorities, and Other Judgment Data," pp. 181–182.
[54] Stake, "Objectives, Priorities, and Other Judgment Data," p. 182.

In systematic courses an analysis of the recommended content of the course and the actual content used by the teacher may provide useful data for evaluation. Content may be analyzed on the basis of the predetermined subgoals for the course, the concepts and generalizations developed by the course, the content of preceding courses in the same subject and of succeeding courses, including those at the postsecondary school level, related courses in other fields of study, the content of similar courses in other schools, and, most important, the relevancy of the content for the students.

Another important aspect of the curriculum which should be included as a part of the evaluation is the organization or design of the curriculum or of any segment of it. Usually attention is primarily directed to the organization of a domain, since, as was discussed in Chapter 5, the domains constitute the basis for organizing the school program. In addition, the organization of individual courses and other kinds of instructional segments should be scrutinized. The question to be faced in the evaluation of design is whether the design used for carrying on instruction in and of itself contributed to the realization of goals and the attainment of outcomes desired or deterred or militated against effective goal attainment.

Data obtained in the evaluation of instruction, considered in the next section, is, of course, essential for program evaluation. In fact, evaluation of the curriculum or any segment of it and evaluation of instruction are parts of the same undertaking, although formative evaluation looms much larger in curriculum appraisal and summative evaluation in instructional assessment.

The fourth responsibility in curriculum evaluation is to determine standards by which outcomes will be judged in terms of what is good, what is acceptable, and what expectations are reasonable in a given situation. This is a difficult matter to decide, and none of the authorities cited previously offer much help. Stake comments on the matter of standards:

> There is a general agreement that the goal of education is excellence—but how schools and students should excel, and at what sacrifice, will always be debated. . . . Today's educational programs are not subjected to "standard-oriented" evaluation. . . . This is to say that standards—benchmarks of performance having widespread reference—are not in common use. . . . Even in an informal way, no school can evaluate the impact of its program without knowledge of what other schools are doing in pursuit of similar objectives. Unfortunately, many educators are loathe to accumulate that knowledge systematically.[55]

[55] Stake, "The Countenance of Educational Evaluation," p. 535.

He offers some suggestions about setting standards—largely the use of expert opinion, as well as the views of parents—but he admits that he has little help to offer. Certainly, standardized test results are no help, for they simply compare groups and do not offer evidence on what is desirable. Similarly, the National Assessment of Educational Progress (see next section) simply reports percentages of students who choose each alternative answer to a test item. It is suggested that setting standards with respect to knowledge and understandings of a subject area or a field in which cognitive outcomes predominate may utilize extensively the opinions of scholars or experts in the area of study; similarly psychologists, sociologists, psychiatrists, and mental health experts may contribute in affective aspects of learning outcomes; highly competent teachers certainly can assist in setting standards, as well as interested parents. In using comparative data from other school systems, as Stake suggests, the evaluator must take full account of antecedent conditions as well as the contingencies, or context conditions of which Stufflebeam and his co-workers write.

Finally, in curriculum evaluation the evaluator must make judgments on the congruence between the outcomes produced by the program or segment of the curriculum and the intended outcomes. Again, he must be alert to the importance of outcomes identified that were not covered in the goals or lists of intended outcomes. The evaluator may be expected also to make cost analyses, which, obviously, adds greatly to his burden.

These judgments, findings, or conclusions must then be prepared for use by the decision-maker. Again, this is a responsibility seldom performed adequately. Stufflebeam's group has provided an excellent section on "work breakdown for providing information."[56] It includes a format for reporting evaluations prepared by Stake.

Examples of Curriculum Evaluation

A considerable number of examples of curriculum evaluation are available in the literature. With the great increase in interest in evaluation many more excellent ones will be forthcoming from state and local school systems. At this point we especially direct attention to projects described by Provus. Chapter 4 of his book describes an application of his model to a standard speech development program and Chapter 9 to several other aspects of the curriculum in the Pittsburgh schools. These illustrations show processes and techniques used in both formative evaluation in the development of a project or program and summative evaluation of the outcomes.

[56] Stufflebeam, pp. 197–213.

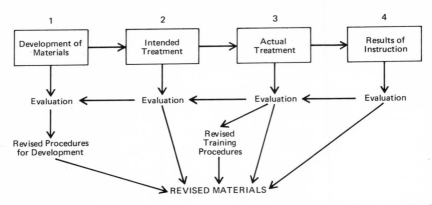

FIGURE 16   Procedures used for the formative evaluation of BSCS instructional materials. (*From "Evaluation Issue,"* BSCS Newsletter *No. 46, February 1972*)

Hulda Grobman has also provided a description of the methods used in both formative and summative evaluation of three curriculum development projects.[57] The steps used in the Biological Sciences Curriculum Study will be described briefly here as an excellent illustration of course evaluation.

The steps and process for the formative evaluation of the three versions of the Biological Sciences Curriculum Study instructional materials are illustrated in Figure 16.

The study staff states that many forms of data collecting and "systematic observations" were used in evaluation: "extent of use, peer group approval, degree of influence both domestically and abroad, formal and informal feedback, and structured evaluation studies."[58] The structured studies included feedback from teachers, students, professional societies, biologists, and educators, the use of specific test instruments, and classroom visitations. The use of test instruments as a basis for revising curriculum materials is described in detail in the report for two recent curriculum projects of the study. Timelines illustrating the interweaving of development and evaluation are helpful guides for understanding the process of formative evaluation of a new course or program. Figure 17 brings the whole process together.

Another example of curriculum evaluation that is attracting attention because of the uniqueness of its approach and techniques is the Minnemast Project. In evaluating segments of the curriculum, in this instance the

[57] Grobman, *Developmental Curriculum Projects*, Chap. 6, and *Evaluation Activities of Curriculum Projects*.

[58] William V. Mayer, "Evaluation and Curriculum Development," *BSCS Newsletter*, No. 46 (February 1972), p. 2.

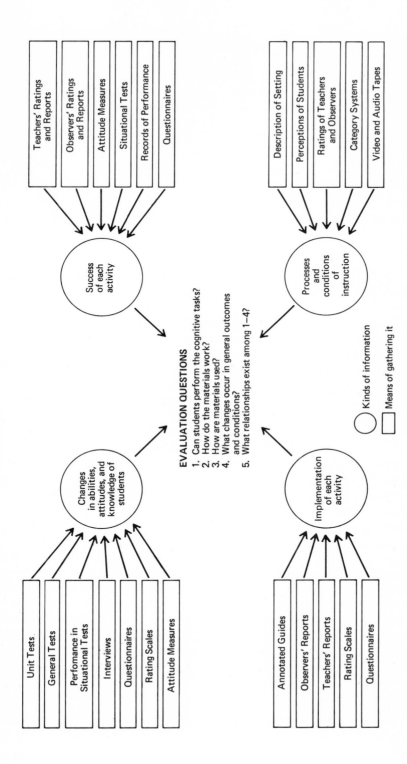

FIGURE 17 Scope of evaluation and data sources in BSCS curriculum projects. (*From "Evaluation Issue,"* BSCS Newsletter, *No. 46, February 1972*)

Minnesota Mathematics and Science Teaching Project, a domain-referenced technique for preparing the evaluation instruments was used.[59]

In concluding this section on curriculum evaluation, we note again that the entire program of educational opportunities made available for the children, youth, and young adults of a community must be evaluated. This matter was treated in the previous section. The evaluation of a course, a set of learning opportunities, or any segment of the curriculum is an aspect of and contributes to the evaluation of the total educational program, and thus the total curriculum plan for a school system or an individual school. Similarly, evaluation of instruction is an integral part of the process, contributing essential data to the other, broader, aspects of curriculum evaluation.

EVALUATING INSTRUCTION

Instruction as implementation of the curriculum must be evaluated in its own right as instruction, so that teachers and other decision-makers may make the best choices of instructional objectives, modes, and content, teaching methods, and evaluative methods for ascertaining outcomes. We now consider this aspect of curriculum evaluation.

The same three models presented earlier in this chapter are adaptable to the evaluation of instruction. For aspects of data collecting the plan for developing tables of specifications presented by Bloom, Hastings, and Madaus, and the *Elementary School Evaluation Kit: Needs Assessment,* and the corollary *CSE Hierarchical Objectives Charts,* issued by the Center for the Study of Evaluation, are helpful.[60]

The procedures in instructional evaluation should follow the same general format outlined in previous sections. The first step is the identification and tentative evaluation of instructional objectives. This is simply an extension of the evaluation of goals and subgoals. An important factor in this aspect of the process, however, is that many or perhaps none of the instructional objectives of a unit of learning activities—which may be as small as a single unit of work or as large as a year's course, a school subject or even all of the courses offered in field of study—may not be explicitly stated. This point was considered in Chapter 4. A curriculum guide may list a number of objectives that sample the possibilities inherent in the unit, leaving it to the teacher to further develop the list. A few more general objectives, comparable to subgoals, may be stated, or only

[59] Hively and others.

[60] The complete kit consists of nine different sets of material. Available from the Center for the Study of Evaluation, University of Califormnia at Los Angeles.

subgoals for the entire course or unitary set of learning opportunities may be defined, leaving entirely to the teacher(s) the responsibility of formulating instructional objectives.

Thus, the evaluator often must take steps to have the teacher or director of an activity or service set down the intended outcomes; in some instances he may have to deduce them entirely from observing instruction or conferring with the teacher. Regardless, the evaluator must have a set of objectives or intended outcomes before he can complete the appraisal. This is not to repudiate goal-free evaluation, which was discussed previously, but rather to state that in the evaluation of instruction it is necessary to be fair to the teacher by taking account of his objectives and ascertaining how well they have been achieved by each member of the participating group.

However, the evaluator, particularly an outside one, although the teacher himself should also be seeking evidence on side effects, will need to take account of concomitant outcomes of instruction. In effect, such data will contribute to the evaluation of the stated or determined objectives themselves, as well as to evaluation of the quality and merits of the total school program, in addition to judgments about the program, course, or segment being evaluated.

The first aspect of instruction to be evaluated, then, will be these objectives. The evaluator will ascertain the congruence between these objectives and the general and subgoals previously defined and evaluated; he will identify important outcomes not included in or consistent with the intended ones and, in turn, appraise their merits in light of goals and subgoals. Procedures for evaluating instructional objectives are the same as for the evaluating of goals already considered earlier in this chapter. It is emphasized that the validity and appropriateness of objectives cannot finally be determined until all data have been collected and the last stages of summative evaluation are reached.

Analyzing Antecedents

The second aspect of instructional evaluation is the determination of antecedent or context conditions. Of primary importance among these data are the characteristics of the students who were instructed in the segment of instruction under assessment. These are the same kinds of data listed in the tables pertaining to students in Chapter 3. Sources of such data were also described. These data are essential for judging intended and actual outcomes, but also in the setting of standards by which to judge the quality and appropriateness of instruction. Moreover, the data ought to be obtained on a personal basis for each student. This is a tremendous undertaking, as noted previously, but evaluation is inadequate, perhaps misleading, and seriously deficient as a basis for decision-making and planning unless these characteristics are taken into account. Examples of such grossly inept and misleading assessments are published in the *New York Times* and the *Washington Post* (and probably in many less widely circulated newspapers) in reporting mean scores in reading by grades on the basis of standard norms for each individual elementary and often secondary school.

The kinds of student data listed in the tables in Chapter 3 of special importance in evaluating instruction include:

1. The capabilities, talents, and aptitudes of each student.
2. Appropriate aspects of the developmental status of each student at the time of the initiation of the segment of instruction being evaluated, particularly knowledge acquired, cognitive development, skills, attitudes, and ability to be self-directive and to direct and carry on his own learning activities.
3. Any evidence readily obtainable on learning styles, learning difficulties, and special learning aptitudes.
4. Nature and character of motivation for participating in the instruction, including personal interest, career plans, and supportive nature of the family and environmental situation.
5. Clues as feasible to obtain about the nature of the social, moral, and intellectual climate of the peer group in which the class members associate.

The difficulty of obtaining reliable and useful data of these sorts is readily acknowledged; but school psychologists and highly trained evaluators are increasingly developing means of studying children and youth. Teachers themselves often have or can develop a considerable degree of competency in analyzing traits and characteristics of these kinds. Sheer hunches, gossip, or invalid stereotypes, as Rosenthal and Jacobson have attempted to show,[61] are not acceptable as a basis for setting standards for evaluating pupil attainments. Norms on standardized tests, the data from the National Assessment of Educational Progress, and most kinds of comparative data are useless or actually detrimental to valid evaluation unless one can ascertain the congruence between his students and the reference group on these relevant items of student characteristics.

Other kinds of antecedent or context data are also necessary, and the reader is referred to Stufflebeam and his committee's book and

[61] Robert Rosenthal and Lenore Jacobson, *Pygmalion in the Classroom: Teacher Expectation and Pupils' Intellectual Development* (New York: Holt, Rinehart and Winston, Inc., 1968).

to Stake's articles. Although other authorities point out the need for these kinds of data, they offer little or no help in identifying such data or in collecting what is needed.

Studying Classroom Interactions

The third major aspect of instructional evaluation is concerned with the interactive process in the classroom. Stake labels this aspect of instruction as transactions and Stufflebeam and his committee as process evaluation (although both of these terms include additional matters), but Rosenshine[62] simply speaks of classroom instruction. That such data is essential for instructional evaluation is, of course, recognized by all of the specialists in the new approaches to evaluation. Not only do data on classroom interactions enable the evaluator to make judgments about the classroom conditions under which the student outcomes were achieved and what these augur for decision-making but the interactive process itself is a major contributor to the achievement of many important instructional objectives. Hence, evaluating student outcomes must be done in the context of these classroom (broadly understood as the locale of instruction) transactions.

Systems for analyzing and classifying the interactive process in classrooms have been described in recent professional literature.[63] The schemes most extensively used are the Flanders-Amidon, Bellack, and the Smith-Meux, although more recent versions of the Flanders method and other approaches may be more appropriate. The use of video taping machines greatly facilitates the gathering of such data. Much use is also made of the students' own reactions to the instructional process in a specific class. This form of data collecting has been widely used at the college level, and it certainly has value at the common school level, prob-

[62] Barak Rosenshine, "Evaluation of Classroom Instruction," *Review of Educational Research*, 40, 279–300 (April 1970).

[63] For a most exhaustive and exceedingly helpful description and analysis of systems and techniques see Barak Rosenshine and Norma Furst, "The Use of Direct Observation to Study Teaching," and Ira J. Gordon and R. Emile Jester, "Techniques of Observing Teaching in Early Childhood and Outcomes of Particular Procedures," in Robert M. W. Travers, ed., *Second Handbook of Research on Teaching* (Chicago: Rand McNally & Company, 1973), pp. 122–183 and 184–217; and the similar earlier reviews, Donald M. Medley and Harold E. Mitel, "Measuring Classroom Behavior by Systematic Observation," in N. L. Gage, ed., *Handbook on Research in Teaching* (Chicago: Rand McNally & Company, 1963), pp. 247–328; Milton O. Meux, "Studies of Learning in School Setting," *Review of Educational Research*, 37, 539–562 (December 1967); Anita Simon and E. Gil Boyer, eds., *Mirrors for Behavior: An Anthology of Classroom Observation Instruments* (Philadelphia: Research for Better Schools, Inc., 1968).

ably as early as the middle school. Reaction sheets, rating scales, and opinionnaires are used to gather such data, but conferences and interviews are also useful. Parents' reactions are also used, especially those obtained by a neutral party.

The information on the classroom interactive process gathered by these various means will, of course, need to be analyzed and treated in as reliable a method as possible. Stake[64] and Rosenshine[65] not only discuss methods of processing the data but list many references that provide additional suggestions. More sophisticated methods may also be used.[66]

Measuring Student Outcomes

We move from the input factors to the output side of the ledger. As professional evaluators of today point out, measuring student outcomes is about the only kind of formal instructional evaluation that was done in years past. It was the process of endless testing. Yet any plan for instructional evaluation even in the most up-to-date models relies extensively on formal test and measurement techniques. The difference between the two approaches lies in the very limited nature of the total plan of evaluation and the kinds of data collected in the traditional procedures contrasted to the plans for instructional evaluation recommended today. What also set present-day approaches apart are the scope and nature of the measurements used and the methods for treating and analyzing the data as a part of the total evaluation process.[67]

A plethora of books, research reports, brochures, and articles on testing and measuring student achievement have been written, and the tests and other devices used to measure outcomes fill many file drawers. Hence, we will not here consider at length the whole field of testing, measurement, statistical analysis, and methods of appraising the achievement of individual students.[68] Rather, we will examine some problems and issues concerning their use.

[64] Stake, "Objectives, Priorities and Other Judgment Data," pp. 195–203.

[65] Rosenshine, pp. 288–296.

[66] Herman Wold, "Causal Inference from Observational Data. A Review of Ends and Means," in Wittrock and Wiley, pp. 351–390; and Richard J. Light, "Issues in the Analysis of Qualitative Data," in *Second Handbook of Research on Teaching*, pp. 318–381.

[67] For an excellent analysis of earlier and current approaches to evaluation of the curriculum and instruction see Glass; and Scriven.

[68] Some of the most useful handbooks and references on the subject include Bloom, Hastings, and Madaus, which includes bibliographies at the end of each chapter; Beatty, especially Section II, "An Inventory of Measures of Affective Behavior"; Fred T. Wilhelms, chairman, *Evaluation as Feedback and Guide*, 1967 Yearbook, Associa-

The first, and most important, point to be made is the extreme difficulty, if not the impossibility, of measuring quantitatively through tests and other instruments many of the most significant outcomes desired, sought, and achieved. The authors of the Rand report, in summarizing their exhaustive analysis of research on school effectiveness, stated the situation:

First, the data used by researchers are, at best, crude measures of what is really happening. Education is an extremely subtle phenomenon. Researchers in education are plagued by the virtual impossibility of measuring those aspects of education they wish to study. For example, a student's cognitive achievement is typically measured by his score on a standardized achievement test, despite the many serious problems involved in interpreting such scores.

But this is only part of the indictment:

Second, educational outcomes are almost exclusively measured by cognitive achievement. Although no one would deny that non-cognitive outcomes and social outcomes beyond the individual student level are of major importance, research efforts that focus on these outcomes are sparse and largely inconclusive and offer little guidance with respect to what is effective.[69]

Many test-construction specialists, researchers, and staff members of test bureaus and colleges of education have endeavored to develop reliable and valid tests not only of the higher levels of the cognitive processes, such as application, analysis, synthesis, and evaluation, so often neglected or minimized in the usual achievement tests used by schools,

---

tion for Supervision and Curriculum Development (Washington, D.C.: The Association, 1967), especially Part 3; W. James Popham, ed., *Criterion-Referenced Measurement: An Introduction* (Englewood Cliffs, N.J.: Educational Technology Publications, Inc., 1971); Joel Weiss, ed., *Curriculum Evaluation: Potentiality and Reality*, Monograph Supplement, Curriculum Theory Network (Toronto: Ontario Institute for Studies in Education, 1972); *Evaluation Comment* and other publications of the Center for the Study of Evaluation, University of California at Los Angeles, 145 Moore Hall; Terry Denny, ed., "Educational Evaluation," special issue, *Review of Educational Research*, 40, 181–320 (April 1970), an excellent review of an extensive body of literature; see especially chapters by Stake, Rosenshine, and Sjorgren; Harvey A. Averch and others, *How Effective Is Schooling? A Critical Review and Synthesis of Research Findings*, Final Report to the President's Commission on School Finance (Santa Monica, Calif.: The Rand Corporation, December 1971, available from the Government Printing Office, Washington, D.C., Catalog No. Pr. 37, Sch 6/Sch 6/2).

[69] Averch and others, p. ix; see also their chapter on "Measuring Educational Outcomes," pp. 16–30.

but in the affective domain of development as well.[70] Nevertheless, such efforts, as the Rand people stated, still do not cover some of the most important aspects of schooling, and far too many schools simply do not use the instruments that are available. Equally serious is the fact that most parents have little interest in measures of student achievement except those that produce comparative norm or percentile scores denoting the extent factual knowledge and communicative and computational skills have been acquired.

A revolt against the excessive and unsound use of standardized tests to measure achievement has taken place in recent years. On the other hand, the accountability movement during the same period and the interest in performance contracting and related approaches have caused greater emphasis to be placed on achievement testing. It is worth noting in this connection that the National Education Association, at its convention in July 1972, passed this resolution: "The NEA strongly encourages the elimination of group standardized intelligence, aptitude, and achievement tests to assess student potential or achievement until completion of a critical appraisal, review, and revision of current testing programs."[71] Stake has commented

> Without yielding to the temptation to undercut new efforts to provide instruction, educators should continue to be apprehensive about evaluating teaching on the basis of performance testing alone. They should know how difficult it is to represent educational goals with statements of objectives and how costly it is to provide criterion testing. They should know that the common-sense interpretation of these results is frequently wrong.[72]

Many other methods in addition to tests may be used to gather information about student outcomes. Admittedly, the evaluator faces a much more difficult problem in obtaining reliable data from these methods, although in many instances the data may be more valid; moreover, the analysis and treatment of the data presents even greater hurdles. As Combs insists, however, judgmental and other methods of assessment must be used: "Judgment frees us to go beyond mere observation. To reject it as a tool for assessment is to limit ourselves to the least important

[70] The review by Donald J. Dowd and Sarah C. West in Beatty, pp. 89–158, lists such tests; and the authoritative handbook edited by Oscar K. Buros, *The Mental Measurements Yearbook* (Highland Park, N.J.: Gryphon Press, periodic editions), is an essential tool for any evaluator.

[71] "Moratorium on Standardized Testing," *Today's Education*, 61, 41 (September 1972).

[72] Robert E. Stake, "Testing Hazards in Performance Contracting," *Phi Delta Kappan*, 52, 583–589 (June 1971); his extensive references are useful.

aspects of our educational efforts and so to assure the increasing irrelevance of a system already desperately ill of that disease."[73] But he much more than advocates the use of other types of assessment; he presents methods for doing so.

Most of the recently published books on testing and measurement provide ample literature on nonquantitative types of data; for this purpose manuals, curriculum guides, and books and articles on curriculum, instructional planning, and teaching methods for a subject field, such as social studies, science, and language arts, usually provide excellent help in collecting evaluative data. Again, we call attention to the handbook by Bloom, Hastings, and Madaus, especially Chapter 10, and the *CSE Elementary School Evaluation Kit*. Both sources provide for the selection and use of a variety of data-collecting methods for the evaluation of instruction.

A number of descriptions of instructional-evaluation programs that provide excellent examples have been published. These should be helpful in planning and conducting evaluative programs in the modern idiom.[74] In addition, surveys or analyses of classroom activities that use observations, survey instruments, interviews, and the like, provide examples of a broad approach to instructional evaluation.[75]

Assessing Educational Progress

Evaluators of instruction will also find the National Assessment of Educational Progress project a help in conducting instructional evaluations. First, the data-collecting instruments developed in this program constitute a significant contribution to the evaluation process; second, the model used by the program for assessing educational achievements has provided techniques that are used and probably will continue to be used in widespread efforts to evaluate educational outcomes on a state, regional, or national basis. Third, the results of the assessments are useful to curriculum planners in making revisions and changes in the curriculum and in instruction. We noted in Chapter 4 that the educational goals

---

[73] Arthur W. Combs, *Educational Accountability: Beyond Behavioral Objectives* (Washington, D.C.: Association for Supervision and Curriculum Development, 1972), p. 14.

[74] Frances R. Link and Paul B. Diederich, "A Cooperative Evaluation Program," and Paul B. Diederich and Frances R. Link, "Cooperative Evaluation in English," in Wilhelms, Chaps. 6 and 7; Grobman, *Evaluation Activities of Curriculum Projects;* and Provus.

[75] Two exceptionally useful studies are Philip W. Jackson, *Life in the Classroom* (New York: Holt, Rinehart and Winston, Inc., 1968); and John I. Goodlad, M. Frances Klein, and associates, *Behind the Classroom Door* (Worthington, O.: Charles A. Jones Publishing Company, 1970).

developed as a part of the program have been widely used by educators as resource material in defining their own sets of purposes.

Professional literature contains ample accounts of the origin and history of the project and the nature of the assessment project as it has been carried out in this country since 1964.[76] It is evident that curriculum planners and evaluators should be fully cognizant of this widespread national project and its contributions to evaluative data.

Project plans call for the assessment of each of ten study areas on a five-year cycle. Thus measures of "progress" will be available in due time for each area. The schedule, which may be changed before it is all carried out, is as follows:

1969–1970	Science, Writing, Citizenship
1970–1971	Reading, Literature
1971–1972	Music, Social Studies
1972–1973	Mathematics, Science—repeat
1973–1974	Writing—repeat, Career and Occupational Development
1974–1975	Art, Citizenship—repeat
1975–1976	Reading—repeat, Literature—repeat
1976–1977	Music—repeat, Social Studies—repeat
1977–1978	Mathematics—repeat, Science—2d repeat
1978–1979	Writing—2d repeat, Career and Occupational Development—repeat
1979–1980	Citizenship—2d repeat, Art—repeat[77]

The test results are reported by the four age groups, by sex, by four large regions of the United States, by seven types of communities

[76] Jack C. Merwin and Frank B. Womer, "Evaluation in Assessing the Progress of Education To Provide Bases of Public Understanding and Public Policy," in Ralph W. Tyler, ed., *Educational Evaluation: New Roles and New Means*, Sixty-eighth Yearbook, Part II, National Society for the Study of Education (Chicago: University of Chicago Press, 1969), Chap. 13; Jack R. Frymier, "National Assessment," in Wilhelms, pp. 249–259; Galen Saylor, "National Assessment: Current Status," in Robert Leeper, ed., *Humanizing Education: The Person in the Process* (Washington, D.C.: Association for Supervision and Curriculum Development, 1967), pp. 104–114; Ralph W. Tyler, "The Purposes of Assessment," in Beatty, pp. 2–13; Ralph W. Tyler, "National Assessment: A History and Sociology," *School and Society*, 98, 471–477 (December 1970), also published in James W. Guthrie and Edward Wynne, eds., *New Models for American Education* (Englewood Cliffs, N.J.: Prentice-Hall, Inc., 1971), pp. 20–34; and Frank B. Womer and Marjorie M. Mastie, "How Will National Assessment Change American Education," *Phi Delta Kappan*, 43, 118–120 (October 1971). The Project publishes a newsletter which reports current news and developments. (Published by the National Assessment of Educational Progress, A Project of the Education Commission of the States, 1860 Lincoln St., Denver, Colo. 80203.)

[77] See "Questions and Answers about the National Assessment of Educational Progress," NAEP brochure, April 1972.

(and hence school systems), by two color groups (black and white), and by four levels of parental education. The reports on national test results for each subject area are published by the Government Printing Office in the form of overall national data and then as supplementary reports by the subpopulations.[78]

The test instruments, as has been stated, have been acclaimed by evaluators as constituting a step forward from the traditional test instruments available in the past. Stake and Denny particularly cite the use of test descriptors as a significant contribution.[79] Other evaluators have also commented favorably on the criterion-referenced, personalized nature of the test instruments. The National Assessment of Educational Progress staff, utilizing advisory committees of competent persons, official advisory boards, and the services of well-known test publishers and service bureaus, undertakes an extensive analysis of the instruments, as well as of the goals formulated for a testing area, and may make revisions in them for the later rounds of the cycle. Moreover, the project office releases for use by school systems, state education departments, or other authorized agencies about half of the exercises used in the previous test administration.

The sampling model is another matter; whether it is a reliable sample of the population for which results are published is difficult to determine. Unlike a sampling technique used by political pollsters, no check on the sample occurs later through an election. If state and local assessment programs use the test instruments for measuring educational outcomes of their student populations, some verification of the adequacy of the sampling may be feasible. The project staff insists that the procedure yields reliable results. This claim, however, may be seriously disputed when one considers that only 2000 students nation-wide responded to any one exercise and that only 28,000 students were included in the entire testing program in three subject areas—citizenship, science, and writing—for each of three age groups tested—nine-, thirteen-, and seventeen-year-olds. At the adult level the number taking any one exercise was 650–900.[80]

The most significant, and major, contribution of the National Assessment of Educational Progress to curriculum and instructional

[78] Available from the Government Printing Office, Washington, D.C., under the title "National Assessment of Educational Progress," Stock No. HE 5.2:As 7/rp. 1 (one in series).

[79] Robert E. Stake and Terry Denny, "Needed Concepts and Techniques for Utilizing More Fully the Potential of Evaluation," in Tyler, *Educational Evaluation: New Roles, New Means*, p. 382.

[80] National Assessment of Educational Progress, *Report I: 1969–1970 Science—National Results and Illustrations of Group Comparisons* (Denver: The Project, 1970), p. 4.

evaluation is, of course, the results of the assessment process. These are analyzed and published in detail, exercise by exercise.

Illustrations may be readily given of such contributions. The results of the first test run in science (1969–1970) showed that

> Blacks performed 12% to 16% below the national average at all four age levels assessed. On the whole Blacks performed best on those Science exercises most dependent upon daily experience and common knowledge and poorly on those which involve the more abstract aspects of Science. . . . National Assessment observed that it is not possible to draw conclusions about the many conceivable sets of factors that explain Black performance at the four age levels.[81]

Another illustration of the findings of the National Assessment is as follows:

> The third report on the Citizenship Assessment revealed that those who live in inner cities, those whose parents have only an elementary school education or attended high school but did not finish, and Blacks understand less than other groups about the functions of government and feel helpless to affect the policy-making process.[82]

Such findings, stated as general conclusions of the study, should —provided the educator accepts them as valid—be of considerable value in evaluating the curriculum and instruction of a local school system or of a state school system. Revision of the curriculum, adoption of new textbooks, purchase of new instructional materials, use of other modes of instruction, improvement of the classroom interactive process, and similar decisions should take account of such findings, although they are for a general population. The conclusions provide clues for local testing with a specific population. Some professional associations of educators have recently been working with the National Assessment project staff not only in the revision of goals and test exercises for the second cycle of testing but in interpretation of data obtained to date, with implications for planning and instruction.

Application of Standards

After data of various kinds have been obtained from all feasible sources, the evaluator must set standards for judging the merits of the instruction. As we observed earlier in the section on curriculum evalu-

---

[81] *NAEP Newsletter*, Vol. 5, No. 1 (January–February 1972), pp. 2–3.
[82] *NAEP Newsletter*, Vol. 5, No. 5 (August–September 1972), p. 3.

ation, this is a difficult and demanding aspect of the process. Techniques and procedures for setting standards were considered briefly at that point; these suggestions and recommendations are equally valid for determining standards for instruction; in fact, the latter step is really part and parcel of the same endeavor. Here we will consider some points on standards in reference to measuring devices used in evaluating instruction.

For tests that yield quantitative measures, standards may, but need not, be set on the basis of a "normal" population of students. The scores made by the normal group are scaled, and the scale then shows how a student making a certain score compares with a group of presumably comparable students. The scale usually is stated in terms of grade-level attainments or percentile rank. Thus, average or median scores for a class, all of a certain class or grade in the system, and similar student populations may be determined. Schools often report the median grade-level score or percentile rank for the fifth grade, say, in a certain school, and similarly for any other class or conglomerate of students.

A second means of deriving norm-referenced scores is to use the test group itself to determine percentile ranks among its members. The normalizing scale is set by the group being tested. It shows only a student's rank in comparison with his fellow participants. This measure may have value for planning instruction for individuals, but it still provides no evidence, in and of itself, concerning the quality of instruction or the acceptability of the level of accomplishments of the class or group.

Criterion-referenced tests[83] have come into extensive use in recent years, particularly in conjunction with performance contracting, some types of accountability, and individualized learning programs. This is the method of measuring used in the National Assessment of Educational Progress project. In these types of tests the standard is individualized, but comparison to a test population is also possible. The standard is the extent to which the student accomplishes the task specified in the test item, or, for a group, the percentage or number who performed the task correctly. In a criterion-referenced test the test item should constitute a valid sample of the kind of behavior specified by an objective for that segment of instruction. If the test is to measure outcomes for a number of closely related specific behavioral objectives, it may contain test

[83] See Popham; Robert Glaser and Richard C. Cox, "Criterion-Referenced Testing for the Management of Educational Outcomes," in Robert A. Weisgerber, ed., *Instructional Processes and Media Integration* (Chicago: Rand McNally & Company, 1969); C. M. Lindvall and Richard C. Cox, *The IPI Evaluation Program*, AERA Monograph Series on Curriculum Evaluation, No. 5, Robert E. Stake, ed. (Chicago: Rand McNally & Company, 1970).

items that only sample evidence of such behavior rather than test for each objective. To measure attainment of a broader nonbehaviorally stated objective or even a goal, a large number of test items may be necessary, and these should constitute a valid sample of such competencies.

Learning for mastery[84] is a part of this same general development. Instruction is usually individualized and the student ordinarily stays with a learning task until he reaches a desired level of proficiency. This level is then measured by a criterion-type test.

Criterion-referenced testing is a highly desirable kind of measurement for evaluating instruction. Its use in recent years has generally been associated with a highly structured, very narrow mode of instruction and is principally a teaching method itself rather than an evaluative device for judging the quality of instruction. But a skilled evaluator working with a teacher or a group of teachers in a local school situation could obtain some valuable data by the use of criterion-type tests. The Rand staff has stated: "Much work remains to be done in developing criterion-referenced tests but they appear to have great promise. Their greatest potential value is that they focus on instructional content, yield information for remediation, and allow for individual differences in performances."[85]

Teacher-made tests for specific situations are usually criterion-referenced, although the validity of the test items and of the scoring may be questioned. Nevertheless, they may provide more significant data for evaluative purposes than the published tests, inasmuch as they should be measures of outcomes desired in specific units of instruction.

Judgments

Drawing on all data and information available on context input and antecedents, and utilizing observations and other data relative to contingencies in which the instruction was carried on, the evaluator makes judgments about the merits of the instructional program in light of the objectives, goals, or intended outcomes. The procedure is similar to those described previously, so little new treatment of the subject is needed here. Suffice it to say that such judgments, obviously, provide more pertinent, useful, and meaningful information than is provided by simply preparing tables of class means, medians, or percentile ranks obtained from sets of test norms published in a manual.

The views of parents, the students themselves, specialists in an area of study, and concerned citizens also should be used in judging the quality of the instruction.

[84] See especially Bloom, Hastings, and Madaus, Chap. 3.
[85] Averch and others, p. 28.

The final responsibility of the evaluator is to report findings to the decision-makers and other planners. Again, this task requires ingenuity and a keen understanding of the purposes of evaluation. An examination of almost any educational evaluation report, especially in relation to instruction, reveals the ineptness and shallowness of the document. Much of this weakness is due to the inadequacy of the evaluation itself, but even in the more commendable projects the reports leave much to be desired.

EVALUATING THE EVALUATION PROGRAM

The total evaluation of the educational program of a school or school system is not complete until the evaluation program itself is evaluated. Such an evaluation follows the same steps and procedures used in all other aspects of the curriculum appraisal.

In all likelihood independent evaluators from outside the school, system, or agency should conduct the evaluation. If this were done consistently throughout the nation, a large number of school testing programs, state education department procedures for school accreditation, state-wide testing programs, research projects of many schools and colleges, and evaluation reports submitted to fulfill requirements of federally supported programs would probably end up with a failing grade, just as do too many students in U.S. schools.

Stake has pointed out one of the problems:

> There is a common belief among educators that ideal programs can only be those tailored to the local community, to a particular teaching style, and sometimes, to each and every child separately. If this belief is well founded, all methods of educational evaluation are going to be very expensive.[86]

In concluding this chapter, reference is made again to Figure 13, which illustrates the scope and nature of curriculum evaluation. A complete effort to judge the quality of the program the school provides the children, youth, and young adults of a community should comprehend all of these types of evaluations. Evaluations of educational programs that are inadequate in conception, shoddy in execution, limited in scope, and misleading in findings are not only of little genuine value to decision-makers but may be highly detrimental in the long run to the education of the students. Philip Kraus, in a longitudinal study of 165 children in two New York City schools from the time of their entrance to kinder-

[86] Stake, "Language, Rationality, and Assessment," p. 25.

garten through the sixth grade, points out the tragedy that results if achievement test scores are wrongly and even stupidly used:

> When children are told that they are deficient until they meet the grade norm, the anxiety which is triggered sometimes becomes a paralyzing force and frequently shows its effects well into the high school years. . . . It is as if we were to line up children in the order of their scores, set the norm at the midpoint, and then proceed to punish all the children who are below this point—although we used them to establish that midpoint or norm.[87]

Kraus' comments on current evaluation practices in New York City schools also apply to many other systems:

> More destructive of teacher morale and pupils' self-image is the practice of the New York City Board of Education of publishing in the newspapers each year the grade equivalency scores obtained in the annual achievement testing program by each grade in every school. It is unrealistic to expect parents to understand that, statistically, half the children will always fall below the norm, no matter how well they actually read. This has resulted, in recent years, in odious comparisons between schools, and militant attacks upon teachers and supervisors by parents of children in schools with low reading scores.[88]

On the other hand, well-conceived and well-executed evaluation programs provide significant information to educators, taxpayers, parents, and the students themselves and can contribute to the development of better programs of schooling.

ADDITIONAL SUGGESTIONS FOR FURTHER STUDY

Ahmann, J. Stanley, and Marvin D. Glock, *Measuring and Evaluating Educational Achievement*. Boston: Allyn and Bacon, Inc., 1971. One of the best of the textbooks on measurement and evaluation; broad in concept and comprehensive in treatment.

Block, J. H., ed., *Mastery Learning: Theory and Practice*. New York: Holt, Rinehart and Winston, Inc., 1971. An extended treatment of the concept of learning for mastery and methods of measuring the results.

---

[87] Philip E. Kraus, *Yesterday's Children: A Longitudinal Study of Children from Kindergarten into Adult Years* (New York: John Wiley & Sons, Inc., 1973), p. 128.
[88] Kraus, p. 143.

Carver, Ronald P., "Special Problems in Measuring Change with Psychometric Devices," in Brent Baxter, chairman, *Evaluative Research: Strategies and Methods*. Pittsburgh: American Institute for Research, 1970. A good discussion of some of the problems facing evaluators.

Eiss, Albert P., *Evaluation of Instructional Systems*. New York: Gordon and Breach Publishers, Inc., 1972. A comprehensive treatment of the evaluation of instruction.

House, Ernst R., *School Evaluation: The Politics and the Process*. Berkeley, Calif.: McCutchan Publishing Corporation, 1973. Emphasis is on the use of evaluation in decision-making, especially with reference to allocation and use of resources. Part 4 deals with evaluation when there is a consensus on goals and Part 5 when there is not.

Kraft, Richard, and others, *Three Examples: Economic, Anthropological, and Narrative*, AERA Monograph Series on Curriculum Evaluation, Robert E. Stake, ed. Chicago: Rand McNally & Company, 1973. Excellent examples of the evaluation program in different types of school communities.

Rippey, Robert M., and others, *Studies in Transactional Evaluation*. Berkeley, Calif.: McCutchan Publishing Corporation, 1973. An excellent set of essays on the use of the methods of transactional evaluation in appraising school programs, projects, and practices. This method makes extensive use of data collected by observation and other means in actual classroom and school situations.

Wynne, Edward, *The Politics of School Accountability: Public Information about Public Schools*. Berkeley, Calif.: McCutchan Publishing Corporation, 1972. Although pointing his study to the accountability movement, Wynne considers the matter of the kinds of data that should be used by evaluators and offers excellent suggestions for reporting them to decision-makers.

PLANNING
SCHOOLS FOR
THE DECADES
AHEAD

Throughout this book we have examined the procedures and processes that we believe are the basis for enlightened curriculum planning. In this concluding chapter we will draw on these models to present important considerations and recommendations for the development of U.S. schools in the years ahead. Principles that have proved to be valid through application to program development over the years constitute the basis for planning schools for the future. Yet the factors that influence the school program, as well as the setting in which learning is carried on, change with the times, so that ever-continuous revisions of the curriculum are necessary. Schools must engage in what John Gardner has designated self-renewal:

Every individual, organization or society must mature, but much depends on how this maturing takes place. A society whose maturing consists simply of acquiring more firmly established ways of doing things is headed for the graveyard—even if it learns to do those things with greater and greater skill. *In the ever-renewing society what matures is a system or framework within which continuous innovation, renewal and rebirth can occur.*[1]

In this chapter, then, we call attention to social, political, and economic changes, both in the United States and world-wide, that necessitate changes in the nature and scope of the educational program at all levels.

Lawrence Cremin, although writing in 1955, in the early years of the current movement to redefine, restructure, and readapt the program of the schools, foresaw the nature and scope of the then-current efforts at self-renewal:

> From the very earliest period in which the American people sensed their uniqueness, the principal theme of their educational history has been the search for a school which in its scope, program, organization, and administration might best support and advance their most cherished ideals. . . . As in the period between 1893 and 1918, new social and intellectual currents are calling for new educational outlooks. . . . Such fundamental reappraisals are extraordinarily difficult and strenuous. They proceed unplanfully, and engender conflict, skepticism, and doubt. . . . And yet the promise of such reappraisal is the abiding faith of the democrat.[2]

SCHOOL SITUATIONS CALLING FOR CHANGE

In planning educational programs for the future, three types of situations may be identified. First, existing schools will need to take account of significant changes that have recently taken place, are currently taking place, or can be reliably predicted to take place in the next decade or two. Second, individual schools in which a significant shift in the data obtained in accordance with Chapter 3 has occurred will need to analyze such new data to ascertain what, if any, changes in the educational program should be made. Finally, when new schools are established programs must be designed to serve the particular needs of the communities in which they are located. These may be existing communities which need new schools because of growth or other factors or newly developed communities built as new-town ventures.

The same basic principles and processes of curriculum planning apply to all three types of situations. The difference among the situations lies in the fact that planning for schools of the second type is often of a

---

[1] John W. Gardner, *Self-Renewal: The Individual and the Innovative Society* (New York: Harper & Row, Publishers, 1963), p. 5.

[2] Lawrence Cremin, "The Revolution in American Secondary Education, 1893–1918," *Teachers College Record,* 56, 296–308 *passim* (March 1955).

crash nature or may require new understandings and considerations that necessitate extensive study and research on the part of curriculum planners. The new-school situation should not be a crash situation, but one that calls for a full-fledged planning program of the kind discussed throughout this book. It is an opportunity to lay out and use a planning system in its full scope, in contrast to a frequent situation in existing schools where curriculum planning may be a spearhead approach on a broken front.

Changed Situation in a Local School

Educators in the United States have been faced with circumstances or events which have necessitated drastic changes in public education within a relatively short period of time. An example familiar to everyone is the Supreme Court decision requiring school desegregation on the basis of race and the subsequent rulings of many federal courts in connection with this issue concerning policies and practices of specific school systems. Obviously, desegregation has caused, and continues to cause, major changes in the data that provide the bases for curriculum planning. Hence, the curriculum too needs to be reexamined and changed in the light of new circumstances.

Another traumatic event in many school systems in recent years has been the increasing failure of citizens to vote funds for public education beyond the level required by law. This reduction in financial support has resulted in significant changes in educational programs in some communities.

In some instances a rapid shift in the characteristics of a school may occur when a new military base or some government agency is established in a community or, on the other hand, when one is closed. The same situation applies for an industry or a new housing complex. All of these developments may bring about changes in the characteristics of the pupil population of a school. Other examples of dramatic occurrences of this kind are apparent.

But the more widespread types of changes in pupil population occur simply as a result of a gradual shift in the composition of the families who live in the attendance area of a particular school. Teachers and other educators in large urban areas are familiar with such changes in the factors that shape the educational program of a school.

Opportunities in New Schools

Many educators might envy those who have the privilege of planning the program for a newly established school. Certainly, here exists an opportunity for curriculum planners unexcelled in educational circles.

A new school may be established to serve a community or an area of a city. Almost every reader knows of such instances; some recent ones, in which the staff took dramatic advantage of the situation to develop a really new program, include John Adams High School in Portland, Oregon, John Dewey High School in New York City, Ridgewood High School in Norridge, Illinois, and Juanita High School in Kirkland Washington. But every reader can recall instances in which the new school, whether elementary or secondary, was established simply on the pattern of the existing schools of the district with little or no effort made to create a program specifically designed for a new situation.

Another exciting situation for educational planners arises when an entire independent community is established. Such examples are Columbia, Maryland; Park Forest South, Illinois; and some of the Levittowns in Pennsylvania, New Jersey, and New York. Social planners insist that many new communities will spring up throughout the United States in the decades ahead; by 1972, as many as 250 were in various stages of planning and development.[3]

The fairly new concept of the middle school represents another example of vision and imagination brought to educational planning. At the elementary school level almost every forward-looking school system has established new schools with programs that constitute a marked break from the usual schools of the community.

Another kind of challenging situation in which to formulate new kinds of programs is the establishment of what are called alternative schools. Originally, many such schools were founded by private groups who wanted to try out approaches to education that differed significantly from existing ones. More recently public schools have joined the movement, and many of the alternative schools are now a part of the program of public education (see Chapter 2).

Regardless of the situation, all schools, whether in existence now or in various stages of planning, will be kept in mind as we apply accepted principles and processes to the task of developing educational programs for the years ahead.

PREDICTED CHANGES IN AMERICAN LIFE

The starting point for planning schools for the decades ahead is to go to the standard data sources and endeavor to predict the significant changes that are likely to occur during this period.

For this task the educator has a number of useful sources and

[3] Myron Lieberman, "Education in New Cities," *Phi Delta Kappan*, 53, 407–414 (March 1972).

may draw on the assistance of various agencies. Listed below are those we consider particularly helpful at the present time; undoubtedly, very useful reports and studies will continue to be made in the future, and educational planners should seek out such material.

Suggested Source Materials

Commission on the Year 2000, "Toward the Year 2000; Work in Progress," *Daedalus*, 96, No. 3 (1967). It is indicated that this Commission will publish later reports.

Herman Kahn and Anthony J. Wiener, *The Year 2000: A Framework for Speculation on the Next Thirty-Three Years* (New York: The Macmillan Company, 1967).

William R. Ewald, Jr., ed., *Environment for Man: The Next Fifty Years* (1967); *Environment and Change: The Next Fifty Years* (1968); and *Environment and Policy: The Next Fifty Years* (1968) (Bloomington: Indiana University Press).

Kurt Baier and Nicholas Rescher, *Values and the Future* (New York: The Free Press, 1969).

Tracey M. Sonneborn, ed., *The Control of Human Heredity and Evolution* (New York: The Macmillan Company, 1965). A basic reference on development in genetic control, genes alteration, and biological developments.

Paul R. Ehrlich and Anne H. Erhlich, *Population, Resources, Environment: Issues in Human Ecology* (San Francisco: W. H. Freeman and Company, 1970). An important handbook and reference work on man and his relations to the environment.

William M. Alexander, J. Galen Saylor, and Emmett L. Williams, *The High School: Today and Tomorrow* (New York: Holt, Rinehart and Winston, Inc., 1971). Chapter 2 summarizes many predicted developments and trends in national life.

Barry Commoner, *The Closing Circle: Nature, Man, Technology* (New York: Alfred A. Knopf, Inc., 1971).

Alfred B. Bronwell, ed., *Science and Technology in the World of the Future* (New York: John Wiley & Sons, Inc., 1970). Speculates on future developments in various technological fields.

Hal Hellman, *Biology in the World of the Future* (New York: M. Evans and Company, Inc., 1971). Reports on recent and prospective advances in biology.

Richard Kostelanetz, ed., *Social Speculations: Visions for Our Time* (New York: William Morrow and Company, Inc., 1971).

Willis W. Harman, "The Nature of Our Changing Society: Implications for Schools," in Philip K. Piele and others, eds., *Social and Technological Change: Implications for Education* (Eugene, Ore.: Center for Advanced Study of Educational Administration, 1970). An excellent, succinct summary of predicted developments in our society.

Foreign Policy Association, *Toward the Year 2018* (New York: Cowles Education Association, 1968).

D. S. Wallia, ed., *Toward Century 21* (New York: Basic Books, Inc., 1970).

Jay W. Forrester, *World Dynamics* (Cambridge, Mass.: Wright-Allen Press, 1971). A study projecting interactions of world population, natural resources, industrialization, and pollution in the decades ahead.

Donella H. Meadows, Dennis L. Meadows, Jorgan Randers, and William Behrens III, *The Limits to Growth*. A report for the Club of Rome's Project on the Predicament of Mankind (New York: Universe Books, 1971). One of the most startling studies on the future.

Fred Warshofsky, ed., *The 21st Century: The New Age of Exploration*, Vol. 1, Twenty-first Century Series (New York: Viking Press, 1969). Describes technological developments that are remaking the nature of human life and society.

Ben H. Bagdikian, *The Information Machines: Their Impact on Men and the Media* (New York: Harper & Row, Publishers, 1971). Surveys the new communications technology; especially significant for educators.

Martin V. Jones, *A Technology Assessment Methodology: Some Basic Propositions* (Springfield, Va.: National Technical Information Service, 1971). Presents a seven-step methodology for assessing a new technological development (or an old one).

Perry London, *Behavior Control* (New York: Harper & Row, Publishers, 1969); and Albert Rosenfeld, *Second Genesis: The Coming Control of Life* (Englewood Cliffs, N.J.: Prentice-Hall, Inc., 1969). These two books explore rather thoroughly what is known about control of human behavior and behavior modification. The picture is frightening, but one that educators must understand.

An interesting social research method, called the Delphi technique, has been used increasingly in recent years to forecast future developments. It was originally developed by the Rand Corporation of Santa Monica, California, as a method of pooling the collective wisdom of selected persons in the solution of a problem, particularly one involving the judgments of competent people with various, but cognate, specializations. The technique has been used somewhat in educational planning circles to identify the most probable developments in education in the years ahead.[4] Harold Shane has formulated a modification of the Delphi

---

[4] W. Timothy Weaver, "The Delphi Forecasting Method," and Frederick R. Cyphert and Walter L. Gant, "The Delphi Technique: A Case Study," *Phi Delta Kappan*, 52, 267–273 (January 1971); see also their citations.

technique for use in future-planning education in his ORPHIC (Organized Projected Hypotheses for Innovations in Curriculum) procedures.[5] It is a group-process procedure for identifying the "more desirable of alternative educational futures."

Predicted Developments That Would Shape Education

It is not our purpose here to treat in detail predicted developments in American life but rather to urge curriculum workers to analyze such forecasts, make some of their own, and then move rapidly but effectively in developing the kinds of educational programs required to educate children of today for life in a future that is foreseen as insightfully as possible. To illustrate the significance of such anticipated developments for curriculum planning and to stimulate reading and discussion we list here what we consider to be the most likely major changes in the United States during the remaining years of this century:

1. *Population will grow, both in the United States and the world.*
2. *People in the United States will seek—and probably demand— more extensive opportunities for formal education.*
3. *In the relation between man and his environment, tremendous efforts, both officially by government and unofficially by citizens' groups, will be made to exercise rigid controls over man's use of the environment.*
4. *Family life, marriage, and child rearing doubtlessly will change to some extent, but the nature, extent, and permanency of the changes are difficult to predict.*
5. *The population will largely become urbanized, living in great megalopolises that pack people, business, industry, and services together on hundreds of square miles of concrete.*
6. *Technology will continue to change modes of living.*
7. *The biological revolution will probably embody the most marked changes in the lives of the people.*
8. *The work-year, that is, the hours a person spends on a job, will undoubtedly decrease markedly.*
9. *Occupational patterns will change gradually.*
10. *Government will become even more omnipresent, become larger in every respect, and employ many more people.*
11. *Patterns of moral behavior, life-styles, modes of living, and value systems in all but the most fundamental matters of group living*

[5] Harold G. Shane, "Future-Planning as a Means of Shaping Educational Change," in Robert M. McClure, ed., *The Curriculum: Retrospect and Prospect*, Seventieth Yearbook, National Society for the Study of Education (Chicago: University of Chicago Press, 1971), pp. 201–217.

will become more diverse, more pluralistic in nature, more per-missive, more unconventional, and more diffuse.

12. *The nations of the world will be tied together much more closely, particularly in economic matters, but also in political and social affairs.*

13. *Citizens will be better informed and more knowledgeable in general as well as on matters of special interest to them.*

14. *The world of the future will be one of rising expectations among all peoples, economically, culturally, and socially.*

Today's students will face a different world during their adulthood than the one in which they are being educated. How can the schools of today best prepare them for the life of the future?

The second phase of planning educational programs that will prepare children for living in the world of the future is to state overtly and comprehensively the basic principles and concepts on which such programs should be founded. In a school or school system that has continuously been engaged in formal programs of curriculum planning, very likely such principles or guidelines will have been stated in some form. Nevertheless, in planning for the future we are especially concerned with long-range plans for schools, with directions in which education should move. Hence, it is recommended that an existing set of principles be revised or a new one be formulated that will be primarily oriented to the kinds of educational programs needed in the years ahead. Then a school staff would be stimulated to proceed at once to develop such programs as rapidly as it is feasible to do so.

ESSENTIAL CHARACTERISTICS OF THE SCHOOL OF THE FUTURE

1. *Fullest personal development.* Each child must have ample opportunities to develop his own potentialities and capabilities within the generally approved system of social values.

2. *Equality of opportunity.* All children must have genuine equality of opportunity for maximum growth; no student should be assigned to a particular program, group or class or subjected to any administrative arrangements on any basis other than his own capabilities and educational needs at that particular point in his development.

3. *Assessment of talents.* As broad and comprehensive an assessment of each student's potentialities, capabilities, talents, and developmental needs as is possible should be made frequently enough to serve as a basis for planning his individual program of schooling from entrance to

termination of the formal program, usually extending through post-secondary and higher institutions.

4. *Personal counselor.* A highly qualified staff member should be responsible for counseling and working closely with each student in planning, carrying out, and assessing his educational development. In fulfilling these responsibilities the counselor should work closely with the parents or whoever is directly responsible for the well-being of the student.

5. *Valid administrative and organizational structures.* The administrative and organizational structure of the school system must facilitate and make possible the kinds of school programs postulated in these principles; hence, rules, regulations, laws, policies, or financial arrangements that arbitrarily deny to some students these opportunities are unacceptable in the schools of the future. A large measure of direct control over program, curriculum, and instruction by the citizens of the community or neighborhood working directly with the teachers and staff of the individual school is highly desirable.

6. *Compassionate staff.* Teachers and other staff members must be primarily concerned with the development of human beings through education, and provide evidence on every hand that the well-being of every student with whom they work is their first and foremost concern.

7. *Comprehensive curriculum.* The curriculum—the class program, the community-experience program, the extrainstructional activities program, and services for pupils—must be comprehensive in nature, providing as ample opportunities as feasible for individual development.

8. *Relevant subject matter.* Within the framework delineated by the educational goals of a school and the curriculum planning goals of an area of instruction content selected for study should be highly relevant; that is, it should constitute the best choice feasible in terms of the goals, educational needs, interests, previous learnings, aspirations, and self-perceptions of each student. Subject matter must be selected on criteria other than one of hoary tradition.

9. *Varied teaching modes.* The instructional program should be so organized and the methods of instruction be so selected that each student will have an extensive body of experiences appropriate for his own learning needs and style. Excessive dependency on only a few or even one instructional mode is unacceptable.

10. *Goals for human development.* Among general goals for curriculum planning should be included those that call for:

a. The acquisition of a large body of knowledge essential for understanding man and his world and for taking rational and considerate action on matters of concern to an individual.

b. Adequate development of the skills necessary for learning and for communicating efficiently and effectively.

c. The development of a desire and a willingness to continue to learn throughout one's lifetime.

d. The conscious refinement and development of a system of values that embodies the basic moral traditions of the American ethos.

e. The development of the ability and desire to make decisions and to choose among alternative courses of action on a rational basis that embodies a high sense of ethical standards.

f. The development of competencies necessary for occupational success.

g. The ability to maintain one's health.

h. The development of the ability and desire to establish good relations with other people.

11. *Cumulative growth experiences.* The total school program should provide learning experiences that will be cumulative in terms of development and continuous in terms of effecting real growth.

12. *The school a center for coordinating learning.* The school must be truly a community agency, coordinating insofar as possible all the educational experiences of its students, whether originating in the school, home, peer group, volunteer agencies, religious center, civic or political organizations, or other sources. The school is responsible for providing a rich body of educational activities and programs not only for children, youth, and young adults but for all citizens and for planning and carrying out community activities directed at improving community life for all inhabitants. The school, in turn, should use the resources and agencies of the community for providing highly relevant experiences for students.

13. *An advocate for children and youth.* There is great need for an advocate for children and youth and for their education. We are not sure if such a role should be performed by a staff member of the school system or by an independent person or agency. The White House Conference on Children recommended the establishment of such an agency at the federal level,[6] and in 1971 steps were taken to establish a National Center of Child Advocacy. The important functions of such an agency have been stated by its first director.[7] But inasmuch as many decisions concerning children, especially those having to do with their schooling,

[6] White House Conference on Children, *Report to the President* (Washington, D.C.: Government Printing Office, 1971), pp. 15, 29, 363, and 389–397.

[7] Frederick C. Green, "Child Advocacy—Reflections," *Young Children,* 27, 82–88 (December 1971).

are made at the local and state levels, it seems desirable to have a child and youth advocate at these levels.

We suggest these principles as guidelines for planning the kind of school program this nation needs, not only in the future but now. As is quite evident, such a list is really a restatement, perhaps in somewhat different form, of what we have advocated throughout this book.

RECOMMENDATIONS FOR SCHOOLS OF THE FUTURE: THE SCHOOL CENTER

The remainder of this chapter will present what we believe to be some of the most important developments that should characterize schools in the years ahead. These recommendations are made not in a spirit of authoritarianism or dogmatism but to stimulate discussion, study, and planning and, perhaps, an advance contribution to a Delphi or ORPHIC process. The sections suggest some of the aspects of development with which educators should be concerned and the kinds of considerations that we believe should be encompassed in programs of curriculum renewal and future planning.

The School as a Learning Center

The formal education of young people in the future will continue to be planned, administered, and carried on in a school building that serves as the center for education. With somewhat more than 50 million U.S. students enrolled in regular day schools, grades kindergarten through twelve, throughout the 1970s, and an even larger number anticipated for the remainder of the century, it seems obvious that places designated as schools will be required.

We emphasize this point because some writers have speculated that much of education in the future may be carried on in the home, and some, at various stages of schooling, in community agencies of all sorts. But even the so-called schools without walls and the store-front schools have a headquarters—a building—from which to administer the program and in which to carry on certain kinds of instruction, such as tutorials, seminars, and small-group activities. However, such schools today serve only an infinitesimal part of the 50 million students.

The school of the future will be primarily a learning center. This concept, introduced in Chapters 1 and 2, envisions the school as a center that will plan, organize, administer, and direct a formal learning program for its students, but it will not provide all aspects of their education directly. Moreover, an important function of the center will be to analyze and assess the total development of each student and then work in full partnership with other agencies that influence the child's development, especially the home, in seeking his maximum self-fulfillment. Finally, the school of the future will be a center for community self-development and self-renewal.

Thus the school center will have these primary responsibilities:

1. Assess the developmental status of each student.

2. Provide extensive learning opportunities of the kinds that best can be offered in a formal, organized school setting.

3. Plan with the student and his parents other kinds of learning experiences needed for maximum development that can better be provided through the home or community agencies: peer-group activities, travel, child- and youth-serving programs of agencies, service with community agencies, camp experiences, participation in the arts, sports, club activities, and so on.

4. Plan experiences away from the school but under the direction of the school: community activities, work-experience programs, self-directed study activities, surveys, research, field experience, study tours.

5. Work closely with parents or foster parents in a counseling or consulting role: cooperatively plan and guide the development of the child, adolescent, or young adult during the period for which the school customarily accepts responsibility. This period would include the time when the person is making the transition to a career.

6. Serve as a center in which people may carry on activities directed at community development and renewal.

Harold Gores, president of the Educational Facilities Laboratories, envisions such a school center in the future:

> These will be exciting years as the schoolhouse—or whatever it will be called—moves to the center stage as the principal instrument for shaping the renewal of our human habitations. In our central cities, schools will be moving into the mainstream of social reconstruction by providing the nexus for neighborhoods and by improving the economy through the recycling of space; in suburbia, the schoolhouse will be only one of the places where people, young and old, will gather to learn from each other; and back in the hills and down in the deltas, there will emerge the general center where all people are entitled to receive the social services that are appropriate to their condition.[8]

[8] Harold B. Gores, "The Schoolhouse of the Future," *National Elementary Principal*, 52, 13 (September 1972). For examples see *Found Spaces and Equipment for Children's Centers* and *Places and Things for Experimental Schools* (New York: Educational Facilities Laboratories, Inc., both 1972).

Organizational Pattern

We have no clear-cut ideas on what should be the organizational structure of these school centers of the future. In any instance it would be antithetical to our concept to suggest that a common pattern should prevail. The overwhelming matter of bringing about real integration on racial and ethnic bases among students must be dealt with politically as well as socially and ethically, and arrangements may vary greatly between large urban areas and smaller communities.

In Figure 18 we suggest a possibility for the organization of learning centers as well as show interrelations that ought to exist. Other patterns should be tried out across the country, and from such experiences may evolve one or more sound plans.

For infants and children up to seven or eight there should probably be small, neighborhood early-learning centers. Formal learning opportunities should be available for all young children whose parents wish them to attend. But racial balance, if deemed desirable at this level of development—valid empirical evidence on this matter is not yet established—greatly complicates the problem in school districts with considerable mixture in racial composition.

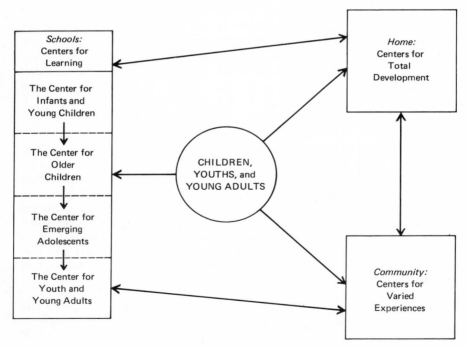

FIGURE 18   Locale of educational opportunities.

The building should have adequate facilities for parent and neighborhood meetings, group activities, and conferences between staff and parents. It is especially important at this level of development to insure the fullest possible cooperation between home and school, and this becomes more difficult if the building is some distance away from the homes of many parents. Without being dogmatic, we suggest that the enrollment in these schools not exceed 300–400.[9]

The school center for later childhood, ages eight or nine to about eleven, in many instances will be on the same campus as the early-childhood center or even in the same building, at least until some day in the future when separate buildings are possible. Perhaps, however, a single building is the most desirable arrangement in many instances, such as in older sections of a city or community.

At this maturity level the matter of racial integration of schools becomes more of a factor in planning, either as a result of court decrees, educational considerations, or public concern. For this age group the enrollment may be somewhat greater, perhaps up to 500–600 students. Again, there should be ample facilities, with multipurpose rooms, for a widespread, comprehensive type of program and for community meetings, parent activity groups, and conferences.

Some urban school districts have already tried out a plan in which a school for early childhood or a common school for both age groups is included as a part of a large building or interconnected complex of buildings that may also house smaller businesses and offices as well as living facilities for families.

At the next age level—about eleven to fourteen years—the dominant trend at present is to establish a middle school. It is anticipated that the middle school movement will spread throughout the country as rapidly as the change can be made in light of the building situation in a district. In those school systems with outstanding educational leadership and with an informed and concerned citizenry that have established middle schools the evidence, largely observational and impressionistic to date, indicates that a better program of education may be provided for this age group.

The building will need adequate facilities to carry out a total program of education for this age group. It should serve as a community center, correlating its efforts, of course, with the two lower sets of schools in the same area. Size will be difficult to set on an ideal basis, inasmuch as existing buildings will usually be used, and, again, the matter of

[9] For ideas on and examples of such school centers see Educational Facilities Laboratories, *The Early Learning Center: Stamford, Connecticut* (New York: The Laboratories, 1970).

achieving racial balance will be a major consideration. We recommend, however, an enrollment of about 600–700 students.

For adolescents and young adults the school center will be the high school. It will serve all age groups from those who have completed the middle school to young adults who are ready to transfer full time to a postsecondary school career—work, social service, homemaking, or further study. Often it will be desirable to integrate or at least correlate the programs of the high school and the community college or vocational and technical institute, if one exists in the district. Although it may not be realistic in terms of present school plants, we believe that high schools should not enroll more than about 800–1000 regular daytime students. Racial integration is assumed at this level. It is at the secondary school level that the school will most completely embody the characteristics of a center for learning and, hence, its facilities need to be appropriate for such a program. The building will also serve the community in many ways.

Voluntary Attendance and Deschooling

In describing the school as a center for learning, it is desirable to examine several movements and studies that question the value and place of schools in our society. One of these movements proposes that children and youth be allowed a large measure, or even complete, freedom in choosing the kind and nature of schooling in which they will participate.[10] In its milder form, it proposes that all compulsory attendance laws be repealed; thus parents could determine for themselves what kinds of schools, if any, their children would attend, and on what basis. In its more radical form, it proposes that schools be abolished, that society be freed of the legal responsibility to establish schools to inculcate values and transmit the culture. Ivan Illich, the leading spokesman for this view, stated that his analysis "of the hidden curriculum of the school should make it evident that public education would profit from the deschooling of society, just as family life, politics, security, faith, and communication would profit from an analogous process."[11]

Citizens have not been disposed to adopt such extreme measures in any form. The fundamental functions of the public schools are still

[10] See Ivan Illich, *Deschooling Society* (New York: Harper & Row Publishers, 1970); Everett Reimer, *School Is Dead* (New York: Doubleday & Company, Inc., 1971); John Holt, *Freedom and Beyond* (New York: E. P. Dutton and Company, 1972); Paul Goodman, *Compulsory Mis-education* (New York: Random House, Inc., 1962); and Paul Goodman, *The New Reformation* (New York: Random House, Inc., 1970).

[11] Illich, p. 2.

accepted as basic to the survival of the nation as well as essential for individual self-fulfillment, and the nature and quality of education is not about to be left to chance or to the whims of parents or their offspring.[12] Regular public and private schools will continue to exist wherever there are children and youth to be educated, and attendance is an accepted way of growing up.

Quality of Schooling and Adult Success

A new body of literature, utilizing sociological and historical research, has appeared within the past several years that plays down the importance of the school as a factor in individual success in adult life, or, more disturbing to us educators, in providing equal opportunities for every child to attain success.[13]

Unlike the advocates of optional schooling, these writers recognize the importance of the school in national life; they simply challenge the role, almost a deific one during the second quarter of this century, assigned the schools historically. Jencks and his associates concluded:

There seem to be three reasons why school reform cannot make adults more equal. First, children seem to be far more influenced by what happens at home than by what happens in school. They may also be more influenced by what happens on the streets and by what they see on television. Second, reformers have very little control over those aspects of school life that affect children. Reallocating resources, reassigning pupils, and rewriting the curriculum seldom change the way teachers and students actually treat each other minute by minute. Third, even when a school exerts an unusual influence on children, the resulting changes are not likely to persist into adulthood. It takes a huge change in elementary school test scores, for example, to alter adult income by a significant amount.[14]

Since its publication, the Jencks and associates study has been the subject of much controversy and debate. Other research workers

---

[12] Robert M. Hutchins, "The Great Anti-School Campaign," in *The Great Ideas Today 1972* (Chicago: Encyclopedia Britannica, Inc., 1972), pp. 154–227. Also available in reprint form.

[13] See Christopher Jencks and others, *Inequality: A Reassessment of the Effect of Family and Schooling in America* (New York: Basic Books, Inc., 1972); Michael Katz, *Class, Bureaucracy, and Schools: The Illusion of Educational Change in America* (New York: Frederick A. Praeger, Inc., 1971); and Colin Greer, *The Great School Legend: A Revisionist Interpretation of American Public Education* (New York: Basic Books, Inc., 1971). See also the significant essay by Wilma S. Longstreet, *Beyond Jencks: The Myth of Equal Schooling* (Washington, D.C.: Association for Supervision and Curriculum Development, 1973).

[14] Jencks and others, pp. 255–256.

found much fault in the methodology, data, and procedures, and educators generally raised serious questions about the scope of the study, particularly its definition of "success" (income of adults as reported to census takers).[15] In any instance, the study, of course, did not compare a "control" group that had not attended school. Perhaps it is well that schooling as measured in this study does not account for a significant difference in the reported incomes of citizens; the schools have many other important goals to fulfill.

Katz and Greer do not denigrate the schools as such, recognizing their importance in a society; however, they present evidence to show that actually U.S. schools have not in the past served in the grand and glorious manner depicted by educational historians. They note particularly the failure of the schools to provide equality of opportunity for minority-group children and those from economically and culturally disadvantaged families.

All of these critical examinations of the schools, ranging from those who strongly support them but wish to see major changes made in the programs to those that want to disestablish them, are salutary: they should prompt the schools as institutions to pursue vigorously a program of self-renewal. If U.S. schools truly become centers for learning, a major step forward will have been taken.

RECOMMENDATIONS FOR SCHOOLS
OF THE FUTURE:
DIRECTOR OF PERSONAL DEVELOPMENT

We recommend that curriculum and instructional planners in developing schools for the future establish a position to be known as the director of personal development, or some suitable title. Such a staff position, we believe, is essential if the schools are to offer the kind of program envisioned here. The principal responsibility of such a person would be to oversee the total development of a student; he would be a coordinator, an adviser, a confidant, a companion, an astute analyzer, a vision-expander, a catalyst, a stimulator, and a teacher. The person would *not* be a superparent or even a surrogate parent, a social worker, a judge, a crutch, a refuge, or a shelter. Ideally, he or she would be simply

[15] See especially Henry M. Levin, "Schooling and Inequality: The Social Science Objectivity Gap," *Saturday Review—Education*, 50, 49–51 (November 11, 1972); and Special Section, "Perspectives on *Inequality: A Reassessment of the Efforts of Family and Schooling in America*," *Harvard Educational Review*, 43, 37–164 (February 1973).

a person who is greatly interested in his clients and able and willing to do anything within reason and feasibility to assist them to attain the fullest measure of self-realization.

Rationale for the Position

The basis for the establishment of a program for personal development, headed by a director, has been stated implicitly throughout this book. If the ultimate goal of the schools is to enable each student to achieve the fullest possible development of his potentialities, the schools must have comprehensive provisions for assessing each student's capabilities, a program that will enhance his development, and methods of appraising his attainments. Each student must be able to work closely with someone if he is to benefit from his school program. This person would be the director of personal development. Young people themselves have recommended much the same kind of a staff responsibility as we envision:

> Counselors should (a) devote a major share of their time and effort to facilitating the student's personal, cultural, and environmental exploration, career and life style planning and decision-making, and building multiple choices within the curriculum, (b) be available in sufficient numbers to work with all students throughout the elementary and secondary schools (one counselor to 50 students), (c) be made more readily available to *all* students.[16]

To meet the ultimate goal of education a school program must be founded on *individualized planning*. Learning opportunities must take account of each student's developmental needs; instruction must be personalized; evaluation of student attainments must be on an individual basis. A director of personal development is envisioned as the staff member who can orchestrate such a complex undertaking.

The total development of each child must be assessed continuously. This process takes account of the full scope of learning acquired in school and out of school. The director will become familiar with the nature and character of a student's intellectual, social, and emotional developmental opportunities in the home, in the neighborhood, in community activities and organizations, in travel, and with friends and relatives.[17]

From his first days in school until completion of his school program the child needs a person to whom he can go for advice, counsel,

---

[16] White House Conference on Youth, *Report of the White House Conference on Youth* (Washington, D.C.: Government Printing Office, 1971), p. 88.

[17] On the importance of such associations see Carle C. Zimmerman and Lucius F. Cervantes, *Successful American Families* (New York: Pageant Books, Inc., 1960).

support, sympathy, understanding, and compassion. This would be his director of personal development.

This staff member would also work very closely with the teachers of his clients and with all other members of the staff. The student's own teacher(s) would participate extensively in all aspects of personal development. The director would direct, coordinate, interpret, and counsel them in their work with students and provide them with the data, information, and assessments suggested in this section.

Requirements of the Position

The director of personal development should be knowledgeable in the fields of psychology, guidance, and education, including teaching methods and curriculum planning. The most important qualification is an understanding of human development and a high level of sensitivity to people. The person need not be a highly competent *specialist* in all of these areas, but he should have access to specialized services from members of the central school staff. He or she would be a director of a service program for persons, not necessarily a specialist in providing all of these services.

At the infant and preschool level, some authorities have recommended a program of family and home consultative and advisory service for parents.[18] Usually it is presumed that such a program would be under the direction of a family service agency, not the school. This service, of course, would be in addition to high-level medical and health service. The coordination of parent service with the work of the school director of personal development would need to be achieved. The family service person might also be a member of the director's staff, or the entire program of child-development service could be carried on under the auspices of the school, with the support and cooperation of appropriate community agencies. Until a nation-wide public program of nursery school education is provided, such a service for families is especially needed. The school system should take the lead in seeing that it is provided under some feasible arrangement.

When the child enters a school, whether at age three, four, five, or six, the school's director of personal development would assume responsibility for providing the family and school services described

---

[18] An illustration of such a program in action is the Parent Education Project at the University of Florida. See Ira J. Gordon, *A Parent Education Approach to Provision of Early Stimulation for the Culturally Disadvantaged*, Final Report to the Fund for the Advancement of Education, November 1967; also reported in Evelyn Weber, *Early Childhood Education: Perspectives on Change* (Worthington, O.: Charles A. Jones Publishing Company, 1970), pp. 55–60.

previously. He or she might be a teacher for part of the school week and serve as director for a reasonable number of children the remainder of the time; perhaps the school could have a full-time staff of directors. How many clients a director should have is difficult to state until schools try out the plan. Perhaps 60–100 for a full-time person is a feasible number. It is assumed that a director would serve his clients as long as they are enrolled in that school, unless personality conflicts or other problems indicate a transfer to another director. The personal development records for children that transfer to other schools would be forwarded to their new schools.

We see no new elements in the program for children enrolled in the upper-level elementary school. The director would need to be very much concerned about learning difficulties, about skill development, and about mental health and emotional and social problems. Moral behavior also looms important for this age group.

In the middle school the job of the director becomes even more demanding, partly because a more comprehensive program of learning opportunities must be provided from which to make an appropriate selection, partly because life outside school becomes more varied and more complex, and partly because students in this age group are emerging into adolescence and face new problems and tensions. Relations with parents assume different dimensions, and the youngster faces new developmental tasks. The techniques for assessing both potentialities and attainments need to be extensive in scope and methodology. Close relations with parents may be more difficult to establish, and often the parents' involvement in school affairs is less extensive.

The same situation exists at the high school level only on an even greater scale. Also, community experience would be a part of the program at this age level, involving community service, work experience, job-training programs, service activities, and the like. We will consider these matters in more detail later in this chapter.

SCHOOLS OF THE FUTURE: EDUCATIONAL PROGRAMS FOR YOUNG CHILDREN

We now turn to a consideration of the kinds of programs U.S. schools should provide for the education of young children in the years ahead. We are not here attempting to predict trends or developments. Rather, we have two purposes in mind: to summarize by school levels what now seem to be the significant characteristics of the kinds of educational programs needed in the future and to suggest school arrangements that will provide such programs. The recommendations made in this section are based on the broad, general guidelines for future development presented earlier in this chapter.

Desirable Characteristics of Educational Programs for Young Children

Research, conventional wisdom, reports of conferences, institutes, and task forces, and the insight and imagination of scholars and other specialists suggest that educational programs for infants and young children in the future should have these primary characteristics:

1. Educational efforts should start at the time of conception. This part of the program should include top-quality parent education provided through an appropriate school agency and provisions for counseling parents, particularly the mother, on steps to take to provide the best prenatal environment possible for fullest development of the fetus and on tests for determining the possibility of genetic defects.

2. The living experiences of the infant from the day of birth should be as rich and lush as can feasibly be provided. Benjamin S. Bloom has stated that:

> marked changes in the environment in the early years can produce greater changes in intelligence than will equally marked changes in the environment at later periods of development. . . . extreme environments may be described as *abundant* or *deprived* for the development of intelligence in terms of the opportunities for learning verbal and language behavior, opportunities for direct as well as vicarious experience with a complex world, encouragement of problem solving and independent thinking, and types of expectations and motivations for intellectual growth.[19]

Play, especially with the parent, is also an important part of these experiences.[20]

3. Formally organized and structured programs of education for children should begin, if at all feasible, by three or four years of age.[21]

---

[19] Benjamin S. Bloom, *Stability and Change in Human Characteristics* (New York: John Wiley & Sons, Inc., 1964), pp. 88–89.

[20] See especially Ira J. Gordon and J. Ronald Lally, *Intellectual Stimulation for Infants and Toddlers* (Gainesville, Fla.: Institute for the Development of Human Resources, 1967).

[21] However, this has become a point of dispute. See the symposium "When Should Schooling Begin?" and a summary of an extensive analysis of research on early childhood education, "The California Report: Early Schooling for All?" by Raymond S. Moore, Robert D. Moore, and Dennis R. Moore in *Phi Delta Kappan*, Vol. 53, No. 10 (June 1972), pp. 610–621; also further comment on the California plan by Elizabeth Lewis, "The Real California Report: A New Approach to Education," and Raymond S. Moore, "Further Comments on the California Reports," *Phi Delta Kappan*, 54, 558–561 (April 1973).

The more economically deprived is the family, the more important are such programs. But as a minimum all children should have the opportunity to attend a school by at least age five.

4. Parent participation in formal educational programs for young children is highly desirable. In fact, if possible, the program should be carried on as much or more so in the home than at school. The director of personal development has a major responsibility in this matter.

5. Within the possibility (not just the feasibility) of arrangements, parents should be allowed to choose the school their child attends.

6. With a large measure of responsibility for program, curriculum, and instruction vested in the local school community, alternative kinds of educational programs should be available as part of the school program; a variety of public and nonpublic schools that conform to desirable standards of excellence should be encouraged. The matter of support, of course, would be up to governmental determination.

7. For the immediate future, until disadvantageness of an educational nature is largely ameliorated, "positive discrimination" should prevail. That is, schools and other developmental programs that primarily serve children in disadvantaged areas should receive a larger share, on a per pupil or per building basis, of school resources—money, equipment, staff, extra services, and the like—than other schools in the system. But such a policy would not in any way be a substitute for racial integration of the schools. This policy would apply to culturally disadvantaged children of any race, ethnic origin, or socioeconomic status.

8. The school for the early childhood years should maintain close working relations with social workers, public health agencies, and voluntary service agencies that serve the same families and children as the school. This partnership is a necessity in disadvantaged neighborhoods.

9. Day-care centers should be available to children from six months to school age where family situation indicates a need for such service. These centers should include an educational component in their service, with a professionally prepared teacher, either under the general supervision of the school system or working closely with the appropriate staff members, in charge of the educational program.

10. The school building should be humming with neighborhood activities—study and discussion groups, conferences and meetings, political and community action projects, workshops in the creative arts, family life, child development, and the like, and cultural and social events.

11. The child advocate proposal is especially appropriate for the early childhood level, but we see no reason to break such an agency into school levels. However, if the concept is not implemented for children and youth of all ages, then someone or some appropriate agency

should be the advocate for the young child. Perhaps the staff for personal development or one or more of its members could serve in the advocate's role.

References on Infant and Early Childhood Education

Curriculum planning committees will need to study significant books, reports, research, and other professional materials as they plan the program for young children. New publications, of course, appear continuously; the following list is suggestive of the most helpful materials currently available.

Central Advisory Council for Education (England), *Children and Their Primary Schools*, Volume 1, *Report* (London: Her Majesty's Stationery Office, 1967).

White House Conference on Children, *Report to the President* (Washington, D.C.: Government Printing Office, 1971).

Ira J. Gordon, ed., *Early Childhood Education*, Part II, Seventy-first Yearbook, National Society for the Study of Education (Chicago: University of Chicago Press, 1972).

Far West Laboratory for Educational Research and Development, *The Early Childhood Information Unit* (San Francisco, Calif. 94103, 1972).

Evelyn Weber, *Early Childhood Education: Perspective on Change* (Worthington, O.: Charles A. Jones Publishing Company, 1970).

James L. Hymes, Jr., *Teaching the Child Under Six* (Columbus, O.: Charles E. Merrill Publishing Company, 1968).

Bernard Spodek, ed., *Early Childhood Education* (Englewood Cliffs, N.J.: Prentice-Hall, Inc., 1973).

Joe L. Frost, ed., *Revisiting Early Childhood Education: Readings* (New York: Holt, Rinehart and Winston, Inc., 1973).

Robert H. Anderson and Harold G. Shane, *As the Twig Is Bent: Readings in Early Childhood Education* (Boston: Houghton Mifflin Company, 1971).

"Early Childhood Education," special issue, *National Elementary Principal*, Vol. 51, No. 1 (September 1971).

Lawrence Kohlberg, "Early Education: A Cognitive-Developmental View," *Child Development*, 39, 1013–1062 (December 1968).

Urie Bronfenbrenner, "Day Care USA: A Statement of Principles," *Peabody Journal of Education*, 48, 86–95 (January 1971).

Task Force on Early Childhood Education, Education Commission of the States, *Early Childhood Development: Alternatives for Program Implementation in the States* (Denver, Colo.: The Commission, 1971).

Edna Shapiro and Barbara Biber, "The Education of Young Children: A Developmental-Interaction Approach," *Teachers College Record*, 74, 55–79 (September 1972).

Some Developments in Early-Childhood Education

It is not our purpose here to present in detail descriptions of innovations and developments in early-childhood education. But it may be helpful to curriculum planners to list some of the programs that may be indicative of the direction that education at this level is taking at the present time.

Informal education   This is the more common term used to designate the new developments in British infant schools. Many schools in this country have or are now developing similar programs. The curriculum and instruction are flexible, enabling teachers to adapt to each pupil's interests and educational needs.

Literature on these programs is voluminous, but listed here are some of the most useful references:

> Lillian Weber, *The English Infant School and Informal Education* (Englewood Cliffs, N.J.: Prentice-Hall, Inc., 1971).
> Vincent R. Rogers, ed., *Teaching in the British Primary School* (New York: The Macmillan Company, 1970).
> Charles H. Rathbone, "Examining the Open Education Classroom," *School Review*, 80, 521–549 (August 1972).
> Maurice Kogan, project coordinator, a series entitled "Informal Schools in Britain Today," consisting of Vol. I, *Curriculum* (1972); Vol. II, *Administration and Organization* (1972); Vol. III, *Classrooms and Teachers* (1972); and a set of 23 booklets on individual topics (1971–1972) (New York: Citation Press).
> Alice Yardley, *Reaching Out; Exploration and Language; Discovering the Physical World; Senses and Sensitivity; The Teacher of Young Children;* and *Young Children Thinking*, a series of six booklets (New York: Citation Press, 1973).
> Casey and Liza Murrow, *Children Come First: The Inspired Work of English Primary Schools* (New York: American Heritage Press, 1971).
> Robert J. Fisher, *Learning How To Learn: The English Primary School and American Education* (New York: Harcourt Brace Jovanovich, 1972).
> "Perspectives on Open Education," special issue, *National Elementary Principal*, 52, 10–81 (November 1972).
> Roland S. Barth, *Open Education and the American School* (New York: Agathon Press, 1972).

Head Start and Follow Through   Educators are familiar with the Head Start and the Follow Through Programs, initiated under the auspices of and supported by the federal government. These programs are designed for young children in disadvantaged circumstances, but the large body of experience accumulated by teachers, staff members, and curriculum planners working with the programs is very useful in developing any program for young children. Details on programs may be obtained from individual schools or government agencies.

More general references include:

> Ellis D. Evans, *Contemporary Influences in Early Childhood Education* (New York: Holt, Rinehart and Winston, Inc., 1971), Chap. 3.
> Jenny W. Klein, "Head Start: National Focus on Young Children," and Robert L. Egbert, "Follow Through," *National Elementary Principal,* 51, 98–109 (September 1971).

Concrete experience and sensory development   World-wide resurgence of interest in the Montessori approach to early-childhood education has resulted in the overt use of her methods in many schools as well as the introduction of more concrete experiences into many programs. The British infant schools have adapted many of the Montessori concepts to their instruction. The toys, materials, play experiences, and outdoor and community activities used in many schools today are in harmony with this method of instruction. Some sources of information are:

> Maria Montessori, *The Montessori Method,* republished (New York: Schocken Books, Inc., 1964).
> Paula P. Lillard, *Montessori: A Modern Approach* (New York: Schocken Books, Inc., 1972).
> Ellis D. Evans, *Contemporary Influences in Early Childhood Education* (New York: Holt, Rinehart and Winston, Inc., 1971), Chap. 2.

Structured language development   Much controversy has raged in early childhood education circles about the merits of plans for highly structured programs of language development for deprived children. The principal advocates of this type of "crash" deficiency schooling are Carl Bereiter and Seigfried Engleman. Their instructional programs are available in both reading and arithmetic (a special form of language). Other highly structured programs for teaching language skills are also in use. Important references are:

> Carl Bereiter and Seigfried Engleman, *Teaching the Disadvantaged Child in the Preschool* (Englewood Cliffs, N.J.: Prentice-Hall, Inc., 1966).
> Seigfried Engleman and Wesley Becker, *Participants Manual: Preservice Workshop* (Chicago: Science Research Associates, 1970).
> Ellis D. Evans, *Contemporary Influences in Early Childhood Education* (New York: Holt, Rinehart and Winston, Inc., 1971), Chap. 4.

Wisconsin Research and Development Center for Cognitive Learning, "The Wisconsin Design for Reading Skill Development" (Madison: The Center, University of Wisconsin, 1973).

Parent involvement   The necessity for extensive parent involvement in the formal program of education has been stated repeatedly in this book. But such cooperative efforts are especially necessary at the early-childhood level. Many schools are developing planned programs of parent participation in various ways, and it seems evident that such efforts will expand greatly in the future. The Head Start and Follow Through programs gave great impetus to parent participation, and the tremendous expansion of nursery schools and child-care centers has greatly accelerated it.

More recent books on the education of young children devote space to this matter, and some additional references of interest include:

Alice M. Pieper, "Parent and Child Centers—Impetus, Implementation, In-Depth View," *Young Children*, 26, 70–76 (December 1970).

Susan W. Gray, "Home Visiting Programs for Parents of Young Children," *Peabody Journal of Education*, 48, 106–111 (January 1971).

Ira J. Gordon, *The Florida Parent Education Model*, and Ira J. Gordon, ed., *Reaching the Child Through Parent Education: The Florida Approach* (Gainesville, Fla.: Institute for Development of Human Resources, both 1969).

William W. Hartup, ed., *The Young Child: Reviews of Research*, Vol. 2 (Washington, D.C.: National Association for Education of Young Children, 1972).

Earl S. Schaefer, "Parents as Educators: Evidence from Cross-Sectional, Longitudinal and Intervention Research," *Young Children*, 27, 227–239 (April 1972).

Evelyn Shelby, "The School Volunteer," *Saturday Review of Education*, 1, 36–40 (February 1973).

Demonstration schools   A highly desirable development is the establishment of demonstration schools for infants and young children. In recent years a number of excellent innovative and model programs which concentrate on one or several types of development have emerged.[22] Studies of the process of educational change and renewal

[22] See especially National Center for Educational Communication, *Model Programs: Childhood Education* (Washington, D.C.: Government Printing Office, 1970); and Evelyn Weber, *Early Childhood Education: Perspectives on Change.*

show the value of such schools when planned and administered wisely. They should be quite typical of schools in an area or region in terms of pupil composition, administrative structure, financing, staffing, and the like. But they should be outstanding in terms of the educational program offered. Exemplary schools are especially needed at the nursery school level, inasmuch as such schools are increasing rapidly in number and there is considerable division of opinion among professionals and parents on programs, practices, and instruction.

Also, a National Laboratory in Early Childhood Education was established in 1967 under the auspices of the U.S. Office of Education. The laboratory is a "coordinated research and development effort"; a National Coordination Center and an ERIC Clearinghouse on Early Childhood Education were established at the University of Illinois. Later, centers for research, development, and demonstration were authorized at six universities. Federal funding has been meager in recent years, but many educators hope that the laboratory will still fulfill a significant function in early-childhood education.

It is difficult to predict the developments that will take place in the years ahead in the infant and early-childhood education programs listed in this section. But they are being tested in school situations, and it is likely that most of those identified will continue to shape school practice in the future.

SCHOOLS OF THE FUTURE: EDUCATIONAL PROGRAMS FOR LATER CHILDHOOD

In addition to the general lines of school development listed on pages 355–358, we consider the following to be some of the highly desirable characteristics of educational programs at the second level of maturity, ages eight or nine to eleven or twelve.

Desirable Characteristics of Programs for Older Children

1. All records and pertinent information about a child should be made available to teachers and the director of personal development as the student progresses through the formal program.

2. Personalization of the total program is especially important at the upper elementary school level.

3. Plans that call for teams of teachers to work with the same group of students and, insofar as feasible, over an extended period of time (several years) are highly desirable.

4. A broad, comprehensive curriculum should be planned, enabling students not only to explore talents and ascertain capabilities in many aspects of development but to make great strides in developing their potentialities. Particularly, the school should provide abundant experiences in the arts and other creative activities, sports and leisure activities, handicrafts, and abstract cognitive processes of inquiry, rational thinking, conceptualization, and generalization.

5. Students should participate in curricular and instructional planning and in setting policies and regulations for student conduct and governance.

6. It is especially important at this level of development that the school become truly a community agency; parent participation in the total program of schooling should continue at a high level.

7. A wholeness in the total program of schooling is essential. This means not only a continuity in the total program of education but the development of relatedness among the various elements in the daily and weekly experiences of the child.[23]

8. At this maturity level significant efforts should be made to develop an understanding of cultural pluralism, particularly with reference to different nationalities, ethnic groups, and races and to assist students to accept and support such cultural diversities within the basic structure of the American ethos.

9. The child should be encouraged and assisted in extending his eagerness to learn. Too often this enthusiasm drops off in the later years of childhood; hence the need to keep the fires of learning burning brightly.

Suggested References

Many of the references cited in the previous section on early childhood education are equally useful for planners of programs for later childhood. Additional references are:

> Mario D. Fantini and Milton A. Young, *Designing Education for Tomorrow's Cities* (New York: Holt, Rinehart and Winston, Inc., 1970).
> Ruth C. Cook and Ronald C. Doll, *The Elementary School Curriculum* (Boston: Allyn and Bacon, Inc., 1973).
> John I. Goodlad and Harold G. Shane, eds., *The Elementary School in the United States*, Seventy-second Yearbook, Part II, National Society for the Study of Education (Chicago: University of Chicago Press, 1973).

[23] For a biting comment on the situation in the traditional graded plan, see Evelyn Weber, pp. 175–178.

U.S. Commissioner of Education, *Education of the Talented and Gifted*, Vols. I and II (Washington, D.C.: Government Printing Office, 1971).

John I. Goodlad, "The Child and His School in Transition," *National Elementary Principal*, 52, 28–34 (January 1973).

Arthur W. Foshay, *Curriculum for the 70's: An Agenda for Invention* (Washington, D.C.: National Education Association, 1970).

Celia Stendler Lavatelli, Walter J. Moore, and Theodore Kaltsounis, *Elementary School Curriculum* (New York: Holt, Rinehart and Winston, Inc., 1972).

Allen Graubard, *Free the Children* (New York: Pantheon Books, 1972).

Urie Bronfenbrenner, "Reunification with Our Children," *Equality in Education*, No. 12, pp. 10–20 (July 1972), Center for Law and Education, Harvard University.

Some Developments in Later-Childhood Education

Much of the material presented in the previous section on early-childhood education is indicative of changes and promising innovations in the upper level of schools for children; indeed, often in practice there is no break between the two levels, and a particular program or approach is used throughout elementary education with appropriate adaptations. Descriptions of additional innovations, especially used at the upper level, follow.

The open-space school   A considerable number of elementary schools have adopted an open-space or open-plan concept for carrying on the educational program. Others have tried the plan and abandoned it. The traditional classroom with rows of desks is eliminated in favor of a large floor space that can be used by a considerable number of students at one time. A greater degree of informality and flexibility usually characterizes the instructional activities. Each area may be regarded as a learning center, with subportions becoming the location of various types of learning resources.

Children of various ages may work together on a learning activity or pursue individual interests in the same subspace. The entire concept usually encompasses team teaching, multiunit or nongraded groupings, and considerable time for work on an individual basis.

Although many of the references for the informal or integrated day program of the British schools also describe an open-space plan, this feature may be used, as it is in many U.S. schools, without adopting fully the instructional and curricular aspects of the British plan. Some useful references on the open-space plan as such include:

I. Ezra Staples, "The 'Open-Space' Plan in Education," *Educational Leadership*, 28, 458–463 (February 1971).
American Association of School Administrators, *Open Space Schools* (Washington, D.C.: The Association, 1971).
Educational Facilities Laboratories, *Profiles of Significant Schools: Schools without Walls* (New York: The Laboratory, 1971).
Alexander Frazier, *Open Schools for Children* (Washington,, D.C.: Association for Supervision and Curriculum Development, 1972), Chapter 2.

Learning and multisensory experience centers Learning centers and open-space schools may be similar in some aspects but quite different in others. An open-space plan almost always embodies a learning center. The large area is usually subdivided on an informal basis (not by walls) into centers for learning activities. Hence, appropriate resources for learning are made available in each interest section of the space. But a learning center may, and often is, established in a school with the traditional box-type classrooms. It is an expanded concept of the library, housing all sorts of instructional materials—books, films, tapes, recorders, play-back machines, projectors, models, toys, simulation games, construction equipment and materials, art materials, duplicating machines, and connections to central facilities for television, play-back, and the like. Often there is also an allied outdoor center with various kinds of activities available.

A multisensory experience center is simply a major aspect of a learning center, but because of the nature of the experiences provided it may be housed separately. It primarily makes use of the communications media—film, sound, television, and the like.

The term "learning center" is also used currently to designate a special facility for offering instruction not feasible to provide in each individual neighborhood school. It may encompass a number of special types of programs, such as a student development center or skills center, arrays of models, exhibits, demonstration equipment, teaching machines, and audiovisual aids. Also included may be a center for teacher development, containing resources for curriculum and instructional planning and the like.

Some references are:

Virginia Rapport, ed., *Learning Centers: Children on Their Own* (Washington, D.C.: Association for Childhood Education International, 1970).
Henry W. Ray, "Designing Tomorrow's School Today: The Multisensory Experience Center," *Childhood Education*, 47, 254–258 (February 1971).

T. Darrell Drummond, "The Learning Center: A Chance for Every
Child," *National Elementary Principal*, 50, 30–39 (September
1970).
Harold Davis, *Organizing a Learning Center* (Cleveland: Educational Research Council of America, 1968).

Children teach children Plans for "family groupings" in which
older children work with younger children are often aspects of the open
classroom or informal plans described previously. Also, the multiunit
plan encourages this practice. Special attention should be focused on this
arrangement because it has promise of adding to the effectiveness of
classroom activities and hence to the education of children. Teachers who
use the plan believe that both parties in the endeavor benefit—those, for
the moment, teaching and those being taught; roles may be reversed
readily. See especially Alan Gartner, Mary Kohler, and Frank Riessman,
Children Teach Children: Learning by Teaching (New York: Harper &
Row, Publishers, 1971).

Outdoor education Camping experience became part of the
elementary school curriculum in a few schools as early as the 1940s. Other
types of outdoor experiences, perhaps as a part of a summer program,
have also existed. Today more definite plans and more facilities are available for outdoor education. Such a learning center may be a part of the
school campus or a separate area made available for school use.[24] Helpful
references are:

Shirley A. Brehm, *A Teacher's Handbook for Study Outside the
Classroom* (Columbus, O.: Charles E. Merrill Publishing Com-
pany, 1969).
Wilbur Schramm, "Classroom Out-of-Doors," *National Elementary
Principal*, 48, 70–81 and .80–90 (April and May 1969).

SCHOOLS OF THE FUTURE: EDUCATIONAL
PROGRAMS FOR THE EMERGING ADOLESCENT

Plans for educating youth of from eleven or twelve to thirteen
or fourteen years of age have changed considerably since the early 1960s.
These changes have centered around the establishment of a new type of
school designated as a middle school and the resultant impact of this
approach on the traditional junior high school program.

---

[24] Excellent examples of the latter type are the Fontenelle Forest in Omaha,
Nebraska, and the Ruth Park Wildlife Area of the University City, Missouri, schools.

Whether a school system changes its organization to encompass this new type of school or retains the junior high school in name, the educational program for pre- and young adolescents will take on a new look in the years ahead. The patterns are rather well established already.

Desirable Characteristics of Programs for the Emergent Adolescent

We consider these to be the main elements in an educational program for the emerging adolescent.[25] These are, of course, in addition to the characteristics that apply to all levels of schooling stated earlier.

1. The school for this age group should be unique in its own way and not a "junior" version of a higher school nor an advanced level of a lower school. However, the total program provided young people from ages three or four to eighteen or nineteen must have a continuity and a cohesiveness that eliminates unnecessary duplication of learning experiences yet tolerates no serious gaps in total development.

2. The program must be especially designed for boys and girls at this level of maturity. It should build on previous learnings and developmental maturation and in turn enable each adolescent to continue without deficiencies or handicaps in the high school program.

3. The world of the emerging adolescent is ever widening in terms of interests, drives and needs, anxieties, ability to perform certain tasks, values, relations with others, and many other traits. Teachers must understand these changes in personality and motivations and act in accordance with them. The school must offer a broad curriculum, not only in the academic area but in extrainstructional programs and community experiences.

4. The services provided by the middle or junior high school must be extensive and planned properly for this age group. Guidance and counseling services, particularly, constitute a major challenge to the school staff, but health services, likewise, should be especially planned for this age group and not be just a perfunctory set of first aid and inspection services. The facilities of a learning center should be extensive and provide ample opportunities for independent study, free-time reading, and viewing and listening to tape recordings, film, and the like.

5. The programs and activities of schools for this age group must be geared to young persons who are considerably better informed, more advanced intellectually, emotionally, and socially, and more competent to assume responsibility for their own activities and for planning

[25] For another excellent set of guidelines see "Guidelines for the Middle Schools We Need Now," *National Elementary Principal*, 51, 79–89 (November 1971).

and carrying on learning experiences independently than were students of this age group a generation ago.

6. This age group is maturing rapidly, yet at individual rates of development, creating a student body that is diverse not only from student to student but from month to month, if not from day to day. Again, such a situation calls for a highly flexible program, ample opportunities for student participation in planning and carrying on learning experiences, and a wide breadth in curriculum plans.

7. A great deal of attention should be given to value development. The school can assist the emerging adolescent greatly in refining his value system. He can learn from school experiences how to appraise his own values, how to apply them to life situations, and to redefine them, if necessary, in terms of American ideals.

8. Students should become familiar with a number of subject areas and fields of study. The exploratory function of the school for this age group has been emphasized from the beginning of school reorganization, but seldom has it been well fulfilled. Each student should have meaningful experiences in the creative arts, literature, handicrafts, sports, home arts, languages, and the like. And, of course, exploration includes opportunities for high-level study in the disciplinary fields.

Selected References

Important references on curriculum and program planning for schools for the emerging adolescent include the following:

William M. Alexander and others, *The Emergent Middle School*, 2d ed. (New York: Holt, Rinehart and Winston, Inc., 1969).

Donald H. Eichhorn, "The Emerging Adolescent School of the Future—NOW," in J. Galen Saylor, ed., *The School of the Future —NOW* (Washington, D.C.: The Association for Supervision and Curriculum Development, 1972), pp. 35–52.

William Van Til, Gordon F. Vars, and John H. Lounsbury, *Modern Education for the Junior High School Years*, rev. ed. (Indianapolis, Ind.: The Bobbs-Merrill Company, Inc., 1967).

"The Middle School," special issue, *National Elementary Principal*, Vol. 51, No. 3 (November 1971).

Theodore C. Moss, *Middle School* (Boston: Houghton Mifflin Company, 1969).

M. A. McGlasson and V. D. Pace, eds., "Junior High School and Middle School Education,'" *Viewpoints* (Indiana University), 47, 1–129 (November 1971).

Thomas E. Gatewood, "What Research Says About the Junior High School versus the Middle School," *North Central Association Quarterly*, 46, 264–267 (Fall 1971). Extensive bibliography.

SCHOOLS OF THE FUTURE:
EDUCATIONAL PROGRAMS FOR OLDER
ADOLESCENTS AND YOUNG ADULTS

Self-appraisal and then self-renewal are perhaps more necessary for the secondary school than for any other level of schooling if education is to prepare young people for the world of the future. Teachers and all others responsible for planning schools for tomorrow should make changes and reforms on the basis of a thoroughly prepared and soundly based conception of the whole process of education, not accepting without examination the demands of pressure groups or those who advocate the disestablishment of schools. As in the previous sections, let us suggest important guiding principles, in addition to the general guidelines stated earlier, for developing the high school of the future.

Desirable Characteristics of Programs for Adolescents and Young Adults

1. The high school student must be a full-fledged participant in every way in planning and carrying on his or her formal education through the school center.

Secondary schools are for students and students should be involved in their school's policy decisions, particularly those concerned with developing curricula and determining rules governing student conduct. Students should also have a voice in determining the criteria for evaluating teachers. . . . Secondary school students should be represented on all boards of education.[26]

2. It is especially important at the high school level that a document of governance be officially adopted. It should set forth students' rights, responsibilities, and regulations concerning conduct and define the social responsibilities and obligations of each to the other, as well as the legal rights, authority, and obligations of the students, teachers, administrators, and board of education.

3. To the fullest extent possible the school-directed program of education should be as broad as the life of the community itself. Obviously, a good deal of formal study, laboratory, studio, and shop programs, extrainstructional activities, use of school services (health, guidance and counseling, learning resources), and seminar activities with the director of personal development will take place in the school center. In addition, however, each student will engage in many planned learning experiences in community or out-of-community settings and in the home.

[26] White House Conference on Youth, pp. 81–82.

4. It is important that a continuing appraisal be made of each student's capabilities, potentialities, achievements, personal development, aspirations, self-concepts, and self-fulfillment. Such analyses must be made by the student, but with the assistance, advice, and direction of appropriate members of the staff and with their input becoming a part of the student's raw data for generating conclusions. This is one of the principal functions of the director of personal development.

5. On the basis of these appraisals the student should be strongly encouraged, though not forced, by his director to participate in courses, activities, programs, and other kinds of experiences that will foster his growth, help him overcome personal deficiencies, and broaden and deepen his interests. Of course, the other domains of the curriculum will be properly and adequately included in the total program of every student. Youth themselves have said: "Secondary school students must be offered opportunities to design individualized educational programs suited to their particular competencies and interests with the help of sensitive, informed advisers and counselors."[27]

6. Personalization of the total program is essential, as at all levels of schooling. But at the high school level methods and procedures for personalization become even more pronounced and more sophisticated.

7. The school staff should encompass collectively persons who possess a variety of competencies, interests, points of view, and personality traits. Such a staff should then work in ways that enable each member to utilize his competencies appropriately, either individually or cooperatively in a team arrangement.

8. A major portion of the total school program, and correlatively of each student, is devoted to attaining carefully defined goals that constitute the four curriculum domains described in Chapter 5. Overt preparation for an occupation is deferred until the postsecondary period of schooling. Orientation to careers and specialization in a subject field basic for occupational preparation is an appropriate function of the high school.

Selected References

Some important references on the program of secondary education needed in the years ahead include:

> White House Conference on Youth, *Report of the White House Conference on Youth* (Washington, D.C.: Government Printing Office, 1971).

[27] White House Conference on Youth, p. 83.

William M. Alexander, J. Galen Saylor, and Emmett L. Williams, *The High School: Today and Tomorrow* (New York: Holt, Rinehart and Winston, Inc., 1971), Chap. 12.

Aase Eriksen and Frederick M. Fiske, "Teacher Adaptation to an Informal School," *Bulletin*, National Association of Secondary School Principals, 57, 1–9 (January 1973).

L. Craig Wilson, *The Open Access Curriculum* (Boston: Allyn and Bacon, Inc., 1971).

Task Force on High School Redesign, *Toward the 21st Century: Recommendations for the New York City High Schools* (New York: Board of Education, 1971).

The Four-School Study Committee, *16–20, The Liberal Education of an Age Group* (New York: College Entrance Examination Board, 1970).

Mario D. Fantini and Milton A. Young, *Designing Education for Tomorrow's Cities* (New York: Holt, Rinehart and Winston, Inc., 1970).

Richard Renfield, *If Teachers Were Free* (Washington, D.C.: Acropolis Books, 1969).

J. Lloyd Trump and Delmas F. Miller, *Secondary School Curriculum Improvement*, 2d ed. (Boston: Allyn and Bacon, Inc., 1973).

SCHOOLS OF THE FUTURE: OPENNESS, FLEXIBILITY, AND PERSONALIZATION

From the previous sections it is apparent that several significant characteristics apply for all four levels of schools of the future: the desirability of openness, flexibility, and personalization in the educational program. In this section we briefly consider these aspects of schooling.

Much has been done in recent years to "individualize" instruction, and these efforts have been beneficial to students. Many aspects of individualization, however, endeavor to adjust the *rate* of learning to differences in pupil capabilities and previous levels of achievement. All students are still expected to master much the same minimum body of content, acquire the same skills and competencies, participate in designated learning activities, and attain much the same outcomes. Performance standards are often a feature of individualized instructional plans.

The term "personalization," which has only recently appeared in the professional literature, is intended to suggest the idea "to make personal," "to ascribe personal qualities to." The point is that it is what the teacher does that counts. In personalized instruction the content, the assignment, the modes for achieving the general goals and the subgoals of a subject or set of learning activities are determined individually in terms of the student's interests, educational needs, capabilities, achievement level, and other personal factors. It is a custom-made model of schooling, while individualization is an alteration of a factory-made model, but a model that has been adapted to size and height. Both approaches are an improvement over traditional practices, but the greater degree of personalization, the more effective the program. However, sharp lines of distinction cannot be drawn.

Individualization in present programs is evidenced by a number of desirable developments in schools:

Nongraded schools and multiunit plans of organization.
Individualized instructional plans, such as continuous progress, individually guided education, individually prescribed instruction, computer-assisted instruction, instructional modules, unipacs, learning activity packets, and the like.
Supervised correspondence courses.
Centers for remedial work, self-study programs, dropouts, education of adults or part-time students, and studying specialized courses and developing competencies.
Differentiated assignments, contracts, options for grades, individual options in unit plans.
Modular schedules.
Variable-sized groupings of students, particularly small groups and seminars.

A greater degree of personalization occurs in the program—although the opportunties for personalization offered by the approaches listed above should not be minimized—when a student engages in learning activities that may be unique in nature to him or to a small group of students. This is to say that alternate routes are available for students to attain the broad general goals of the school and, to a considerable extent, depending on their nature, the subgoals of a curriculum domain. The objectives for a segment of instruction may be personal or shared by only some of the instructional group, provided they are judged by both student(s) and teacher(s) to be appropriate for the attainment of goals.

Some of the more significant efforts to provide for personalization of a school program include:

1. Student selection from a number of possibilities, the learning activities in which he will engage during a particular period of the school day. Flexibility is provided by the student's choice of the time he will work on a set of activities and the time to be spent on them, with general control by the teacher, and choice among a number of alternative kinds of learning experiences available in an area of study. Flexible arrange-

ments such as these characterize the informal programs of English and U.S. schools and to some extent the open classroom plan. Some individually guided instructional programs also enable the student to make these kinds of choices.

2. Choice of learning activities in the development of a unit of work or other planned set of instructional activities. Teachers may permit or urge students to select the kinds of learning activities in which they will engage during the development of a segment of instruction from among many possibilities offered by the teacher or from those proposed by the student or a group of students. This kind of openness usually characterizes the cooperative planning of instruction by teacher(s) and students so evident in the "child-centered" and the core curriculum programs of the "progressive education" era, but now widely used in seminar-type courses, tutorials, and problem-centered and discovery-type programs. Students often work individually or in small committees on a project, investigation, research activities, or products.

3. Independent study. This is one of the most significant developments in schools in recent years, especially at the high school level. Reference here is made only to those plans which the students carry out individually selected and approved study projects or activities of a broad scope. Independent study is distinct from class work, even when freely planned; it designates a significant undertaking outside or in lieu of class activities. Usually a student proposes a study, investigation, survey, research, or creative project to an appropriate sponsor and then carries it out under his or her general supervision. Sometimes the project is undertaken by two or more students jointly.

4. Mini or unit courses. Many middle and high schools have developed short-term courses in lieu of or as an alternative to traditional courses. Such courses may meet for as short a time as a week, but usually they extend for a number of weeks up to half a semester. Such an arrangement provides students with a greater choice of subjects for his or her program. The offerings often include unit courses dealing with current issues and problems, but may also include subjects of a highly abstract or historical nature. The teachers of mini courses are more inclined to involve students in planning, provide a wide choice of learning opportunities, and use student-centered modes of instruction.

5. Community experiences. In carrying out a program of community experiences, such as has been recommended previously, students choose the activities in which they will participate within the limits of those made available.

6. Learning resource centers. In contrast to the traditional school library, learning resource centers provide students much better

opportunities to read, listen, and view a greater variety of materials, to browse, to follow up on interests, to play back lectures, and the like.

7. Skills laboratories. Some schools provide laboratories in which students may improve study, reading, and computational skills and, hopefully, social skills.

8. Subschools, house plans, and learning communities. The "school within a school" concept has been used by a number of high schools and a few junior high schools or middle schools for several decades. Such plans are variously known as house plans, divisions, or subschools. During the 1972–1973 school year the Institute for Development of Educational Activities (/I/D/E/A/) worked with a number of secondary schools in developing "Learning Community" schools. Students in a school are organized into Learning Communities. These groups are composed of about an equal number of students from each age group comprising the population. The Learning Community is the central point for counseling and, hence, for planning the student's educational development. In the plan

> students spend part of their time in their Community. They exit in their Community when they need human resources or facilities that do not exist within their Learning Community. . . . Students, depending upon their goals, need to spend anywhere from thirty to seventy per cent of their time outside of their Learning Community."[28]

Within the Learning Community a variety of learning opportunities are provided. A student may choose from among short courses (designated mini courses above), cooperatively planned units, or "open structure" programs (designated independent study above). Some students may leave the school for work experience, community service, or special learning opportunities. The program of the Learning Community is highly personalized; the courses available in the school outside the Communities follow the more traditional pattern of instruction.

9. Extrainstructional activities. Providing a comprehensive program of school activities and letting students plan, manage, and carry them out, with only minimal supervision or direction, is an excellent method of personalizing the extrainstructional program.

10. A comprehensive curriculum. Inclusion of the arts, handicrafts, learning skills, and units on issues and problems at the elementary school level and a broad program of studies at the middle and high school levels, which includes seminars, tutorials, advanced-level courses, work experience, and community services, makes possible a much greater

[28] /I/D/E/A/, High School Change Program, *The Learning School Community: Guide for Implementation and Continuous Improvement* (Kettering, O.: /I/D/E/A/, 1972).

degree of personalization than is possible in a school with a limited program. But desirable personalization is not possible if, in turn, rigid requirements are enforced for promotion or graduation.

Moreover, the program offered—formal course work, mini-courses, extrainstructional activities, community experiences, and the informal hidden "curriculum," the content, and instructional modes should be selected and planned on the basis of the kind of world and the kind of society in which these adolescents and young adults will live, insofar as it can be forecast by scholars, planners, task forces, and work committees. These educational opportunities should be relevant—to what? To the kind of world in which they will live their lives in terms of its value structures, its institutions, its political structures, its economic conditions, and its concern for the dignity of all people.[29]

Schools that will prepare children for life in the future should be social agencies that are (1) diverse in nature and program, (2) comprehensive in scope, (3) an integrated aspect of the total life of the community, and (4) concerned with insuring the fullest development possible for their students. Thomas F. Green, a former director of the Educational Policy Research Center at Syracuse University, wrote:

> The most fundamental changes that we might make happen in the period 1980 to 1990 are those that reshape the polity of American schools and redefine their purposes to reflect a national commitment less managerial in intent. . . . The significant question is "Dare the social order build a new system of schools?"[30]

ADDITIONAL SUGGESTIONS FOR FURTHER STUDY

Broudy, Harry S., *The Real World of the Public Schools*. New York: Harcourt Brace Jovanovich, 1972. An eminent educational philosopher examines today's schools and considers accomplishments as well as shortcomings. Implications for self-renewal are foresightful.

"Community Involvement in Curriculum," special feature, *Educational Leadership*, 29, No. 8 (May 1972). An editorial and six articles deal with community-related schools.

Edison, William, and others, *Hunters Point Redeveloped: A Sixth Grade Ven-*

---

[29] In a challenging essay Michael Scriven proposes an educational program for survival in the world of the future: "Education for Survival," in David E. Purpel and Maurice Belanger, eds., *Curriculum and the Cultural Revolution* (Berkeley, Calif.: McCutchan Publishing Corporation, 1972), pp. 166–204.

[30] Thomas F. Green, "Schools and Communities: A Look Forward," *Harvard Educational Review*, 39, 252 (Spring 1969).

ture. Washington, D.C.: Association for Supervision and Curriculum Development, 1970. The authors present an exciting description of what young students have done about their community.

Fischer, John H., "Public Education Reconsidered," *Today's Education—NEA Journal,* 61, 22–31 (May 1972). A well-known educator examines pleas for deschooling and voluntary attendance and proposes instead desirable reforms to improve schooling.

Frymier, Jack R., and others, *A School for Tomorrow.* Berkeley, Calif.: McCutchan Publishing Corporation, 1973. In this set of essays the president of the Association for Supervision and Curriculum Development in 1972–1973 and a group of coworkers present plans for the development of the school's program.

Hack, Walter G., and others, *Educational Futurism, 1985.* Berkeley, Calif.: McCutchan Publishing Corporation, 1971. Although directed principally to educational administrators, the book merits reading by curriculum planners as well. The bibliography and addenda are extensive.

Institute for Development of Educational Activities, *The Greening of the High School.* Dayton, O.: The Institute, 1973. This report of a conference on how to improve high school programs also gives a summary of promising developments and activities.

Noar, Gertrude, *Individualized Instruction: Every Child a Winner.* New York: John Wiley and Sons, Inc., 1972. A widely acclaimed educator presents a broad approach to individualization that is positive in its recommendations. She draws extensively on procedures and plans that have proved successful in schools; most are readily usable by any teacher.

Rubin, Louis, and others, *Facts & Feelings in the Classroom.* New York: Walker and Company, 1972. Rubin and seven associated authors focus on changes that can happen now in U.S. classrooms. They discuss the role of emotions in making the school a "satisfying place" as well as a center for learning.

Saxe, Richard W., ed., *Opening the Schools: Alternative Ways of Learning.* Berkeley, Calif.: McCutchan Publishing Corporation, 1971. Readings include a number of articles related to new trends and developments in education.

Shane, Harold G., "Looking to the Future: Reassessment of the Educational Issues of the 1970's," *Phi Delta Kappan,* 54, 326–337 (January 1973). The leading advocate of future-planning examines the most significant issues facing U.S. public education and presents insightful recommendations for resolving the issues and developing the most effective schools possible.

Stanford Research Institute, Educational Policy Research Center, *Alternative Futures and Educational Policy,* Research Memorandum EPRC 6747-6. Menlo Park, Calif.: The Institute, 1970. This interesting and thought-provoking report considers possible trends in the world of the future, and offers recommendations concerning the kinds of educational programs that are needed to prepare citizens to solve the world's "macroproblem."

NAME INDEX

A

Abott, M. M., 292
Adams, D., 126
Agne, R. M., 285
Ahmann, J. S., 346
Alcorn, M. D., 256
Alexander, W. M., 3, 17, 27, 45, 62, 72, 100, 229, 239, 266, 321, 352, 380, 383
Alioto, R. F., 317
Alkin, M. C., 284
Alpren, M., 210
Amidon, E. J., 335
Anderson, R., 300
Anderson, R. H., 229, 370
Archambault, R. D., 122
Atkin, J. M., 174
Ausubel, D. P., 252, 276
Averch, H. A., 278–279, 337, 344

B

Bachman, J. G., 107
Bacon, P., 259, 262
Bagdikian, B. H., 353
Baier, K., 352
Bailyn, B., 118
Baker, E. L., 201–202, 295
Baker, R. L., 172, 173
Banks, J. A., 114
Barker, L. L., 171
Barlow, M. L., 204
Barth, R. S., 371
Barton, R. E., 262
Bassett, T. R., 188
Beatty, W. H., 178, 304, 305, 336, 338, 340
Beauchamp, G. A., 4, 14, 29, 212
Beck, C. E., 132
Becker, W., 372
Behrens, W., III, 353
Belanger, M., 244, 387

Belford, E., 174
Bell, T. H., 286
Bellack, A., 335
Benjamin, H., 211–212, 238
Bereiter, C., 372
Berman, L. M., 225–226
Bhaerman, S., 84
Biber, B., 370
Bidwell, C. E., 271, 272, 273
Bilodeau, E. A., 254
Bilodeau, I. M., 254
Bingham, R. M., 259
Binzen, P., 117
Birmingham, J., 60
Black, J., 80
Block, J. H., 346
Bloom, B. S., 180, 187, 275, 276, 299, 304, 312, 313, 332, 336, 339, 344, 368
Bobbitt, F., 2, 4, 71, 199–201
Boehme, R., 155
Bongo, J., 46
Boocock, S. S., 262
Bostwick, P., 19
Boyer, E. G., 335
Brameld, T., 188, 218
Brehm, S. A., 378
Bremer, J., 68, 218
Brewin, C. E., Jr., 317
Brickell, H. M., 56
Briggs, L., 45
Bronfenbrenner, U., 114, 370, 376
Bronwell, A. B., 353
Brooks, G. D., 1, 243
Broudy, H. S., 45–46, 126, 129, 145, 146, 167, 168, 170, 174, 175, 188, 223–224, 295, 387
Brown, B. F., 266
Brownell, J. A., 129, 208, 210
Bruner, J. S., 127, 131, 210–211, 213–214, 257, 276
Bryan, C. E., 142
Buber, M., 131

SUBJECT INDEX

A

Accountability, 283–295
  aspects of, 285
  Cooperative Accountability Project, 292
  criticism of, 287–289
  data for, 289–291
  definition of, 283–284
  scope of, 285–292
  standards for, 291–292
  state programs of, 292–293
Accreditation, as factor in planning, 31–32, 319–323
Achievement testing (*see* Evaluation)
Adams Morgan School, 82
Advisory Commission on School District Budgeting and Accounting (California), 317
Aims, definition of, 148
Alternative schools, 79–84, 233–235
American Association of School Administrators, 377
Aptitude–treatment–interaction (ATI), 277–279, 280–281
Assessment (*see* Evaluation)
Association for Supervision and Curriculum Development, 19, 48, 72, 76, 142, 187, 213–214, 226, 228, 240
Audiovisual (*see* Instructional materials)

B

Behavioral objectives (*see* Objectives)
Berkeley, California, Unified School District, 82
Biological Sciences Curriculum Study, 212, 299, 313, 314, 327, 330–331

C

California State Department of Education

Task Force on Early Childhood Education, 324, 368
Cardinal Principles of Secondary Education, 121, 163–164, 168, 185
Career education, 40, 114–116
Carnegie unit, 206
Center for the Advanced Study of Educational Administration, 315, 317–319
Center for the Study of Evaluation, 151, 180–181, 187, 304, 332, 337
Center for Vocational and Technical Education, 116, 317
Central Advisory Council for Education (England), 111, 114, 370
Central Midwestern Regional Educational Laboratory, 54
Change process, 51–69, 90–100
  See also Curriculum planning
Child-centered designs, 230–240
Citizens, participation in planning, 67–69, 149–152, 323
  See also Curriculum planning
College Entrance Examination Board, 229
Colorado State Department of Education, 310, 320
Commission on the Reorganization of Secondary Education, 163–164
Commission on the Social Studies, 222
Commission on the Year 2000, 352
Community councils, 67–69
Community school, concepts of, 68–69, 215–216, 217–218, 267–268, 357
Competencies, as a curriculum design, 198–205
Congruence-Contingency Model (*see* Stake, R. E.)
Cooperative Accountability Project, 157–158, 292, 300
Council for Educational Development and Research, Inc., 54

DATE DUE